THE GARDEN
An English Love Affair

'To own a bit of ground, to scratch it with a hoe, to plant seeds, and watch their renewal of life – this is the commonest delight of the race, the most satisfactory thing a man can do.'

My Summer in a Garden, Charles Dudley Warner, 1876

THE GARDEN
An English Love Affair

One Thousand Years of Gardening

Jane Fearnley-Whittingstall

TED SMART

For my grandchildren

CONTENTS

INTRODUCTION

Our England is a garden, and such gardens are not made
By singing: – 'Oh, how beautiful' and sitting in the shade,
While better men than we go out and start their working lives
At grubbing weeds from gravel paths with broken dinner-knives…

The Glory of the Garden, Rudyard Kipling, 1911

I'VE JUST SPENT some time on my knees, doing more or less what Kipling describes: weeding the cracks between flagstones with a knife that has seen better days. Now the flagstone cracks are clean, and the cracks in my fingernails are dirty. But I have a sense of achievement, the petty annoyances of life have receded, and I look forward to an evening among the sights, scents and sounds of the garden I love.

A love affair with a garden seems to be an especially English form of love. I have lived in several gardens, some in the country, some in the town, and one in Africa, but still an 'English' garden. The common denominator of these gardens is that they have all been cherished, sometimes by several generations, and over the years I have wondered why it is the English love their gardens so much. Much of my working life has been spent restoring period gardens in England and adapting them to suit modern needs. As a result I have become intrigued by the history of gardens and their makers, and the nature of each garden maker's love affair with his or her plot.

The enduring parts of a garden often have a story to tell. Stone or brick walls and terraces enriched with mosses and lichens, old trees and hedges, show changes of style from one generation to the next, reflecting architectural fashions, horticultural and botanical developments, and economic, cultural and social changes. Such gardens are peopled by the ghosts of their makers and evoke the events that shaped their lives. The personalities involved may have

Much of the satisfaction of gardening comes from nurturing plants and seeing them thrive. Summer Garden, *Patricia O'Brien, 1990.*

been delightful, difficult, even eccentric, perhaps all three. They may have little in common except garden making, but that is not a little thing to share. They share a relationship with nature, which has, over the last thousand years, come full circle.

The evolving relationship between man and nature is at the heart of English garden history. The first gardeners were at war with nature, building high walls and planting impenetrable hedges as fortifications against the savage world of the forest and the wild beasts that lived there. Their achievement was the medieval *hortus conclusus*, the enclosed, secret garden. At other periods men have sought to dominate nature, driving avenues through the forest, carving hillsides into terraces and manipulating plants to form elaborate topiary. Occasionally art has fused with nature to achieve perfection in an eighteenth-century Brown or Repton landscape; or a twentieth-century woodland garden distilling the essence of a Himalayan gorge in a Welsh or Cornish ravine; or an orchard in a meadow spangled with native flowers. As we enter the twenty-first century, we are retreating again into the security of the *hortus conclusus*, designed, this time, to exclude the ugliness of an industrial landscape.

The history of English gardens is an enormous subject and the development of diverse garden styles reflects a rich and varied political, economic, social and cultural life: life lived in cottages and terraced town houses, as well as in mansions and manor houses. No survey in a single volume could paint a complete picture and each writer on the subject has his own approach and interests, which will influence his way of telling the story. Miles Hadfield wrote in his

The earliest gardeners grew mainly vegetables and herbs. This is a modern version of the Garden of Eden. Chelsea Flower Show, 2001.

classic *A History of British Gardening*: 'The great eighteenth-century landscape must not squeeze out the garden whose length is dictated by the clothes-line,' and I have tried to bear this in mind. When forced by lack of space to choose what to leave out, my policy has been to write less about large and famous historic gardens (the information is available elsewhere) and more about the 'clothes-line' gardens.

I wanted to set the gardens and the people who made them in their context and to see how changes in garden style were linked to changes affecting architecture, clothes, manners and other aspects of daily life. From the days of the crusaders, travellers have brought home new ideas about architecture and gardens; immigrants introduced new horticultural skills; new plants were discovered by intrepid and sometimes eccentric explorers.

All these elements went into a melting pot from which they emerged, transformed, into unique expressions of the English art of garden making. It is a complex, exciting story, and there is a rich reservoir of written and pictorial sources to draw on: poetry, fiction, diaries, memoirs; illuminated manuscripts, embroideries, paintings, drawings and photographs.

Artists and writers, including satirists, described the garden styles of their day, and garden makers were influenced, not only by accounts of real gardens but also by fantasy gardens imagined by poets, novelists and artists, and by philosophers' ideas about gardens. In due course, images of plants and gardens appeared in paintings, textiles, wallpapers, furniture and ceramics, reflecting back each period's horticultural fashions as if in a mirror.

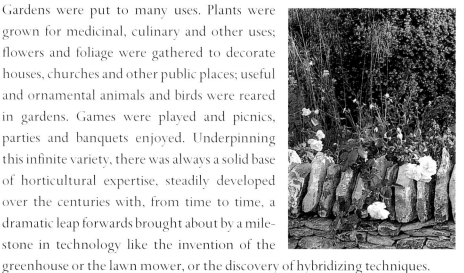

A stone wall in a modern cottage garden. The rural gardening tradition in England has remained unchanged for centuries.

Gardens were put to many uses. Plants were grown for medicinal, culinary and other uses; flowers and foliage were gathered to decorate houses, churches and other public places; useful and ornamental animals and birds were reared in gardens. Games were played and picnics, parties and banquets enjoyed. Underpinning this infinite variety, there was always a solid base of horticultural expertise, steadily developed over the centuries with, from time to time, a dramatic leap forwards brought about by a milestone in technology like the invention of the greenhouse or the lawn mower, or the discovery of hybridizing techniques.

Today the techniques, materials and designs of the past are available to garden makers: knots, arbours, fountains, grottoes, statues, urns and classical furniture can be made by those who want to create a garden in tune with a period house, or who simply love history. For modernists, concrete, steel and glass form stylish backdrops to water features pumped by electricity or solar power.

Above all, the love of plants, especially flowering plants, continues to inspire English gardeners. At the beginning of the story the flowers grown in gardens could be listed on a single page. Today, The Royal Horticultural Society's *A-Z Encyclopedia of Garden Plants* describes more than 15,000 plants. They are the culmination of a thousand years of gardening, of discovery and development, all catering for the English passion for plants. To return to Kipling:

So when your work is finished, you can wash your hands and pray
 For the Glory of the Garden, that it may not pass away!

1

MEDIEVAL GARDENS

Keeping Nature at Bay

IT SEEMS RIGHT TO begin the story of English gardens with the Norman Conquest, not because there were no gardens before 1066, but because there is little evidence to show what they were like. The Roman Palace at Fishbourne in Sussex is a remarkable exception. There, archaeologists are able to show in detail what the garden of an important local ruler looked like in about AD75: large, elaborate and formal. Perhaps lesser Roman officials also created gardens, albeit on a more modest scale than Fishbourne, and some of the better-off Britons may have emulated their rulers. The British would certainly have been employed in Roman gardens, vineyards and orchards, and would have learned something of the craft of gardening. But the Roman administration came to an end in the early fifth century, and after that our knowledge of gardens and gardening comes mainly from northern European sources.

After the Roman legions were called home, life for most people was, in Thomas Hobbes's words, 'nasty, brutish and short'. During the depressed period between the end of Roman occupation and the Norman invasion, known as the Dark Ages, the average Englishman's home was a hovel. The

---

Saint Fiacre, c.610–70, an Irish monk, is the patron saint of gardeners. Here he is shown in a fifteenth-century French manuscript reproduced in 'Les Arts Somptuaires'.

nearest he would come to having a garden of his own, even if he were comparatively well-off, was a small plot in front of his cottage where he could grow a few coleworts (cabbages and kales), onions, roots, peas and beans to help feed his family. There might be garlic, parsley and other herbs growing beside the path. A few villagers would also have had room behind their cottages to grow one or two fruit trees: perhaps apples, pears or cherries. A monotonous diet might be supplemented with additional herbs, berries and fruit gathered from wild places. As far as home-reared meat was concerned, the more prosperous families might own a pig in a poke and a few hens, ducks or geese. To own a cow was rare.

The struggle for survival

There was not much difference between gardening and agriculture. A peasant's work was agriculture, growing wheat, barley, oats or vegetables on a strip of land next to his neighbours' strips, or herding swine, sheep or cattle as they grazed the forest floor. During the winter following a poor harvest, there was a real risk that a family might starve to death. So, with what little time and strength they had left over from the back-breaking work of manual cultivation of the land, a man, his wife and any children old enough to work, would grow additional food crops in the yard or garden.

The pattern of settlement and land tenure established in the Middle Ages is still recognizable today. In country villages, cottages have front gardens divided by a path connecting the cottage to the lane, still sometimes planted with neat rows of cabbages, onions and beans. The traditional layout of front and back gardens has not only survived in the country, it has also been adopted in the town, in rows of terraced houses; and in the suburbs, in semidetached and detached villas set back from leafy avenues.

In the Middle Ages getting and keeping a garden was a gruelling battle against nature. The forest was quick to reclaim hard-won cultivated land, and clearing encroaching scrub was a constant struggle. The forest was a dark and sinister place where wolves lurked, wild boar hurtled out of thickets, and the brambles and briars of those thickets might tear your flesh and entrap you. Mythical as well as actual monsters threatened those who ventured into the forest, and people were afraid they might get lost and never find their way out. Stories like Little Red Riding Hood and the Babes in the Woods inculcated a fear of untamed nature in children from an early age.

For a few, however, the forest was a friendly, long-established source of food, fuel and building materials. Woodlanders had learned, probably in pre-Roman days, to stool and coppice forest trees to provide a sustainable source of timber, and among the trees their cattle, sheep and goats grazed, and pigs rooted for acorns.

'…great joy and liking to the hunter's heart'

The Norman Conquest brought the symbiotic relationship between wood and woodsman to an end. Forests were taken into royal ownership and managed principally for the royal sport of hunting deer and wild boar. Other creatures such as hares, swans and peacocks were also fair game. Hunting, then as now, was not simply a way of getting food. It was, for the rich and noble, a recreation, a way of taking exercise in the fresh air, an opportunity to show off and to practise skills of marksmanship which would also be useful in times of war, and a joyous excuse for a party.

All this is evident in the 'Devonshire' series of tapestries depicting hunting scenes, made at Arras in the 1420s to 1440s and now displayed in the Victoria and Albert Museum in London. Ladies and gentlemen are dressed up to the nines, with huntsmen and dogs in attendance, in an idealized countryside. In the panel depicting 'Falconry', pretty shepherdesses tend flocks of sheep near a mill with a water wheel, and there are ducks, a cow and a goat. In 'the Otter and Swan Hunt' a bear hunt also seems to be going on and a lady is fishing.

The tapestries were clearly designed by people who knew and loved the countryside; their work includes accurate representations not only of birds and animals but also of trees, shrubs and flowers. These works were not made in Britain and cannot be assumed to show British scenes, but by the time the tapestries were commissioned, the imported tastes and pursuits of the Norman and Plantagenet courts depicted in them had been thoroughly assimilated. The hunt may have been cruel and brutal, but with it went an enjoyment and love of the countryside that was to underpin the attitudes of the English gentry to the landscape and to gardens in centuries to come. Edward, Duke of York, a cousin of King Henry V, wrote in *The Master of Game*, the oldest known English book on hunting:

> For when the hunter riseth in the morning, and he sees a sweet and fair
> morn and clear weather and bright, and he heareth the song of the small
> birds, the which sing so sweetly with great melody and full of love… and
> when the sun is arisen, he shall see fresh dew upon the small twigs and
> grasses, and the sun by his virtue shall make them shine. And that is great
> joy and liking to the hunter's heart.

In the twelfth century, the forest had already become, as Richard FitzNigel wrote, 'the sanctuary and special delight of kings, where, laying aside their care, they withdraw to refresh themselves with a little hunting. There, away from the turmoils inherent in a court, they breathe the pleasure of natural freedom.' This natural freedom did not extend to the king's subjects. Infringements of his majesty's rights over 'vert and venison' (trees and beasts) were punishable by the grisly penalty of removal of the offender's eyes and testicles. Court records show, however, that most cases were dealt with by means of a fine rather than mutilation. The new laws were bitterly resented, and those who resisted them, like the legendary Robin Hood and his band of outlaws in Nottingham's Sherwood Forest, became folk heroes.

Vast acreages were fenced in for royal hunting forests, and lodges were built where kings and queens and their courtiers could eat, drink and rest. Henry III's deer park at Clarendon, near Salisbury, was the largest in England, surrounded by a wall 18km (11 miles) long to keep the deer inside. Recent excavations have shown that at the centre of the park was no mere lodge but a palace, with a magnificent marble-pillared hall 24m (80ft) long, rooms decorated with gold and lapis lazuli, and a wine cellar.

Clarendon and other palaces served a political purpose. The Courts of Norman and Plantagenet kings were always on the move, travelling from one palace or castle to the next with a retinue of some 300 people. The royal residences, often set within deer parks, demonstrated the power and wealth of the king. Rulers were already rich and confident enough to manipulate the English landscape for their pleasure. Royal parks, fenced or walled around and well stocked with deer, were managed so that the king and his guests could indulge their passion for hunting. These, and the parks owned by noblemen, were the forerunners of the great landscaped parks of the eighteenth century, and often provided the sites for them.

Most of the king's subjects still avoided the forest, although it was no longer the harshness and cruelty of nature they feared, but that of the king's foresters and the sheriff's men.

'… the beauty and savour of sweete flowers'

As peace and prosperity increased, people began to appreciate the benefits of the countryside and to develop a love for trees, flowers and the refreshing greens of the landscape. In good weather it was a delight to leave their cramped living accommodation and spend time in the open air. Fresh air was in itself highly valued. In about 1180 William FitzStephen, Thomas Becket's clerk and biographer, praised London as a beautiful and splendid city 'known for its healthy air and honest, Christian burghers [and] excellent suburban wells with sweet, wholesome, clear water', such as Clerkenwell, Holy Well and St Clement's Well. He was impressed by the fine timber-framed houses of London's well-to-do citizens in suburbs like Smithfield, and described these houses as having beautiful gardens planted with trees.

Advice on the site and laying out of small pleasure gardens, such as those at Smithfield, is given by Albertus Magnus, Count of Bollstadt, Dominican churchman and scholar of Padua University, writing in the thirteenth century. He said that the garden should allow health-giving breezes from the north and east to circulate freely, and trees should be planted far enough apart to prevent spiders spinning their webs between the branches and catching on the faces of people walking below.

Medical opinion was also in favour of fresh air. Johannes Mirfield of St Bartholomew's, also in Smithfield, gave the following sound advice: 'The first and most important [exercise is] to walk abroad, choosing the uplands where the air is pure; this is the best of all. Riding is another form of exercise but this is only for the wealthy.' Those who wished to ride and had the means could equip themselves at the horse fair held every Saturday at Smithfield. Farther afield, beyond the suburbs, there were meadows and mill-streams, and forests where Londoners might hunt deer, boar and bulls with merlins, falcons and dogs. Londoners also had the right to hunt in the Chiltern Hills.

On high days and holidays, Londoners headed out of town. On May Day, FitzStephen wrote, 'every man, except impediment, would walke into the sweete meadows and greene woods, there to rejoice their spirites with the beauty and savour of sweete flowers, and with the harmony of birds.'

Young men and girls would go to the woods, accompanied by a group of musicians, to gather May blossom. They used it, bound in wreaths, to decorate the windows and doors of their cottages and brought back 'their Maie pole, whiche they would bring home with great veneration' as William FitzStephen describes

> They have twentie or thirtie yoke of oxen, every oxe having a swet nosegaie of flowers tyed on the tippe of his hornes, and these oxen draw home this Maiepole… which is covered all over with flowers and hearbes, bounde rounde about with strings, from the top to the bottome, and sometyme painted with variable colours, with two or three hundred men, women and children following it, with great

devotion. And thus beying reared up, with handkerchiefs and flagges streamying on the toppe, they strawe the ground aboute, binde greene boughs aboute it, sette up Sommer haules, Bowers and Arbours hard by it. And then fall they to banquet and feast, to leape and daunce aboute it, as the Heathen people did at the dedication of their Idolles, whereof this is a perfect patterne, or rather the thing itself.

Vita Sancti Thomae, William Fitzstephen

In country villages the maypole sometimes stood in place 'in the whole circle of the year, as if it were consecrated to the goddess of Flowers.' Sometimes the celebrations included archery displays, with the contestants dressed up as Robin Hood and his merry men. There were processions of young men with garlands on their heads of ivy leaves and hawthorn, and girls in blue kirtles, wearing primrose garlands and leading a cow decorated with ribbons and flowers. Other girls wore garlands of blue and white violets and cowslips. Today few of us observe the rites of spring, but at Christmas, people still go through the same rituals of decoration as in the Middle Ages. According to Fitzstephen, 'Every man's house, as also their parish churches, were decked with Holme [holly], Ivie, Bayes, and whatsoever the season afforded to be greene.'

For decorations and for wreaths and garlands used in processions on Church festivals and Saints' days, flowers brought in from the wild would be grown in monastery gardens, as well as other precious flowers like roses, lilies and carnations. In private pleasure gardens, these would be grown for the sheer delight of studying their shapes and colours and smelling their scents.

'Now was there made, fast by the towris wall/a garden fair'
The need for a peripatetic court to maintain authority over their possessions in France and England left royal landowners little leisure for the creation and enjoyment of pleasure gardens. They were seldom in one place for long enough and were often too occupied with fending off military threats from their relations and neighbours. Henry II and his Queen, Eleanor of Aquitaine, moved, sometimes together and sometimes separately, from one fortified castle to another. They travelled with large retinues, from Winchester to Romsey to Abingdon to Oxford, then made the dangerous Channel crossing to show their strength and adjudicate in their courts in Anjou, Normandy or Toulouse. Landowners were frequently summoned to accompany the court or obliged to feed and entertain in their own castles the hundreds of men and women who made up a royal court on the move.

Against the odds, several royal pleasure gardens were created. What they looked, sounded and smelled like can be deduced from the painted images of illuminated manuscripts and Books of Hours, the woven and embroidered scenes on tapestries, and from written evidence in the Royal Pipe Rolls (the equivalent of account books), records of the King's Works and contemporary chroniclers. Such gardens were small enclosures inside the fortified walls of a castle and modelled on the earlier gardens of monasteries and convents. In 1415, James I of Scotland, a prisoner in Windsor Castle, looked wistfully down into just such a secular garden and wrote:

> Now was there made, fast by the towris wall
> A garden fair; and in the corners set
> An herbere green with wandis long and small
> Raillit about and so with treeis set
> Was all the place and Hawthorn hedges knet
> That life was none warkyn therefore bye
> That might within scarce any wight esppye.

Sacred gardens

Virtually the only places where secure, settled communities were to be found before and immediately after the Norman Conquest were the monasteries. The architecture and layout of their buildings and the form and content of their gardens were a Roman legacy. It was a legacy bequeathed, not directly to the descendants of Rome's British subjects (very little survived the period of anarchy and unrest that followed the departure of the Romans), but indirectly, through the Christian Church in Europe. It was the Norman conquerors who brought the Romanesque architectural style with them to Britain from mainland Europe.

Clearing the ground for a religious building or complex of buildings, and the associated gardens, involved the same battle against nature for the monks as it did for the serfs of an Anglo-Saxon or Norman baron. Perhaps, though, they set about the work more cheerfully because for them it was an act of praise and worship. In *The Making of the English Landscape* W.G. Hoskins quotes from an early life of the fifth-century St Brioc, who established a monastery in Brittany. It describes how the brethren 'gird themselves to work, they cut down trees, root up bushes, tear up brambles and tangled thorns, and soon convert a dense wood into an open clearing…some cut down timber and trim it with axes…some turned up the sod with hoes…'.

A monastic community is, of its nature, enclosed and so mysterious to outsiders. To the peasant in his hovel, a monastery or abbey must have seemed an awesome and holy place. A glimpse into a walled monastery garden must have seemed like a foretaste of Paradise.

We know fairly accurately what a Benedictine monastery and its surroundings, including the gardens, looked like. A drawing, a blueprint for the ideal monastic foundation dating from the early ninth century, was found at St Gall in Switzerland. We also know that the plan was adapted for numerous sites in northern Europe, including the twelfth-century abbey at Fontevraud in France and Peterborough Abbey in England.

The St Gall model provided, compactly arranged, everything necessary to sustain a self-sufficient community. There was space for pigs, sheep, goats, cows and pregnant mares and foals; there was a granary, threshing floor, mill, bakery and brewery. In the kitchen garden were long, narrow beds planted with vegetables, including beans, beetroot, cabbages, celery, garlic, leeks, onions and peas. The herbs recommended for the kitchen were chervil, coriander, dill, parsley and savory.

Fruit and nut trees are shown in the orchard: apples, pears, peaches, plums, quinces, cherry laurel, hazelnuts and almonds. These would either have been improved, selected forms of wild fruit trees, or grafts imported from other religious foundations in Europe. Other fruits originally brought into cultivation by the Romans included cherries, medlars, mulberries, figs, walnuts and sweet chestnuts.

The orchard also served as the monks' cemetery. The 13 trees shown on the St Gall drawing perhaps symbolize Christ and the 12 apostles, adding a contemplative dimension to this part of the garden.

Monks derived sensual pleasure from the gardens, even if their primary purpose was practical and spiritual. The tenth-century monk Walafrid dedicated his poem *De Cultura Hortulorum* to his mentor Father Grimald:

> I can picture you sitting there in the green enclosure of your garden
> Under apples which hang in the shade of lofty foliage,
> Where the peach-tree turns its leaves this way and that
> In and out of the sun, and the boys at play,
> Your happy band of pupils, gather for you
> Fruits white with tender down and stretch
> Their hands to grasp the huge apples…

Translation by Raef Payne, 1966

Walafrid is remembering a late summer scene. The Yorkshire monk Alcuin's *Elegy on his life at Aachen* expresses nostalgia for a similar garden in late spring:

> Throughout your enclosed gardens apple boughs smell sweetly,
> and white lilies are mingled with little red roses.

In monastery gardens, in order to achieve complete self-sufficiency, plants had to be grown for other practical uses beside food. The infirmary (hospital) garden, presided over by the infirmarer, provided medicinal herbs, and plants were needed for various domestic uses. Aromatic strewing herbs were spread on indoor floors to sweeten the air and discourage bugs. Woad (blue), Dyer's chamomile (yellow) and meadowsweet (black) were among the dye plants grown, and flowers, particularly those with symbolic significance, like roses and lilies, were used to decorate the church. Scented flowers and foliage were made into nosegays and pomanders, to be carried and sniffed at when the smells of the street became unbearable.

Miscellaneous uses of plants included onion juice to eliminate freckles (perhaps not often resorted to by monks, but many nuns came from wealthy families and had a worldly attitude to their looks); quince seed, cherry gum and marshmallow root for glue; and twisted strips of hazel bark for twine.

Medicine and magic

The infirmary garden must have been pretty as well as practical; roses, lilies, flag irises, sage, rue, rosemary and savory were grown for their medicinal properties, as well as kidney beans, cumin, fenugreek, lovage, fennel, pennyroyal and mint. The boundaries between medicine, religion and magic were blurred. In the fourteenth century, Johannes Mirfield of St Bartholomew's, Smithfield, gives this advice: 'Taking the herb cinquefoil and, while collecting it, saying a Paternoster on behalf of the patient, and boiling it in a new jar with some of the water the patient is destined to drink, and if the water be red in colour after this boiling, then the patient will die.'

Mirfield also proposed an anaesthetic ointment to be used before surgery, made up with henbane, mandragora, hemlock and black and white poppies. In addition, the seed of henbane 'giffen in wyne to drynk maketh the drinker alsone for to sleep that he schal noght fele whatsoever is done to hym'.

At this time, when herbal remedies were applied for every complaint from constipation to a broken heart, botany and medicine went hand in hand. Henry Daniel (*c*1315–85), a Dominican friar and scholar, studied medicine for seven years. His description of, and instructions for, the use of medicinal plants are the earliest known in England. Among more than 40 authorities he cites are 'a Christian man that long had woned [lived] among Saracens and Jews' and 'a Christian man that mickle had learned among Saracens'. The latter recommended the juice of tansy to treat boils and sores. If applied in a circle around the infected part, 'that sor passeth not that cercle'.

Contact with Saracen doctors, botanists and scientists may have come through Moorish Spain, where gardening knowledge came from Arabic tradition and experience and was advanced compared to northern Europe. In about 1080 Ibn Bassal, director of a large botanic garden in Toledo, wrote a treatise for Al-Ma'mun, the Moorish king of Toledo. It is written from his own experience, with few traces of earlier Classical or Arabic texts, and was much translated and copied. Friar Henry Daniel may well have known this work. Daniel himself had a large garden at Stepney with 252 different kinds of plant: many more than most monastic herbaria, which list 100. Daniel studied plants for their own sake as well as for their medicinal attributes. He described new introductions like cypress, germander, gourd, sweet marjoram, pomegranate and rosemary (said to have been first brought to England from the Netherlands in about 1340 by Queen Philippa, wife of Edward III), and gave instructions for their acclimatization. He studied the preferred growing conditions for different plants, commenting on habitats such as dry banks, hedges, feeble soil, meadows, marshes, in or near water, or in woods.

To most people medicine and magic were much the same thing. For them, preventive medicine meant planting a rowan tree or a clump of *Helleborus niger* (Christmas rose) beside their door to ward off witches and evil spirits. If that failed and a member of the family fell ill, they might consult a 'wise woman', an unofficial practitioner who would prepare lotions and potions from ingredients gathered in the wild, or tended in her own garden plot. An ill-judged dose of some of the remedies described in medical treatises could easily result in the death of a patient, and a changed perception of the practitioner from wise woman to wicked witch.

The monastic complex

It was safer to take your ailments to the monks at the infirmary. Your children, too, might be admitted to the monastery to attend the school run by the monks. But no layman could penetrate the inner sanctum of the abbot's (or abbess's) private garden, or the area described on the St Gall plan as 'paradise'– the burial ground for abbots and others of high status. These gardens were for

relaxation and contemplation and probably had a similar layout and the same fragrant plants and flowers as a nobleman's pleasure garden.

At the heart of the monastic complex was the cloister-garth (the Middle English word 'garth' means yard or garden), an area where the monks or nuns walked at set hours under the cover of a roofed arcade. There is no evidence that the centre of the cloister court was planted with anything except grass and perhaps a single evergreen tree or shrub. The plain green lawn was considered an important source of spiritual refreshment, symbolizing renewal and ever-lasting life. The colour green was also known to refresh eyes strained by the close work of reading, copying or illuminating manuscripts.

Absent from the St Gall plan are the fishponds, or stew-ponds, where the carp that supplied the monks' Friday and Lenten protein were nurtured. A meatless diet was mandatory on Fridays and in Lent and virtually every monastery or manor had ponds, streams or moats stocked with fish. Sometimes there was also a fish-house and curing furnace. Often incorporated later into more sub-stantial stretches of ornamental water, fishponds are virtually the only element of monastic life to have survived the destruction of Henry VIII's Dissolution of the Monasteries (under which monastic lands were broken up and sold off). Examples can be seen in several gardens today, including Deans Court in Dorset, Stanton Harcourt near Oxford, and Elsham Hall, South Humberside.

Although tools and techniques have changed over the centuries, garden tasks remain much the same. This couple is mowing and raking up the grass in their orchard. 'Labours of the Months' (detail). Alsace, mid-fifteenth century.

At Mettingham Castle in Suffolk, a survey made in 1562 described 'The Inner orteyarde, inclosed with the mote… [and] little pondes in it called fridaye pondes. Werein is small store of fyshe or none but they s(er)ved to p(re)s(er)ve fishe taken on ye weke dayes tyll fridaye.'

There was also a 'greate orteyarde' west of the moats with a 'fayre pond', containing at the time of the survey a few bream and perch. In the moat there were roach, bream, tench and perch, 'sore destroyed with a otter and some pickerel.' These features may have been installed when the castle was built in 1342 for Sir John, Lord de Norwich. By the end of the century it was a religious college, dissolved in 1542.

In some medieval monastic and castle gardens the ponds and orchards are the only features still identifiable today. They are often in close proximity to each other. The 'Inner orteyard' at Mettingham Castle, where the 'fridaye pondes' were, was 'sette with dyvers trees of fruite', and there were pears, apples, wardens (cooking pears) and plums in the 'greate orteyarde'. Gerald of Wales, describing his birthplace at Manorbier Castle, wrote in 1188

> just beneath its walls is a very good fishpond, notable both for its
> majestic appearance and the depth of its water. On the same side
> there is likewise a most beautiful orchard, enclosed between the
> pond and a wooded grove – itself remarkable both for rocky crags
> and tall hazel trees.

His comments on the 'majestic appearance' of the fishpond and the beauty of the orchard indicate that gardens were appreciated for their aesthetic as well as their practical attributes, and his pleasure at the remarkable rocky crags shows sensitivity to the kind of landscape that was to be admired as 'picturesque' and 'sublime' 600 years later.

'Profane' gardens: 'The Garden of Earthly Delight.'

The St Gall Monastery plan described above was prepared for the Benedictine order. Its founder, St Benedict, lived in Rome in the early sixth century. He belonged to a prosperous social class and became disillusioned by the shallow frivolity and licentiousness of the life he and his companions lived. With his twin sister, Ste Scolastica, he retired to live as a hermit in a cave at Subiaco, to the east of Rome. He planted a rose bush, *il roseto*, outside his cave so that the flowers could tempt his sensuality and the thorns chastise his flesh. His sacred cave, *sacre speco*, can still be visited, and there is a rose garden to commemorate his *roseto*.

The symbolism of St Benedict's rose bush is reflected in the dual role that gardens were developing during the relatively stable period when Henry II and Eleanor of Aquitaine ruled England and much of what is now France. Monastic gardens and the private devotional gardens of kings, queens and princes fulfilled a sacred role. But what we might call, for the sake of contrast, 'profane' gardens, clearly made for worldly pleasures, began to appear in literature and paintings.

It was a time when people believed very literally in heaven and hell. But it was also the age of chivalry, when knights jousted and troubadours sang of love. Eleanor was an enthusiastic patron of troubadour poetry and music at her court at Poitiers, where lords and ladies were elegantly and sumptuously dressed in rich silks, furs and jewels. It would be hard to exaggerate the luxury enjoyed by kings and courtiers. For example, at his marriage to Berengeria on 12 May 1191 at the Chapel of St George, Limassol, Cyprus, Richard I wore a rose-coloured belted tunic of samite (a heavy silk fabric often woven with gold and silver threads), with a mantle of striped silk tissue threaded with gold crescents and silver suns; a scarlet bonnet embroidered with gold beasts and birds; and buskins of cloth of gold with gilded spurs on his heels. True, this was a special occasion, but at court, almost every day brought a special occasion.

Even so, the living conditions of courtiers were in many ways as squalid as those of the peasants. The sensual delights of a garden planted with sweet roses and lilies, with clear water flowing from a fountain, were valued all the more in contrast to the dirt and stench of banqueting halls, where bones and other scraps of food lay festering on the floor and men as well as dogs often urinated against the walls.

Such pleasure gardens, like the monastery gardens, probably owed their existence to a religious tradition, but it was a tradition very different from the austerity of the Christian monastic orders. Islamic culture brought sophisticated gardens and advanced horticultural knowledge from Baghdad to Spain, where the Arabs ruled from 711 to 1492. They made ravishingly beautiful gardens following a traditional Persian pattern, which had been eagerly adopted for Islam in the seventh century. In Spain there were said to be 50,000 gardens in and around the city of Córdoba. Few traces of the gardens of Córdoba remain today, but there are still exquisite examples in the Alhambra and Generalife palaces in Granada.

Islamic gardens, like the biblical Eden of the Book of Genesis, symbolized the four quarters of the universe, separated by four great rivers in the form of a cross. There was usually a central pavilion, and shade provided by trees. Oranges, pomegranates and other fruit, along with headily scented jasmine, hyacinths, tulips, pinks and, above all, roses ornamented the gardens. And there was always the sparkle and splash of running water gushing from a fountain or spring.

Muslims did not share Christian inhibitions about the sensual enjoyment of gardens. In Arabic, paradise is *al-janna*, the garden. The Koran promises that the faithful will be amply rewarded. They will spend eternity in a beautiful garden, where they will find not only flowers and fruit, but also 'maidens good and comely'. Earthly Islamic gardens were designed to give a foretaste of the sensual pleasures to come.

Diplomats and other travellers from northern Europe would have seen and wondered at the sophisticated luxury of these gardens. Crusaders travelling to the Holy Land would also have encountered Islamic gardens. Some Crusaders remained as rulers of the four crusader states, including the kingdom of Jerusalem, established after the First Crusade to capture the Holy Land from the Turks in 1096–99. Such a prince was Raymond of Poitiers, uncle (and some said lover) of Eleanor of Aquitaine and England. Raymond became ruler of Antioch in 1134. His court enjoyed an incredibly luxurious lifestyle with, among other delights, beautiful hanging gardens. Eleanor was one of the visitors who had the opportunity to see them, when she went with her first husband, the French King Louis VII, on the disastrous Second Crusade of 1147.

Although the crusade was a serious military enterprise, it was also a wonderful chance for adventurous travel. It involved moving the French court more or less lock, stock and barrel, with a second army of retainers to look after the royal party. The Queen travelled with silk and wool dresses, furs, jewellery, veils, household plate, goblets, washbasins and soap, fully equipped for the 11 months she spent in Jerusalem. There is a legend that she brought *Rosa gallica* back from the Holy Land to France and thence, later, to England, where it became the badge of the house of Lancaster. She may also have introduced silk worms into Aquitaine, along with the mulberry trees for them to feed on.

The wars of the crusades were fought with harsh brutality on both sides, but there seems to have been a code of chivalry between the commanders of the two armies: when Richard I fell ill with malaria during the siege of Acre in 1191, Saladin, who greatly admired Richard's bravery in battle, sent him gifts of fruit and food. When he was ill again the following year, Richard sent to Saladin asking for fruit and snow to relieve his fever.

This fifteenth-century Italian illumination shows a walled pleasure garden where there is wine, food, music, lovemaking and mixed bathing. The garden contains flowering trees, a flowery meadow and an elaborate marble fountain.

So it seems likely that elements of Islamic culture, including medical and horticultural expertise, and the tradition of garden making perfected over a long period, found their way to Europe directly from the Holy Land, as well as from those parts of Spain under Arab rule.

In northern Europe, Christian authorities initially frowned upon pleasure gardens based on the Islamic pattern. But before long their symbolism was adapted to suit Christian iconography. The Old Testament described how: 'The Lord God planted a garden eastward in Eden', and the Garden of Eden became the pattern of perfection towards which all earthly garden makers must strive. The cruciform pattern formed by the four rivers of Eden came to signify Christ's cross. Perhaps too much is made of this symbolism. After all, if you are faced with a rectangular piece of ground and you wish to divide the space to make it easier to cultivate, your first instinct is to halve it then to quarter it. At the centre of an enclosed garden, or *hortus conclusus*, there was often a fountain, sometimes with a waterspout on each of its four sides, the water falling into a round, square or octagonal pool. The water might symbolize purification, re-birth and eternal life.

Flowers grown purely for pleasure were also 'christianized'. The red rose, the flower of voluptuous passion in Persian gardens, when grown in a Christian garden was said to be stained with the blood of martyrs. With lilies and violets, roses also became the special flowers of the Virgin Mary. The Venerable Bede, the great scholar and monk of Jarrow, who died in 735, explained that the whiteness of *Lilium candidum* represented the purity of the Virgin and the golden anthers the glowing light of her soul. We still call it the Madonna lily. The cult of the Virgin Mary was so potent that some devotional gardens were designed specifically to honour her.

Enclosed gardens appear again and again in medieval paintings and French and Flemish Books of Hours, both as the setting for sacred groups of Mary, Jesus and the Saints, and as the more secular 'Garden of Earthly Delight'. Many of these illustrations show imagined, fantasy gardens, but even fantasies are based in reality, and similar gardens existed at the time for the enjoyment of royal ladies and their attendants within the safe walls of fortified castles. The gardens made in the various kingdoms and dukedoms of what is now France were brought to England by rulers and their entourages, and by bishops, priests and scholars of the Church. In spite of the many difficulties and hardships of travel, there was a great deal of movement between England and Europe, making possible a constant exchange of ideas about horticulture and the dissemination of plants.

Queen Eleanor's Garden

After her marriage to Henry II, Eleanor of Aquitaine did much to introduce Norman and French culture to England. Her former husband, Louis VII of France, had brought her to Paris as his bride in 1137. They lived in the Cité Palace, which had gardens 'enclosed by walls and trellised vines, they had paths ordered with acanthus and shaded by willow, fig, cypress and pear trees; in the flower beds grew roses, lilies and poppies, and there was a herb garden smelling fragrantly of mint, rue, watercress and absinthe'.

There is also evidence of a royal, enclosed garden in England at Winchester Castle: £22.13s.2d was paid in 1159 'for the repair of the chapel, the houses, the walls and the garden of the Queen, and for the transport of the Queen's robes, her wine, her incense and the chests of her chapel, and for the boys shields, and for the Queen's chamber, chimney and cellar'. At this time, Winchester had still not been overtaken by London as the principal city. It was also near Southampton, the port most often used to travel between Normandy and England, so the King and Queen spent more time at Winchester than at their other English castles.

Henry III succeeded to the throne in 1216 and horticultural knowledge continued to grow during his reign and those of the three Edwards who followed him. When Henry III built the Great Hall at Winchester Castle in 1235, he also embellished the Castle with 'three herbers' (a herber was a small enclosed garden). This has been recognized by the creation, just outside the Great Hall, of an historically accurate medieval garden, known as 'Queen Eleanor's garden'. Designed for Hampshire County Council by two distinguished scholars of medieval garden history, Sylvia Landsberg and John Harvey, it commemorates, not Henry II's Eleanor of Aquitaine, but Eleanor of Provence, Henry III's queen, and Eleanor of Castile, the wife of his son Edward I.

The garden is open to visitors all the year round. Its design is based on a finely detailed French fourteenth-century painting. The painting shows a small garden, perhaps four yards square, enclosed by a wooden trellis with double red and white roses trained on it. The garden is entered through an elaborately carved gothic arch, also of wood. Outside the trellis there is a shady walk beneath vines trained over arches. In front of the trellis a lady sits on a low turf bench under a tree, threading red and white roses on to a headband to make a coronet. She is wearing a brilliant blue dress trimmed and lined with ermine and her golden hair falls over her shoulders to below her waist. Besides the roses, the painting shows pinks or carnations, a hollyhock, columbines and violas. The picture tells Boccaccio's story of two noble kinsmen imprisoned in a castle.

From their window they see the lovely Emilia and both fall in love with her. They can be seen in the picture, gazing out from behind bars, rather lustfully, or perhaps merely wistfully.

Eleanor of Castile was the first wife of Edward I who reigned from 1272 until 1307. She loved gardens. Her husband's wedding present to her was an island garden at Leeds Castle, and she is thought to have introduced several Mediterranean plants to Britain, such as hollyhocks, pot marigolds, lavender and wallflowers. They have been planted in 'Queen Eleanor's Garden' at Winchester. She is also known to have had a garden within the walls of Rhuddlan Castle in Wales. There, in 1282, a garden is recorded which had a roofed well, surrounded by a small fishpond lined with four cartloads of clay, with seats constructed around it. In the castle courtyard 6000 turves were laid and edged with staves from discarded casks. The well still remains. The following year, 1283, a lawn was made for the queen at Caernarfon Castle, where her son Edward, the first English Prince of Wales, was born in 1284. In 1285 a 'King's Pool' was added. Eleanor died in 1290, but in 1295 further improvements were made, the 'King's Garden' being dug and hedged around. During 1304–5 a touch of fantasy was added, an artificial swans' nest being placed in the middle of King's Pool.

The Legend of Rosamond's Bower

An earlier royal garden was the setting for the legend of Rosamond's Bower. Henry II was said to have imprisoned his mistress, Rosamond Clifford, in a garden of love in the middle of a maze. Only the King, the story goes, could find his way through the maze until his wicked and cunning queen (Eleanor of Aquitaine again) discovered the secret and arranged for Rosamond to be poisoned. Tradition puts Rosamond's Bower in the deer park at Woodstock Park, in Oxfordshire, were Henry I had built a hunting lodge on the site of a Saxon manor house. Henry II's affair with Rosamond de Clifford probably began in 1165 and lasted till shortly before her death (almost certainly from natural causes) in 1176. No evidence exists that Rosamond lived at Woodstock or that there was ever a maze there. The story of her living in a bower at the centre of a labyrinth was started much later, in the early fourteenth century by Ranulf Higden, a monk from Chester. Henry II used Woodstock to house a menagerie

The design of Queen Eleanor's Garden at Winchester is based on this picture, 'Emilia in the Garden' (detail), from The Hours of the Duke of Burgundy, 1454–55. The painting is one of the most detailed and valuable sources of information about medieval gardens.

of lions, leopards, lynxes, camels and a porcupine, gifts from foreign rulers, and Richard I kept a crocodile there.

But Henry II did make a cloistered garden nearby at Everswell in 1166, with bench seats and pools fed from an existing spring. It is possible that he installed Rosamund Clifford there. The remains of the Everswell garden were described and sketched by John Aubrey in the seventeenth century. Although there was no maze at Woodstock and Rosamond Clifford died in a nunnery at Godstow, the myth of the secret bower is a potent one.

'Le Roman de la Rose'

The enclosed garden was a safe haven for women, a place where, both metaphorically and literally, their chastity was inviolate. Religious paintings show the Madonna and Child sheltered by a rose arbour or playing on a flower-studded lawn, attended by various female saints. Much of our knowledge about secular gardens of the Middle Ages comes from the numerous paintings and woodcuts made to illustrate the allegory of love known as *Le Roman de la Rose*. One of the most popular works of medieval literature, the poem was completed in about 1270–7 and is thought to be the work of two authors: Guillaume de Lorris and Jean de Meun. The story tells of a lover's quest for a perfect rose, which he is allowed to pick only when he has overcome various obstacles. The illustrations vary greatly in quality. Some versions of the story show a simple and crude representation of a circular wattle fence enclosing a single rose tree, with the lover about to enter through a simple wooden gate. Others are much more elaborate. A very detailed Flemish painting *c.*1485 gives a clear picture of a wealthy nobleman's garden at that time.

In the painting, the entire garden is enclosed by a strong, castellated stone wall. Outside a sturdy wooden door in the wall, stands a rather hesitant lover, his hand firmly grasped by a lady called Idleness. In her other hand she holds a large iron key with which to unlock the door. Once inside the garden, he passes through an area laid out with rectangular raised beds, shaded by fruit trees. A waist-high fence of diagonal wooden trellis, with a peacock sitting on it, separates this area from the garden beyond.

The lover makes his way towards an arched gate leading into a pleasure garden where Lady Idleness will, no doubt, tempt him to waste some time when he ought to be questing for his perfect rose. At the centre of the garden is an ornate eight-sided fountain with water spouting from eight lions' heads into a circular stone pool at ground level. The stone sections forming the rim of the pool are joined with metal rivets, and a straight-sided rill carries the water away,

through an arched grille in the garden wall. Just inside the boundary wall is an open wooden fence with climbing plants trained on it: sweetbrier roses, perhaps. Birds swoop and dive in the sky or settle on the branches of tall trees. Some fashionably dressed young men and women are having a musical party, some reclining or sitting on the lawn while others stand and listen to the music. One man with a dashing feathered hat is playing a lute, and two of the ladies are singing from song-sheets. It is a delightful scene, often repeated with minor variations in other medieval documents. There are fruit trees in the background, and a turf-covered bench along one side of the garden. The bench and the lawn around the fountain are spangled with daisies.

The story illustrated in the medieval manuscript 'Le Roman de la Rose' (c.1487–95) would have been familiar to English readers through Chaucer's translation. The garden shown here is divided into separate enclosures within a strong stone perimeter wall.

Flowery meads

The flower-strewn lawn or meadow and the flowery turf seat are well-documented components of medieval gardens, and are shown in a number of illustrations, including the series of *millefleurs* 'Unicorn' tapestries in the Cloisters Museum in New York. They show a flowery carpet of such density and variety that the grass can hardly be seen.

In the thirteenth century, scientist, philosopher, and theologian Albertus Magnus gave instructions for making such a garden; these were later translated by Piero de Crescenzi and widely read:

> Certain gardens may be made only of herbs, others with trees and yet others of both… The whole plot shall be filled with fine turf, and the sods themselves thoroughly compressed by wooden mallets, and the grass trodden underfoot will grow little by little like hair and cover the surface like a green cloth… Let the site… be planted with fragrant herbs of all kinds, such as rue, sage, basil, marjoram, mint, and the like, and similarly all kinds of flowers, such as violet, columbine, lily, rose, iris and the like. Between the level turf and the herbs let there be a higher piece of turf made in the fashion of a seat, suitable for flowers… Trees [should have] sweet scented flowers and give pleasant shade, such as vines, pears, apples, pomegranates, sweet bays, cypresses and such like.
>
> Beyond the lawn there may be a great variety of medicinal and scented herbs, not only to delight the sense of smell, but to refresh the eye… If possible a fountain of clear water should be in the middle… Delight rather than fruit is the objective in a pleasure garden.

Albertus/de Crescenzi also gives useful practical advice, explaining how to clear and cultivate the plot and recommending rue to keep away vermin.

Alexander Neckham in *De Naturis Rerum*, written in the 1190s, lists plants suited for different purposes: for adornment, 'roses and lilies, the turnsole or heliotrope, violets, and mandrake, there you should have parsley, cost [costmary], fennel, southernwood, coriander, sage, savery, hysop, mint, rue, ditanny [an herbaceous plant], smallage [possibly wild celery], pellitory, [*Anacychus pyrethrum*] lettuce, garden cress, and peonies.' For food, 'There should also be beds planted with onions, leeks, garlic, pumpkins, and shallots,' and pottage herbs, such as beets, herb mercury, orach, sorrel, and mallows. For medicinal use, Neckham recommended borage and purslane, hazelwort, colewort and ragwort, valerian and myrtle, thyme and saffron.

Apart from enjoying the sight and scent of the flowers, the coolness of the breeze, the splashing of the fountain and the song of the birds, how did people use their gardens?

Contemporary paintings and prints show couples or small groups eating, drinking, reading, playing music, dancing and playing chess. In the 'greate orteyard' at Mettingham Castle in Suffolk there was a bowling alley, as well as apples, plums, pears and wardens (cooking pears). Games in which children as well as grown-ups could take part were hoodman blind (blind man's buff), frog-in-the-middle, handball, whip and top and nine-pins.

'La Main Chaude' and other games
A tapestry dating from the early sixteenth century shows the game of 'La Main Chaude', known in England as 'Hot Cockles'. One person is blindfolded and another hits her on the hand or the back. She has to guess whose 'hot hand' it is. In the tapestry, the game is played in an idyllic rustic scene, a flowery meadow inhabited by sheep, goats, pigs, a fox, a pheasant, woodcutters and peasants carrying agricultural implements.

This was the age of 'courtly love', and there is a series of pictures illustrating 'the Garden of Earthly Delights' with lovemaking (flirting, wooing, and some-times winning) as their subject. It was a time when marriages were made not for love but as property mergers, and for the getting of heirs to kingdoms, duke-doms and lesser properties. The emotional vacuum left by this system was filled by the idea of courtly love: that is to say, by love as practised at court. One court where the game of love (it was a game, and there were rules by which to play it) flourished was that of Marie, Countess of Champagne, daughter of Eleanor of Aquitaine. Both women extended their patronage to the troubadours of southern France, peripatetic poets who made their living composing and

Ornamental gardens were for fun and games as well as for contemplation. The game of blind man's buff has never quite lost its appeal. Here, in this illustration in a book of sixteenth-century French love poems by Pierre Sala, it is played in a garden surrounded by rose-clad wooden trellises.

singing stories of knightly chivalry and love, mostly unrequited. In his book *The Allegory of Love* (1936), C.S. Lewis defined courtly love as Humility, Courtesy, Adultery and the Religion of Love. The humble lover is the slave of his 'mistress'. He expresses his adoration by means of all the courtesies he can contrive to make her life delightful: considerate attention, bouquets, presents, songs, poems. The relationship is extramarital, therefore adulterous, even if it remains unconsummated, as it was supposed to. Sublimated love acted out in the gardens at court set the pattern. In less-aristocratic circles, flirtation probably gave as much, or greater, satisfaction.

'The square garden of Henry the Poet'

And if you could not be making love in the garden, you might be inspired to write about it. Chaucer's translation of *Le Roman de la Rose* was short on details about the flowers growing in the garden of the rose. But John Skelton (?1460–1529) gives us plenty of flowers in two poems, extolling the charms of two very different ladies:

> To Mistress Margery Wentworth
> With margerain gentle,
> The flower of goodlihead,
> Embroidered the mantle
> Is of your maidenhead.
> Plainly I cannot glose;
> Ye be, as I divine,
> The pretty primrose,
> The goodly columbine.

> To Mistress Isabell Pennell
> By saint Mary, my lady,
> Your mammy and your daddy
> Brought forth a goodly baby!
> My maiden Isabel,
> Reflaring rosabel,
> The flagrant camamel;
> The ruddy rosary,
> The sovereign rosemary,
> The pretty strawberry;
> The columbine, the nept,

The gilliflower well set,
The proper violet;
Enewed your colour
Is like the daisy flower
After the April shower…
Star of the morrow gray,
The blossom on the spray,
The freshest flower of May.

Gardeners were poets and vice versa and, in the tradition of classical Latin treatises on horticulture, gardening manuals were often written in verse, which sometimes degenerated into doggerel. There was at least one poet who was also a garden maker.

A vivid picture of 'The square garden of Henry the Poet' has been built up by Dr John Harvey from a fourteenth-century manuscript in the British Library. Henry the Poet, also a physician described by Friar Henry Daniel as 'leche and noble poete', probably lived between 1235 and 1313. Dr Harvey describes a garden surrounded by trellis fixed to posts, with a grass lawn at the centre and perhaps a pool or fountain. The four borders around the perimeter were planted with the tallest plants along the fence and the lowest plants at the front. Most gardens of this period are known to have followed the St Gall Plan, with each bed occupied by a separate species. So this garden is remarkable for following a different system, hinted at in Albertus Magnus's 1260 description of a pleasure garden, arranging the plants in what later came to be known as herbaceous borders.

Henry the Poet's four borders had 25 plants in each, mainly pot herbs, salads and medicinal plants, but some with purely ornamental flowers. They include hollyhock, lavender, clary, thyme, myrtle, hellebore and calamint.

War and pestilence

During the 419 years between the Norman Conquest and the end of the turbulent years of the Wars of the Roses, crisis followed crisis, and England enjoyed few prolonged periods of peace and economic stability. In just two years, between 1348 and 1350, there was a cataclysmic event, which would bring about

Overleaf: 'Pallas expelling the Vices from the Garden of Virtue', c.1499–1502, Andrea Mantegna. The elaborate topiary architecture of Renaissance gardens like Mantegna's fantasy Garden of Virtue appeared later in Tudor gardens.

permanent changes and leave deep and lasting scars. The epidemic of bubonic plague that swept through the country became known as the Black Death because of the black spots it produced on the skin. Caused by the bacterium *Pasterurella pestis*, it arrived, carried by fleas on black rats, by sea on a ship that docked at Melcombe in Dorset (now Weymouth). Most historians agree that the disease wiped out at least 25 million people, one-third of the population of Europe. Perhaps surprisingly, England's economy improved as a result. Because labour was scarce, wages increased, and the standard of living for the majority improved.

The fall in population led to villages being completely abandoned and left to fall into ruins. Their outlines can still be traced in humps and bumps beneath the ground's surface. In some areas man was again on the losing side in the battle against nature; there were simply not enough able-bodied workers to prevent the scrub encroaching on cultivated land.

If you add to the devastation caused by the Black Death the insecurity of fluctuating waves of civil war as the Yorkists fought the Lancastrians for the crown, it would not be surprising if no gardens were made in this period. But there were families that benefited from the war and from the fall in land values after the Black Death. They built houses and probably also made and maintained new gardens, or altered and improved old ones. Their gardens would have been composed of the same, traditional elements as the monastic and royal gardens of the twelfth and thirteenth centuries.

There were raised beds for vegetables, salads, flavouring herbs, medicinal herbs and other useful plants, with the earth contained by wooden planks or low brick walls and the beds divided by trodden earth or sand paths. There was a separate area for rest, spiritual refreshment or social recreation, enclosed by walls or by wooden trellis covered with climbing plants. There might be turf benches and a table, and underfoot would be close-cut turf planted with low-growing flowering plants such as daisies, wild strawberries and periwinkle. Ideally, there would be a fountain in the centre. Most gardens had a shaded walk, consisting of a pergola covered with vines, and one or two shade trees. Beyond the garden might be greater or lesser orchards and fish ponds or a moat. And beyond the orchards and moat there might be a park, enclosed for hunting deer and other wild creatures.

The cultivation of medicinal herbs; physicians conferring about their uses; apothecaries preparing herbal remedies; and a very sick patient being dosed (clockwise from top right) are detailed in this woodcut of the English School, 1531.

One family to benefit from the Wars of the Roses was the Vaughan family at Tretower Court in Powys, Wales. Sir Roger Vaughan was given Tretower Court in about 1450 by his half-brother William Herbert, who later become Earl of Pembroke. The brothers supported the Yorkist side in the Wars of the Roses, and were well rewarded for their loyal service to Edward IV. Roger Vaughan became the richest commoner in Wales, and greatly extended and modernized his house at Tretower. But in 1471 Vaughan, in pursuit of the Tudors fleeing after their defeat at the Battle of Tewkesbury, was himself captured at Chepstow by Jasper Tudor and beheaded.

Although there is no evidence for a medieval garden at Tretower, it is very likely that such a rich and influential family would have made a pleasure garden as part of the general improvements to their property, and such a garden has recently been made, with layout and planting as authentic as meticulous research can make it.

The Tretower garden incorporates most of the standard medieval features and themes described above. All the themes were already in place and, over the next 500 years, these would be developed in various permutations at different times to form richly diverse garden styles suited to the cultural and political life of each period.

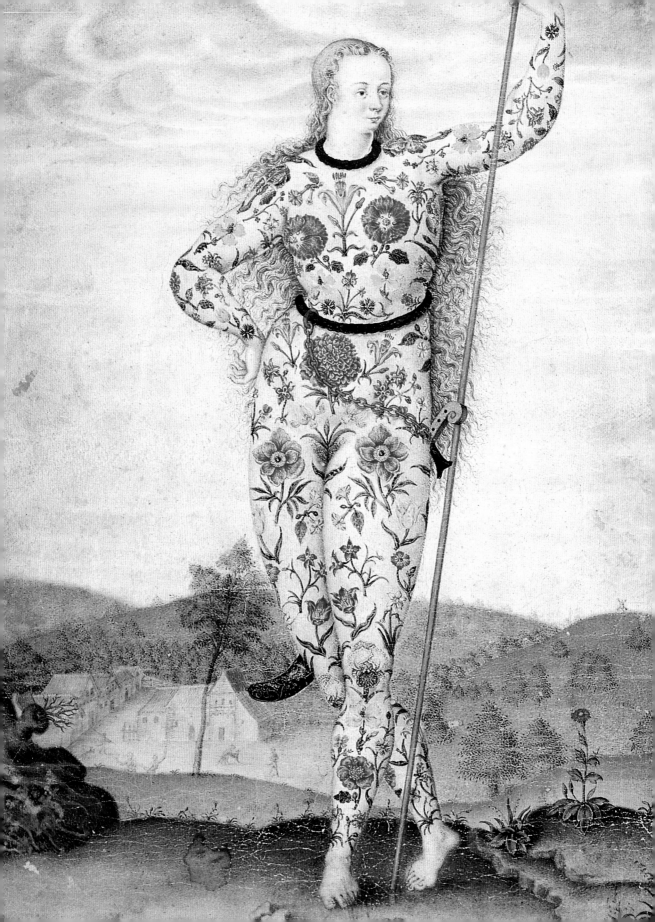

2

TUDOR GARDENS

Taming Nature

T HE WARS OF THE ROSES began (according to Shakespeare, at any rate) in a garden and ended on Bosworth Field in 1485, when the Lancastrian Henry Bolingbroke, whose emblem was a red rose, defeated Richard of York (King Richard III), whose emblem was a white rose.

Thirty years of sporadic warfare and unrest ended, as they are said to have begun, with a rose. When Bolingbroke became Henry VII, he united the two warring factions by marrying Elizabeth of York, daughter of Edward IV. He made a symbolic affirmation of this union, by choosing a double red and white rose as the new royal emblem.

We have seen the rose's power as a medieval religious and secular symbol, and over the centuries it has retained this power, adopted by sundry organizations including, in the twentieth century, Britain's Labour Party. And, while Scotland has its thistle and Wales its leek, Henry VII's Tudor rose remains the emblem of England. For more than 500 years it has been carved in wood and stone, moulded in plaster, fashioned in precious metals, embroidered in silk and gold or silver thread. It decorates cathedrals, palaces, coats of arms and robes of state. Look in your pocket or purse and you will find the Tudor rose embossed on a

The body paint of this young female warrior celebrates the Tudor love of decoration and of flowers in particular. 'Young Daughter of the Picts', Jacques le Moyne de Morgues, c.1585.

twentieth-century 20-pence coin. Roses have long been valued above all other flowers. In 1398 Franciscan encyclopaedist Bartholomeus Anglicus wrote in his *De proprietatibus rerum* ('On the Properties of Things').

> Among all floures of the world the floure of the rose is chief and beereth ye pryse... for by fayrness they feed the syghte, and playseth the smell by odour, the touch by soft handlynge. And wythstondeth and socouryth by vertue against many siknesses and evylles.

Henry VII spent his reign building a stable and prosperous economy that would make possible the extravagant consumption of his son Henry VIII. It was a rural economy, and the most valuable commodity was wool. At the end of the fifteenth century the devastation caused by the Black Death was still felt. The population of England and Wales had fallen to between 2.5 and 3 million people: not enough to work the land in the traditional combination of arable and pasture. But there were at least three times more sheep than people, and landowners realized that their future success lay with sheep. Less than one-third of the land had been cleared and brought into cultivation and, throughout the Tudor period, much of that land was enclosed to form productive agricultural units, including open areas grazed by sheep. By the end of the sixteenth century the landscape had become the patchwork of fields, hedges and woods, with tracts of heath on high ground and marsh on low ground that we still recognize today.

The more profitable the export of wool turned out to be, the more land was given over to sheep production, and the more profits the landowners made. Piety, or at any rate its outward appearance, was the norm, and many gave thanks to God for their new riches by building new churches or adding chapels or towers to existing churches. Others invested their fortunes in making their houses more comfortable, improving and extending medieval hall houses, or building from scratch. With the new houses went new gardens, larger and more elaborate than those that had gone before.

Pomp and ceremony: gardens for kings and courtiers

The surest way to succeed at the court of Henry VIII was to follow his example of ostentatious display. It has always been necessary for kings and queens to impress foreign rulers and their ambassadors by putting on a lavish show to entertain them. The most celebrated example is Henry VIII's own meeting with François I, King of France, at the 'Field of Cloth of Gold', but the custom has not died out. The Queen of England still hosts banquets in honour of visiting heads

of state, when several hundred guests, some wearing silk and satin, and jewels if they have them, sit down to an elaborate menu of dishes served on gold or silver plates, and drink the best wine from crystal glasses.

What sets Henry VIII apart from most monarchs is that he seems actually to have enjoyed dressing up and showing off, and expected those around him to enjoy it too. But nobody must be allowed to rival the king in splendour, as Cardinal Wolsey discovered to his cost. The story of Hampton Court Palace is well known: Thomas Wolsey, born in about 1475 in Ipswich (his father was probably a butcher), became Archbishop of York and by 1515 was a cardinal and Lord Chancellor of England. In 1514 he took a 99-year lease on Hampton Court and set about a costly and ambitious building programme, including lodgings for the king and his family, and elaborate gardens.

Wolsey's fall from grace came in 1528, after he failed to get the Pope to agree to Henry's divorce from Catherine of Aragon. The king took Hampton Court for himself and spent a further £62,000 (£18 million is today's equivalent) on building and rebuilding, including much work on the gardens.

A Tudor needlework image of a garden. The fountain can be compared with the medieval one shown in the illustration to 'Le Roman de la Rose' on page 31, and the elaborate green arcade to Mantegna's 'Garden of Virtue' on page 36.

What you see today at Hampton Court is the restoration of the gardens as they were redesigned for William and Mary in 1702, but we know from contemporary descriptions about some of the features made for Wolsey and Henry VIII.

There was a 'splendid, high and massy fountain with an ingenious waterwork whereby you can, if you like, make the water play upon the ladies and others who are standing by and give them a thorough wetting.' Some beds were 'planted with nothing but rosemary, others laid out with various other plants which are trained, intertwined and trimmed in so wonderful a manner and in such extraordinary shapes that the like could not easily be found.' These topiary shapes would have been made with hawthorn and rosemary. Yew was not used, and box not reintroduced till 1595, although we know from the excavations at Fishbourne that the Romans used it to make low, shaped and clipped hedges.

A mount was built for Henry in 1533 on a base of 256,000 bricks, with an elaborate three-storey banqueting house on the summit. A spiral path 'like turnings of cokilshilles [cockle shells], to cum to the top without payn' led up through flowerbeds edged with green and white painted rails and planted with

The garden at the Tudor House Museum at Southampton, Hampshire, was planned by the garden historian Sylvia Landsberg, and includes a knot based on a pattern in 'L'Agriculture et Maison Rustique' by Estienne and Liebault, 1570.

evergreens: bay, cypress, holly, juniper, yew; and 400 roses. In his biography of Wolsey, George Cavendish describes the garden as if in the cardinal's own words, in verse. It is a surprising and rather touching description considering the garden was noted for its grandeur rather than its intimate atmosphere, so perhaps Wolsey really did love the tranquil refuge his garden provided.

> My gardens sweet enclosed with walles strong
> Embanked with benches to sytt and take my rest
> The knots so enknotted it cannot be exprest
> With arbors and allyes so pleasant and so dulce
> The pestylent ayres with flavours do repulse.
>
> *The Life and Death of Cardinal Wolsey*, George Cavendish, *c.*1557

'the knots so enknotted it cannot be exprest'

The verse above describes the essential elements of lesser as well as great Tudor gardens. Most are already familiar from images and descriptions of earlier, medieval gardens: enclosure to create a place apart from, and safe from, the world outside; seats still constructed as 'embankments' covered in turf or creeping herbs; alleys and arbours to provide shaded and sheltered walks in all weathers; and scented plants to repulse the 'pestylent ayres'.

'Knots', however, were a novelty. They were rectangular beds planted with interlaced linear patterns of low, evergreen plants such as germander, hyssop, thrift, santolina and, later, box; variations on the kind of pattern a skilled practitioner of 'cat's cradle' can make with a loop of string. Some were extremely elaborate, others quite simple. They expressed a love for complex geometrical ornament also found in the new architecture, on plaster ceilings and carved panelled walls, and in fashionable clothes, with patterns woven into brocade or embroidered overskirts, doublets and sleeves, as shown in portraits of the time.

Knot gardens are the first garden features that can be regarded as uniquely English, and they remained popular for a century. The interstices of the pattern might be filled in with flowers or with coloured gravels, sands, brick dust, coal or seashells. The word 'knot' was also used to describe a relatively simple, symmetrical pattern of flowerbeds outlined with evergreen edging plants. Henry VIII's beds at Hampton Court were surrounded by posts and rails painted with green and white stripes.

A visitor to Hampton Court during Elizabeth I's reign, noticed 'rosemary so nailed and planted to the walls as to cover them entirely, which is a manner exceeding common in England.... [the gardens] laid out with various other plants, which are trained, intertwined and trimmed in so wonderful a manner, and in such extraordinary shapes, that the like could not easily be found.' The idea of training rosemary to grow up a wall is a reminder that many shrubs, if planted against a wall, will grow a great deal taller than in the open. The 'extraordinary shapes' he referred to would have been topiary, tied to its frame using strips of hazel, or flexible willow twigs. This method is still used to tie in climbing roses at the Roseraie de l'Hay gardens in Paris.

One feature of Hampton Court was unique to Tudor royal gardens. Large numbers (perhaps as many as 200) of carved heraldic animals were set up on painted wooden poles throughout the gardens: lions, tigers, bulls, dragons, griffins, deer, leopards, horses, rams and greyhounds. The vast scale of Hampton Court's gardens is indicated by an order for the great orchard of 600 cherry trees, 'at 6d the hundred'.

'the best house that has been built in this age': competitive courtiers

During Elizabeth's reign, peace and prosperity led to an increase in foreign trade and travel. Influences from Italy, France and the Netherlands were assimilated and incorporated into a confident English building style. Men of wealth and influence vied with each other to build houses and gardens of a size and magnificence equal to or greater than the royal palaces, in the hope that the queen would be lured to visit them with her considerable retinue. Vast sums were spent on the construction and upkeep of the gardens as well as the houses.

Sir Christopher Hatton, Elizabeth's Lord Chancellor, built Holdenby House, near Althorp in Northamptonshire, in the late 1570s, finishing it in 1583. Nearly double the size of Blenheim Palace (built later as a present to the Duke of Marlborough from the grateful nation), Holdenby was described at the time as 'altogether even the best house that has been built in this age'. The house was reached by a long green and a series of courtyards. South of the house were terraces and a 'rosery', and to the west more gardens, an orchard and a pond with two mounts at the farthest corners. A three-storey banqueting house, completed in 1585, had six rooms on each floor. Sir Christopher Hatton came close to financial ruin equipping his house to receive the queen. But although he was a great favourite with her, he died in 1591 without having had the pleasure of entertaining her at Holdenby. The entrance forecourt and a small part of the

An allée of clipped trees at Hatfield House in Hertfordshire: part of the Marchioness of Salisbury's brilliant twentieth-century interpretation of a late Tudor/Jacobean nobleman's garden, celebrating pattern and symmetry.

house survive, with two grass terraces and a fishpond. Visitors today will also find a reconstructed Elizabethan garden with plants of the 1580s.

Perhaps the queen found the hunting at Holdenby not up to scratch. She adored the sport and, unlike other court ladies, who shot from a stand at deer driven past them by hounds, she rode fast and furious with the men, even at the age of 67, shooting with a heavy crossbow and killing a 'great and fat stagge with her owen Hand.'

One garden the queen did visit was that of Lord Burghley, at Theobalds in Hertfordshire. Burghley told a friend that Her Majesty 'found fault with the small measure of her chamber (which was in good measure for me). I was forced to enlarge a room for a larger chamber'. John Gerard, author of *The Herball or Generall Historie of Plantes* (1597) supervised Burghley's gardens in the Strand in London and at Theobalds where, in addition to the regular garden staff, 40 poor people were employed for total of £10 a week. No trace of Theobalds remains, but Paul Hentzner, who visited it in 1598 on the day of Cecil's funeral, described it in his *Travels in England in the Reign of Elizabeth*:

> One goes into the garden, encompassed with a ditch full of water, large enough to have the pleasure of going in a boat, and rowing between the shrubs; here are great variety of trees and plants; labyrinths made with a great deal of labour; a *jet d'eau* with its basin of white marble; and columns and pyramids of wood, up and down the garden. After seeing these we were led by the gardener into the summer-house, in the lower part of which, built semi-circularly, are the twelve Roman emperors in white marble, and a table of touchstone; the upper part of it is set round with cisterns of lead, into which the water is conveyed through pipes, so that fish may be kept in them, and in summer time they are very convenient for bathing.

The Tudor layout at Theobalds included a square Privy Garden below the private apartments, with raised walks, arbours and knots; and a Great Garden divided into nine squares with the fountain mentioned by Hentzner at the centre. It may have featured knots decorated in the traditional way with dazzling sands and gravels. In the next generation, James I bullied Robert Cecil into accepting Hatfield House, a shabby, neglected royal property in exchange for Theobalds.

The life of Robert Cecil's father, Lord Burghley, builder of Theobalds, was plagued by the queen's passion for Robert Dudley, Earl of Leicester. Burghley deplored his strong influence over the queen and feared, above all, that she would marry him. Like other ambitious courtiers, Dudley made a garden fit for a queen. It was at Kenilworth Castle in Warwickshire and, though not much more than an acre in extent, was clearly spectacular. At its centre was a marble fountain spouting into a fishpond surrounded by jets to drench the unwary spectator. The garden was described by court official Robert Laneham in his account of a 19-day festival of pageants, masques and sport in 1575:

> Close to the wall is a beautiful terrace ten feet high and twelve feet broad, quite level and covered with thick grass which also grows on the slope. There are obelisks on the terrace at even distances, great balls and white heraldic beasts, all made of stone and perched on artistic posts, good to look at. At each end is a bower, smelling of sweet flowers and trees… There are also four parterres cut in regular proportions; in the middle of each is a post shaped like a cube, two feet high; on that a pyramid, accurately made, symmetrically carved, fifteen feet high; on the summit a ball ten inches in diameter.

The rise of the town garden: merchants and lawyers

The successful statesmen, politicians and courtiers of the time did not all start with the advantage of noble birth. For many the route into politics was by means of a career in law, as it still is today. Sir Christopher Hatton was at the Inner Temple, and William Cecil entered Gray's Inn in 1541. About 50 years earlier, Thomas More, Cardinal Wolsey's successor as Lord Chancellor to Henry VIII, studied law first at New Inn, then at Lincoln's Inn.

Thomas More was a great scholar, closely involved with European thought and art; Erasmus stayed with him when he was in London, and Holbein spent three years in the More household in Chelsea, and painted portraits of Thomas and his family. More was a dedicated family man, and made a garden to which he was devoted and where he spent much of his time after resigning the chancellorship in 1532. He wrote fluent and elegant Latin prose and poetry, his best-known work being *Utopia*, completed and published in 1516. On the imaginary island of Utopia the system of government is communism, there is education for women as well as men, and religious toleration. The inhabitants

> set great store by their gardens. In them they have vineyards, all manner of fruit, herbs and flowers, so pleasant, so well furnished, and so finely kept, that I never saw thing more fruitful nor better trimmed in any place. Their study and diligence herein cometh not only of pleasure, but also of certain strife and contention that is between street and street, concerning the trimming, husbanding and furnishing of their gardens, every man for his own part.

In noticing the beneficial results of 'a certain strife and contention', More touches on a perennial motive for keen gardeners: the desire to keep up with, or better still, to outdo the Joneses. The immaculate bedding scheme, the weed-free lawn, the biggest onion, the longest runner bean: these are goals to be striven for with the zest that only competition with your neighbour can provide. Today, the same spirit is applied street by street, in competition for 'Best Kept Village' and 'Britain in Bloom' awards.

Towns in general, and London in particular, were expanding rapidly under the Tudors. The antiquary John Stow in his *Survey of London and Westminster 1598* complained about the

> inclosure of the fields for Gardens wherein are builded many fayre summer houses, and as in other places of the Suburbs, some of them like Midsomer Pageantes, with Towers, Turrets, and Chimney tops, not so much for use or profite, as for shewe and pleasure, bewraying the vanity of men's mindes, much unlike in the disposition of the ancient Cittizens, who delighted in the building of Hospitals and Almes houses for the poore…

Stow had every reason to take a jaundiced view of the enclosure of land to make gardens for new men. His father, a tailor, lived next to Austin Friars, a monastic property acquired for his own use by Thomas Cromwell, the devious, ruthless

Gardeners pruning and tying in climbing roses on an arbour sheltering a table and turf benches are shown in this woodcut from the popular 'Gardeners Labyrinth' (1577) by Dydymus Mountaine, a pun on the name of Thomas Hill.

and very successful politician (yet another member of Gray's Inn), who presided over the Dissolution of the Monasteries. Without warning Cromwell had his neighbour's house dug out, placed on rollers and moved 6m (20ft) from his own boundary so that Cromwell could extend his garden.

After the Dissolution, the new owners of former religious houses turned them into dwellings, sometimes selling off parts of the gardens for building and turning chapels into parish churches, pulling them down or converting them. The chapel of the Crutched Friars became a tennis court; that of St Martin-le-Grand a wine tavern; and Whitefriars Carmelite priory became tenements, ale-houses and poor men's shops.

In 1580, new building was prohibited in London and outside the walls, but it made little difference. Tenements were still built, encroaching on church precincts and on roads. Gardens of big houses were turned into bowling alleys and dicing houses. The moat at Walbrook was covered over with carpenters' yards, kitchen gardens and tenements. John Stow describes new suburbs just outside Bishopsgate:

> Hogge Lane… within these fortie yeares had on both sides fayre hedgerows of Elme trees, with bridges and easie stiles to pass over into the pleasant fields, very commodious for Citizens therein to walke, shoote and otherwise to recreate and refresh their dulled spirites in the swete and wholesome ayre, which is now within few yeares made a continuall building throughout, of Garden houses, and small Cottages: the fields on either side be turned into Garden plottes, teynter yards, Bowling Allyes, and such like, from Houndes Ditch in the West, so farre as white Chappell, and further towards the East.

'crowned with almost perpetual verdure:' Beaufort House

The house Sir Thomas More built was not in London at all. Chelsea was still a country village, yet it was easily accessible from the City by river. Beaufort House seems to have been a comfortable but unpretentious family house, according to Erasmus, 'neither mean nor subject to envy yet magnificent and commodious enough.' The playwright John Heywood, who was married to More's niece Elizabeth Raskell, thought the garden

> Wonderfully charming… both from the advantage of its site and also for its own beauty. It was crowned with almost perpetual verdure; it had flowering shrubs and the branches of fruit trees interwoven in so beautiful a manner that it appeared like a tapestry woven by Nature herself.

Each of More's servants was given his or her own plot in the garden to look after. He could not bear anyone to be idle, and expected them to spend their leisure time with gardening, music or books. In 1532, More resigned the chancellorship and spent the next two years at home in Chelsea with his family. It is easy to imagine him keeping an eye on how the servants tended their gardens, and also taking quiet pleasure in his own gardens and orchard at this difficult time in his life. More wrote:

> As for Rosmarine I lett it run alle over my garden walls, not onlie because my bees love it, but because 'tis the herb sacred to remembrance, and therefore to friendship; whence a sprig of it hath a dumb language that maketh it the chosen emblem of our funeral wakes and in our burial grounds.

Although not extending as far as Chelsea, development did follow the River Thames west from the City of London. The Earls of Arundel and Essex had palaces west of the Temple, then came the Lord Protector's great Renaissance mansion, Somerset House, built between 1547 and 1550 from monastic ruins. Northumberland House, the town house of the Dukes of Northumberland followed, and farther west were the king's palaces of St James's and Whitehall.

Across the river at Lambeth Palace, Archbishop (later Cardinal) Pole planted fig trees between 1554 and 1558, and they are still there today outside the south wall of the old library. Cardinal Pole's successor, Archbishop Parker, put his wife in charge of the gardens, as was usual. He committed the gardener's job description to paper, giving us a good idea of what was involved in the maintenance of a grand town garden:

> His office is to see the garden, orchard and walks to be kept well weeden, rould [rolled], the grass walks and plats not suffered to be much growne but kept lowe with the sythe To see that there be planted in the grounds flowers, hearbs and roots, both for the provision of the kitchen and chambers; and with all sorts of good fruits, hearbs, plants and flowers for use and pleasure. That he keep nurseries of all sorts of good plants, to supply any defect that may happen, and that he delve and manure the grounds to the best commodity of the owner.

Before leaving London altogether, let us look more closely at Gray's Inn, the cradle of so many ambitions. In 1576, Francis Bacon was admitted to Gray's Inn and in 1586 became a bencher. In due course he became Lord Chancellor to

James I. A philosopher and a versatile and distinguished man of letters, his best-known work was a volume of essays first published in 1597. The opening words of his essay 'Of Gardens' are famous: 'God Almighty first planted a garden and, indeed, it is the purest of human pleasures; it is the greatest refreshment to the spirits of man.' Bacon goes on to describe his fantasy 'princely' garden, listing the flowers and fruit month by month, with much attention paid to plants which give off scent, in the air and underfoot. He then discusses the layout. The total area should be 30 acres, and the main, central garden 12, 'best to be square, encompassed on all four sides by a stately arched hedge.' This might be enclosed by a brick wall and form a shady, arcaded gallery. There are covered alleys on frames of carpenters' work; beds edged with 'little low hedges, round, like welts, with some pretty pyramids'; a mount 9m (30ft) high 'with three ascents and alleys, enough for four to walk abreast' (a very ambitious mount); a banqueting house; fountains and a bathing pool. Some of his more radical ideas will be discussed in the next chapter – but much of what he said was not new.

'the pleasantest place about London'

Bacon's interest in gardens must have been known by the authorities at Gray's Inn years before his essay saw the light of day. In 1591, when he was 30, he was asked, jointly with a Mr Angel, to make arrangements for the enclosure of 'parts of our back field' with a brick wall. The back field became the pleasure garden and 'Walkes'. In 1583, 91 elms, a young ash and three walnut trees had been recorded, but in 1598 there was an order for the 'supply of more yonge elme trees in the place of such as are decayed and that a new Rayle and quicksette hedge bee set upon the upper long walks at the good discretion of Mr Bacon and Mr Wilbraham soe that the charges thereof doe not exceed the sum of seventy pounds.' In 1600, £60.6s.8d was paid for the 'garnishing of the walkes' with ornamental trees, roses and other flowers. In 1609, Bacon made a mount in the northwest corner of the garden, surmounted with a summerhouse in memory of Jeremy Bentham, a former reader of Gray's Inn. It was octagonal and open sided, with the roof supported on slender pillars. From it you could see the distant wooded hills of Hampstead and Highgate. The mount and summer-house were demolished in 1755 and 'the Walkes' altered.

Bacon's work at Gray's Inn seems to have been much appreciated over a long period. John Stow wrote that the gardens 'lie open to the air and the enjoyment of a delightful prospect of the Fields. And the garden hath been, for many years, much resorted unto by the gentry of both sexes and are the chief ornament be-longing to the Inn.' In 1621, James Howell, author and diplomat, called it 'the pleasantest place about London and that you have there the choicest society.' It seems to have been a fashionable place to promenade. In 1661, Pepys went 'to Graye's Inn Walk, all alone, and with great pleasure seeing the fine ladies walk there.' And in 1662, 'When church was done, my wife and I walked to Graye's Inn, to observe fashions of the ladies because of my wife making some clothes.' By 1701 the gardens had become a less desirable venue. A duel was fought there and the survivor tried for manslaughter. Nevertheless, a century later Charles Lamb was able to say, 'They are still the best gardens of any of the Inns of Court, my beloved Temple not forgotten – have the gravest character, their aspect being altogether reverend and law-breathing. Bacon has left the impress of his feet upon their gravel walks.' The gardens are still a quiet, contemplative place.

'a City in an Orchard, or an Orchard in a City'

By the second half of Elizabeth I's reign most towns were pleasant places to live in. New building took place mostly outside city walls, and each house occupied a generous plot. Norwich seemed to be 'either a City in an Orchard, or an Orchard in a City, so equally are Houses and Trees blended in it', and at Exeter, of the 37 hectares (93 acres) enclosed by the city walls, at least a quarter, perhaps even a third, were not built over. Most people had either a garden or an allotment, and many were able to keep a few animals or fowls. Cottages were usually situated in individual plots, not in rows or terraces, and old maps show a pattern of business-like rectangular beds in each garden, with an occasional arbour, orchard or pond. Nobody lived more than a short walk from open countryside.

Expanding overseas trade, coupled with the need for strong coastal defences, led to the development and expansion of cities such as Southampton and Bristol. Sir Richard Lyster, Lord Chief Justice of England under Henry VIII, lived at what is now called 'The Tudor House' in Bugle Street, Southampton, from 1520 until he died in 1554. Sylvia Landsberg has designed the sort of garden Sir Richard might have made. Although Lyster held such an important post, the house is not grand and the garden is small. But there is space for a square plat surrounded by striped wooden railings, with a central knot; beds of flowers, herbs and vegetables; a fountain; an arbour and a tunnel of climbing plants. It is a restful, intimate garden of a kind that citizens of far more modest means than the Chief Justice might have aspired to.

Another sensitive reconstruction of a small Tudor garden has been made at The Red Lodge in Bristol. The Red Lodge, and its counterpart The White Lodge, were built in about 1590 in the gardens and orchards of Sir John Younge's Great House, part of the estate of a Carmelite priory sold at the Dissolution of the

Monasteries in 1538. In the eighteenth century, houses were built over the two-acre gardens, and now all that remains is a small walled area. There is a knot with a pattern taken from a plaster ceiling in the house, a trellis copied from a seventeenth-century design and herbs and flowers of the period.

Monasteries and manors: gardens for gentlemen

The kind of countryside people liked to see, when they strolled out of town after the day's work was done, or surveyed the landscape from their garden mount or from the summerhouse at the end of a terrace, was the tamed countryside of well-farmed fields, carefully managed woodland, or close-cropped deer park. Anything wild was abhorred. In 1586, in the first edition of his *Britannia*, William Camden, antiquarian, historian and headmaster of Westminster School, declared Wales to be 'Rough all over and unpleasant to see, with craggy stones, hanging rocks and rugged ways' and Radnor, 'hideous after a sort to behold, by reason of the turning and crooked by-ways and craggy mountains.' A very different opinion from that of the chronicler Gerald of Wales, who much admired the deep majestic pool and the rocky crags at Manorbier Castle in 1188, but then, Camden was not a Welshman. It would be a long time before rugged landscapes were admired.

The countryside admired then was not so different from the landscape we still love. It was the product of a successful rural economy and a particular pattern of land tenure, uniquely English. The same factors have contributed to certain specifically English elements in our garden making and gardening.

The pattern that first developed under the Tudors, and especially under Queen Elizabeth, was one of country houses surrounded by their own land. From the viewpoint of the urban merchant or tradesman, the country seemed to be occupied not, as you might expect, by rustic bumpkins, but by cultured gentlemen living in modern, comfortable houses with fine paintings on the walls, full of beautiful furniture. The owners and their wives were able to look out of large glass windows (a sign of conspicuous wealth) at symmetrically laid out, productive gardens. They ate and drank well. There were joints of venison, beef, bacon and mutton in the larder, jellies, preserves and pickles in the still room, fish in the fishponds, and wine in the cellar.

Some country gentlemen were connoisseurs of art and literature. Others were of a philosophical or scientific bent. There were some whose passion was the breeding of cattle or sheep to improve the quality and yield of their stock. Country pursuits, as they have come to be known, were part of the allure of rural life, particularly the hunting of deer. Foxes and badgers were occasionally hunted, and hare coursing was popular, but deer were still the favourite quarry. Dogs were used in the chase and it may be at this time that the proverb, 'He cannot be a gentleman who loveth not a dog' was first coined. Greyhounds and spaniels were considered suitably sporting dogs for a gentleman to own. His wife might have a pretty little lapdog or two in the house.

The gentler occupation of fishing was extolled by Dame Juliana Berners in *A Treatyss of Fysshynge with an Angle* written in about 1496. The angler

has his wholesome and merry walk at his ease, in the swete ayre and smelling the swete savoure of the meede floures… He hears the melodious harmony of birds, He sees the young swans, herons, ducks, coots and many other birds and their broods. And if the angler catches fish, surely then there is no man merrier than he is in his spirit.

The hunter, on the other hand, 'must alwas renne and folowe his hounds… swetynge full sore. He bloweth tyll his lyppes blyster, and when he wenyth it be an hare full oft it is an hegge hogge.' He gets home tired, clothes wet and torn, hounds and hawks lost, with 'ryght evyll a thurste'. Dame Juliana is said to have been the Prioress of Sopwell Nunnery near St Albans, Hertfordshire, and had a reputation for scholarship, wisdom and charm. But there is some doubt as to the authenticity of the *Treatyss*, and, indeed, as to whether she ever existed.

There is no doubt however, that fishing was a pleasurable pursuit for gentlemen. The delightful Richard Carew of Antony in Cornwall, a scholar as well as a gentleman, 'ever delighted so much in reading… if he had none other hindrance, going or riding he would ever have a book and be reading.' He celebrated his estuarial fish pond, a short walk from the house, stocked with sea fish including bass, mullet, whiting, plaice and sole, in verse:

In heat the top, in cold the deep
In spring the mouth, the mids in neap
With changeless change by shoals they keep
Fat, fruitful, ready, but not cheap
Thus mean in state, but calm in sprite
My fishful pond is my delight.

Games were sometimes played in the garden, including bowls, tennis, fives, fencing and archery. In his *Proffittable Arte of Gardening* Thomas Hill gives advice on the maintenance of 'Bowlyng allies…you shall sift over with the finest sand'.

The new landowners were gentlemen of leisure, with time to enjoy the wealth their land produced. They loved the country and the life outdoors, and although they visited London from time to time, and perhaps were obliged to spend time at court, they spent most of their lives in the country through choice, not through necessity.

Carew described the moderate, comfortable life of Elizabethan gentlemen like himself:

> They keep liberal, but not costly builded or furnished houses, give kind entertainment to strangers, make even at the year's end with the profits of their living, are reverenced and beloved of their neighbours, live void of factions amongst themselves (at leastwise such as breakout into any dangerous excess), and delight not in bravery of apparel…A gentleman and his wife will ride to make merry with his next neighbour, and after a day or twain those two couples go to a third, in which progress they increase like snowballs, till through their burdensome weight they break again.

The Dissolution of the Monasteries

This was the life that farmers newly rich from the wool trade aspired to. It was the life successful tradesmen and merchants aspired to. And it could be achieved relatively easily. In 1510 Sir William Compton obtained a licence to enclose 2000 acres. He razed the village of Compton Superior in Warwickshire, simply turning the villagers out, and built Compton Wynyates, one of the loveliest of early Tudor houses, using brick from the nearby deserted village of Fullbrook. Others enclosed land without applying for a license at all, and often got away with it.

The Dissolution of the Monasteries, carried out between 1536 and 1540, made it even easier to become a country gentleman. The suppression and sale of some 8000 monastic properties had an enormous and permanent effect. The operation was masterminded by the unpleasant Thomas Cromwell — we met him earlier, shifting his neighbour's house in London to give himself a bigger garden. The ostensible purpose of the Dissolution was to purge the country of a corrupt and venal clergy. In fact, Henry VIII desperately needed to raise money without raising taxes. He also had no scruples about taking any monastic property he coveted for himself.

In 1539 he had the 'Daughters of Sion' expelled from their convent at Syon House on the Thames. The convent had been endowed by Henry V to pray for his soul and those of his family in perpetuity. The conduct of the nuns was irreproachable, but Henry VIII wanted the property and grabbed it for himself.

Katherine Howard stayed there under house arrest for three months before her trial and execution. Furthermore, the king was not above a bit of petty pilfering for his own garden. The year before he acquired Syon, when the Charterhouse, the Carthusian monastery at Clerkenwell, was dissolved, three loads of bay trees, 91 fruit trees, rosemary and other shrubs found their way to the king's garden at Chelsea, and two gardeners were sent from Hampton Court to dig up cypress, bay and yew trees.

In 1547 Edward VI gave Syon to his uncle, Protector Somerset. We know there were walled gardens, later swept away by Capability Brown, and a mount which, when Somerset was accused of treason, was declared to be a fortification and demolished. Dr William Turner probably laid out the gardens. He was Somerset's chaplain and physician, a scholarly botanist who wrote *Names of Herbes* in 1548. Mulberry trees brought from Persia and planted at Syon in that year still survive.

The Dissolution provided the newly rich with a unique opportunity to purchase Church property from the Crown, and with it the means of achieving their ambition to become landed gentry. Sir John Thynne came from a farming family and, thanks to the patronage of an uncle, obtained a post as steward to Protector Somerset. He was able to acquire the Augustinian Priory at Longleat in Somerset, where he set about increasing his land-holding and building a house designed to impress, surrounded by an equally impressive garden.

The building boom

The pattern was repeated elsewhere, albeit usually on a smaller scale. Most monastic communities had been remote from the cities, surrounded by well-watered, fertile land, so they were self-sufficient. This reinforced the idea that country life was at least as comfortable and civilized as life in the city, if not more so. The rate at which country houses were built increased throughout the sixteenth century and the early years of the seventeenth. Between 1570 and 1620 more country houses were built in the counties of Derbyshire, Essex, Somerset and Shropshire than in any other half-century.

Farmers were more prosperous than ever before, and they either improved existing houses to make them more modern and comfortable or built new ones. Farmhouses were on a modest scale, but built to last, timber being replaced by local stone where it was available. In brick-earth districts, bricks were used for building and the soil was also good for growing fruit, so orchards of apple, pear and cherry were planted, giving the landscape a distinctive local character. Where neither stone nor brick was available, houses were of half-timbered, beam and plaster construction.

Local building materials gave the gardens, as well as the landscape in general, a distinctive look. They were used for the building of walls, shelters and summer-houses, for the edging of beds and the edging or paving of paths. The gardens of 'lesser' gentlemen and farmers were not large. They were practical and down to earth, logic dictating a rectangular enclosure, walled or hedged, immediately in front of the house, to be admired from windows and terrace. The area might be subdivided by paths into quarters, with a central fountain, sundial or other feature. Around the perimeter there might be covered alleys, either open-sided or completely enclosed like tunnels, formed of pleached trees or vines. The paths were gravelled or sanded and occasionally turfed or carpeted with scented herbs.

Each quarter of the garden might be treated differently, but one at least would have rectangular raised beds, edged with planks, bricks or wooden railings, and planted with vegetables, herbs or flowers. Of the other three quarters, one might be turfed, with a clipped evergreen shrub at the centre. In another, there might be a knot made with interlacing low hedges of lavender, rosemary, hyssop, or box, with coloured gravel or sand in the interstices. The pattern for the knot could be taken from one of the new books on gardening, such as Thomas Hill's *The Gardener's Labyrinth*. Knot patterns were also copied from the fretwork of a plastered ceiling or panelled frieze inside the house. The more you aspired to fashion, the more complex your knots would be. Another area of the garden might be decorated with a maze cut into the turf.

Exercise and entertainment

Larger, more ambitious gardens had mounts and terraced walks around the perimeter, from which to enjoy views of the park or farmland outside, and a bird's eye view of knots and other garden patterns within. The alleys designed for exercise in all weathers were sometimes elaborate, roofed wooden 'galleries' or cloisters, rather than simple pleached tunnels. Beyond the immediate garden there would be at least one, and perhaps several, orchards.

The emphasis on alleys and paths reflects one of the main functions of a garden: to provide a sheltered area for gentle exercise. A walk is always more amusing if it has a goal, and in grander gardens the banqueting house served this purpose. Today 'banquet' implies a large, formal meal where numerous guests sit down to consume several courses. In the sixteenth century it had a different meaning. The banqueting house was a small summerhouse where you would go at the end of a meal to take dessert: the equivalent of coffee and chocolates today. Most banqueting houses were for small family parties, with room for no

more than half a dozen people. They were sometimes quite near the house, like the two at each end of the front courtyard wall at Montacute in Somerset.

More fanciful, and perhaps not built as a banqueting house at all, is Freston Tower, near Ipswich in Suffolk. Built in about 1549, it is generally described as the earliest known folly. There are six small rooms one above the other, and an explanation sometimes offered is that it was built for Ellen de Freston to study in, with one floor for each of her subjects.

Triangular Lodge is equally remarkable. Built in 1595 at Rushton in Northamptonshire by Sir Thomas Tresham, its plan is triangular and each of the three walls is 10m (33ft) long and has three gables with tall finials. Everything about it relates to the number three. Tresham was a Catholic convert, imprisoned for his faith during Elizabeth's reign. The lodge is a pun on his name, 'Tres' meaning 'three', but, more importantly, by representing the Holy Trinity, it bears witness to his faith. It was referred to in the Rushton accounts as the 'warryner's lodge', the warrener being the keeper of rabbits which were slaughtered and sent to market in London. But it was also an 'eyecatcher' to be seen from

The west front of Lyveden New Bield at sunrise. Sir Thomas Tresham's elaborate banqueting house, begun in 1594, was never finished and is now a roofless shell, but parts of the garden, including a moated orchard, are still intact.

Rushton Hall, and so perhaps may be claimed as a garden building. It seems likely that such an elaborate and unusual building was used by the family as well as the warrener; there is one fireplace in the lodge, on the top floor, from where fine views across the countryside can be enjoyed.

Another fascinating Tresham building in Northamptonshire has the remains of a very interesting garden: Lyveden 'New Bield' was never finished; it is a roof-less shell, but the stonework is pristine and crisply carved. A large and elaborate garden lodge, or banqueting house, it was big enough for family occupation on short visits when it was not worth opening up Lyveden 'Old Bield', of which a small part survives half a mile off.

New Bield is built on the plan of a cross and, like Triangular Lodge, it is full of complex Christian symbolism. Half a mile of gardens was planned to link Old Bield with New, and the water garden that has survived is remarkable and strongly evocative of its time. It consists of a large, level square, surrounded by broad moats. Tresham referred to 'my moated orchard', so the square was prob-ably planted with neat rows of fruit trees. At two corners of the square are large 'snail' mounts, with paths spiralling to the top, almost completely surrounded by water. On the opposite side a raised terrace has smaller, pyramid-shaped mounds at each end. The banks of the terraces and moats would have been planted with sweetbrier roses and other scented plants to be enjoyed by boating parties. Immediately around the lodge, Tresham planned a formal garden with eight arbours, gravelled or grassed walks, a bowling green and raised terrace, but there is no evidence that this plan was executed.

A sixteenth-century needlework valance in the Victoria and Albert Museum (see page 65) illustrates the kind of garden Tresham may have had in mind. It shows a garden enclosed by a wooden fence of diamond trellis, with flowers in pots, a fountain, ducks, a rose arbour, an elaborate architectural pavilion and arcade covered in greenery and more roses, various animals in a flowery meadow and, in the background, a castle and mountains. The people in the garden are listening to a group of female musicians, a cellist, a flautist and a lutist, their sheet music held aloft by a small black boy.

Husbandry for housewives: the first gardening books

Because much of the garden was given over to produce for domestic use, its management was generally considered to be women's work. A detailed picture of the women's work involved in running a well-to-do household can be built up from Lady Hoby's diary, kept between 1559 and 1605. At her home in Yorkshire, she dried fruits, made quince jelly and damson jam, dried rose leaves, prepared syrups and candied sweetmeats and distilled cordials. All this was still-room work, but the ingredients she used would have come from her garden, where vegetables and kitchen herbs were also grown, along with herbs for strewing on the floor or spreading in cupboards to sweeten the air and keep lice, fleas and other bugs away. Lady Hoby mentions dyeing wool and, on one occasion, 'After private prayer, I saw a man's leg dressed'. For this and other fairly minor medical treatments, such as preparing poultices and bandages, or potions to cure headaches or constipation, a good housewife would be able to provide the right healing herbs from the garden. Lady Hoby also supervised the making of lights from beeswax and 'went to take my bees and saw my honey ordered… went to talk to my old women… After supper I talked a good deal with Mr Hoby of husbandry and household matters.'

Farmers' wives were just as busy, and the wives of farm labourers must have found it difficult to find time for their cottage gardens. For a while, during the reign of Queen Elizabeth, all newly built cottages were required by law to have four acres at least, so although most of the four acres would have been used to rear livestock or grow fruit, there would have been enough land to make a garden. The orchard, bridging the gap between garden and farm, seems always to have been the husband's responsibility rather than the housewife's.

In the Middle Ages, gardening knowledge was passed from one generation to the next by word of mouth and by demonstration. Monasteries were centres of learning and monks were able to read and copy classical Latin texts, including Pliny's descriptions of plants and gardening techniques, but there were no printed books and the vast majority of people could not read. Even kings and queens often needed a secretary or clerk to read their letters to them, and write the answers. The great leap forward in the dissemination of knowledge came with William Caxton's printing press, set up at Westminster in 1477. This was followed by a rapid increase in literacy, the result of a stable, prosperous economy.

By 1557, most gentlemen and some farmers and their families could read, and owned a few books. In that year, Thomas Tusser published *A Hundreth Good Pointes of Husbandrie*. It was a great success and he expanded it in 1573 into *Five Hundred Pointes of Good Husbandrie*, a title which went through many reprints. Tusser was educated at Eton, where he was flogged by the infamous headmaster Nicholas Udall, and at King's College and Trinity Hall, Cambridge. Later, he farmed in the Stour valley on the borders of Suffolk and Essex. The husbandman for whom Tusser wrote was a farmer or small-holder, and much of his advice is about farming, but there is also plenty of information on gardening, addressed specifically to the housewife. The book is in the form of a calendar, written in an engaging doggerel:

September   Wife into the garden, and set me a plot
                 Of strawberry rootes, of the best to be got:
                 Such growing abroad among thornes in the wood
                 Well chosen and picked, prove excellent good.

[The large, cultivated strawberry varieties we grow today were not available in Tusser's day]

                 The Gooseberry, Respis and Roses, al three'
                 With Strawberries under them trimly agree.

In December he tells you to cover up the 'gilleflower' and 'rosemarie gaie' and other plants in 'the knot, and the border,' and 'Go looke to thy bees'. January is the time to trim the bower and arbour: 'What greater crime/Than losse of time?'

February   Stick plenty of bowes [sticks]
                 among runcivall [large, sturdy] pease
                 to climber thereon,
                 and to branch at there ease.

In winter beans and 'perseneps' were sown, in spring 'cabbegis, turneps, carrets' – 'Herbes and rootes to boile or butter'. Tusser's March list of 'Seedes and Herbes' is divided into 'for the kitchen', 'for sallets and sauce', 'to boile or to butter', 'strowing herbes', 'herbes, branches, and flowers, for windowes and pots', 'herbes to still in summer' and 'necessarie herbes to grew in the garden for Physick'.

January: What greater crime
              than loss of time?

March: In March and in April, from morning to night,
              In sowing and setting good huswives delight;
              To have in a garden, or other like plot,
              To trim up their house, and to furnish their pot.'

              'Through cuning with dibble,
              rake, mattock, and spade,
              by line and by leavell,
              trim garden is made.

One forms a picture of an orderly row of neat plots, tended by an industrious, housewife, her skirt hitched up to keep it from trailing in the mud. The plants are all regarded as useful, but they include primroses, columbines, daffodils, roses, carnations and hollyhocks, so the garden looks pretty as well as tidy. Poor Thomas Tusser, in spite of the success of his book, died in debtors' prison.

A Most Briefe and Pleasant Treatyse

The first book in English with gardening as its sole subject was Thomas Hill's *A Most Briefe and Pleasant Treatyse*, published in 1563. In 1568, it appeared, revised, as *The Proffitable Arte of Gardening*, and after his death it came out as *The Gardeners Labyrinth* by Didymus Mountaine (a pun on Hill's name). Unlike Tusser, who was clearly writing from his own experience, Hill used classical sources freely, quoting from Cato, Varro, Pliny the Elder and Palladius. He gave a lot of information about the multiple medicinal uses of each plant.

He described and illustrated various 'modern' elements, showing drawings of an extremely elaborate knot and two mazes. The illustrations include a circular pattern like the maze at Saffron Walden, and a square one, to be set out in 'Isope and Tyme, winter Savery... Lavender Cotton, Spike, Marioram and such like...

for these doe well endure all the Winter thorow greene.' He explains how to make a shady arbour using 'Ashen poles, or the Willow', with vines melons or cucumbers trained over them.

One more popular book, first published in 1597, was the Herball or *Generall Historie of Plantes* by John Gerard. Gerard's knowledge of plants came to him, as it did to other experts at that time, through studying medicinal plants during a long apprenticeship as a barber-surgeon. He abandoned this career to take charge of the gardens of Lord Burghley, Queen Elizabeth's lord treasurer, in Holborn and at Theobalds. His herbal drew on Latin and French sources, and was concerned with the medicinal (and magical or superstitious) uses of plants more than with horticulture. Here is an example:

> '*Of Red Lillies… The Vertues.*
> The leaves of the herbe applied are good against the stinging of Serpents.
> The same boiled and tempered with vineger are good against burnings, and heale green wounds and ulcers.

Part of the panoramic picture on the embroidered valance described on page 62. The arcade and pavilion are covered in roses, as is the arbour, just visible in the top left corner. A garden party is in progress, with music and dancing. English or French, 1570–99.

The root rosted in the embers, and pounded with oile of Roses, cureth burnings.

The same stamped with honey cureth the wounded sinews and members out of joint. It takes away the wrinkles, and deformities of the face.

The roots boiled in Wine, saith Pliny, causeth the cornes of the feet to fall away within a few dayes, with removing the medicine untill it have wrought this effect.

Poets' gardens

The appetite of gardeners for gardening books would soon increase and multiply faster than bindweed and ground elder. But other forms of literature can also indicate changing attitudes to gardens and gardening. Readers in medieval England absorbed the idealized European *Hortus conclusus* from Chaucer's translation of *Le Roman de la Rose* and were familiar with the Christian symbolism of sacred songs and verses.

Sixteenth-century poetry showed different preoccupations. The enclosed garden was the symbol of woman's sexuality, and the imagery could be overtly erotic, as it was in B. Griffin's *Fidessa, More Chaste than kinde Sonnet 37* of 1596:

> Fair is my love that feeds among the lilies,
>   The lilies growing in that pleasant garden
>   Where Cupid's Mount, that well beloved hill is,
>   And where that little god himself is warden.
> See where my love sits in the beds of spices!
>   Beset all round with camphor, myrrh, and roses.
> And interlaced with curious devices
>   Which, her from all the world apart incloses.
> There, doth she tune her lute for her delight!…

There was not much descriptive poetry directly concerned with gardens. Shakespeare, Spenser and their contemporaries loved and celebrated the natural landscape, its hills and woods, springs and streams, fields and flowers, birds and bees. John Skelton, however, wrote about a dream garden:

> The clouds began to clear, the mist rarified;
> In an herber I saw, brought were I was,
> There birds on the briar sang on every side
> With alleys ensanded about in compass,

The banks enturfed with singular solas,
Enrailed with rosers, and vines engraped;
It was a new comfort of sorrowis escaped.

In the midst of a conduit, that curiously was cast
With pipes of gold, engushing out streams;
Of crystal the clearness these water far past,
Enswimming with roaches, barbellis, and breams,
Whose scales ensilvered against the sunbeams,
Englistered, that joyous it was to behold…

The Garlande of Laurell, John Skelton, 1523

Skelton was created poet laureate by both Oxford and Cambridge universities, and was tutor to Prince Henry (later King Henry VIII), so his poetry would have had wide circulation. Later, he became rector of Diss in Norfolk:

The flowers in Spenser's *Ditty* were a mixture of wild (daffodils, cowslips and kingcups), and garden flowers:

Bring hither the Pincke and purple Cullambine,
    With Gellifloures;
Bring Coronations, and Sops-in-Wine
    Worne of Paramours;
Strowe me the ground with Daffdowndillies,
And Cowslips, and Kingcups, and loved Lillies,
    The pretie Pawnse
    And the Cevisaunce,
Shall match with the floure Delice.

A Ditty, Edmund Spenser

The columbines mentioned by Spenser had certainly been planted in medieval gardens. With their dove-like petals they were thought to symbolize the Holy Ghost. In 1460, they are shown in the illustration of the Boccaccio story described on page 29. A very beautiful columbine with almost black flowers appears in the Portinari Altarpiece, commissioned by Tommaso Portinari, a Florentine who represented the House of Medici in Bruges, and painted by Hugo van der Goes in 1475–76. Gilliflowers, carnations and sops-in-wine were all variations on the same theme, and, with irises, pansies (Pawnse) and lilies (Floure Delice or Fleur de Lis), were old favourites in Spenser's time.

'Strange herbs, plants, and annual fruits are daily brought unto us'

There were plenty of exciting new introductions, even if they remained unsung by the poets. William Harrison, Dean of Windsor wrote in *A Description of Elizabethan England* (1577):

> If you look into our gardens annexed to our houses, how wonderfully is their beauty increased, not only in flowers…and… curious and costly workmanship, but also with rare and medicinal herbs sought up in the land within these forty years: so that, in comparison with the present, the ancient gardens were but dunghills and laystows [rubbish heap] to such as did possess them…Strange herbs, plants, and annual fruits are daily brought unto us from the Indies, Americas, Taprobane [Ceylon], Canary Isles, and all parts of the world.

The Huguenots, much respected for their gardening skills, brought new plants when they came to England to escape religious persecution; and tulips were beginning to arrive from Asia Minor via the Netherlands; there were sunflowers from Peru, lilacs from Persia, nasturtiums from America. Edmund Grindal, Bishop of London 1559–70, brought a tamarisk from Germany to his garden at Fulham Palace and sent presents of its fruit to Queen Elizabeth. Other arrivals were tobacco, crown imperial, fritillary, snapdragon, larkspur, love-in-a-mist, martagon lily and many more. The age of plant collecting was about to begin.

Nostalgia for Tudor gardens

There are no complete and genuine Tudor gardens remaining today, but there are careful reconstructions informed by meticulous research, such as those by Sylvia Landsberg described earlier; there are structural remnants like fishponds, terraces and mounts; and there are authentic elements like knots taken from sixteenth-century pattern books and used in modern gardens.

There is also a special category of garden that deserves attention. A long time before the scholarship of late twentieth-century garden historians revealed the authentic components of a Tudor garden, owners of medieval and Tudor houses longed to create gardens in sympathy with the period of the house. Where they have succeeded, these 'Tudor' gardens probably give today's visitors more

A woodcut from a sixteenth-century book shows two gardeners working in symmetrical raised plots of flowers and vegetables. One uses a dibber, the other digs up a lettuce with a spade. All the tools illustrated are still in use today.

pleasure and a greater sense of history than a trip in a time capsule to view the genuine article could provide.

We can feel reassured by the enduring bulk of Montacute's elephantine yew hedges, although they were never intended to be taller or much wider than a garden wall. At Athelhampton in Dorset, the yew pyramids in the Great Court have grown out of proportion to the site, reaching a height of 9m (30ft). But this only adds to the charm and mystery of the garden. At Ightham Mote, a moated manor house in Kent dating from 1340, The National Trust is restoring the gardens to the nineteenth-century romantic ideal of an old English garden, and at Packwood House in Warwickshire, another National Trust property, a sixteenth- and early seventeenth-century layout of walled courtyards and brick pavilions has survived. Packwood has the famous 'Tudor' topiary of the Sermon on the Mount, actually planted in the 1850s, and a spiral mount planted with yew and box. The gardens were lovingly maintained and developed with planting for all seasons by G. Baron Ash who owned the house in the 1930s and '40s and gave it to the Trust.

Cothay Manor in Somerset must also be mentioned. At Cothay, the grassed and gravelled walks framed by yew hedges were laid out in the 1920s around a moated manor house built in 1480. Within the 1920s framework the gardens have been replanted with great skill and a sure instinct for what is appropriate.

In Wales, at Aberglasney, there is a project underway to restore a cloister garden and other elements dating from about 1600. Archaeological excavation has uncovered sufficient evidence to reconstruct a fairly complete and authentic garden. It will be interesting to see if, in time, Aberglasney garden develops as strong a feeling for the past as the fantasy Tudor gardens mentioned above.

3   THE SEVENTEENTH CENTURY

THERE WERE NO dramatic changes after the death of Elizabeth I. England continued to prosper at home, and the English increasingly travelled abroad on missions of trade and diplomacy.

During the reigns of James I and Charles I, the design of gardens remained much as it had under the Tudors. But there were subtle changes. Religious and literary symbolism had vanished almost completely from gardens. The Dissolution of the Monasteries had destroyed gardens with Christian themes, designed for quiet prayer and contemplation, and the *hortus conclusus* no longer displayed the allegory of mystical virginity expressed in *Le Roman de la Rose*. Instead, it provided an opportunity for discreet amorous dalliance within its arbours and behind its hedges. The nearest most gardens came to symbolism was a coat of arms or the owner's initials carved out of turf, or sculpted in box: symptoms of a trend, started under Henry VIII, continued under Elizabeth I and accelerated in the seventeenth century, to treat the whole garden as a symbol of the owner's wealth, power and culture.

At Theobalds Park in Hertfordshire, James I had the royal arms planted out in mignonette and pinks. Occasionally history repeats itself. Theobalds, with its

In the seventeenth century it was fashionable to have a knowledge of flowers. In this detail of a portrait by Van Dyck, Cupid, himself crowned with flowers, offers a basket of roses, c. 1637.

extensive and well-stocked deer park, belonged to Lord Burghley. James I, who had a passion for hunting and a keen interest in gardens, looked with envy at it, just as Henry VIII had coveted Cardinal Wolsey's Hampton Court. King James made Burghley an offer he couldn't refuse: to swap Theobalds for Hatfield House, a poor bargain from Burghley's point of view, as the garden at Theobalds, built by his father William Cecil between 1575 and 1585, was acknowledged as one of the finest in the land. Hatfield, by comparison, was a neglected and rundown estate around a former Episcopal palace.

Elaborate two-dimensional patterns laid out on the ground and decorated with coloured sand and gravel were still popular in 1690, when John Morgan built his orangery at Tredegar House in Wales and laid out a parterre in front of it. Gervase Markham describes the process in *The English Husbandman* (1613):

> You shall make your yellow, either of a yellow clay usually to be had in almost every place, or the yellowest sand, or for want of both, of your Flanders Tile, which is to be bought of every Iron-monger or Chandelor: and any of these you must beat to dust. For your white you shall make it of the coarsest chalk beaten to dust, or of well-burnt plaster, or, for necessity, of lime, but that will soon decay. Your black is to be made of your best and purest coal-dust, well cleansed and sifted. Your red is to be made of broken useless bricks beaten to dust and well cleansed of spots. Your blue is to be made of white-chalk, and blacke coal dust well mixed together, till the black have brought the white to a perfect blueness.

Archaeological evidence has enabled Newport Borough Council to restore the Tredegar parterre with complete accuracy. The result appears bright and garish, even vulgar, to modern eyes.

James Howell, royalist, diplomat and politician, has left us a description, written in a letter of 1619, of a more outward-looking garden, fairly typical of that of a nobleman or gentleman with a large country estate. These are the elements he admired at Sir Thomas Savage's Melford Hall in Suffolk:

> The stables butt upon the park, which for a cheerful rising ground, for groves and browsings for deer, for rivulets of water, may compare with any, for it shines in the whole land; it is opposite to the front of the great house, whence from the gallery one may see much of the game when they are a hunting. Now, for the gardening and costly choice flowers, for ponds, for stately large walks green and gravelly, for orchards and choice fruits of

all sorts, there are few the like in England: here you have your Bon
Christian pear and Bergamot in perfection, your Muscadel grapes, in such
plenty that there are some bottles of wine sent every year to the king.

At Melford Hall, now in the care of The National Trust, parts of the garden are
being restored to the Edwardian phase of their history. But a bowling green
survives and a beautiful Tudor brick pavilion overlooking the village green on
one side and the garden on the other. No doubt there were knots, arbours and
trelliswork in 1619, but Howell did not think them worth mentioning. They
were not the latest fashion. He is more interested in the view of the deer park
from the house, the 'costly, choice flowers' and, significantly, the orchards.

'That lovely recreation': growing fruit trees

In the seventeenth century, gardening became a recreation, and in some cases a
passion, for many of the aristocracy and landed gentry. The political situation
forced a leisured rural life on those reluctant to take sides during the Civil
War, on Royalists and Catholics during Cromwell's Protectorate, and on
Parliamentarians and Puritans immediately after the Restoration. Before the
Civil War, travel in France, Italy and Holland resulted in a cosmopolitan attitude
to garden design and an exchange of botanical and horticultural knowledge;
gentlemen developed an interest in and knowledge of new and rare flowering
plants. But in many cases it was the orchard rather than the flower garden that
captured the aristocratic imagination. Ben Jonson celebrated the orchards at
Penshurst Place in Kent in his poem 'To Penshurst' (1616):

> Then hath thy orchard fruit, thy garden flowers,
> Fresh as the air and new as are the hours.
> The early cherry, with the later plum,
> Fig, grape, and quince, each in his time doth come;
> The blushing apricot and woolly peach
> Hang on thy walls, that every child may reach.

Sir William Temple was one of those gardeners whose hobby became his passion.
He grew up at Penshurst, in the care of Dr Henry Hammond, and must have

Overleaf: *Parterres de Broderie with patterns infilled with flowers or with coloured gravels
continued to be popular both before and after William and Mary made the Dutch style fashionable.
'The Garden of the Former Amsterdam Leprozenhuis', Louis Chalon, 1735.*

known well the extensive orchards at Penshurst Place, where much remains of the Tudor garden layout. We don't know how his own garden at Sheen, just outside London (part of the site of a vast Carthusian monastery) was laid out, except that it was probably in the Dutch style, since he was Ambassador at the Hague, where he helped negotiate the marriage of William of Orange to Princess Mary, who was a niece of Charles II. The  garden would have been relatively modest in size; Sir William wrote 'I think from 4 to 5 or 7 acres is as much as any gentleman need design,' whereas Francis Bacon in his famous essay *On Gardens* suggested 30 acres. But Bacon had in mind a 'princely garden'.

Fruit was Temple's first love. He considered flowers 'more the ladies' part than the man's.' His wife Dorothy Osborne certainly played her part with enthusiasm. Like all keen gardeners, she enjoyed plant-swapping. 'Sir Sam', she wrote of a neighbour, 'has grown so kind as to send to me for some things he desired out of this garden, and withal made the offer of what was in his, which I had reason to take for a high favour, for he is a nice florist.' ('Florist' in those days meant not a person who sells flowers but a gardener or nurseryman with a good knowledge of flowers.)

Sir William Temple understood fruit growing from personal experience, and his cosmopolitan connections increased his knowledge. He wrote:

> perhaps few countries are before us; either in the Elegance of our Gardens;
> or in the number of our plants, and I believe none equals us in the Variety
> of Fruits which may be justly called good; and from the earliest Cherry
> and Strawberry to the last Apples and Pears, may furnish every Day of the
> circling year.

Temple's French guests assured him that the peaches he served were as good as any in Gascony, and his grapes 'as good as any they have eaten in France, on this

The immaculately espaliered or fan-trained fruit which Sir William Temple and his contemporaries aspired to can still be seen at Westbury Court, Gloucestershire and at Erddig, Clwyd (shown here), which has been restored by The National Trust.

side Fountainbleau… Italians have agreed, my white figs to be as good as any of that sort in Italy.' His success was due to the great care he took with cultivating his fruit. John Evelyn, the author of *Sylva*, whose expertise extended from arboriculture and forestry to all branches of gardening, wrote after a visit to Sheen in 1688, '…the wall-fruit trees are most exquisitely nail'd and train'd, far better than I ever noted.'

The same skilful work can be seen today in the gardens of Westbury Court in Gloucestershire, where apple and pear trees are trained immaculately against a long brick wall. The Westbury Court garden, restored by The National Trust, is in the Dutch style, its main feature being a long canal, flanked by yew hedges, with a tall summerhouse at one end. It was made by Maynard Colchester between 1696 and 1705, to a scale small enough to create an atmosphere of domesticity rather than grandeur. Maynard Colchester loved flowers as well as fruit; his account books show that he bought hundreds of bulbs, including tulips, irises, crocuses, jonquils, hyacinths, double narcissus, anemone and ranunculus. Shrubs were grown at Westbury Court for their scent, including syringa, mezereon and phillyrea.

In the 1650s Sir Thomas Myddleton, an officer in the Parliamentarian army, felt secure enough to develop his garden at Chirk Castle, Clwyd in Wales. He owned copies of Parkinson's Herbal and his *Paradisi in sole Paradisus Terrestris*, and successfully grew licorice plants, vines, damsons, red currants, gooseberries, a fig tree, apples and pears. Sir Thomas built several summerhouses, paying a blacksmith in 1653 for ten weathercocks to adorn them. He may have used the summerhouses to entertain visiting judges who are recorded as stopping at Chirk for beer and biscuits. In 1684, in Sir Richard Myddleton's (Sir Thomas's son?) day, Thomas Dineley, accompanying the Duke of Beaufort to south Wales, wrote of Chirk Castle:

> an admirable walled garden of trees plants and flowers and herbs of the greatest variety as well forreigne as of Great Britain, orrenge and lemon trees the sensitive plant and where in a Banquetting house a collation of choice fruit and wines was lodged by the sayd to entertein his Grace.

Wales was by no means behind England as far as gardening fashions were concerned. French influence is seen in Sir John Wynn's garden at Gwydir, Gwynedd, where there was a 'labyrinth', or maze, and a summerhouse on a hill above the house, commanding distant views. In 1613 Sir John's son wrote from France suggesting oranges and lemons would grow well there. Five years later, Sir John's brother-in-law was offering to send nectarine and fig trees from London, and in 1625 bay trees and 'slivings' of tamarisk were sent to Sir John from Penrhyn in Gwynedd to plant in his garden.

Fruit was grown in orchards or trained against the walls of country-house gardens. But even the meanest cottage plot supported one or two fruit trees, and in parts of the country where soil and climate were suitable for fruit trees to thrive, landscape and gardens were seamlessly integrated:

> From the greatest to the poorest cottager, all habitations are encompassed
> with Orchards and Gardens; and in most places our hedges are enriched
> with rowes of fruit trees, pears or apples, Gennetmoyles, or crab apples...
> All our villages... are in spring-time sweetened and beautified with the
> bloomed trees, which continue their changeable varietyes of Ornament
> till in the end of Autumn they fill our Garners with pleasant fruit and
> cellars with rich and winey liquours.
>
> *Herefordshire Orchards*, John Beale, 1657

'there is scarce a Cottage ...but hath its proportionable Garden'
It was not only the landed gentry who were making gardens. The building boom in villages and towns had started in the reign of Elizabeth I and gathered pace until the Civil War brought prosperity and expansion to an end for a while. During the two generations between 1570 and 1640, medieval houses were modernized to make them more comfortable and new houses were built for an increasing, and increasingly prosperous population. Each house had its garden, and although the layout and content of the gardens had changed from one generation to the next, and some had been divided and built over, nevertheless in many villages and towns the size and shape have remained the same. John Worlidge in *Systema Horticultura* (2nd edition, 1683) wrote:

> there is not a Noble or pleasant Seat in England but hath its gardens for
> pleasure and delight; scarce an Ingenious Citizen that by his confinement
> to a Shop, being denied the priviledge of having a real garden, but hath
> his boxes, pots or other receptacles for Flowers, Plants, etc... there is
> scarce a Cottage in most of the Southern Parts of England but hath its
> proportionable Garden, so great a delight do most men take in it.

In other words, English people love to grow plants, and if they have no garden, they make do with a window box.

For many people the pattern of their daily lives had also changed during the years of economic prosperity and expansion. W.G. Hoskins, in *The Making of the English Landscape* (first published 1955), explains, 'There was no need to go out at the end of a hard day's farming to hack down more trees and clear more ground… The Stuart or the Georgian yeoman reached for a book in the evenings, rather than for the axe or mattock of his forebears.'

It might well have been a gardening book, if not that of John Worlidge, quoted above, perhaps William Hughes's *The Flower Garden* (1672), written for 'Flowrists, Gardeners, or others… but chiefly for more plain and ordinary Country men and women as a perpetual Remembrancer.'

John Rea's *Flora, Ceres and Pomona*, published in 1665 with further editions in 1676 and (posthumously) 1702, was a popular and reliable manual. Rea was a nurseryman at Kinlet in Shropshire, specializing in tulips, rare primroses and other unusual flowers. His commercial experience prompted him to write dourly: 'I have known many Persons of Fortune pretend much affection to Flowers, but very unwilling to part with anything to purchase them; yet if obtained by begging, or perhaps by stealing, contented to give them entertainment.' John Rea's book catered for hands-on owner-gardeners on a modest scale. He offered 40 years of practical experience, and affirmed that 'A choice collection of living Beauties, rare Plants, Flowers and Fruits, are indeed the Wealth, glory and delight of a Garden.' He believed

> It is knowledge that begets Affection, and Affection increaseth
> knowledge… It is chiefly that, which hath made my Flowers and Trees
> to flourish, though planted in a barren Desart, and hath brought me to
> the knowledge I now have in Plants and Planting.

The book suggested a garden 100m (110yd) square as suitable for a nobleman, and 55m (60yd) square for a gentleman, of which two-thirds would be for fruit and one-third for flowers, the whole to be surrounded by a brick wall 2.7m (9ft) high and should, if possible, be on level ground. The elements were those of a Tudor garden, with some additional practical suggestions. His 'handsome Octangular Somer-house… serveth not onely for delight and entertainments… but for many other necessary purposes; as, to put the Roots of Tulips, and other Flowers in, as they are taken up, upon Papers, with the names upon them, until they be dried.' A banqueting house and potting shed combined.

John Rea's gardening philosophy is expressed in the dedication at the beginning of the book:

Into your garden you can walk
And with each plant and flower talk;
View all their glories, from each one
Raise some rare meditation.

The pleasures of a flower garden were emphasized, but gardens also continued to be an important source of useful plants and food. The boundary between gardening and husbandry was blurred, and many of the increasing number of books available offered advice on both fronts.

Fit up thy gardens, orchards and walks handsomely

The account books of Sir John Oglander give a vivid picture of the concerns of a gentleman running a small estate. He went to live at Nunwell in the Isle of Wight in 1609, and from 1620 until 1650 recorded his income from rents and his daily expenditure. The accounts are interspersed with notes on other matters, and observations for the benefit of his descendants. These *Observations of Sir John Oglander which he found useful in his time and which thou must observe till experience hath better instructed thee* vary from sound, practical farming advice to the kind of admonitions Polonius made to Horatio in Shakespeare's *Hamlet:*

> Lend moneys to thy friends but be bound for none. It is the best point of good husbandry; observe it. Nor to thy friends, whereas thou shall thereby make them thy enemies.

> Keep thyself out of debt if thou canst for as Solomon sayeth; the borrower is a slave to the lender… Meddle of no man's money but thy own.

> Next hate London as to live there (without thou hast a vocation that calleth thee to it). Dice and whores as the instrumental causes that bringeth many to beggary. Serve God and thou shalt inherit thy land.

Sir John set out his 'Good Rules in Husbandry' clearly and in great detail. His farming interests were diverse and he was an efficient and conscientious farmer. He gave advice about improving the soil by various methods including green manuring ('sow phatches and … turn them in again purposely to enrich the land'), making hay and growing wheat, barley, oats and peas. He also recommended hops as a lucrative crop. Forestry, including planting and maintaining hedges and coppice for firewood, was an important part of husbandry. Sir John's

notes included advice on the treatment of sick animals. At Nunwell he kept
cattle, oxen, hogs, sheep, and horses: 'Keep a good folde mare or 2 and every year
breed a colt or 2 and if thou hast a good stallion it is the better, but although this
Island seldom breed good horses yet they will be very useful to thee.' Near the
house Sir John advised his descendants to

> Have a small warren for some rabbits when thy friends cometh. Build
> a pigeon house and fit up a fishpond or two that at all times thou mayst
> have provisions at hand. Pale in a place to breed or keep pheasants and
> partridges in.
> Keep a good goshawk or lanard which will be good help to thy kitchen.

The self-sufficient larder was completed with home-brewed mead (he recommended keeping bees for this purpose), cider and beer, and the produce of a
well-organized kitchen garden and orchard.

Sir John was a dedicated family man, advising his descendants to 'Love they
wife and children otherwise thou canst never love thy home' and 'Fit up thy

*Fishing, either in the remaining monastic stew ponds or in ornamental canals in the new Dutch style,
became a leisure pursuit as well as an exercise in self-sufficiency. The subject of this painting by
Arthur Devis (1711–87) is believed to be Francis Popham of Upton House, Warwickshire.*

gardens, orchards and walks handsomely about thee that thou mayst give content both to thyself and wife to enjoy the place.' He loved his garden, and flowers were his one extravagance. He noted at the end of a list of rents due on 26 March 1633,

> I have been so foolish as to bestow more moneys than a wise man would have done in flowers for the garden. It was my content, wearied with study to solace myself in the garden and to see the sports of Nature how in every several species she showeth her workmanship.

A brief description in a later entry shows his how proud he was of his garden:

> I have with my own hands planted 2 young orchards at Nunwell; the Lower with pippins, pearmains, putes, hornies and other good apples and all sorts of good pears: in the other, cherries, damsons and plums. In the upper garden, apricocks, mellecatoons and figs. In the Parlour Garden, in one knot, all sorts of gillie flowers in the other knot all sorts of French flowers and tulips of all sorts: some roots cost me 10s a root. In the Court, vines and apricocks... I have now made it a fit place for any gentleman, and had hopes that my son George would have succeeded me and have en- joyed the fruits of my labours.

The last sentence is poignant, since George, his eldest son, died of smallpox when he was 22. In the margin of the notebook Sir John added this sad verse:

> But he is gone, my hopes are lost,
> And with him my fare, charge and cost.
> Forbear: Thou hast another son, whose worth
> Will raise thy spirits and advance thy mirth.
> Though dead in sorrows, he will them revive,
> Bids thee go on and for his sake to thrive.
> I go, I go, but to my grave,
> To find out him I could not save.

Seventeenth-century landowners aspired to create Eden in their gardens, and both poets and practical garden writers saw gardens as a metaphor for Paradise, with delicious fruit always playing an important part. 'Adam and Eve in the Garden of Eden' (detail), Lucas Cranach, 1530.

'You might… angle a peckled Trout'

Most gentlemen were able to supply their family's Friday fish from domestic sources. Great houses might have great ponds where fish could breed, and the houses of lesser gentry and farmers often had a stew pond, a relic perhaps of earlier monastic occupancy, used as a holding tank to keep fish until needed for the table. Roger North recommended positioning a pond in the garden where 'your Journey to them is Short and easy, and your Eye will be often upon them [to prevent theft], which will conduce to their being well kept and they will be a Ornament to the Walks.' He also drew attention to the fun to be had from a fish pond: 'young People love Angling extremely; then there is a Boat, which gives Pleasure enough in Summer, frequent fishing with Nets, the very making of Nets, seeing the Waters, much Discussion of them, and the Fish, especially upon your great Sweeps, and the strange Surprises that will happen in Numbers and Bigness…'

William Lawson, a country clergyman and a Puritan, also extolled the delights of angling in *A New Orchard and Garden* (1618): 'I could highly recommend your Orchard, if either through it, or hard by it there should runne a pleasant River with silver streames: you might sit in your Mount, and angle a peckled Trout, or sleightie Eele, or some other dainty Fish. Or moats, whereon you might row with a Boate, and fish with Nettes.'

'Cheape and Good Husbandry'

John Rea's and William Lawson's books were just two among many gardening books published in the seventeenth century. Lawson's *The Country Housewife's Garden* is of special interest as the earliest book addressed specifically to women gardeners. His chatty, easy-going style and sound practical knowledge made his two titles, usually bound together, popular. They went into many editions, the last appearing in 1683. They included diagrams showing patterns for knots.

Gervase Markham brought out *The English Husbandman* in 1613, followed the very next year by *Cheape and Good Husbandry*. The most comprehensive book was John Parkinson's *Paradisi in Sole Paradisus Terrestris* (1629). The title was a pun on his name, translated as 'park-in-sun'. In general, a Latin title lent dignity to a book, but the texts were in English. Parkinson was apothecary, or herbalist, to James I and, after the publication of his book with a dedication to Queen Henrietta Maria, Charles I gave him the title of 'Botanicus Regius Primarius'. His *Paradisi* is an illustrated account of the cultivation of fruit, including 60 apple varieties, vegetables and nearly 1000 different flowers. As well as being a compendium of current botanical and horticultural knowledge, Parkinson's book was highly persuasive, his love of plants leaping off the page: 'so delightsome flowers that the sight of them doth enforce an earnest longing desire to be a possessoure of some of them at the leaste.'

These books satisfied a thirst for practical gardening knowledge both among the rich, with their many acres of gardens and orchards, and those of more modest circumstances, with perhaps an acre or less. Other books, essays and letters indicate that garden making had become a subject for philosophical and intellectual discussion.

'The purest of human pleasures': Gardens in prose and poetry

The play on words in the title of Parkinson's book uses the word 'Paradise' twice, once to mean 'Park' and again in the phrase '*paradisus terrestris*', meaning earthly paradise. Reminders of the first and perfect garden, the Garden of Eden, crop up frequently in the seventeenth century, and for some garden makers the biblical Eden was interchangeable with Elysium, the heaven of Greek and Roman mythology. English gentlemen were classicists by education and some, having travelled to avoid being caught up in the Civil War, had first-hand knowledge of the Italian Renaissance. John Evelyn called his gardening book, which was never published, *Elysium Britannicum*. In some of the literature of the time, comparisons began to be made between the elaborate formality of gardens and the natural beauty of the landscape. In Book IV of *Paradise Lost*, written between 1655 and 1665, John Milton saw the Garden of Eden as a 'happy rural seat' where flowers grow naturally, 'not like Art in Beds and curious knots.'

> Flours worthy of Paradise which not nice Art
> In Beds and curious knots, but Nature boon
> Poured forth profuse on Hill and Dale and Plaine,
> Both where the morning Sun first warmly smote
> The open field, and where the unpierc't shade
> Imbround the noontide Bowrs: Thus was this place
> A happy rural seat of various view.

Milton's colleague and fellow-republican, Andrew Marvell, in the often-quoted, sensuous lines from his poem *The Garden*, also implied that 'natural' informality is to be preferred to manicured symmetry:

> What wondrous life is this I lead!
> Ripe apples drop about my head;

The luscious clusters of the vine
Upon my mouth do crush their wine;
The nectarine and curious peach
Into my hands themselves do reach;
Stumbling on melons, as I pass,
Ensnared with flowers, I fall on grass.

Thoughtful prose writers on the subject of the ideal garden included Sir William Temple, who expressed his philosophy of gardening in a long essay, *Upon the Gardens of Epicurus* (1685). He mingled the biblical with the classical, seeing imitation of Eden as his goal; a Platonic ideal for a garden. After retiring to his garden at Moor Park, in Surrey, Temple emulated the Greek philosopher Epicurus, who 'passed his life wholly in his garden; there he studied, there he exercised, there he taught his philosophy… the sweetness of air, the pleasantness of smell, the verdure of plants, the cleanness and lightness of food, the exercises of working and walking; but above all, the exemption from cares and solicitude, seem equally to favour and improve both contemplation and health.'

'Gardens should be irregular'

Temple and a few others began to speculate whether a 'regular' garden layout was the only option, or even the best option:

What I have said, of the best forms of gardens, is meant only of such as are in some sort regular; for there may be other forms wholly irregular, that may, for aught I know, have more beauty than any of the others… Something of this I have seen in some places, but heard more of it from others, who have lived much among the Chinese; a people, whose way of thinking seems to lie as wide of ours in Europe, as their country does. Among us, the beauty of building and planting is placed chiefly in some certain proportions, symmetries, or uniformities; our walks and our trees ranged so, as to answer one another, and at exact distances. The Chinese scorn this way of planting, and say a boy, that can tell an hundred, may plant walks of trees in straight lines… But their greatest reach of imagination is employed in contriving figures, where the beauty shall be great, and strike the eye, but without any order of disposition of parts, that shall be commonly or easily observed… they have a particular Word to express it; and where they find it hit their Eye at first sight, they say the Sharawadgi is fine or is admirable.

'Sharawadgi' bears no relation to any known Chinese word or phrase and it is possible Temple invented the word to express the design principle he had heard about. He drew back from advocating its implementation in English gardens, saying, 'I should hardly advise any of these attempts in the Figure of Gardens among us, they are Adventures of too hard Achievement for any common Hands; and though there may be more honour if they succeed well, yet there is more Dishonour if they fail and 'tis twenty to one they will; whereas in regular figures 'tis hard to make any great and remarkable faults.'

Temple was not the only leader of opinion to feel early whisperings of a breeze of change. In *Elements of Architecture* (1624) Sir Henry Wotton, a well-travelled diplomat who lived for some time in Venice, suggested:

> Gardens should be irregular, or at least cast into a very wild regularity…
> I have seen a garden (for the manner perchance incomparable) into
> which the first access was a high walk like a terrace, from whence
> might be taken a general view of the whole plot below; but rather in a
> delightful confusion, than any plain distinction of the pieces. From this
> the beholder descending many steps, was afterwards conveyed again by
> several mountings and vailings, to various entertainments of his scent
> and sight, which I shall not need to describe (for that were poetical) let
> me only note this, that every one of these diversities was as if he had been
> magically transported into a new garden.

Wotton might almost be describing, in seventeenth-century terms, a twentieth-century garden of luxuriant informal planting within a formal framework, divided into 'rooms' in the fashionable Sissinghurst and Hidcote style.

Francis Bacon, in his essay *Of Gardens* (1625) described his ideal garden with its shady walks, flowers, singing birds and elaborate fountains sprinkling or spouting. As well as these conventional elements, Bacon describes a 'heath or desert' occupying 6 acres out of a total of 30 acres. There were to be

> …thickets made only of sweetbriar and honeysuckle, and some wild vine
> amongst and the ground set with violets, strawberries, and primroses; for
> these are sweet, and prosper in the shade… I like also little heaps, in the
> nature of mole-hills (such as are in wild heaths), to be set, some with wild
> thyme, some with pinks, some with germander that gives a good flower to
> the eye, some with periwinkle, some with violets, some with strawberries,
> some with cowslips, some with daisies, some with red roses, some with

Lillium convallium, some with sweet-williams red, some with bear's foot, and the like low flowers, being withal sweet and sightly; part of which heaps to be with standards of little bushes pricked upon their top, and part without: the standards to be roses, juniper, holly, barberries (but here and there, because of the smell of their blossom), red currants, gooseberries, rosemary, gays, sweet-briar and such-like: but these standards to be kept with cutting, that they grow not out of course.

It seems radical, but Bacon may not have had in mind anything less formal than the beautifully restored seventeenth-century 'Wilderness' to be seen today at Ham House in Richmond, Surrey. The Wilderness is divided into compartments by hornbeam hedges in a strictly symmetrical layout. Only the planting, in the style of a flowery meadow, is wild.

At the very turn of the century, in 1700, Timothy Nourse in *Campania Felix or a Discourse of the Benefits and Improvements of Husbandry* echoed Bacon almost word for word in his description of a country-house garden 'with Flowers for every month or season of the Year...A Grove of wilderness... [where] there are tufts of cypress trees; laurels, Philyreas, Bays Tumarist,... Pyracanthe, Yew, Juniper, Holly, Cork tree and in a wood with all sorts of winter Greens'. Nourse also describes 'little banks or hillocks' planted with flowers, like Bacon's 'mole-hills',

Most of the features of a grand seventeenth-century garden are here: a wide avenue, stone balustrades, statuary, a fountain, orange trees in wooden tubs. This painting, 'An imaginary view of the garden of a mansion with a fountain and trees', is attributed to Robert Robinson.

and paths planted with camomile, water mint and other scented plants, 'for these being trod upon yield a pleasant smell': another Baconian conceit. But, as Christopher Thacker points out in *The Genius of Gardening*, it is when Nourse stops copying Bacon that he becomes interesting: looking from the highest point in the garden, he proposes '…at length the Prospect may terminate on Mountains, Woods, or such Views as the Situation will admit of.' Here is the first hint that the landscape may become part of the garden.

'As near as possibly to the Garden of Eden'

John Evelyn, diarist and author of, among other works, *Sylva, or a Discourse of Forest Trees* was, according to Samuel Pepys, a most excellent humoured man. He was also a keen garden maker and wrote on the subject. He thought gardens should be made 'As near as possibly to the Garden of Eden', and that the layout of a garden should 'agree with the nature of the place', anticipating Alexander Pope's maxim 'in all let nature never be forgot'.

Evelyn was in tune with Bacon's contempt for 'knots, or figures with divers coloured earths'. Bacon wrote, 'they be but toys; you may see as good sights many times in tarts,' and Evelyn criticized 'Those painted and formal projections of our cocknet gardens and plotts, which appear like gardens of past board and March pane [marzipan], and smell more of paynt than of flowers and verdure.' His vision was of

> …a noble, princely, and universall Elysium, capable of all the amenities
> that can naturally be introduced into Gardens of pleasure… We will
> endeavour to shew how the aire and genious of Gardens operate
> upon humane spirits towards virtue and sanctitie… How Caves,
> Grotts, Mounts, and irregular ornaments of Gardens do contribute
> to contemplative and philosophicall Enthusiasms… for these expedients
> do influence the soule and spirits of man, and prepare them for converse
> with good Angells.

Evelyn's feeling for the mysticism of gardens finds a faint echo in the remains of a walled garden at Vaynol Old Hall, Gwynedd, where the arched gateway is inscribed '1634 T W K Thomas and Katherine Williams YE MYSTIC GARDEN FOLD ME CLOSE I LOVE THEE WELL'.

Evelyn put his garden ideas into practice at Sayes Court, Deptford, where he lived quietly during the Commonwealth, He was a royalist and had spent much of the Civil War abroad. He bought the house with 100 acres) of farmland in 1653, and immediately 'began to set out the oval garden… which was before a rude orchard… This was the beginning of all succeeding gardens, walks, groves, enclosures and plantations there.' We gather from Evelyn's diary that making the garden was a gradual process, spread over many years. In March 1664, he 'Planted the Home Field and Westfield about Sayes Court with elms, being the same year that the elms were planted by His Majesty in Greenwich Park.' He was also sent cones and seeds of cedar trees from Lebanon and ordered trees from America: larch, lime, walnut, sumach and firs. In December he was planting 'the lower grove next the pond at Sayes Court. It was now exceeding cold and a hard long frosty season, and the Comet was very visible.'

Twenty years later, in another hard winter, Evelyn's diary entry for 4 February will strike a sympathetic chord with every gardener: 'I went to Sayes Court to see how the frost had dealt with my garden, where I found many of the greens and rare plants utterly destroyed. The oranges and myrtles very sick, the rosemary and laurels dead to all appearance.' 'Greens' in a garden history context does not mean vegetables, as in 'eat up your greens', but evergreen shrubs.

Pepys, who served with Evelyn on a commission dealing with prisoners of war, thought the Sayes Court garden, '… for variety of evergreens, and hedge of holly, the finest things I ever saw in my life.' He also remarked on Evelyn's '…hive of bees so as being hived in glass you may see the bees making their honey and combs mighty pleasantly.'

We also know from John Gibson's *A Short Account of Several Gardens near London* (1691) that Evelyn's 'pleasant villa' had '…a fine garden for walks and hedges (especially his holly one, which he writes of in his *Sylva*), and a pretty little greenhouse with an indifferent stock in it. In his garden he has four large round phillyreas, smooth clipped, raised on a single stalk from the ground, a fashion now much used. Part of his garden is very woody and shade for walking; but his garden, not being walled, has little of the best fruit.'

When Evelyn was not busy with his own garden at Sayes Court, he was helping friends with theirs. At Renishaw in Derbyshire, Mr Justice Sitwell planted a lime avenue in 1680 on Evelyn's advice.

'the prettiest garden that I ever beheld': Albury Park

At Albury Park in Surrey, Evelyn designed a garden for his friend Thomas Howard. It is of special interest because it is still there, and little changed. A few miles from Evelyn's family home at Wotton, Albury was one of those gardens to benefit from the decision of their owners to rusticate during the Civil War and Commonwealth. Thomas Howard, Earl of Arundel, was a Royalist and settled in

Italy at this difficult time. John Evelyn, whose father had died in 1640, joined him and spent some time travelling in France and Italy with Howard's grandson Henry (later the 6th Duke of Norfolk).

From 1648 onwards, John Evelyn's diary mentions visits to the Countess of Arundel or Thomas Howard at Albury. Howard referred to the house as 'my darling villa' and by 1655 'had begun to build, and alter the gardens much'. On 21 September, 1667, Evelyn recorded: 'I accompanied Mr Howard to his Villa at Alburie, where I designed for him the plot for his Canale & Garden, with a Crypta thro the hill &c'. Three years later, almost to the day, 'to Alburie to see how that Garden proceeded, which I found exactly done according to the Designe & Plot I had made, with the Crypta through the mountaine in the parke, which is 30 pearches [50m/165yd] in length, such a Pausilippe is no where in England besides: the Canals were now digging, & Vineyards planted.'

'Pausilippe' refers to a classical site at Posilippo near Naples, which Evelyn and Howard probably visited together. It consists of a grotto and a tunnel going into a mountain, with what are said to be the ruins of Virgil's tomb above.

In 1822, William Cobbett's *Rural Rides* took him to Albury. Because the garden is so little changed since his visit, I quote his description at length:

At the end of the village we came to a park, which is the residence of Mr *Drummond*. Having heard a great deal of this park and of the gardens, I wished very much to see them….

They say that these gardens were laid out for one of the *Howards*, in the reign of Charles the Second, by Mr EVELYN, who wrote the *Sylva*. The mansion house, which is by no means magnificent, stands on a little flat by the side of the parish church… It looks right across the gardens, which lie on the slope of a hill which runs along at about a quarter of a mile distant from the front of the house. The gardens, of course, lie facing the south. At the back of them under the hill is a high wall; and there is also a wall at each end, running from north to south. Between the house and the gardens there is a very beautiful run of water, with a sort of little wild narrow sedgy meadow. The gardens are separated from this by a hedge, running along from east to west. From this hedge there go up the hill, at right angles, several other hedges, which divide the land here into distinct gardens, or orchards. Along at the top of these there goes a yew hedge, or, rather, a row of small yew trees, the trunks of which are bare for about eight or ten feet high, and the tops of which form one solid head of about ten feet high… This hedge, or row, is *a quarter of a mile long*. There is a nice hard sand-road under this species of umbrella; and, summer and winter, here is a most delightful walk! Behind this row of yews, there is a space, or garden… about thirty or forty feet wide as nearly as I can recollect. At the back of this garden, and facing the yew-tree row is a wall probably ten feet high, which forms the breastwork of a *terrace*; and it is this terrace which is the most beautiful thing that I ever saw in the gardening way. It is a quarter of a mile long, and, I believe, between thirty and forty feet wide; of the finest green sward, and as level as a die.

The wall, along at the back of this terrace, stands close against the hill, which you see with the trees and underwood upon it rising above the wall. So that here is the finest spot for fruit trees that can possibly be imagined. In the middle of the wall there is a recess, about thirty feet in front and twenty feet deep, and here is a basin, into which rises a spring coming out of the hill. The overflowings of this basin go under the terrace and down across the garden into the rivulet below. So that here is water at the top, across the middle, and along at the bottom of this garden. Take it altogether, this, certainly, is the prettiest garden that I ever beheld. There was taste and sound judgment at every step in the laying out of this place. Everywhere utility and convenience is combined with beauty. The terrace is the finest thing of the sort that I ever saw, and the whole thing altogether is a great compliment to the taste of the times in which it was formed.

In the valley, Evelyn had dammed the Tillingbourne River to form an 24-m (80-ft) wide canal running the full 366m (400yd) length of the terraces above, but by Cobbett's time the canal was gone and the river reinstated, falling over weirs from a lake on the east side to follow a swift-flowing, natural course. Today the basin and 'overflowings' are dry, and the orchards and hedges dividing them are gone, but otherwise the garden is much as Cobbett described. Beneath the upper terrace there is also a brick-built underground bath house in the Roman style. Behind the basin a large archway leads into the 'Pausilippe', a tunnel of generous dimensions, running back into the hill at rightangles to the terrace The hillside above the top terrace is steep and densely wooded; a picturesque mature oak clings with gnarled roots to the slope above the tunnel entrance. The yew trunks are bare, just as Cobbett saw them, allowing views between them across the valley to the house, with a background of massed rhododendrons and woodland. Thomas Howard's 'darling villa' was altered and enlarged in the mid-nineteenth century by Pugin for the banker Henry Drummond.

Cobbett noted, 'At both ends of this garden the trees in the park are lofty, and there are a pretty many of them… chiefly beeches and chestnut: so that, a warmer, a more sheltered, spot than this, it seems to be impossible to imagine.' It is still true today, and some of the trees may be the same ones he saw. In 1822, Albury garden must have seemed old-fashioned to many observers, but you could hardly hope for a commentator less influenced by fashion than Cobbett, so his opinion is especially valuable.

'Choice flowers'

Neither Cobbett nor Evelyn mentions flowers or a flower garden at Albury, but Evelyn did grow flowers in his own garden at Sayes Court. He seems to have postponed making a flower garden until 1671, 18 years after he moved to Sayes Court. In that year, his friend Sir Thomas Hanmer sent him roots and bulbs of bear's ears (auriculas), anemones, ranunculus and tulips. Sir Thomas's letter says, 'I suppose your flower garden, being new, is not very large, and therefore I send you not many things at this tyme.'

Hanmer, of Bettisfield in Flintshire, came from a family of aristocratic Welsh landowners. In spite of having been a page to Charles I and receiving a commission in the Royalist army, he managed to spend much of the Civil War abroad, returning, like Evelyn and Howard, to devote the Commonwealth period to his garden. He wrote of his passion:

> Persons of quality and ingenuity have in all ages delighted themselves
> with beautiful gardens, whose chiefest ornaments are, choice flowers,
> trees and plants.

Enthusiasm for gardening can sometimes override politics, and the royalist Hanmer was friendly with Cromwell's general, John Lambert, supplying him with tulip bulbs. Hanmer's gardening skill and knowledge were greatly respected by his gardening friends, including John Evelyn and John Rea, who dedicated his book *Flora, Ceres and Pomona* to him, describing the collection of plants at Bettisfield as 'incomparable' with 'many noble and new Varieties'.

Hanmer's own *Garden Book* was not published until nearly 300 years after it was written, but it is full of carefully observed, first-hand information on the right soil for each plant, the best time of year to plant it, and how to propagate it. He was a tulip fancier, recommending that tulip beds be four feet wide and raised in the centre 'that all the flowers may bee seen the better.' The tulip 'Agate Hanmer', first grown at Bettisfield, was described by Rea as 'a beautiful flower, of three good colours, pale gredeline [grey], deep scarlet and pure white, commonly well parted, striped, agoted and excellently placed.' His book gives a vivid picture of the plants in each bed in his garden. Some beds are planted just with tulips, in seven rows, one of each named variety, and

> All the little bordered beds… are full of anemones on the outsides and tulips and narcissuses in the midst, with some gilly flowers and some buses at the ends of the beds and cyclamens at the four corners.
> The border under the south wall in the Great Garden is full of good anemones, and near the musk rose are two roots of the daffodil of Constantinople from Rea and a martagon pomponium. In the border under my Lady's closet are anemones and two piece of Liere de Paris and 2 double yellow ranunculuses and a great root of Georgina tulips and a root of Queen Mab and some tulips I know not what and 2 good red cowslips and 2 roots of two sorts of rare Virginian martagons. In the border under the stack of chimneys by the door are tulips and crocuses.

Hanmer may have got his 'rare Virginian martagons' from those other great gardeners of the seventeenth century, John Tradescant, father and son. John Tradescant the Elder was gardener to Robert Cecil, Earl of Salisbury, creating the gardens at Hatfield House for his master and collecting plants abroad on his behalf. Later he became Keeper of His Majesty's (Charles I's) Gardens. Tradescant's own garden at Lambeth became a fashionable venue for sightseers, not just for the rare plants he grew, but for his 'Closett of Rarities', also known as 'The Ark', a collection of strange objects acquired on his travels, which later formed the nucleus of the Ashmolean Museum at Oxford.

John Tradescant the Younger inherited his father's royal post, and it was he who collected plants in Virginia in 1637, 1642 and 1654. The careers of the Tradescants show that successful professional gardeners were held in high esteem. John the Elder came from humble origins, but ended as a 'gentleman' with his own coat of arms.

Willing nature's wild and fragrant innocence

While ideas about the countryside as Eden or Elysium were developing, the landscape itself was changing. In most parts of England, the countryside beyond the garden was no longer wild and dangerous, but the scene of idyllic pastoral life. In Bedfordshire Dorothy Osborne, before she married Sir William Temple, was happy to go for a walk alone on the common where, on summer evenings:

A great many young wenches keep sheep and cows and sit in the shade singing of Ballads. I talk to them, and find that they want nothing to make them the happiest people in the world, but the knowledge that they are so. Most commonly when we are in the midst of our discourse, one looks about her and spies her cows going into the corn, and then away they all run as if they had wings at their heels.

Much of the landscape had been tamed by clearing forests and by enclosure. By the end of the seventeenth century, Gregory King, author of *Natural and Political Observations and Conclusions upon the State and Condition of England* (1696), reckoned that roughly half the land in England and Wales was cultivated as arable, pasture or meadow. In addition, he estimated three million acres of woods and coppices and three million of 'forests, parks and commons.' This still left more than ten million acres of 'heaths, moors, mountains and barren land.'

> Tis all enforced the fountain and the grot
> While the sweet fields do lie forgot
> Where willing nature does to all dispense
> A wild and fragrant innocence
> > 'The Mower, Against Gardens', Andrew Marvell, 1681

Woods and coppices were almost as valuable, in terms of rent, as arable land. During the century, the amount of woodland was greatly reduced, a problem identified by John Evelyn, who expressed his concern so eloquently, and set out his proposed remedy so practically, that he almost solved it. As W.G. Hoskins pointed out in *The Making of the English Landscape*, timber served the purposes of coal, steel and concrete today, as domestic and industrial fuel, and as a building material. Hoskins cites the example of one Durham man who felled more than 30,000 oak trees in his lifetime.

Woodland was still being grubbed up to provide more agricultural land. In Nottinghamshire 'numberless numbers of goodly oaks' were replaced by sheep and oxen 'grazing upon a Carpet Green'. Enclosure of land newly claimed from forest, and other land formerly farmed by the feudal strip system, led to the pattern of fields bounded with stone walls, banks or hedges that we still see today, alternating with open parkland reserved for hunting. The builders of new country houses went some way towards reafforesting this landscape, extending their formal gardens by striking out with bold, confident avenues and rides through symmetrical plantations, following the precepts of John Evelyn's *Sylva*.

The bird's-eye views of Kip and Johannes Knyff in *Britannia Illustrata* (1707) are invaluable sources of information, showing the quite extraordinary extent and complexity of grand, formal gardens, and the dominance in the landscape of avenues, woods and rides.

The painted garden

In the late seventeenth century, owners were so proud of their houses and gardens, and the status they conferred, that they commissioned paintings to record them. Earlier, fragments of 'real' gardens could sometimes be glimpsed in the background of portraits, and fantasy or imaginary gardens were seen in illustrations to books or in pictures showing the life of the Holy Family. But now pride of possession demanded portraits of gentlemen's gardens. Artists devised bird's eye techniques to show the extent and grandeur of garden and park to best advantage. Paintings showed grand carriages approaching the house, deer and horses grazing, and well-dressed people strolling: all status symbols. We are

A rare three-dimensional representation of a small formal garden complete with fruit trees and statuary fits into the lid of this casket. The sides of the box are embroidered with biblical scenes, flowers, fruit and foliage. English, 1650.

lucky to have these pictures as a record of gardens – swept away for ever, soon after they were painted – by 'Capability' Brown and other advocates of the natural landscape style.

Painted gardens include *The Garden of Pierrepoint House, Nottingham,* by an unknown artist. It shows a walled town garden, laid out in the 1690s, in front of a large house next to the church. It includes all the elements of a fashionable garden: a broad terrace runs around a sunken parterre, with a pattern of stone-edged flower beds punctuated by tall, narrow trees, probably cypresses. Trees are trained against the walls and the terrace wall and grand flights of steps are decorated by marble (or faux marble) statues and glazed urns alternating with topiary. It is, as Roy Strong points out in his book *The Artist and the Garden* (2000), a hugely expensive garden.

The House and Gardens of Llanerch, Denbighshire, also the work of an unknown artist was painted in 1662. Sir Peter Mutton, a prosperous judge, built the house and the gardens were made for his grandson, Mutton Davies, between 1654 and 1662, soon after his return from an Italian tour. He seems to have thrown every fashionable element he could think of into his garden, with no expense spared. Somewhere in the garden was a sundial which spouted water in the faces of the unwary; its inscription read 'Alas! My friend, time soon will overtake you; And if you do not cry, by G-d I'll make you.'

The Sermon on the Mount: topiary gardens

Not all houses and gardens were conceived as expressions of grandeur. Levens Hall in Cumbria is a large but manageable family house, and its garden, though ambitious, is on a domestic scale. Colonel James Grahme was a victim of political upheavals. He was Privy Purse and Master of the King's Buckhounds under James II and his wife Dorothy had been a Maid of Honour to Catherine of Braganza, wife of Charles II. When the Glorious Revolution led to the abdication of James II in 1688, there was no future for the Grahmes at court. They retired to Westmorland, where Colonel Grahme bought the Levens estate, acquiring part of it, so legend has it, in payment of a gambling debt won with the ace of hearts. That is why the lead downspouts on the house are decorated with hearts.

Grahme's interest in gardening and estate management was fostered by a friendship with John Evelyn (yet another example of Evelyn's widespread influence), and he set about planting the park and making a spectacular garden. He was advised by Guillaume Beaumont, a French garden designer who had worked for James II and was also out of a job after 1688. In the Hall there is a portrait of M. Beaumont inscribed 'Gardener to King James II and Col James

Grahme. He laid out the Gardens at Hampton Court Palace and at Levens.' Levens Hall gardens are a rare and precious survival. They correspond almost exactly to a map drawn in about 1730 showing Beaumont's layout. The gardens were much visited and admired in the 1690s and still are today. Colonel Grahme held an annual 'Radish Feast' on 12 May to coincide with the Milnthorpe Fair. He served his guests Morocco ale, a potent local brew, then asked them to cross the bowling green in a straight line. If they succeeded they were given another glass, and no one ever managed the return journey.

Levens Hall has a strong claim to the first ha-ha (a boundary set in a trench so as to allow the landowner an uninterrupted view of the countryside), but it is most famous for its topiary garden. In Beaumont's time, the 90 or so yew and box pieces would have been neat, vertical punctuation marks in the pattern of his parterre. Now they are huge, romantic and fantastical shapes with names like the Judge's Wig, the Howard Lion and the Great Umbrellas, and we love the garden all the more for the air of antiquity they give it. The rest of the gardens has been brought up to date with beautifully chosen modern planting in the seventeenth century framework, never at odds with the strong period atmosphere of the whole.

Overgrown topiary bestows a similar charm on the seventeenth-century garden at Packwood House in Warwickshire, although some of the yews were planted in the 1850s. John Fetherston set out the garden between 1650 and 1670. His father and grandfather were yeomen, with no pretensions to fashion, but John's generation were educated as gentlemen, John training as a barrister and his brother Thomas as a physician. A letter from John to his brother in about 1642 expresses a dilemma of conscience that concerned many families during the Civil War:

> Good Brother, I am in a distraction concerninge my armor (beinge alltogeither unable to satisfy my self in judgment and conscience what to do) by reason of the severall commands of the Kinge and parliament; my protestation putts me in mind that I am bound in conscience to serve both, and yet there seems now a very great difference betweene them; which I humbly desyer allmighty god, if it be his will may be peaceably & timely composed and settled.

Part of the famous topiary garden with its fanciful shapes at Levens Hall in Cumbria. The layout of the gardens today is almost exactly the same as when it was first made by Guillaume Beaumont for Colonel James Grahme in the 1690s.

John Fetherston satisfied his conscience by putting up Cromwell's general, Henry Ireton before the Battle of Edgehill in 1642, and offering refreshment to Charles II after the Battle of Worcester in 1651. But it was only with the Restoration in 1660 that he felt secure enough to embark on a building programme. The garden he left consisted of an area south of the house walled with mellow brick with small gazebos, one of which dates from the 1660s to 1670s, at each corner. Today it encloses a lawn with a sunken garden to one side, but Fetherston may have laid out a knot garden or parterre to be viewed from the raised terrace on the south side. The south face of the terrace wall is constructed with a row of 30 brick niches in the wall built to house not statues or urns, but bee skeps.

From a pretty early eighteenth-century wrought-iron gate, steps descend from the terrace into the famous Yew Garden. At the north end is that rarity, a spiral mount, the path hedged in box. At the top is a venerable yew, which has come to be known as 'the Master'. He is flanked by four 'Evangelists' and twelve 'Apostles'. On the lawn below are numerous yews, known as 'The Multitude'. Much as one might like to attribute the whole conceit of the Sermon on the Mount to John Fetherston, who hoped so much for God's guidance in the Civil War, there is no evidence that he planted the yews. However, elsewhere in the garden his sundial dated 1667 survives, and his cold plunge bath built in 1680 is still there, bearing witness to the hardiness of our ancestors.

'The sweetness and satisfaction of this retreat': the rural idyll

The exile to their country estates of Royalist landowners during the Civil War and Commonwealth, and, following the Restoration, the rustication of many of Cromwell's former supporters, augmented a trend already significant during the Tudor period: a preference among the rich and influential for country life over town life. Courtiers had built mansions with elaborate gardens in the hope they might play host to Queen Elizabeth during her summer 'progresses', taken each year to avoid the insalubrious conditions of hot weather in London.

These conditions worsened, reaching a climax with the epidemic of bubonic plague in 1665. The capital was cleansed the following year by the Great Fire of London ('sixteen sixty-five, not a man alive/sixteen sixty-six, London burnt to sticks'), but by then the habit of country living was well established. Fresh, unpolluted air was considered immensely important. Pepys wrote, in the year of

This eighteenth-century Delftware plate depicting the month of April shows a lady meeting her gardener in a typical seventeenth-century garden with features such as symmetrical beds, wall-trained fruit and a summerhouse.

the Fire of London, 'Of the present fashion of gardens to make them plain, that we have the best walks of gravell in the world, France having none nor Italy and our green of our bowling alleys is better than any they have. So our business here being Ayre, this is the best way'.

Sir William Temple was so entranced by the rural idyll that he refused the post of Secretary of State under Charles II. He moved from Sheen and spent the last years of his life making a garden at Moor Park near Farnham, perhaps inspired by the Countess of Bedford's Moor Park in Hertfordshire which he thought 'the perfectest figure of a garden I ever saw.'

He praised 'The sweetness and satisfaction of this retreat, where since my resolution taken of never entering again into any public employments, I have passed five years without once going to town, though I am almost in sight of it, and have a house there always ready to receive me.' Temple so loved his own garden that in his will he did 'desire and appoint that my heart may be interred six foot underground on the South East side of the stone dyal in my little garden at Moreparke.' And this was done.

The bucolic ideal came naturally to men like Temple, educated in the classics and familiar with the poetry of Virgil and Horace. It filtered down to yeomen farmers, merchants and prosperous tradesmen, and the generally accepted goal for an ambitious man became a country house with a small estate. Enormous numbers of such houses were built, with gardens of just a few acres. Destined to evolve into England's great glory, they were constructed on traditional lines, an enclosed rectangle in front of the house being subdivided by paths into smaller rectangles. There might be a raised terrace and mount from which to survey the garden on one side and the landscape on the other. There were certainly vegetable plots and orchards, for self-sufficiency was important.

The flower garden was an innovation. Its development was tentative at first. Pepys, in the garden of gravel walks that he admired, would allow only 'a little mixture of statues or pots' as decoration. '…for flowers', he wrote, 'they are best seen in a little plot by themselves.' Nevertheless, this is the time when the great English love affair with plants began. Botanists, collectors, nurserymen and discerning garden owners like Sir Thomas Hanmer and his influential friends were developing a pool of knowledge and, thanks to traffic with the rest of Europe, a rapidly increasing stock of plants. It was a development of great significance for the future.

4 THE EIGHTEENTH CENTURY I

Geometry Triumphant  103

THE FASHION FOR geometric formality was not yet over. In fact the early decades of the eighteenth century could be regarded as its high point. George London and Henry Wise were Purveyors of Geometry: their expertise lay in designing formal gardens and no job was too big or too complex for them. The first really famous and fashionable garden designers in England (in France there had already been André Le Nôtre, 1613–1700), in partnership they were able to develop and maintain a virtual monopoly of the big prestigious projects of the time. They worked for royalty, laying out gardens at Hampton Court and Kensington Palace for William and Mary; among their other aristocratic clients were Viscount Weymouth at Longleat in Wiltshire, the Duchess of Beaufort at Badminton in Gloucestershire and the Duke of Devonshire at Chatsworth House in Derbyshire.

This client list was reassuring to the *nouveaux riches* wishing to establish themselves as gentlemen. They wanted gardens and landscapes of appropriate status for their newly built mansions. To them, money was no object, but they needed to know they were buying the best, and London and Wise's credentials were impeccable. Their clients could be sure they were buying fashion and the best

In the eighteenth century, architecture and gardens were subjects for passionate discussion among landowners, poets and philosophers. 'The Hervey Conversation Piece', William Hogarth.

possible taste. A 40-hectare (100-acre) garden for Sir Richard Child at Wanstead in Essex was one successful project for the partnership; gardens for Sir John Harpur at Calke in Derbyshire was another.

Attention to detail was one of the contributing factors in London and Wise's success. They paid very careful attention to planting plans, using material from the famous nursery at Brompton Park in Fulham, another successful business in which George London and Henry Wise were partners. Formal flower borders were often planted in the French *plate-bande* style recommended by the French writers Louis Liger and Antoine-Joseph Dezallier d'Argenville. In 1706 London and Wise published *The Retir'd Gard'ner*, a translation of Liger's *Le Jardinier Fleuriste et Historiographe*. In this book they explained that the objective was 'a Cloth of Tissue of divers Colours, wherein the chief Beauty of a Garden consists.' It could be achieved by planting, to a strict grid system, a repeat pattern of tulips, narcissus and hyacinths, with a narrow box edging in front and they described it thus

> The great Vacancys in the middle of the Borders, are to be fill'd with clipt
> Yews and Flowering Shrubs cut into Balls... You likewise put in the
> middle such flowering Plants as are of a middle Stature, as Snapdragons,
> Chrisanthemum, Indian Rose, Poets Pink, Amaranthus, &c. and the large
> Bulbs of the Lilly, Crown Imperial, martigon, &c.

The result was a graded effect, with the tallest plants in the middle, and the lowest on the outside. The width specified for the border was just 1.2m (4ft), so the plan was easily adaptable for small gardens, or for a border against a wall or fence with the tallest plants at the back.

The famous 'Birdcage' made for Thomas Coke's formal garden at Melbourne Hall in Derbyshire by local iron-worker Robert Bakewell. The garden at Melbourne is a remarkable survival of an English garden in the French style.

The fashion in England was for plain grass plats, with or without flower borders around them, rather than elaborately patterned parterres, but the grass plats themselves were sometimes decorated with flowers, as recommended by Peter Aram, the gardener at Newby Hall in North Yorkshire in the 1720s. He wrote that 'Pritty Figures & embellishments may be contriv'd & easily made with Snow-drops, common Crocus's & Daffodils in slope Banks in Grass-plants…'. He gives instructions for lifting the turf, laying down the pattern of bulbs, then replacing the turf. What he had in mind was not the millefleurs meadow effect seen in medieval tapestries, but patterns and images coloured in with solid blocks of flowers.

However, at about the same time, in the 1728 edition of his *The Theory and Practice of Gardening* (first published in 1712), a translation from d'Argenville, John James added a section on plants for 'Grass-plots enamel'd with Flowers,' 'enamelled meadow' being the traditional phrase for turf spangled with multi-coloured flowers. Among the flowers suggested by James were auriculas, violets, daisies, pansies, primroses, cyclamen, sea-thrift and chamomile.

George London came, as far as is known, from nowhere (his pupil Stephen Switzer said he had 'little opportunity… in laying a Foundation of Learning') to become immensely rich. Henry Wise was younger than London and, having started his career as London's apprentice, did very well out of the business. The combination of the fashionable design consultancy with the nursery business, which supplied all the plants they specified for their clients, was very profitable .

'To suit with Versailles': the French style

Thomas Coke of Melbourne Hall in Derbyshire was a client of London and Wise's. Coke had studied architecture and garden design in France, and as soon as he inherited Melbourne, on his coming of age in 1696, he started to plan the development of the garden, ordering large quantities of trees and shrubs from Brompton Park Nursery, including 600 limes at a shilling each. Mr Wise also sent him '… two drafts to form and plant the ground. One you have made choice of, to suit with Versailles.' The grounds of Melbourne Hall were doll's-house sized compared to Versailles, but the new gardens were certainly in the French style.

Before he laid them out, Coke had to negotiate the freehold of his land with the Bishop of Carlisle. This was eventually achieved in 1704, and he lost no time in appointing a contractor to reconstruct the existing gardens as 'a division of Partare work' with 'terrasses, sloops, verges and fleets of steps. A second contract soon followed for 'divisions of wilderness work', 'reservoirs or bassoons for water', fruit walls, kitchen gardens, orchards, plantations and hedged alleys.

Melbourne is a composition of lawns, trees, water and statuary. The garden is L-shaped, the main axis running from west to east, descending in terraces from the house down to 'The Great Basin', a generous expanse of water. Beyond the Basin the vista is terminated by Melbourne's *pièce de résistance*, the dark green and gilded ironwork arbour made by Robert Bakewell for £120, and known as 'The Birdcage' (see page 104). From here the other leg of the 'L' runs from north to south. A network of straight paths hedged with lime and hornbeam radiates through groves of trees, linking *ronds-points* where fountains splash into pools of various shapes. Each vista is completed with a stone urn or statue. Thomas Coke bought his statuary from John Van Nost's workshop in Piccadilly, the acknowledged best source. Van Nost's bill in 1706 listed '4 pr. Of Boyes cast in Mettall £42-00-00, Perseus & Andromeda Do. £45-00-00, and Indian Slave & Black Moor Do. £30-00-00'.

When completed, the Melbourne Hall garden was elegant and immaculate, truly a mini-Versailles. Amazingly, except for the replacement of the 'Partares' in front of the house with plain lawns, they are almost exactly the same today as when Thomas Coke planned them. It is ironic that the style he chose was going out of favour fast. By 1712 his garden was described as 'curious', and in 1789 it was considered downright old-fashioned.

'A delightful Cannell': the Dutch style

London and Wise also had a hand in another garden completed at about the same time as that of Melbourne. The gardens at Castle Bromwich Hall owe more to the Dutch style than the French, having an intimate, domestic quality. The Hall and its gardens are a miraculous survival, surrounded as they are by suburbs of Birmingham, close to Junction 5 of the M6 motorway. Neglect seems to have protected them from the vagaries of fashion, and in 1982 a Trust was set up to restore the gardens, which, although derelict, still retained their historic structure. The restoration has been successfully completed, including plants of the correct period.

In 1657 Sir John Bridgeman, son of Sir Orlando Bridgeman, Lord Chief Justice under Charles II, bought the Tudor hall. Sir John married in 1662, and he and his wife Mary began altering the Hall by adding a second floor, balcony and porch and redecorating the interior. With great enthusiasm they also set about laying

A typical Dutch garden of the kind made fashionable in England by William and Mary, with a formal parterre, canal and two-storey pavilion like the one at Westbury Court, Gloucestershire. The painting is by the Flemish artist Pieter Gysels (1621–91).

out new gardens. On the north side, two existing courtyard gardens separated the house from the church; to the east, the house was screened from the Chester road by functional buildings: a dovecote, malthouse, bakehouse, brewhouse and laundry; the main entrance and forecourt was on the south, fronting the Birmingham road. So the only available site for new gardens was west of the Hall. Fortunately, there were fine views in this direction.

The Bridgemans enlisted the help of their cousin, Captain William Winde, who had been involved with designing gardens at Coombe Abbey, Cliveden and Powys Castle, and it was Winde who consulted London and Wise. Later, between 1710 and the 1730s, the garden was extended by John and Mary Bridgeman's son, John Bridgeman II. He completed the building of the boundary walls, planted the holly walk and built the charming brick and stone Summer House and Green House in the Palladian style. The two buildings face each other from each end of the Holly Walk. The garden plan is symmetrical, centred on the west front of the house, from which a vista runs through the Best Garden and Upper Wilderness, across the Archery Ground and Holly Walk, through the Lower Wilderness to the west *claire-voie*. From that point there is a view across a pond down a broad avenue, out into the former park.

The garden is divided into self-contained areas, some ornamental, some working. The Best Garden, My Lady's Border, the Holly Walk, planted with variegated hollies – then the height of fashion – the parterres, wildernesses and maze are in the former category. The working areas include the melon ground, the nut ground, two orchards and a kitchen garden for vegetables and herbs. Although functional, these areas are also extremely decorative.

The fashion for gardens in the Dutch style came to England with William and Mary, both keen gardeners. The style can be seen at its grandest in London and Wise's Privy Garden at Hampton Court, laid out to suit the taste of the new King and Queen and now meticulously restored. The new royal gardens at Kensington Palace, also by London and Wise, included a sunken garden, which is still virtually unchanged in its structure. In general, Dutch gardens were designed for more limited spaces than those in France and made greater use of water. The element of conspicuous display was missing: Dutch gardens were smaller in scale, more inward looking, more domestic, and perhaps more suited to the English temperament and way of life. A classic example is to be found at Westbury Court at Westbury-on-Severn in Gloucestershire, mentioned in the previous chapter for its beautifully trained espalier fruit. Like Melbourne, it is a supremely harmonious composition of water, grass walks and hedges, but its style is quite different. There are long, straight canals contained by immaculate yew hedges and focussing on a wrought-iron *claire voie*; clipped holly balls, a parterre with box topiary, a quincunx of small trees; and two charming brick buildings: a two-storey pavilion, its height doubled by reflection in the long canal, and a gazebo in a small walled enclosure.

If Dutch influence is to be judged by the number and length of canals, then that influence was certainly strong in Suffolk. According to Edward Martin's article 'The Discovery of Early Gardens in Suffolk', written for the Suffolk Gardens Trust in 2000, 40 examples of canals have survived. The largest, at Battlesea Hall, is 300m (985ft) long and 17m (56ft) wide. It was probably built by Joseph Fox, who died in 1748. The canal at Little Thurlow Hall was made before 1735, as part of a large walled garden with a terrace and orchard, and was described in an eighteenth-century survey as 'a delightful Cannell running all along on the south side of the house & Gardens stored with fish.' A good supply of fish for Fridays and other fast days was still an important part of the economy of a country household. At Parsonage Farm, Boxford (formerly the Rectory), the Reverend John Warren (Rector of Boxford, 1683–1721) made a 'Canal of a great Length [68m/223ft by 10m/33ft wide] & well stockd with Fish… in a place where before was nothing but a foul stinking Ditch.' The ditch was actually the remains of a medieval moat.

Canals could be delightful ornamental as well as practical features. At Ickworth the canal built by John Hervey, 1st Earl of Bristol, mirrored in its waters an orangery flanked by walled gardens. He was lucky to live to enjoy it, having been, in 1717, as he later related, in '…imminent danger from being some time under water in my new-made canal here, with the boate (out of which I fell topsy turvy) driven by the wind over my head.'

Another Suffolk canal reflects in its waters a large mound, measuring 55m (180ft) across at the base and 7.9m (25ft) high, ascended by a spiral path. This is not a survival from a Tudor garden, but was built in the first part of the eighteenth century by someone with the unusual name of Hunn Wyard. In his will, he decreed that it should be known as 'Hunn Wyard's Mount', and so it is. He added the request that it should be 'for ever preserved in as good order or condition as the same now is and no ways defaced or demolished but with free liberty nevertheless to Add unto and Increase the said Mount in such manner as they shall think proper.'

Overleaf: *Thomas Coke's formal landscape at Melbourne Hall 'to suit with Versailles'. Avenues of pleached lime trees radiate from the urn of the Four Seasons by the Flemish sculptor John Van Nost. The garden was already considered old-fashioned soon after it was completed.*

The Italian style

In the first two decades of the eighteenth century, the Grand Tour was an essential part of the lives of aristocratic and fashionable young men. The equivalent of today's 'gap year' between school and university, the Tour was intended to broaden the horizons of the young and impart a working knowledge of European culture. With many Grand Tourists, the culture did not 'take'; they spent more time fooling around and getting drunk with other young

Englishmen than studying the art and architecture of France, Italy and Germany. The political economist Adam Smith expressed the cynical view that:

> A young man who goes abroad at seventeen or eighteen and returns home at one-and-twenty…commonly returns more conceited, more unprincipled, more dissipated and more incapable of any serious application either to study or to business, than he could well have become in so short a time had he stayed at home.

However, the culture of Italy did take very effectively with Richard Boyle, 3rd Earl of Burlington. He visited Italy at the age of 19 and again when he was 25, and returned home with a deep interest in, and sound knowledge of, Palladian architecture. The Renaissance reinterpretation of ancient Roman building styles, the style was perfected by Andrea Palladio (1508–80) and explained in his *I Quattro libri dell'architettura* (Four Books on Architecture), published in 1570.

Lord Burlington also brought home with him from Italy William Kent, a Yorkshireman some ten years older than himself. Kent had been travelling in Italy for nine years, visiting Rome, Florence, Venice and Bologna. He earned his living by making architectural drawings and copies of Old Master paintings and sending them home to English patrons. Their shared enthusiasms led to a close friendship between the two men. Kent joined Burlington's household, and Burlington involved him in architectural and decorating projects for other friends. Kent went on to produce innovative and historically significant work at

---

William Kent was an early and brilliant designer of classically inspired landscape gardens. His masterpiece at Rousham House is intact. This portrait is by William Aikman (1682–1731).

Stowe in Buckinghamshire and at Rousham House, Oxfordshire, for Sir Charles Cottrell Dormer in 1738. His earlier involvement in Burlington's own dream of creating a Roman Villa and garden in the grounds of his house at Chiswick was a creative triumph.

Chiswick House, restored and looked after today by English Heritage, was reported by Sir John Clerk of Penicuik to be 'rather curious than convenient', and Lord Hervey described it as 'too little to live in, and too large to hang to one's watch.' There were bedrooms and a wine cellar but no dining room, so the family and their guests presumably ate in the adjacent old house. The villa may have been intended mainly for entertaining, but its function is still uncertain. What is certain is that Burlington, with Kent, fully and triumphantly realized his fantasy of a classical villa set in a classical garden. We can see exactly how the garden looked from a series of paintings by Pieter Andreas Rysbrack, and, although there are maintenance problems, visitors today can get a fair idea of what it was like in the eighteenth century.

There was a formal stretch of water, a cascade (the hydraulics gave endless trouble in Kent's time, and the cascade never flowed properly, but, thanks to modern technology, it does now), two *pattes d'oie* (paths radiating from a central point, like a goose's foot) with walks terminating at different classical buildings, including an Ionic Temple designed by Burlington, in a charming, circular Orange Tree Amphitheatre. Classical statues were displayed in an exedra with clipped yew niches. The elements which bear out Kent's reputation for innovative irregularity are the twisting paths through the wilderness groves, the mildly serpentine shape of the lake, adapted by Kent from a straight canal, and a ha-ha between a deer house and the Inigo Jones gatehouse, a present from Sir Hans Sloane brought from Beaufort House in Chelsea.

Classical garden buildings and statuary were an important element in the English interpretation of an Italian garden. Timothy Nourse, in his *Essay of a Country-House* (1700) discussed the layout of the Pleasure Garden and recommended a fountain as a central feature, with a statue of Neptune, a sea monster, Diana and her nymphs bathing, or 'some other naked Female Figure with water letting out at her Nipples'. Stephen Switzer took a more prudish line in *The Nobleman, Gentleman, and Gardener's Recreation* (1718), warning, in his section 'of Statues' against 'impropriety in the Gesture and Habiliments of these Gods… Neptune in the Management of his Sea-Affairs embracing Amphitrite; and Mars in his Armorial Array in his Amour with Venus' were to be avoided. 'Of course', as Sir George Sitwell wrote two hundred years later, 'the proper place for Venus is in a private or a public bath.'

A Wind of Change

In his book *Polite Landscapes: Gardens and Society in Eighteenth-Century England*, (1995) Tom Williamson describes the attitude to gardening early in the eighteenth century as follows:

> By the start of the eighteenth century the frontiers of cultivation in England were being pushed to their limits: subsequent enclosures and reclamations removed the last vestiges of wilderness. Nature was now tamed, wildness no longer a threat, and as a result the old popular aesthetic preference for fertile, tamed and cultivated schemes was in retreat. More natural landscapes were increasingly valued, and this became the model for the pleasure grounds of the wealthy.

The French and Dutch styles, more or less part of a formal mainstream, nevertheless showed subtle changes from what had gone before. The Italian style as interpreted by Kent was more innovative, and radical changes were to follow.

It is in the nature of fashion that its aficionados tire of it. A style that has been adopted by lesser mortals is no longer desirable to the elite, and so, after a good run for its money, the formal, geometric style of gardening began to seem dowdy. Politically, all that Louis IV stood for and Versailles was designed to reflect – despotism, centralized government, absolute control – were out of tune with the times, and gardens modelled on Versailles went out of favour. Men of culture began to feel their way towards a style that expressed British democracy and freedom, as it was then understood, with all its imperfections. They found the new style in the peaceful rural landscape just outside the garden. 'The sight of a mountain is to me more agreeable than that of the most pompous edifice; and meadows and natural winding streams please me before the most beautiful gardens, and the most costly canals,' wrote poet and literary critic John Dennis in 1717, in his lengthy description of the view from Leith Hill in Surrey.

There were also very practical reasons for change. The construction of formal gardens, the earth-moving needed to form terraces, and the building of retaining walls, flights of steps and balustrades were expensive operations. The cost of upkeep was also exorbitant. The built elements had to be kept in good repair, greenswards had to be carefully cut and gravel paths weeded several times a

The Orange Tree Garden at Chiswick House: part of the serene classical landscape designed by Lord Burlington for his Roman villa with assistance from his protégé William Kent. The garden included water, vistas enclosed by tall hedges, and classical statuary.

week; box parterres, edging and topiary had to be clipped several times a year. After a decade or so, topiary figures and shapes grew too big for their neat, precise outlines to be maintained, and so the proportions of garden patterns were distorted. Today we love to see old box or yew hedges or topiary grown into billowing, organic, sculptural shapes, but eighteenth-century garden critics did not share our sentimentality about antique plants. When topiary became unwieldy it was removed and often not replaced. Sir John Clerk noted in 1721 that plain lawns had replaced 'evergreen trees and shrubs which were formerly planted in so great numbers that now they grow up and choak the aire'.

Alexander Pope dealt topiary a blow in a satirical article in *The Guardian* in 1713, with a catalogue of evergreens for sale:

Adam and Eve in yew; Adam a little shattered by the fall of the tree of
Knowledge in the great storm; Eve and the serpent very flourishing…
St George in Box; his arm scarce long enough, but will be in a condition to
stick the dragon by next April.
A green dragon of the same, with a tail of ground-ivy for the present.
NB – these two are not to be sold separately.
An old Maid of honour in wormwood.
A toppling Ben Johnson in Laurel.
Divers eminent modern poets in bays, somewhat blighted, to be disposed
of a penny worth.

Stephen Switzer noted that many gardens were 'stuffed too thick with Box, a Fashion brought over out of Holland by the Dutch Gardeners', and by 1735 Thomas Hamilton declared that the yew 'Arrives at Great Beauty and Value… If not kept down by Formal Clipping.' Arguments for and against topiary were to boil up again in the early part of the twentieth century.

Change was gradual and many garden makers continued with the formal style. We should remember all the time that the gardens we know about from contemporary pictures and written descriptions are, inevitably, the remarkable gardens: those of the rich and fashionable, or those of gifted and creative innovators. Most gardens of average size, made by and for lesser gentry or those aspiring to become gentry, were low-key. They had only one avenue, and that a short one, centred on the main frontage of the house. The garden was walled, and laid out in plain grass rectangles divided by sand or gravel paths, and bordered with narrow flower beds. Topiary, if it featured at all, consisted of a few pieces in simple geometric shapes.

Just such a pleasant, conservative garden of modest size was made at Canons Ashby in Northamptonshire. The structure of the garden is still intact and has been restored by The National Trust, with appropriate planting. Edward Dryden laid out the garden between 1708 and 1717 as part of his 'modernization' of the sixteenth-century property. Four terraces descended from the south front of the house: these were known as the 'best garden', the 'upper garden', the 'lower garden' and the 'little one below'. The central vista through the terraces led into a double avenue of elms half a mile long, a grand gesture in an otherwise discreet and modest scheme.

Today, single rows of limes replace the elms and the terraces are planted with Portugal laurels and sixteenth-century varieties of apples and pears. The house and garden are of a comfortable domestic scale, and show clearly how a self-sufficient estate would have been run. The buildings around the pebble-paved central courtyard include a brewhouse, bakehouse and laundry, as well as a great hall, kitchen and drawing room range and staircase tower. There is a romantic connection with Edmund Spenser, a cousin of Sir Erasmus Dryden. Spenser stayed at Canons Ashby so often that he had his own room there, where he may have written *The Faerie Queen*. Poetic genes emerged again in the family with the Poet Laureate John Dryden (1631–1700).

'A man might make a pretty Landskip of his own Possessions'

The pace of change began to accelerate. Negative ideas decrying formal gardens were replaced by positive new ideas for bringing gardens closer to nature. In 1712 Joseph Addison suggested, in an article in *The Spectator*, that 'a Whole Estate be thrown into a kind of Garden by frequent Plantations…a man might make a pretty Landskip of his own Possessions'. He felt this could be achieved by making use of the 'pleasant Prospect' of cornfields and 'the natural Embroidery of the Meadows' with just 'some small Additions of Art'. On a smaller scale, he enjoyed 'the beautiful Wildness of Nature' in his own garden at Bilton Hall near Rugby. He described his garden as 'an Confusion of Kitchin and Parterre, Orchard and Flower Garden', where the flowers grew 'in the greatest Luxuriancy and Profusion.' It sounds as if he had an unusually *laisser-faire* gardening regime for his time. Nevertheless, his garden was still laid out with strict symmetry defined by yew hedges and uniformly spaced trees.

Other men and women with an appreciation of art and literature were coming to value 'natural' scenery and to compare the elaborate gardens of the day unfavourably with its beauty. Two things began to happen: people in the vanguard of gardening fashion started to think about altering their gardens so that the landscape beyond the boundaries could be better appreciated. New gardens were planned, or old ones changed, to give views of the existing farm, woods, water or, most desirable of all from the status point of view, the deer park. Further changes might be made to make the mood of the garden harmonize with the landscape beyond.

The second revolutionary event was the designing of the landscape itself. We have seen how, in the seventeenth century and the early part of the eighteenth, landowners declared the extent of their possessions by driving formal plantations out from a mansion that sat like a spider at the centre of a web of ramrod-straight rides and avenues. The avenue forming the main approach to Badminton House in Gloucestershire, for example, was 4km (2½ miles) long. Such expressions of power came, in time, to seem crude, and a different attitude to 'nature' began to gain ground. Instead of dominating nature, a few landowners became interested in the idea of actually improving nature, attempting to increase its beauty.

This seems the right place to say that this book is about the history of English gardens, including 'landscaped gardens' of a manageable size. But 'designed landscapes' or 'landscaped parks', like many of those planned by 'Capability' Brown and Humphrey Repton, are outside its scope. Stephen Switzer in his book *The Nobleman, Gentleman and Gardener's Recreation* (1715) pointed out that there was no need for broad, extensive rides and walks in a garden designed for walking rather than riding and hunting. A garden designed for walking rather than riding seems a sensible limit to set, so Kent's Rousham and Hoare's Stourhead may count as gardens, but the vast, great classical landscapes of Castle Howard, Stowe and Blenheim do not.

Switzer was quick to embrace and disseminate the newly fashionable idea that the garden should be, as he wrote, 'open to view, to the unbounded felicities of distant Prospect and the expansive Volumes of Nature herself,' echoing Timothy Nourse's idea, expressed in *Campania Felix*, about the desirability of views looking outward from the garden.

Switzer had two categories, city gardens for flowers, etc., country gardens for 'Woods, Coppices, Groves…and Agriculture, with which gardening is unavoidably mixed', an idea which would be further developed by the creators of *fermes ornées*. Rural life should be celebrated as it was by Virgil and Horace, and the forms suggested by the 'best landskip painters' should be followed. The text of Switzer's book was more radical than its illustrations, which show large, elaborate formal gardens in the French mode. A few of his wildernesses have twisty paths, but the twists are mathematically set out with a compass.

Arbiters of taste: Alexander Pope and his circle

No one was more enthusiastic for change than Alexander Pope and few were in a better position to spread the word. Pope had many rich and influential friends and others in the forefront of intellectual life. They included Allen, Earl Bathurst at Cirencester Park; Richard Boyle, Earl of Burlington at Chiswick House; the Earl of Peterborough at Parson's Green and Robert, 5th Lord Digby at Sherborne in Dorset. The two innovative landscape designers of the time, Charles Bridgeman and William Kent, were both Pope's friends, as were Ralph Allen at Prior Park, Bath (he took on Pope's gardener, John Searle after Pope died), and several members of the Royal Society, including the Reverend William Borlase, who sent stalactites and marbles from Cornwall for Pope's grotto at Twickenham, and Sir Hans Sloane, who also contributed to the grotto with specimens from the Giant's Causeway.

Pope stated the theoretical case for Nature and against the more artificial manifestations of Art by attacking the extravagances of topiary, just as Bacon had attacked 'pastry-cooks' parterre patterns a generation earlier and Addison had complained of 'The Marks of the Scissars upon every Plant and Bush.' In 1713 Pope wrote in *The Guardian*:

> I believe it is no wrong Observation, that Persons of Genius, and those who are most capable of Art, are always most fond of Nature, as such are chiefly sensible, that all Art consists in the Imitation and Study of Nature. On the contrary, People of the common Level of Understanding are principally delighted with the Little Niceties and Fantastical Operations of Art, and constantly think that finest which is least Natural. A Citizen is no sooner Proprietor of a couple of Yews, but he entertains Thoughts of erecting them into Giants, like those of Guild-hall. I know an eminent Cook, who beautified his Country Seat with a Coronation Dinner in Greens, where you see the Champion flourishing on Horseback at one end of the Table, and the Queen in perpetual Youth at the other.

The landscape of his friend Robert Digby's estate at Sherborne in Dorset may have been influential in the formation of Pope's ideas about garden design. It belonged originally to Sir Walter Raleigh, but the Digby family altered the house and grounds between 1624 and 1639.

High woods on the tops of hills formed an amphitheatre sloping down to the house, with a 'depth of groves' on each side of the garden. The garden consisted of formal walks and six terraces descending the slope. At the bottom there was a bowling green 55m (180ft) long, with a regular grove of horse chestnuts at each end, a T-shaped canal and beyond it a natural river and more terraces on the other side of the valley. It is the impression Pope formed of the ground beyond these formal terraces that is interesting. Writing in 1722 or 1724, he described a landscape later to be destroyed by 'Capability' Brown. Pope was specially interested in the natural and informal aspects of the garden.

> The gardens are so irregular, that it is very hard to give an exact idea of them except but by a plan. Their beauty rises from their irregularity, for not only the several parts of the garden itself make the better contrast by these sudden rises, falls, and turns of the ground; but the views about it are let in… in very different figures and aspects.

Pope also outlined plans for the two terraces farthest from the house which

> …are to be turned into a line of wilderness with wild winding walks for the convenience of passing from one side to the other in shade, the heads of whose trees will lie below the uppermost terrace of all, which completes the garden and overlooks both that and the country. Even above the wall of this, the natural ground rises, and is crowned with several venerable ruins of an old castle…

He went on to describe two walks leading out of the formal part of the garden:

> One walk winds you up by a hill of venerable wood over-arched by nature, and of a vast height, into a circular grove, on one side of which is a close high arbour, on the other a sudden open seat that overlooks the meadows and river with a large distant prospect. Another walk under this hill walks by the riverside quite covered with high trees on both banks, overhung with ivy, where falls a natural cascade with never-ceasing murmurs. On the opposite hanging of the bank (which is a steep of 50 feet) is placed, with a very fine fancy, a rustic seat of stone, flagged and rough, with two urns in the same rude taste upon pedestals, on each side from whence you lose your eyes upon the glimmering of the waters under the wood, and your ears in the constant dashing of the waves. In view of this, is a bridge that crosses the stream, built in the same ruinous state… Hence you mount the hill over the Hermit's Seat (as they call it)… and so to the highest terrace again.

There is also, behind some 'inexpressibly awful and solemn' old trees, a ruined castle 'to complete the solemnity of the scene'.

Pope's description is interesting because it anticipates almost every feature of the landscape gardens at such sites as Rousham (William Kent 1738), Painshill (Charles Hamilton 1738–73) and Stourhead (Henry Hoare 1741–65). Parts of Pope's interpretation of Sherborne, including the ruined bridge (an early example of a fake ruin), the Hermit's Seat, the 'awful and solemn' trees, and the ruined castle with its 'venerable broken walls', anticipate the Picturesque landscape style of the late eighteenth and early nineteenth centuries. We expect Pope to have a sensitive appreciation of all these elements. What is surprising is that they were in place, with a route around the garden planned to take best advantage of them, so early in the seventeenth century.

Pope rather undermines his *avant-garde* credentials by suggesting the ruin at Sherborne could be improved with evergreens and parterres and its rooms decorated with circles or octagons of grass or flowers. However, he redeems his reputation by suggesting ' seats…to enjoy those views, which are more romantic than imagination can form them,' and

> …a little temple [to be] built on a neighbouring round hill that is seen
> from all points of the garden and is extremely pretty. It would finish some
> walks, and particularly be a fine termination to the river to be seen from
> the entrance into that deep scene I have described by the cascade, where it
> would appear as in the clouds, between the tops of some very lofty trees
> that form an arch before it, with a great slope downward to the end of the
> said river.

'The Ha! Ha! Is digging'

In 1739 an article in *Common Sense* magazine summed up the fashion for gardens and gardening:

> Every Man now, be his fortune what it Will, is to be doing something
> at his place, as the fashionable Phrase is; and you hardly meet with any
> Body, who, after the first Compliments, does not inform you, that he
> is in Mortar and moving of Earth; the modest terms for Building and
> Gardening.

Pope laid down three areas which he believed the designer should consider: 'The Contrast, the Management of Surprises and the Concealment of Bounds', sound

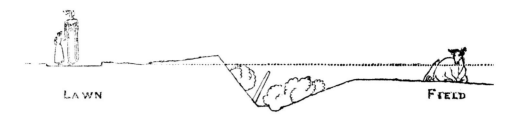

LAWN   FIELD

principles to apply to garden design in any era. His friend Joseph Spence (1699–1768), professor of poetry at Oxford, looked beyond the bounds when he helped design the pleasure grounds at Oatlands, Surrey, for the 9th Earl of Lincoln. He had this preliminary advice to offer:

> to study the ground thoroughly, one should not only take a view of
> the whole and all its parts, and consider the laying of it in general, and
> all its beauties and advantages or inconveniences and impediments, in
> particular, but also walk around it in the line without your own bounds;
> to see what beauties may be added by breaking through your outline.

Today we would call it 'borrowed landscape', an effect the ha-ha would help to achieve. We have seen how political stability and economic prosperity encouraged landowners to look confidently beyond the immediate surroundings of house or castle with feelings of pleasure rather than anxiety. Fortifications from which the horizon had once been scanned anxiously for approaching enemy bands had become redundant in the sixteenth century, and nature, enclosed and tamed to make undulating parkland or well-husbanded farmland, could be contemplated with satisfaction.

The desire to see the view beyond the garden walls was served initially by the construction of mounts, elevated walks and gazebos, or by the device of the *claire voie*. But it was not until the eighteenth century that the means of fully appreciating the landscape, and creating the illusion of its integration with the garden, became available in the form of the ha-ha. Nobody is quite sure who first devised a sunken fence or a retaining wall and ditch to form an invisible, stock-proof barrier. Horace Walpole attributed it to William Kent, when

---

*The ha-ha – a device allowing 'lady and cow to gaze at each other across the ditch'. This
cross-section from 'The Art and Craft of Garden Making' by Thomas Mawson,
1900, sshows how a sunken fence, or ha-ha, is constructed.*

> He leaped the fence, and saw that all nature was a garden...The contiguous ground of the park without...was to be harmonised with the lawn within; and the garden in its turn was to be set free from its prim regularity, that it might assort with the wilder country without.

By 'wilder country', Walpole meant extensive grassy slopes of well-kept parkland, grazed by picturesque herds of deer, forming a sward almost as smooth as the lawn within the garden. In the background he envisaged woodland, probably managed for sport as well as for timber.

Why 'ha-ha'? Walpole's theory was that, when 'the common people' came across a sunken fence, or fosse, they exclaimed Ha! Ha! 'to express their surprise at finding a sudden and unperceived check to their walk.' Less kindly, 'Ha-ha' was what your friends might exclaim if you failed to spot the hazard and fell into the ditch.

We think of the ha-ha as quintessentially English, but its origin may be the French device known as *saut de loup* (wolf's jump). This was a deep ditch, made at the end of an *allée* or broad path, to deter trespassers and animals. A small ha-ha of this kind was made at Levens Hall in Cumbria for the Bagot family in the 1690s, under the direction of James II's French gardener, Guillaume Beaumont. It is still there today. The ha-ha's French connection is confirmed by John James's publication in 1712 of *The Theory and Practice of Gardening*. It was a translation of *La Theorie et la Pratique du Jardinage*, a popular and influential book first published anonymously in 1709 by A.J. Dezallier d'Argenville. After describing how parterres should be laid out immediately in front of the house, he writes:

> The principal walk must be in the front of the house and another large walk ought to cross it at right angles. If they be double and very wide, you may cause the walls to be pierced with grilles at the end of those... to extend the view, and to show the country to advantage. At present we frequently make through views, called *Ah. Ah*, which are openings in the walls, without grilles, to the very level of the walks, with a large and deep ditch at the foot of them, lined on both sides to sustain the earth, and prevent the animals getting over, which surprises the eye upon coming near it, and makes one cry Ah! Ah! from whence it takes its name.

Early ha-has at Houghton in Norfolk and Bramham in Yorkshire, were based on traditional military fortifications, with straight walls running between bastions. By the 1730s and 1740s, ha-has were all the rage. It seems everyone had to have one. Most were informal in shape. Their purpose, described by Stephen Switzer, was to open up 'the extensive charms of nature, and the voluminous Tracts of a pleasant Country.' As described in 1987 by George Clarke, the ha-ha allowed 'lady and cow to gaze at each other across the ditch, but Art and Nature are kept strictly apart.' At Claremont in Surrey the 'ramparts' were converted in 1738 to a serpentine shape. Work on the serpentine 'Ah! Ah! terrass' at Nostell Priory in Yorkshire, designed by Switzer, was in progress at about the same time, and a survey of Bovingdon House in Devon records in about 1735, 'The Ditch of the ahh to inclose the wilderness'.

Some estates had literally miles of ha-ha, and the cost was reckoned by the mile. In 1795 at Moseley Hall, Warwickshire, a ha-ha was built 2.7m (8ft 9in) deep for £696 a mile. Its depth seems excessive; another Switzer ha-ha, made in 1735 at Wolterton Hall in Norfolk, consisted of 'A wall of four foot high, set in a fosse.' Four feet is the height recommended today by The National Trust as being reliably stock proof.

In 1749 Lady Luxborough wrote in great excitement to her gardening friend William Shenstone, 'the Ha! Ha! is digging.' Shenstone had a ha-ha of his own at The Leasowes at Halesowen in Warwickshire, which we will visit in due course.

Properties like The Leasowes were intermediate between the grand classical estates such as Stowe, where political and philosophical ideas were expressed allegorically, and small-scale gardens like that of the naturalist Gilbert White at Selborne in Hampshire. White's ha-ha was correspondingly modest, but served its purpose: to provide uninterrupted views across fields to the beech woods on the hillside above.

The spread of fashion

Descriptions of up-to-date garden designs must have influenced readers of such popular works of fiction as Samuel Richardson's *The History of Sir Charles Grandison*. Published in 1753, the novel contains this account of Sir Charles's grounds:

The park itself is remarkable for its prospects, lawns and rich-appearing clumps of trees of large growth.

The gardens, vineyard, &c. are beautifully laid out. The orangery is flourishing; every-thing indeed is, that belongs to Sir Charles Grandison. Alcoves, little temples, seats are erected at different points of view; the orchard lawne and grass-walks, have sheep for gardeners; and the whole being bounded only by sunk fences, the eye is carried to views that have no bounds.

The orchard, which takes up near three acres of ground, is planted in a peculiar taste. A neat stone bridge in the centre of it, is thrown over the river: It is planted in a natural slope; the higher fruit-trees, as pears, in a semicircular row, first; apples at further distances next; cherries, plumbs, standard apricots, &c all which in the season of blossoming, one row gradually lower than another, must make a charming variety of blooming sweets to the eye, from the top of the rustic villa, which commands the whole.

The outside of this orchard, next the north, is planted with three rows of trees, at proper distances from each other, one of pines; one of cedars; one of scotch firs, in the like semicircular order. Which at the same time that they afford a perpetual verdure to the eye, and shady walks in the summer, defend the orchard from the cold and blighting winds.

Sir Charles' garden seems to combine the old-fashioned symmetry of the orchard and the shady walks under trees 'at proper distances' with an up-to-the-minute ha-ha carrying the eye to boundless views, and grass grazed by sheep.

In the eighteenth century as in the twentieth, the dissemination of new garden styles was much helped by tourism. You simply turned up at the front door of a grand house, and if the housekeeper or the head gardener liked the look of you, you would be shown round, as Elizabeth Bennett and her aunt were shown Mr Darcy's house and grounds in Jane Austen's *Pride and Prejudice*. Visitors were expected to tip the servants who showed them round.

Writing in 1839, John Claudius Loudon reflected on the changes since 1806, commenting that then 'few persons, after being shown through such houses as Chatsworth, Bretby Hall, Wentworth House, &c. thought of giving less than gold; but now 5s. and even 2s. 6d. are received with thanks'. He thought it important that 'the houses of men of wealth and taste' should be shown, for the purpose of 'improving the taste of the spectators, and showing the wealthy tradesman or manufacturer what he may aspire to. Some owners, including William Shenstone at The Leasowes, even went to the trouble of having descriptive brochures printed for visitors.

By 1753 *The World* (a weekly 'paper of entertainment' edited by Edward Moore) was ready to mock the practitioners of the new landscape style:

Clipt hedges, avenues, regular platforms, strait canals have been for some time very properly exploded. There is not a citizen who does not take more pains to torture his acre and half into irregularities, than he

formerly would have employed to make it as formal as his cravat. Kent, the friend of nature, was the Calvin of this reformation but like the other champion of truth, after having routed tinsel and trumpery, with the true zeal of a founder of a sect he pushed his discipline to the deformity of holiness: not content with banishing symmetry and regularity, he imitated nature even in her blemishes, and planted dead trees and mole-hills, in opposition to parterres and quincunxes.

Fashions in flowers were changing, too. An ever-increasing supply of novelties from abroad meant that many old favourites were, in John Rea's words, 'by Time grown stale, and for Unworthiness turned out of every good garden.' He thought the red lily a vulgar flower which could be seen in every country-woman's garden and he described peonies, daffodils and tulips as 'the more ordinary sorts of flowers' – a sure guide to what was grown and would continue

'Le Petit Parc', c.1762–63, by Jean-Honoré Fragonard, depicts the kind of scene much admired by English travellers on the Grand Tour. Classical architecture and statuary are combined with picturesquely rugged trees to give strong contrasts of light and shade

to be grown in the gardens of the more ordinary sorts of people. Nourse recommended that 'The Borders [should be] replenished with Flowers, for every Month or Season of the Year, with little bushes of evergreens at equal spacing: Cypress, Phillyrea, rosemary, Lavender, bay, lime, Savine, Rue.' He also suggested constructing 'lathe-walkes' (pergolas of a fairly basic kind) for honeysuckle and other scented climbers.

The smaller the space available, the more flowers were sought after and enjoyed. In *The City Gardener*, Thomas Fairchild wrote in 1722,

> Most persons whose business requires them to be constantly in town will
> have something of a garden at any rate. One may guess the general love my
> fellow citizens have of gardening, in furnishing their rooms and chambers
> with basons of flowers and Bough pots, rather than not have something
> of a garden before them. [window boxes had been in fashion from 1603].
> …everything will not prosper… because of the smoke of the sea-coal.

In spite of London's smoke-polluted atmosphere, Fairchild found a vine bearing good grapes in Leicester Fields, figs in Cripplegate and Chancery Lane, lilies of the valley behind Guildhall, and pear trees thriving in narrow alleys near Aldersgate, Bishopsgate and the Barbican.

Regularity and uniformity were recommended for small gardens 'especially if it be a small spot incapable of much grandeur or much variety. The house is regular, so must the garden be…'. All the gardening experts insist on the need to avoid 'the scorching heat of the sun'. Small groves of trees were planted close to the house, to keep the house cool in summer, as well as providing welcome shade outdoors.

There was an increasing feeling that the occupation of gardening – active gardening rather than simply being in the garden – was a delightful activity. Nourse called it 'a *Recreation*, not only from the Refreshment it gives to the Mind, but from the *Restauration of Nature*, which may be lookt upon as a *New Creation* of things.' And Switzer, in the enthusiastic, garrulous preface to his book, asks,

> when carried out in a well-regulated Manner, what solid Pleasure is
> there that is not found there-in? Its Pursuit is easy, quiet, and such as put
> neither the Body nor Mind into those violent Agitations or precipitate
> and imminent Dangers that many other exercises… do. The End of this
> is Health, Peace and Plenty, and the happy Prospect of Felicities more
> durable than any thing in these sublunary Regions…

5 THE EIGHTEENTH CENTURY II

Appreciating Nature

By THE MIDDLE of the eighteenth century, gardening was not only recognized as a pleasurable leisure occupation, it was also considered, among a small, exclusive group, to be an intellectual pursuit. England had become a prosperous and supremely confident nation. Foreign visitors

repeatedly stressed the comfortable circumstances in which most people seemed to be placed, the complacent contentment with which they regarded their country and their own lot, the satisfaction which the middle classes took in making money and all but the very poor took in spending it. *The English – A Social History 1066–1945*, Christopher Hibbert

The change is illustrated by Horace Walpole's comment to Sir Horace Mann, who had lived in Florence from the 1730s to the 1780s as assistant to the British Envoy: 'You left [England] as a private island living upon its means. You will find it the capital of the world.'

In 'the capital of the world', towns were growing rapidly. Nevertheless, more than two-thirds of the population still lived in the country, and town-dwellers

---

A garden in transition between a formal Dutch canal and the serpentine flow of a Brownian lake.
'The Brockman Family at Beechborough Temple Pond', Edward Haytley, c.1744.

were beginning to spend more time there, as improved roads made the country-side increasingly accessible. The introduction of the turnpike system led to roads being kept in better repair so that, although journeys became more expensive, they were more comfortable and much speedier. For example, the time taken to travel from Norwich to London was reduced from 50 hours in 1700 to 19 hours in 1800. Landowners who were members of Parliament, sat in the House of Lords, or had business interests in London, were able to move between town and country more freely; country-house visits could be made more easily; and social intercourse between neighbouring estates became possible over greater distances. All these factors contributed to a liberal interchange of ideas about farming, gardening and landscaping. There were discussions about what a garden should be like, how it should relate to the surrounding landscape, and what feelings it should inspire. Gentlemen began, tentatively at first, to put their theories into practice.

The land itself was, as Tobias Smollett wrote, 'smiling with cultivation: the grounds exhibiting all the perfection of agriculture, parcelled out into beautiful enclosures, corn fields, ley pasture, woodland and commons.' By 1770, Thomas Whately, in *Observations on Modern Gardening. Illustrated by Descriptions* was able to write, 'Gardening, in the perfection to which it has been lately brought in England, is entitled to a place of considerable rank among the liberal arts.'

The adoption of new ideas was not sudden – very few owners decided to get rid of their parterres and avenues all in one go and replace them lock, stock and barrel with a Kentian or Brownian landscape. But we have already seen, at the end of the seventeenth century and beginning of the eighteenth, formal gardens modified, knots and elaborate *parterres de broderie* replaced by plain grass plats, and serpentine paths made to wind through 'wildernesses' where there was formerly a starburst of straight paths.

Pope at Prior Park

As we saw in the last chapter, Alexander Pope, perhaps more than anyone else, spread the new ideas about landscape gardening, both through his writing, and through his wide circle of friends and acquaintances. He encouraged them to think of garden making as an art and to debate how best to practise it. He demonstrated his ideas in his own small garden at Twickenham, and he did the rounds of visits to his grand friends, making himself agreeable and useful by offering suggestions. When he was not visiting his friends, he was writing to them. His network was extensive, and his influence far-reaching. His connections in the West Country, for instance, took in, as well as Lord Bathurst at Cirencester and Lord Digby at Sherborne, a number of landowners busy making gardens in Somerset and Cornwall.

Ralph Allen of Bath was a self-made millionaire and philanthropist. He began his working life in the Post Office at his birthplace, St Columb Major in Cornwall. After two years in Exeter he moved to Bath and became deputy post-master in 1712, at the age of 19. By the time he met Pope, Ralph Allen had already made his fortune by creating a super-efficient postal service and running a business quarrying the beautiful golden Bath stone. Allen and the architect John Wood together created much of Georgian Bath, using stone from Allen's quarries. Wood's great skill in planning Bath's layout and siting the city's terraces, squares, parades and circus was also shown in positioning Prior Park, the Palladian mansion he designed and built for Allen outside Bath. The house with its two wings embraces the head of a steep-sided valley like a long triangle, broad at the top and narrowing as it descends.

From 1741 when he moved into Prior Park, Allen entertained friends there, among them the elder William Pitt who became MP for Bath, standing at Allen's suggestion, Samuel Richardson and Henry Fielding, who portrayed Allen as Squire Allworthy in *Tom Jones* (1749):

> Neither Mr Allworthy's house nor his heart were shut against any part
> of mankind, but they were both more particularly open to men of merit.
> To say the truth, this was the only house in the kingdom where you were
> sure to gain a dinner by deserving it.

Allen got to know Pope by offering to sponsor a new edition of Pope's letters, and first visited him at Twickenham in 1736. From then until his death in 1744, Pope stayed with Allen from time to time, sometimes for as long as three months. He bought stone urns from Allen and introduced him to other customers, including Sir Thomas Lyttleton at Hagley, who ordered a 'Pillar'. During one stay at Prior Park, Pope wrote that he planned to 'read, and plant away my time, leaving the Madness of the Little Town beneath me.'

The planting, jointly planned by Pope and Allen, sheltered a circuit walk, down one side of the valley and back up the other. Part of the route led through a densely planted wilderness, concealing and revealing, among other views and features, a grotto, a serpentine lake and a sham bridge. The grotto was the burial place of Miss Bounce, daughter of Pope's beloved Great Dane (see page 132), given to the Allens by Pope when she was a puppy. By 1754, 20 years after Allen began to plant, the landscape was settled and maturing:

… he has pursued only what the natural situation has pointed out to him; and by that means rendered it one of the cheapest, and at the same time one of the most beautiful seats in England. He has levelled no hills, but enjoys the beauty of the prospects they afford; he has cut down no woods but struck through them with fine walkes… *Universal Magazine*

We cannot know the exact amount of guidance Ralph Allen received from Pope, but this assessment implies that he did 'consult the Genius of the Place' with wonderful results. It is surprising to learn that the enthusiastic account given in the *Universal Magazine* was written before the construction of the Palladian bridge, which today seems to be the focus and *raison d'être* of the landscape. It was built in 1755. In the 1760s Ralph Allen employed 'Capability' Brown to deformalize the planting and the lakes. After that, the landscape remained much as we see it today, although replanting has been necessary, and The National Trust's recent shrub planting along the walks has still to mature. However that simply means that we are seeing something approximating to what Pope and Allen saw before their vision could become reality. Ralph Allen left one more legacy to Bath, and that was the 'Sham Castle' built to Sanderson Miller's design in 1762, to be seen from his town house near the Abbey.

'The finest seat I have ever seen' : Pope's Cornish connections

One of Pope's neighbours at Twickenham was Lord Edgcumbe of Mount Edgcumbe in Cornwall. He rented York House from Thomas Vernon who was also Pope's landlord. Edgcumbe was a Lord of the Treasury to Walpole after the latter became prime minister in 1721, so spent much of his time in London. In 1742 he was ennobled, reputedly to prevent the House of Commons questioning him about Walpole's corruption in his part of the world, and then retired from politics. He arranged for sparry marble from the Mount Edgcumbe quarries to be sent up to decorate the underground grotto which connected Pope's house

'Alexander Pope and Bounce, his Great Dane', c.1710, attributed to Jonathan Richardson. Pope gave one of Bounce's puppies to Mr and Mrs Ralph Allen of Prior Park, Bath.

to his garden on the other side of the road, so presumably he knew Pope's garden, and discussed gardening with him.

We know what the garden at Mount Edgcumbe was like before it was landscaped, from a description by Celia Fiennes in *Through England on a Side-Saddle*, an account of her travels on horseback through every county in England between 1685 and 1712. She saw:

> … a hill all bedeck'd with woods which are divided into several rowes of trees in walks… the finest seat I have ever seen and might be more rightly named Mount Pleasant; there is a long walke from one part of the front down to the waterside, which is on a descent guarded with shady rows of trees, there is a fine terrass walled in at the water side with open gates in the middle and a summer house at each end from whence a wall is drawn round the house and gardens.

It was the sort of garden you would expect to find on a prosperous estate towards the end of the seventeenth century, with avenues and rides driven in straight lines through the woods. Its coastal position, with unrivalled views across Plymouth Sound and out to sea, lifted it out of the ordinary. A bird's eye view made by Thomas Badeslade in 1735 from an estate map of 1729 shows what Celia Fiennes saw, with one significant change; the Wilderness in the left foreground of the picture, also known as the Maze, is divided up by a network of coiled and convoluted serpentine paths, protected from salt-laden gales by tall hedges. At the heart of the wilderness is an open circular space with a Palladian garden house. Another painting by Badeslade shows a party in progress there, with about a dozen guests sitting down to eat, accompanied by a small orchestra.

These changes were made by Richard Edgcumbe, Pope's contemporary. He was mildly eccentric and kept the skeleton of a favourite dog in the garden house so that he could talk to it. Later, the skeleton was taken out and buried, but a ghostly dog can still be heard in the English garden, scratching to get back into the garden house. There are no claw marks on the door. Richard Edgcumbe also built a circular, domed, Ionic temple: almost an obligatory feature in a fashionable landscape garden. Known as Milton's Temple, it carried an inscription from *Paradise Lost*, 'overhead up grew,/ Insuperable heights of loftiest shade…' His other built contributions to the landscape were the Battery, a saluting platform mounted with twenty-one guns to greet visitors, and the Folly, a fake Gothic ruin built with stone from the churches of St George and St Lawrence in nearby Stonehouse.

After Richard's death in 1758, his sons, Richard and George, continued to develop the gardens in the Picturesque style. Both sons belonged to Horace Walpole's 'Strawberry Hill' set, so the Twickenham connection continued. They made the Zigzags, steep cliff paths also known as 'The Horrors'. A description of the wilder part of Mount Edgcumbe's grounds, written by William Beckford in 1781, carries a reminder that the benign Cornish climate permitted plants to thrive there which might struggle elsewhere, as long as shelter from the salt winds could be provided. Beckford wrote, 'Here I am breathing the soft air of Mount Edgcumbe standing upon the brink of a Cliff overlooking the sea and singing Notturnos with Pacchierotti. Innumerable bees are humming about the Myrtles and Arbutus which hang on the steeps and are covered with blossoms.'

To trace Pope's other Cornish connections, we must return to Prior Park at Bath, remembering that Pope's host there, Ralph Allen, was born at St Columb Major, near Newquay. On one occasion Pope fell ill, and his host summoned his own doctor, William Oliver, a fellow Cornishman from Trevarno near Helston. Dr Oliver was Physician to the Bath Mineral Water Hospital from 1740 to 1761, inventor of the Bath Oliver biscuit and author of an essay on gout and a 'Pastoral' called *Myra*. He was made a Fellow of the Royal Society in 1729.

The Palladian bridge at Prior Park, Ralph Allen's eighteenth-century landscape garden just outside Bath. The design of the Prior Park bridge echoes that of the famous bridges at Stowe in Buckinghamshire and Wilton House, Wiltshire.

During Pope's stay with the Allens, Dr Oliver was visited by another Cornish friend, the Reverend William Borlase, also a Fellow of the Royal Society. Borlase was a keen and scholarly antiquarian and geologist. His *Natural History of Cornwall* was published in 1758. Allen clearly thought both Oliver and Borlase would interest his guest, and when Pope had regained his health, invited the Cornishmen to meet him on more than one occasion. Since Pope was helping Ralph Allen with his new landscape garden, the little group would certainly have discussed garden design with enthusiasm, perhaps with passion. Borlase told Pope about the quartz crystals found in the Cornish tin mines, and later sent him some to decorate his grotto, along with those already contributed by Lord Edgcumbe and other interested friends. The list of those Borlase gave can be seen at the Morrab Library in Penzance.

Several of Borlase's friends in Cornwall were building and garden making, and he must have been delighted to relay to them the ideas of such an acknowledged expert as Pope. Borlase's circle included some of Cornwall's foremost landowners and politicians. He was rector of Ludgvan near Penzance from 1722 onwards, and ran a sort of tutorial establishment at the rectory: a small group of students boarded with him to get their classics up to scratch before going to university. They represented Cornwall's *jeunesse dorée*, and all came from families that were staunch Royalists in the Civil War. One student was a member of the Bassett family, which owned St Michael's Mount before selling it to the St Aubyns, and was connected by marriage to several prominent Cornish families;

another was John St Aubyn of Clowance near Camborne, who, like Borlase, gained an MA at Exeter College, Oxford; Philip Hawkins's estate was at Trewithen, near Truro; and Richard Vyvyan lived at Trelowarren near Helston.

These four Cornish estates and their owners were also connected by another thread; the architect Thomas Edwards of Greenwich worked on alterations to all their houses. The landscaper Dionysus Williams is also known to have worked at several Cornish properties at this time, and his plans for the park and pleasure grounds at Trelowarren have survived. Of the other estates where, owing to Borlase's friendship with the owners, Alexander Pope's principles may have been followed, Clowance has been broken up and is now a holiday resort, and the landscape of Trewithen is overlaid by one of Cornwall's finest collections

The elegant, light-hearted Rococo style is exemplified in Thomas Robins the Elder's paintings of gardens such as Painswick House in Gloucestershire and, shown here, the Chinese Kiosk at Woodside, Old Windsor, Berkshire. The painting dates from the late 1750s.

of trees and shrubs, started by George Johnstone in 1912. We have a clear picture of Trelowarren before Sir Richard Vyvyan's improvements from Charles Lyttleton, Dean of Exeter 1747–62 and later Bishop of Carlisle. He wrote on 16 May 1752:

On Sunday, after morning service was over, I left Falmouth accompanied by Mr Borlase and after viewing some amazing rocks and Druid monuments arrived early in the morning at Lady Vyvyan's at Trelowarren. The site of Trelowarren is so bad, the country all around being wild and dreary to the last degree, that nothing would have carried me thither but the prospect of finding a sweet bed to sleep in…. the house and its inhabitants are exact pictures of the old style of living in good Queen Bess's days.

Lady Vyvyan was a formidable dowager, managing the estate after her husband died for 32 years, first on behalf of her son, Sir Francis, then for her grandson Richard. The Dean wrote. '…the greatest curiosity of all is the old lady herself… [she] ate a pound of Scotch Collops for supper and wondered I could not do the like…' Four years after his visit, she died and Sir Richard lost no time in modernizing his house and grounds.

Between 1756 and 1760, Vyvyan employed Thomas Edwards to re-model parts of the Tudor house in the Gothic style. This was not merely a matter of being in the vanguard of fashion. It conveyed a political message to those who were aware of such things. Although gothic and classical ornaments were often found in the same garden, in places like Trelowarren, adoption of the Gothic style implied rejection of the Classical style preferred by Whig sympathizers who admired the republican politics of ancient Rome. By contrast, Gothic architecture expressed a preference for native English qualities. As the Trelowarren site had been inhabited for 5000 years, contained an Iron age fort and was recorded in the Domesday Book, there was every reason for its owners to prefer the Gothic style. It was also a statement of Jacobite sympathies and could mean the owner had been involved in the 1715 and '45 rebellions, as indeed the Vyvyans had.

The political overtones do not mean that the Gothic style was solemn. On the contrary, 'Strawberry Hill Gothic', the style in which Sir Vyell Vyvyan decorated the interior of the chapel for the next generation, was airy, lighthearted and even frivolous. This also applied to the pleasure gardens at Trelowarren, made by Dionysus Williams for Sir Richard in the 1750s. Williams may have been introduced to Sir Richard Vyvyan by Borlase, as Williams, too, was a Fellow of the Royal Society. His design for the gardens at Trelowarren was in a style that has come to be known as 'Rococo', of which very few examples survive. Sir Ferrers Vyvyan, the present owner, is in the process of restoring the gardens to their rococo phase.

The word 'rococo' describes a style of architectural decoration consisting typically of curves and scrolls executed with a free, light touch. It has only been used comparatively recently to describe a garden style, although, from its derivation the word is well suited for the purpose. It is a composite of two French words: *rocaille* meaning rockwork or pebble-work and *coquille* meaning shell. Nor surprisingly, therefore, grottos, shell rooms and the like are typical rococo elements. The lightness and elegance of some gothic garden buildings, with pointed arches, tracery, slender turrets and pinnacles, are also characteristic. The same delicacy of touch, with a dash of fantasy, also qualifies chinoiserie, as found in pavilions, bridges, trelliswork and fences.

The rococo style represented by these elements is best understood by looking at the watercolour paintings by Thomas Robins of gardens at Woodside in Berkshire and at Painswick in Gloucestershire. The paintings show what the gardens looked like, and are framed with sinuous borders of flowers, birds, butterflies and shells. Their elegance and prettiness are the essence of rococo. Robins's drawings of the Painswick garden were so detailed that it has been possible to wake the bramble-covered sleeping beauty and restore it to something approaching its original form. The only other rococo garden in a good state of preservation is at Hampton Court House in Middlesex, close to, but not to be confused with, Hampton Court Palace. It has a superb shell-work grotto.

The rococo style of garden was transitional between the formal, geometric style and the free, landscape style, and lasted roughly from the 1730s until 1770. Perhaps in form as well as in spirit it was too fragile to endure, although new gardens have been made since and are still being made, which have the same quality of elegant fantasy.

'I now, when alone, live in my Gardens': rural life idealized

A rather different kind of fantasy was inspired by the domestic landscapes formed by successful agricultural enterprises. One family who enthusiastically combined an interest in farming with a love of gardening were the Yorkes, a prominent Yorkshire Whig family. The small Richmond estate known today as Temple Grounds came to John Yorke by marriage in 1651 and his grandson, another John, grew up on the estate. This second John, at the age of 47, married a

Richmond girl, Anne d'Arcy, a member of another old Yorkshire family. His life as MP for Richmond took John, and sometimes Anne as well, to London frequently, but they spent as much time at home as they could. Their correspondence reveals their love for the place. In June 1753 Anne Yorke wrote to a nephew, 'I am never absent from this place three or four months but it appears the most charming of any I see at my return. I now, when alone, live in my Gardens where the works now going on afford me greater pleasure than ever they did...'

When she wrote this, Mrs Yorke had been married for 21 years, during which time she and her husband were closely involved in running the estate farm and planning and planting the gardens. It was a childless marriage, and if that was a sadness, perhaps their pleasure in farm and garden provided some compensation. Letters written to their steward Francis Lodge in the 1730s illustrate their concerns about their horses, cows and chickens, about the spreading of dung, about their apples and asparagus and about yew and hawthorn hedges. Farm and garden concerned them equally. Anne Yorke wrote from her brother-in-law's house at Helperby near Boroughbridge in February 1734,

> I would have you tell Tom Leaming not to neglect fireing air into my greenhouse in the middle of the days. I want to know how all our quick goods [livestock] does of every species, and if either of my cows are calved yet...

and again from Helperby on 31 March two years later,

> I hope my seeds I sent to Tom Leaming came safe, if he can spare us a little baskitt of Apples, to keep some for your masters eating for he returns, send me some by next weeks carrier hither, I enclose you both Telfords [Telfords of York, a distinguished nursery] receipts if you may book them according to order.

Presumably Tom Leaming was the head gardener at Yorke House; Mrs Yorke's polite and tentative request that he 'spare us a little baskitt of Apples' hints at the nervousness, perhaps even awe, with which some owners have always regarded their head gardener. John Yorke spent the month of February in London on more than one occasion, and fired off a request for news on how the work in the garden was progressing in that month in 1735. In the same month two years later he wrote, 'I hope the weather continued and favoured manuring the low close without any damage to the walk. When the season offers you must take care to have my ground well dressed and scal'd (lime) att a reasonable charge.'

The estate consisted of not much more than 35 acres of hillside above a sweeping bend in the River Swale. Yorke House, which stood just above the river, no longer exists, but two of the garden buildings remain. John and Anne Yorke inherited formal gardens, probably laid out by his father Thomas in the seventeenth century. Their own efforts were directed towards creating a model farm – even, in the newly fashionable phrase, a *ferme ornée* – and improving the landscape. In 1746 they built the Culloden Tower, also known as the Cumberland Temple or just the Temple, to commemorate the Hanoverian victory at the Battle of Culloden. Rescued in 1981 by the Landmark Trust, and well looked after, it is a delightful three-storey building in the Gothic style, with a balconied roof. The Temple's prominence in the landscape is equalled only by the church tower and the tower of Richmond Castle.

An interesting problem encountered by the Yorkes was 'the Rabble', referred to by Mrs Yorke in a letter of 1734, '…I am glad the Rabble are so civil in our absence not to spoil our gardens but as the fine weather approaches should be glad to hear the wall was up to prevent mischief.' Vandalism, apparently, is not an entirely modern problem.

John Yorke died, appropriately, in his garden in 1757. The estate was inherited by his brother Thomas who, in 1769, built the gothic menagerie known today as Temple Lodge. His son, another John, did away with the formal gardens and made some changes to the landscape according to Picturesque principles, a style we will consider in the next chapter. The natural scenery at Richmond, with the river, woods, hills, rocky cliffs, distant views and, always dominating the scene, the ruined castle, needed little improving.

The idea of an ornamental, or idealized farm originated with Philip Southcote, who married an heiress and made his *ferme ornée* at Woburn near Weybridge in Surrey, in about 1735. Nothing of it remains except descriptions by various commentators, including Thomas Whateley, Secretary of State in Lord North's government. In his popular book *Observations on Modern Gardening*, he described Southcote's

> … ornamented farm, as the means of bringing every rural circumstance within the verge of a garden…. The decorations are… communicated to every part; for they are disposed along the sides of a walk, which, with its appendages, forms a broad belt around the grazing grounds… This walk is properly the garden; all within it is farm.

This was a new idea: a linear garden, with a circuit ranging a considerable distance from the house – the farm at Woburn was 150 acres, two-thirds pasture, and a third arable. According to Whately, nearly 35 acres were 'adorned to the highest degree'. Whately makes it clear that the charm of the 'garden' walk lies in the mingling of farm with garden:

> The lowings of the herds, the bleating of the sheep, and the tinkling of the bell-wether, resound thro' all the plantations; even the clucking of poultry is not omitted; for a menagerie of a very simple design is placed near the Gothic building; a small serpentine river is provided for the water-fowl; while the others stray among the flowering shrubs on the banks, or straggle about the neighbouring lawn; and the corn fields are the subjects of every rural employment, which arable land, from seed time to harvest, can furnish.

'The envy of the great, and the admiration of the skilful' Dr Johnson

William Shenstone's *ferme ornée* at The Leasowes in Warwickshire found a prominent place on the route of fashionable sightseers. Shenstone found it necessary to admonish the 'Sunday starers' in one of the engraved inscriptions along his circuit walk:

> And tread with awe these favour'd bowers,
> Nor wound the shrubs, nor bruise the flowers;
> So may your path with sweets abound
> So may your couch with rest be crown'd!
> But harm betide the wayward swain,
> Who dares our hallow'd haunts profane.

Visitors may sometimes have seemed a nuisance, but in reality the approval of the fashionable world was what Shenstone craved. 'My *ferme ornée*', he wrote, 'procures me interviews with persons whom it might otherwise be my wish, rather than my good fortune to see.' His farm was of about the same acreage as Southcote's at Woburn, but there the resemblance ended. Southcote married an heiress. Shenstone remained an impecunious bachelor all his life. Woburn was attached to a mansion, The Leasowes to a farmhouse.

According to Robert Dodsley, William Shenstone was the son of 'a plain uneducated country gentleman... who farmed his own estate' and 'sensible of his son's extraordinary capacity, resolved to give him a learned education'. William went to Pembroke College, Oxford, but failed to take his degree. He was himself a poet, although not much published until after his death, and his study of classics bore fruit, Virgil's *Georgics* and Horace's poetry having a strong influence on his ideas about the countryside. The farm he inherited might have been in answer to a prayer from Horace's *Satires* I.vi.1:

> Hoc erat in votis: modus agri non ita magnus,
> Hortus ubi et tecto vicinus iugis aquae fons
> Et paulum silvae super his foret.

It translates,

> This was one of my prayers: for a parcel of land not so very large, which should have a garden and a spring of ever-flowing water near the house, and a bit of woodland as well.

The landscape around the Leasowes is dramatic and beautiful. Today, with no ornamental planting, the remaining sections of Shenstone's circuit take the visitor through a series of contrasts, from light to shade, from steep inclines to gentle slopes, from rushing streams to still pools. The views seen from strategic points are spectacular. Much restoration work has been done and continues to be done, and the landscape can still be appreciated with the eyes and felt with the heart, despite the fact that Shenstone's farm has been replaced by a golf course. There are golfers, not cows, on the grassy slopes, and dog-walkers give way to joggers, who in their turn give way to mountain bikes on the eroded paths.

Shenstone's walk took the visitor by twisting and turning paths to 39 viewing points, each with a seat on which to rest and contemplate the view. Thomas Whateley described The Leasowes in detail:

> The variety of The Leasowes is wonderful; all the enclosures are totally different… The lower field comprehends both sides of a deep dip; the upper is one large knowl; the former is emcompassed with a thick wood; the latter is open; a slight hedge, and a serpentine river, are all its boundary…. The path is conducted along the bank to the foot of a hill, which it climbs in an awkward zig-zag.

Among the incidents on the walk were a tenant's house masquerading as the ruins of a medieval priory, constructed economically with stone from the remains of Halesowen Abbey. Its rent brought him 'a tolerable poundage'. There were also a 'fairy vision' of a cascade, a view of the steeple of Halesowen Church,

Right Hon
Henrietta Lady
Luxborough

an Egyptian pyramid (the smelting house of a glassworks), a giant goblet inscribed with the old Shropshire toast, 'To all friends around the Wrekin', and 'Virgil's Grove', a quiet, shady wood. Shenstone never forgot that the basis of his Virgilian idyll was a farm. He wrote 'I find no small delight in rearing all sorts of poultry; geese, turkeys, pullets, ducks, &c.'

Shenstone had some success with his book *Unconnected Thoughts on Gardening*, in which he described his ideas about 'landskip, or picturesque-gardening' and how to execute them. But his regular income was only £300 a year. According to Dr Johnson in *Lives of the Poets,* Shenstone 'spent his estate in adorning it and his death was probably hastened by his anxieties'. He was not the first or the last man to overspend on his garden and end up nearly bankrupt, and he suffered bouts of depression.

At such times his friendship with Henrietta Luxborough was a great consolation. Lady Luxborough's husband ('unquestionably a man devoid of morals' according to a contemporary) accused her of being unfaithful and banished her to Barrels, a derelict estate near Henley-in-Arden, Warwickshire, about 25km (16 miles) from The Leasowes. This lively and energetic woman corresponded with and visited the shy, overweight and not physically attractive poet, seeking his advice about the improving of her house, garden and estate. The friendship gave both of them great pleasure. She was nearly 50 when she began gardening, and she died in 1756 aged 57, after suffering from poor health for several years. But she set about gardening with great gusto and became a real addict. We know about her garden from her letters. It sounds unusual and delightful.

The prospect is a very near one, being surrounded by hills, but is diversified and pretty enough, and I have made a garden which I am filling with all the flowering shrubs I can get. I have also made an aviary, and filled it with a variety of singing birds, and am now making a fountain in the middle of it, and a grotto to sit and hear them sing in, contiguous to it.

Charles d'Agar's portrait of Henrietta, Lady Luxborough, neighbour of the poet William Shenstone of The Leasowes and fellow gardening enthusiast.

An urn to the memory of the poet William Somerville was placed in a prominent position, visible from the shrubbery, terrace, bowling green, long walk and kitchen garden. With her Scottish gardener, and occasional help from Shenstone's 'trusty Tom', she built a hermitage, designed for her by Shenstone, made a bowling green and laid out serpentine paths. Some of her alterations were designed to make the garden less formal. One idea was to 'plant that straight walk, which is now gravelled, full of shrubs, and not let it lead to the hermitage, but return in a serpentine manner on one of my crooked sand walks.' She un-gravelled a lime walk, made the 'seven plots in the shape of Lord Mayor's custards' into one big one, modified slopes and, as noted in the last chapter, built a ha-ha (see page 124). She reported her progress to Shenstone,

> I am now busy in planting the lane that joins the coppice, and have chosen trees according to my years. The abele is what I plant; which in four years time will produce a multitude of setts, and grow to be a good shade.

When not in the garden near the house she was in the woods from 11 o'clock until 5, day after day, 'planting and displanting, opening views, etc'. Another correspondent of Lady Luxborough's, the Duchess of Somerset, was doing the same sort of gardening. She wrote to her friend on 15 May 1748 about making a turf-walk around a cornfield on what had been waste ground. The walk was

> about eight Feet wide… close to a flourishing Hawthorn Hedge; on one Side, there is a thatched Seat open on three Sides, which pretends to no Name of greater Dignity, than justly belongs to what it represents, namely a Shepherd's Hut… and as you are sitting down there, you have… a direct View of *Windsor* Castle. There are Sweet-Williams, Narcissus's, Rose-Campions, and such Flowers as the Hares will not eat, in little Borders round the foot of every Tree: and I almost flatter myself, that you would not be displeased with the rural Appearance of the whole… our Lawns and Meadows are enamelled with a Profusion of Daisies and Cowslips, and we have the greatest Appearance of Fruit that has been seen these many Years.

Lady Luxborough wrote to Shenstone on another occasion to tell him about presents from various gardening friends, 'exquisite sorts of melon seeds, and lettuce' from her brother, Lord Bolingbroke; 'seeds of the greatest curiosity of a flower which the world produces…a water engine made of lignum vitae, which will water my garden with much ease' from a Mr Hall and a double snowdrop from another source. In the same letter she offered Shenstone some Spanish broom, which her gardener was raising from seed. The plants in her garden included a 'great variety of cowslips, primroses, ragged-robbins, wild hyacinths both white and blue, violets… large bushes of Whitsun-roses… lilac… syringa… sweetbriar… roses.'

Shenstone, in turn, confided in her, 'I have been embroidering my Grove with Flowers, till I begin to fear it looks too like a *garden*… If there arrive a Flowering-shrub, it is a Day of rejoicing with me; or (to use a term in *Methodism* now so much in Fashion) a *Day of fat things*.' Among the plants embroidering his grove, he was pleased with his peonies, placed among ferns and brambles in a 'gloomy Place by the water's side.'

At The Leasowes as elsewhere, fashionably winding paths through wildernesses were lined with flowering shrubs, chosen partly for their scent. It was a style that worked just as well in smaller gardens as it did at immensely grand sites like Kedleston in Derbyshire, where 1000 lilacs, 350 honeysuckles and several hundred laburnums, as well as roses and philadelphus were planted in the Long Walk. In 1756 Admiral Boscawen's wife Fanny bought 700 shrubs for her gardener to grow on in boxes before planting them out in her walk.

James Meader, gardener to the Duke of Northumberland at Syon Park and Alnwick Castle, and later in his career, gardener to Catherine the Great in Russia, wrote *A Planter's Guide or Pleasure Gardener's Companion* in 1779. One of his recommendations was to keep deciduous trees separate from evergreens, and to plant each in clumps. His plan for 'The Disposition of deciduous trees and shrubs for a Plantation', showed seven rows of plants, graded by height and including lilac, daphne, jasmine, roses, spiraea, syringa, hydrangea, rubus, honeysuckle, lavatera and tamarisk. The spaces between the shrubs were to be filled with perennial, biennial and annual flowers to 'not only fill up the vacancies but be very ornamental to the new plantation.' As the shrubs developed and spread, the perennial plants would disappear, and finally the tree canopy would shade out the shrubs, leaving just trees, grass and water: the enduring elements we think of as forming a typical eighteenth-century landscape garden.

'The most engaging of Kent's works. It is Kentissimo:' Horace Walpole
Trees, grass and water, and of course, architecture and statuary, are all that today make up the magic of William Kent's intimate 25-acre landscape garden at Rousham Park in Oxfordshire, made for the Dormer family from 1738. Horace Walpole's description, in a letter of 1760, still holds good today,

…as elegant and antique as if the Emperor Julian had selected the most pleasing solitude about Daphne to enjoy philosophic retirement… The garden is Daphne in little, the sweetest little groves, streams, glades, porticos, cascades and river imaginable, all the scenes are perfectly classic.

Rousham is another linear garden. To enjoy it and feel its potent attraction, it is essential to follow the route planned by Kent. It leads past a fine statue of a Dying Gladiator, through Venus's Vale, where a statue of Venus, guarded by two swans, presides over a cascade flowing into the Octagon Pond. From the Octagon Pond, a narrow, stone-edged rill winds a serpentine route through dark woods, to deliver water into a circular Cold Bath. It is hard to imagine anyone could ever have taken the plunge with any motive other than masochism, but the Rousham rill is one of the most mysteriously evocative elements to be seen in any garden. The visitor can pause at the rustic Doric Temple on the way to the statue of Apollo. He is in a key position, with views along the River Cherwell to the ancient (1255) Heyford Bridge, to the Temple of the Mill, and, on the skyline, an arched ruin as an eyecatcher. The route returns to the house by the Lime Walk, and the famous Praeneste Arcade. The rarity and beauty of Rousham's

The ruined abbey beside the 14-acre lake in the Honourable Charles Hamilton's landscape garden at Painshill Park, Surrey. The restored 160-acre park includes a waterwheel, grotto, hermitage, mausoleum, Gothick temple, Turkish tent and Gothick Tower.

landscape are so special that the walled gardens near the house are often over-looked. But they are delightful, and their contrasting formality enhances the landscape garden.

The garden at Rousham makes an idyllic short walk, and several other designed landscapes still offer circuit walks for visitors to enjoy. Stourhead in Wiltshire and Painshill Park in Surrey are incomparable examples. They are large parks involving long walks. At Painshill, eighteenth-century visitors paid five shillings to be driven round the circuit in a pony trap. Both places give a feeling of moving through a fantasy garden, which dissolves into and merges with the 'natural' landscape, a landscape not really the work of nature, but carefully designed to appear like it.

The Painshill landscape was the life's work of the Honourable Charles Hamilton, fourteenth child of the 6th Earl of Abercorn. Hamilton went on two Grand Tours, one in 1725 at the age of 20, the other two years later. He was 34 when he bought the Painshill estate and it became his obsession for the next 35 years. It ruined him financially, and soon after his vision was completely realized, he had to sell it. In 1773, having finished his work at Painshill by flooding the eastern part of the lake, he sold the estate, paid his debts and retired to Bath, where died in 1786.

Large parks like Stourhead and Painshill concern us here because of the influence they have had on the design of gardens. Hamilton's planting at Painshill was exciting and innovative and can be seen today, meticulously reconstructed by the Painshill Park Trust. Hamilton was among the first to introduce the shrubbery into the landscape, using the ever-widening range of plants available, including those newly imported from North America, many of which had spectacular red, orange and yellow autumn colour. The shrubs close to the house at Painshill were rigorously maintained and pruned into tidy shapes, and at first this practice was followed with the shrubs that lined the walks throughout the park; but towards the end of the century, they were allowed to develop their natural luxuriance.

The 'supreme masterpiece of the art of the landscape gardener'

The great landscaped terraces of Duncombe and Rievaulx in the north of England and at Farnborough Hall in the Midlands showed a different response to the idea of bringing the landscape into the garden. They combined grandeur with simplicity, and they provided linear, but not circular, walks. You stroll to the end of the grassy, close-mown terrace, admiring the changing views as the terrace gently curves, you pause when you reach the temple at the end of the walk, and then, although there are alternative routes to follow, you may go back, covering the same ground. There is nothing monotonous about returning the way you went, because the views are different, and the walk is terminated by a different architectural feature.

These terraces have a military quality, as if they started out as defensive ramparts, but in fact they have been purpose-built for admiring the view. They are descended from Tudor and Jacobean raised terraces, commanding views out from formal walled gardens. The classical temples of the eighteenth century are directly descended from the banqueting houses of the sixteenth and seventeenth centuries, and served the same purpose. The Ionic temple at Rievaulx had a kitchen in the basement, equipped to serve roast meat and sauce, wine and beer, followed by fruit, tea and coffee, for up to 12 people.

Duncombe Park and Rievaulx Terrace were created by the same family. The Duncombes, having committed the social crime of making their fortune in banking, were able to buy, for the huge sum of £90,000, the Rievaulx and Helmsley estates in Yorkshire on the death of their previous owner, the profligate and dissolute 2nd Duke of Buckingham. Alexander Pope expressed the snobbish attitude of the fashionable world:

And Helmsley, once proud Buckingham's delight,
Slides to a Scrivener or City Knight.

Moral Essays, Alexander Pope, 1733

Thomas Duncombe, nephew and heir of Sir Charles (the banker), built the mansion and, between 1713 and 1718, excavated the terrace walk, building the Ionic rotunda at the north end on a promontory supported by a massive serpentine ha-ha (a very early example) and a circular Doric temple to the south. The gently curving, half-mile long terrace approximately followed a loop in the River Rye, deep in the valley below. The curve concealed each temple from the other and provided ever-changing views down into the valley. At that time it was an astonishingly radical design. A few miles away at Rievaulx, the terrace built by Thomas Duncombe's son, Thomas II, between 1749 and 1757, has a more free-flowing, loosely serpentine form, showing the development of a taste for the 'natural' from one generation to the next. Both depend for their success on their position in a beautiful landscape and the views they command: at Duncombe the majestic valley, and at Rievaulx the large and picturesque ruins of Rievaulx Abbey, in an equally spectacular valley.

They attracted much attention and, together with advantageous marriages

into aristocratic families, helped establish the Duncombes as desirable neigh-bours. Author and traveller Arthur Young wrote in 1768:

> Mr Duncombe's ornamental grounds… cannot be viewed without
> yielding a most exquisite enjoyment…. The temple commands such
> various scenes of the sublime and beautiful as to form a theatre worthy
> of the magnificent pencil of nature.

Farnborough Hall, Warwickshire, in contrast to the vast mansion at Duncombe Park, is a manageable family house. It has belonged to the Holbech family since 1684, and owes its present handsome exterior and charming interior to the second William Holbech, who spent much loving care and quite a lot of money in improvements, mainly during the 1740s. He spent much of his youth in Italy, far more than the average Grand Tourist, trying to mend, according to family tradition, a broken heart. His love of Italy and appreciation of classical art and

*Thomas Duncombe's grass terrace above the valley of the River Rye presents a sequence of views of
the ruins of Rievaulx Abbey. From 'The Monastic Ruins of Yorkshire', William Richardson,
engraved by George Hawkins, 1843.*

architecture are reflected in the house and in the landscaping at Farnborough.

William Holbech's gentle S-shaped grass terrace rises from the house for three-quarters of a mile, commanding panoramic views over the Hanwell valley towards Edgehill. Today, in order to appreciate the view, visitors must, by a great feat of imagination, blot out the M40 motorway, and stop their ears to the hum of its traffic. Holbech took the walk regularly, to say 'hullo' to his brother who lived in the next village. The gentle slope is sheltered on the left by a belt of beech, oaks and sweet chestnuts, with hollies, Portugal laurels and laurustinus in front. Extensive views to the right are broken by regular planting. In Richard Jago's poem 'Edge-Hill' (1767), he describes in florid terms the construction of the terrace and its eye-catcher obelisk:

> Where the tall pillar lifts its taper head
> Her spacious terrace, and surrounding lawns
> Deck'd with no sparing cost of planted tufts,
> Or ornamental building, Farnborough boasts.
> Hear they her master's call? In sturdy troops,
> The jocund labourers hie, and, at his nod
> A thousand hands or smooth the slanting hill
> Or scoop new channels for the gath'ring flood,
> And, in his pleasures, find substantial bliss.

Holbech almost certainly had help with planning his landscape from Sanderson Miller, gentleman architect and landscape designer and his neighbour at Radway. Miller was also a friend of Shenstone at The Leasowes which was not far away. A letter of 1756 from Shenstone to Jago, a fellow poet and close friend since their schooldays at Halesowen, implies that Holbech had already visited The Leasowes. It reads, 'Pray remember me to Mr Talbot, Mr Miller and Mr Holbech; should they call upon me next year, they will find my place better worthy of their notice.' Beside the Terrace Walk, half-hidden in the trees is Farnborough's jewel, the Oval Pavilion. Its upper room is decorated with light-hearted rococo plasterwork, echoing the decoration in the house. It may have been designed by Sanderson Miller, along with the Ionic temple, the obelisk, and a hexagonal game larder built within a colonnaded loggia.

'A minor Stow on Clifton's crown': Thomas Goldney's Garden
Many successful industrialists, like Thomas Goldney of Bristol, put part of their fortune into making gardens to give themselves and their family pleasure and to

show the world how fashionable and sophisticated they had become. Two things make Thomas Goldney stand out from the rest; one is the fact that much of his garden has survived. The other is the passion and energy he put into creating his garden and, very particularly, his grotto, with triumphant results.

> And each congenial guest with joy invades
> The fountains, grottos, and the clear cascades;
> A minor Stow on Clifton's crown we find,
> In Epic meekness, like its master's mind.
>
> 'Clifton', Henry Jones, 1766

Much of the credit should surely be shared by Goldney's gardener, Adam Sixsmith, who came in summer 1732 and stayed for over 36 years, but Goldney himself was closely involved on a daily basis, as his 'Garden Book', a small home-made notebook, shows.

We know from John Kelsall's journal that the garden was already impressive in 1735. Kelsall, a Quaker like Goldney, was connected with Coalbrookdale iron works in Shropshire, a firm in which the Goldneys had a stake, and where Thomas had worked before returning to Bristol to become the firm's agent there. Kelsall wrote that on 3 June 1735 he walked up from the Hotwell 'to Thos. Goldneys at Clifton, went thro his Gardens &c which are very fine with Walks, Greens, Waterworks, Summer Houses &c there were many Lemons and Orange Trees with fruit on them.' Goldney's notebook for that year refers to the extension of a 'Filbeard [filbert] Grove', a new holly hedge, a long walk with box edgings, fruit trees and a small vineyard. He records sowing sunflower seed in May and broccoli in June. He marked his best anemones with notched sticks, indicating the flower colours.

In the summer of 1727, Goldney embarked on a project that would bring the fashionable world to his garden gate. He began to construct a grotto, perhaps inspired by his father's account of a tour of the Netherlands, where he visited a merchant near Utrecht who had in his garden, a 'most curiouse Grotto in Shell-Work, very admirable Workmanship… variety of Fancys as if twas in paint & all this compos'd by assortment of Shells in colour & shape to answer ye designe of ye compiler.'

Goldney's first step was to buy a plot of land from his neighbour. This was not adjacent to his own garden, so he negotiated permission 'to make a Sub-terranious passage or Footway under Ground of commodious dimensions (not exceeding Eight Foot Wide & Eight Foot high in the clear when walled and

arched over) from the said TG's garden to the said piece of ground.' Work on the grotto went ahead speedily, but it would not be finally finished for 27 years. In September 1749 the Reverend Alexander Catcott, vicar of Temple church in Bristol, visited Goldney, with whom he was on plant-swapping terms, and described '3 rooms, parted by pillars, that on the left hand finished with regard to the Shell-work.' The pillars are encrusted with 'Bristol diamonds', clusters of small quartz crystals, according to Catcott 'not to be found now in the Plenty they were formerly, for Mr Goldney of Clifton has employed men for 7 last years on purpose to gather them, to adorn his Grotto.'

Mrs Delany, the Irish traveller and diarist, sightseeing in November 1756 approved of the grotto as

> one of the few things that answers expectations... I will not say a very
> elegant fancy might not have made the whole better, but it is by much
> the finest thing of the kind I ever saw... the master is reckoned a great
> humourist and a niggard, but I was so fortunate as to take his fancy, and
> he gave me two or three pretty specimens of coral and said I should have
> what I pleased.

In the early 1760s the Duchess of Northumberland thought it 'most magnificent', with its

> Pavement of Tiles glaz'd wch nearly resemble Egyptian Pebbles... at one
> End of the Grotto sitts a River God who from an Urn throws a clear
> Stream wch trickles over the Shells &c in a wild Cascade into a Bason... on
> each Side of this Cascade is a large rough kind of Scollop the inside Mother
> of Pearl wch came from the E Indies.

It was, the Duchess wrote, 'impossible to describe the Variety there is of Shells Fossils Oars Sparres Petrifactions &c &c to adorn this place most of wch were placed here by the hand of Mr Gouldney himself.'

The grotto was the main attraction, but visitors were also impressed by the other features in Mr Goldney's garden. There was a formal canal full of gold and silver fish, an octagonal pleasure house and a rotunda with a colonnade. The Duchess

The grotto at Painshill Park was built for Charles Hamilton, probably by Joseph Lane of Tisbury, Wiltshire. The tunnels and 3sq m (40sq ft) main chamber of the grotto are in the process of being restored and once again glitter with spars and crystals.

of Northumberland re-marked on 'a row of varie-gated standard hollies of incredible height.' She liked the fine, extensive views over the downs, the Wells, the fields and Dundry Tower, and Mrs Delany also admired the view: 'hedge rows, clumps of trees and woods all happily placed; the city of

Bristol; the windings of the river, and sailing boats and barges; the stupendous rocks,... from a terrace in Mr Golding's garden we saw everything in the utmost perfection.' The views are spoiled in many ways, but still extensive.

Paying the price

That great English work of art, the landscaped park, could not have existed without the system of enclosure by which landowners were able to increase and consolidate their land-holdings, bringing about the ideal conditions for 'Capability' Brown, Repton and other designers to ply their trade successfully and profitably. But the enclosure system was not always fair and was often resented. This anonymous verse expresses widespread feelings on the subject:

> The law condemns both man and woman
> Who steals a goose from off the common
> But lets the greater robber loose
> Who steals the common from the goose.

Humphrey Repton's 'before' and 'after' drawings of his own cottage garden in Essex seem to show that he may himself have been guilty of 'stealing the common'. His 'before' picture shows a little village green beyond the garden fence, occupied by a flock of geese and a blind beggar with a wooden leg, a war veteran perhaps, cap in hand. On the left of the picture a stagecoach rattles by, the outside passengers looking down into the garden, and we can see hams hanging

Repton's 'Before' and 'After' drawings show the gentrification of his own garden at Hare Street,
Essex. 'Fragments on the Theory and Practice of Landscape Gardening',
Humphrey Repton with J. Adey Repton, 1816.

outside the butcher's shop across the street. Repton got permission to take 20 yards of green into his garden. He enclosed it with a hedge and in the 'after' version, the beggar and the geese have vanished, and a carefully placed screen of shrubs and a rose-clad obelisk hide the stagecoach and hams.

Repton's cottage had been gentrified. In contrast, the garden of a genuine labourer's cottage is described by Thomas Bernard in 1797, and its form has changed very little in 250 years:

> Two miles from Tadcaster, on the left-hand side of the road to York, stands a beautiful little cottage, with a garden that has long attracted the eye of the traveller. The slip of land is exactly a rood [quarter of an acre], inclosed by a cut quick [hawthorn] hedge; and containing the cottage, fifteen apple-trees, one green gage, and three wine-sour plum trees, two apricot-trees, several gooseberry and currant bushes, abundance of common vegetables, and three hives of bees; being all the apparent wealth of the possessor.

The cottage's owner, Britton Abbot, had himself been the victim of enclosure. He was a married man with seven children, two cows, a rented cottage, two acres and grazing rights on the common. After nine years of successful husbandry, the land was enclosed and his cottage repossessed by the landowner. Abbot's new plot was given to him by a Squire Fairfax. His neighbours helped him build a cottage and he set about making the garden described above. Besides growing, in neat rows, enough vegetables to feed his family, he earned a few pounds a year from his fruit crop and produced about 40 bushels (320 gallons) of potatoes a year.

The *cottage orné* (like the *ferme ornée*, plus chic in French) takes us from the eighteenth century into the nineteenth. Repton, notably at Endsleigh House in Devon, and his son John Adey Repton at Blaise Hamlet outside Bristol, were among the first designers in this branch of the Picturesque style, and must be held at least partly responsible for a new fashion for quaintness, an attribute which would become much admired in the next century.

6

THE EIGHTEENTH
CENTURY III

Romanticizing Nature

T HE IDEAS BEHIND the new 'landscape gardening'
reflected a new liberalism in politics and philosophy.
Among the English intelligentsia, French formality was
thought to reflect authoritarianism in politics and the
arts and was therefore despised. In the second half of the
eighteenth century, fluidity and freedom of thought was
reflected in a similar freedom and relaxation in clothes
and manners. The Duc de la Rochefoucauld was shocked by it. After a visit to
Bury St Edmunds in 1784, he wrote:

> Formality counts for nothing, and for the greatest part of the time one
> pays no attention to it. Thus, judged by French standards, the English, and
> especially the women, seem lacking in polite behaviour. All the young
> people… sit down in a large armchair and put their feet on another, they
> sit on any table in the room and do a thousand other things which would
> be ridiculous in France, but are done quite naturally in England.

Fashionable women no longer dressed in stiff silks and satins with voluminous
skirts which restricted movement and dictated ramrod posture. They lounged

---

*The Landscape Movement did not, as is sometimes thought, banish all flowers from the garden as is
evident from 'The Elysian Fields at Audley End, Suffolk' (detail), William Tomkins, 1788.*

sinuously or, like Jane Austen's heroines, raced up hill and down dale, through mud and puddles, wearing muslin and sprigged cotton. They were able to play naturally and comfortably with children, and the children were no longer got up as stiff miniature adults. The admission of fresh air to blow away stuffy customs also occurred, quite literally, in domestic architecture. Breakfast rooms and morning rooms had French windows opening into the garden, like those of the Prince of Wales' *cottage orné* at Royal Lodge in Windsor Park. It was a time of freedom and new creativity. With the freedom went an unusual degree of domesticity compared to society elsewhere in Europe, which also surprised de la Rochefoucauld:

> Husband and wife are always together and share the same society. It is the rarest thing to meet the one without the other. The very richest people do not keep more than four or six carriage-horses, since they pay all their visits together. It would be more ridiculous to do otherwise in England than it would to go everywhere with your wife in Paris. They always give the appearance of perfect harmony, and the wife in particular has an air of contentment which always gives me pleasure.

'Cabbage walks, potato beds, bean perfumes, and peas blossoms'

M. and Mme d'Arblay were just such a couple as the duke described. He was French, she, English. When Humphrey Repton declared 'A cottage is a dwelling where happiness may reside unsupported by wealth', he might have been describing the d'Arblays' residence at Camilla Cottage, West Humble, near Dorking in Surrey. Mme d'Arblay was Fanny Burney, author of *Evelina*, published in 1778 when she was 26, and *Cecilia* in 1782. The cottage was named after another of her best-selling novels, *Camilla*, published in 1796. Fanny, lively, good-natured and impecunious, made a virtue out of necessity and settled happily for love in a cottage when, at the age of 40, she married General D'Arblay, a refugee from Napoleon's France. Like Fanny, he had no money.

Fanny had spent her youth at the hub of London intellectual and artistic life, her circle including Dr Johnson, Burke, Reynolds and Garrick. In her rural retreat she may have missed the stimulating social life, but since she suffered permanently from poor health it may have been a relief. She kept up a lively correspondence with her family and friends, and that is how we know something about her garden. Her husband rolled up his sleeves and got on with the work but, like everyone new to the game of gardening, he made mistakes. Fanny wrote to her father from the rented cottage that preceded 'Camilla':

Seeds are sowing in some parts where plants ought to be reaping, and plants are running to seed while they are thought not yet at maturity. Our garden, therefore, is not yet quite the most profitable thing in the world; but Mr d'A. assures me it is to be the staff of our table and existence…

Another time, too, with great labour, he cleared a considerable compartment of weeds, and when it looked clean and well, and he showed his work to the gardener, the man said he had demolished an asparagus bed! M. d'A. protested, however, nothing could look more like *les mauvaises herbes*.

In due course M. d'A's labours were rewarded:

…we have had for one week cabbages from our own cultivation every day! Oh, you have no idea how sweet they tasted! We agreed they had a freshness and a *goût* we had never met before. We had them for too short a time to grow tired of them, because, as I have already hinted, they were beginning to run to seed before we knew they were eatable.

Home-grown vegetables are among the high spots of a gardener's life, but only the most dedicated grower could eat cabbage for seven days in a row and still enthuse so extravagantly about the freshness and flavour. In the ornamental department, M. d'Arblay lost no time in rearranging the plants and on 22 March 1794 Fanny's diary records:

His greatest passion is for transplanting. Everything we possess he moves from one end of the garden to another, to produce better effects. Roses take the place of jessamines, jessamines of honeysuckles and honeysuckles of lilacs, till they have all danced round as far as the space allows; but whether the effect may not be a general mortality, summer only can determine.

After they moved to Camilla Cottage things didn't go much better. The dreamed-of prospect of 'cabbage walks, potato beds, bean perfumes, and peas blossoms' never quite materialized.

M. d'Arblay has worked most laboriously in his garden, but his misfortunes there, during our absence, might melt a heart of stone.

The horses of our neighbouring farmer broke through our hedges, and have made a kind of bog of our meadow, by scampering in it during the wet; the sheep followed who have eaten up all our greens, every sprout and cabbage and lettuce destined for the winter, while the horses dug up our turnips and carrots; and the swine, pursuing such examples, have trod down all the young plants, besides devouring whatever the others left of vegetables. Our potatoes, left, from our abrupt departure, in the ground, are all rotten or frost-bitten, and utterly spoilt; and not a single thing has our whole ground produced us since we came home. A few dried carrots, which remain from the indoor collection, are all we have to temper our viands.

The pleasures of the garden are sometimes few and far between, and won in the teeth of adversity, and the absentee gardener is especially accident prone.

A particular friend of Fanny Burney's, although more than 50 years her senior, was Mary Delany, née Granville, whom we met briefly on a visit to Mr Goldney's grotto in Bristol (see page 153). She praised Fanny's 'admirable understanding, tender affection, and sweetness of manners' and did her best to alleviate her difficult financial circumstances by using her influence at Court to get her appointed as second keeper of the Robes to Queen Charlotte in 1786. But the post was arduous, and Fanny, always in poor health, got permission from the queen, with some difficulty, to retire after four years.

Mary was a close friend of King George III and Queen Charlotte. She drew and painted well, and did exquisite embroidery. But she was, and still is, best known for raising the ladylike occupation of decoupage, or 'paper mosaicks' as she called them, to an art. Some of her highly original flower pieces can be seen at the British Museum. She was passionately interested in gardens and garden design, and was a keen sightseer. She thought the landscaping at The Leasowes was reminiscent of Claude's paintings: an early appreciation of the Picturesque landscape style.

After visiting Dr Delany's house near Dublin some ten years before they married, she wrote, 'I already delight in your garden; pray have plenty of roses, honeysuckles, jasmine and sweet briar, not forgetting the lily of the valley.' The garden seems to have been, partly at least, in the style of a *ferme ornée*. Later, she

Neat rows of healthy cabbages and leeks in the kind of well-tended, productive vegetable plot that author Fanny Burney and her husband M. d'Arblay aspired to in their garden at Camilla Cottage, near Dorking in Surrey.

wrote 'the rurality of it is wonderfully pretty.' After her marriage, Mrs Delany divided her time between London and Ireland, where she gardened happily. She wrote to her sister describing her London house in Upper Brook Street,

> You think, madam, I have no garden, perhaps? But that's a mistake; I *have one* as big as your parlour at Gloucester, and in it groweth *damask-roses, stocks* variegated and plain, some purple, some red, *Pinks, Philaria,* some dead some alive; and *honeysuckles* that never blow. But when you come to town to weed and water it, it shall be improved after the new taste, but till then it shall remain dishevelled and undrest.

London gardeners have always had their share of difficulties to contend with, among them air pollution and dry shade. Perhaps the phillyrea more dead than alive and the honeysuckle that wouldn't flower were symptoms of these problems. By comparison, the garden at Lambeth Palace was far enough from the city not to suffer in this way. It remained, for the time being, quite countrified. A member of the household wrote to a friend describing the Palace in the 1760s as:

> …quite a town. It is a town of blooms and perfumes, however. The forecourt, inhabited by full 200 very amusing chickens, is quite fragrant with lime-blossoms… jessamine… cluster[s] round the windows: the rose-walk is to-day in its highest bloom. At every spot one moves to in the garden is some variety of sweets; here a gale of spicy pinks; there the breath of lillies… [the] whole border of the serpentine canal is filled with single pinks, red and white, which perfume the air and look sweet and soft beyond imagination.

'English gardens are not made to a plan, but to a feeling…' Goethe

Like the d'Arblays, two remarkable and courageous Irish women, Lady Eleanor Butler and Miss Sarah Ponsonby chose love in a cottage. In 1778, they ran away together from their families in Kilkenny and in 1780 set up house together at Plas Newydd, outside Llangollen in Wales. For 50 years the Ladies of Llangollen, as they became known, dedicated their lives to friendship, learning and the arts. Their aim was to create a perfect home and garden, and live off the produce of their four acres. The latter proved an unrealistic ambition: they were in debt from start to finish.

In other respects the Ladies succeeded so triumphantly that it became impossible to lead the simple life they had planned. Although remote, Plas Newydd

became a compulsory stopping place on the cultural tours of fashionable and intellectual travellers. Visitors included Burke, Sir Walter Scott, the Duke of Wellington, Josiah Wedgewood, Charles Darwin, Percy Shelley, Sheridan, Robert Southey and William Wordsworth, who wrote a sonnet referring to them as 'Sisters in love, a love allowed to climb/ E'vn on this earth, above the reach of time'.

What did the visitors come to see? Many came out of curiosity, eager to see the eccentric ladies who had defied the usual conventions for the sake of their romantic friendship. But the house and garden were charming and unusual, and as much as the constant stream of visitors permitted, the two ladies were living an ideal life, true to their philosophy and their rigorous system of self-improvement. As the years went by, the square stone cottage, with its five rooms, became more and more *orné*, ending up gothicized from top to bottom.

The surrounding landscape (completely built over today) was wild, romantic and beautiful, with picturesque views of the ruined medieval Castell Dinas Bran, the Trevor rocks and the Berwyn mountains. Below the house the ground sloped down to a small ravine where the river Cufflymen flowed. In due course, the Ladies had the river altered to fall through cascades and pools.

In four acres they could not achieve self-sufficiency. But their needs were at least partly served by a small dairy and poultry yard, and a walled vegetable garden stocked with the best varieties of melons, asparagus, strawberries and peas. They also managed, or their servants did, to make wine, preserves, dairy produce and bread. The whole was laid out as a miniature *ferme ornée*, on the same lines as those of Philip Southcote and William Shenstone 50 years earlier. A

Lady Eleanor Butler and Miss Sarah Ponsonby, out walking with their dog. The font from Valle Crucis Abbey, placed to catch the flow from a spring in the hillside, can be seen in the background in this colour lithograph by J.H. Lynch.

gravel path followed the 'Home Circuit' through the shrubbery, past the dairy, the fowl yard, the drying green and the gardens. There was a rustic summerhouse overlooking the valley and a font, originally in Valle Crucis Abbey, was positioned in a shady place to catch the water flowing from a spring, with moss and ferns encouraged to grow around it.

The ladies loved their garden and spent a great deal of time planning it, working in it, and simply enjoying it. There were thickets of shrubs, white lilac to light up moonlight walks and, elsewhere 'Lilaks, Laburnums, Seringas, White Broom, Weeping Willow, Apple Trees, poplar.' There were lime trees near the cottage, to sit under and enjoy their shade and scent. Flowerbeds were filled with dahlias, geraniums, carnations and roses. As time went by, more and more wild plants were brought from the woods into the gardens, including gentians, strawberries, primroses, Snowdon pinks, white violets and snowdrops.

'How unlike nature!': Gilpin

Eleanor Butler and Sarah Ponsonby sought inspiration for their garden in the books of William Gilpin. They had copies of all of them in their library. In 1772, he published *Picturesque Tours*, an illustrated account of journeys in the more mountainous and rugged parts of the British Isles: the Wye Valley, the Lake District and the Scottish Highlands. He arrived at theoretical principles relating to landscape, which he published in 1792 as *Three Essays: On Picturesque Beauty; On Picturesque Travel; and on Sketching Landscape*. Briefly summarized, his conclusions were that 'beauty' was an attribute of gentleness, smoothness and harmony, whereas Picturesque beauty implied roughness and contrast. He knew which he preferred with reference to the landscape, and wrote, 'How flat, and insipid is often the garden scene, how puerile, how absurd! The banks of the river, how smooth, and parallel! The lawn, and its boundaries, how unlike nature!'

Gilpin echoed the philosophy of Edmund Burke expressed in *A Philosophical Enquiry into the Sublime and the Beautiful* (1757). Burke distinguished between beauty, which implied smoothness, delicacy, smallness and light, and the sublime, which implied power, darkness, solitude and vastness. Terror was an attribute of the sublime, 'Whatever is fitted in any sort to excite the ideas of pain, and danger… or is conversant about terrible objects, or operates in a manner analogous to terror, is a source of the sublime; that is, it is productive of the strongest emotion which the mind is capable of feeling.'

Plas Newydd, Denbighshire, home of the famous Ladies of Llangollen, who ran away together from their respective families in Ireland to create an idyllic, small-scale ferme ornée in the rugged hills of North Wales. This engraving by an unknown artist dates from c.1830.

Similar ideas had been expressed much earlier by the 3rd Earl of Shaftesbury in *The Moralists* (1709). He admired

> Things of a *natural* kind: where neither *Art*, nor the *Conceit* or *Caprice* of Man has spoil'd their genuine order… Even the rude Rocks, the mossy *Caverns*, the irregular unwrought *Grottos* and broken *Falls* of waters, with all the horrid graces of the *Wilderness* itself, as representing NATURE more, will be the more engaging, and appear with a magnificence beyond the mockery of princely gardens.

Shaftesbury used the word 'horrid' in its original, Latin sense, to mean unkempt and savage. 'Horrid' can also mean, 'with hair standing on end', so Shaftesbury's horror equates with Burke's terror as an attribute of the sublime. By the end of the eighteenth century, when Gilpin was making his tours, the greater part of the landscape consisted of well-managed agricultural land or tidy, grazed park-land. The wilderness had shrunk, and scarcity gave it an aesthetic value it had not had before. Rough, irregular, rocky terrain; craggy cliffs and steep valleys; waterfalls and rushing torrents; gnarled, misshapen trees with mossy roots; features that inspired a *frisson* of danger; these were the elements in the landscape that were admired as Picturesque.

Wealthy young men still went on the Grand Tour, but its centre had shifted from Rome and Florence to the Alps. The emphasis was on rugged, grand scenery rather than classical architecture, and the most admired artist was Salvator Rosa who painted wild and macabre mountain scenes. Horace Walpole described the Alps as, 'Precipices, mountains, torrents, wolves, rumblings – Salvator Rosa.

The Sublime and the Picturesque found their way into literature. Walpole himself wrote the first 'Gothic' novel, *The Castle of Otranto*. Typical of the new genre were fantastic and macabre plots in which beautiful, wronged heroines were threatened by, and rescued from, a series of horrible fates. Supernatural agencies were usually involved and the settings were haunted castles, grave-yards, ruined abbeys, hermitages and caves. In the 1790s, the young people observed by de la Rochfoucauld lolling around with their feet on the chairs, were probably either reading or discussing a Gothic novel. The best known was Mrs Radcliffe's bestseller, *The Mysteries of Udolpho*, the book that inspired Catherine Morland's endearing silliness in Jane Austen's *Northanger Abbey*.

Catherine Morland was an addict of gothic novels (she asked her friend Isabella, 'but are they all horrid? Are you sure they are all horrid?'). Later, while a guest at the forbidding medieval Northanger Abbey, Catherine allows her romantic imagination free rein and terrifies herself into believing her host capable of immuring his wife. Jane Austen reminds her readers drily that it is not in the works of Mrs Radcliffe that 'human nature, at least in the midland counties of England, is to be looked for.'

In *Sense and Sensibility*, Jane Austen gently mocks the fashion of the time for the Picturesque, making Edward Ferrars put the case for Sense as far as the landscape is concerned:

> …the woods seem full of fine timber, and the valley looks comfortable and snug – with rich meadows and several neat farm houses scattered here and there. It exactly answers my idea of a fine country, because it unites beauty with utility… I like a fine prospect but not on picturesque principles. I do not like crooked twisted blasted trees. I do not like ruined tattered cottages. I am not fond of nettles or thistles or heath blossoms. I have more pleasure in a snug farmhouse than a watch tower and a troop of happy tidy villagers pleases me better than all the banditti in the world.

The noble art of picturesque gardening

Opinions were divided as to whether landscapes made by 'improvers' like 'Capability' Brown should be preferred to wilder, but often just as contrived, scenery. Some observers found the Brownian landscapes too tamed and bland for their taste. Others thought it absurd to go to the lengths of Richard Payne Knight, one of the most articulate champions of the Picturesque, to achieve his goal. Dead trees were transplanted and 'Large fragments of stone were irregularly thrown amongst the briars and weeds, to imitate the foreground of a picture.' The controversy attracted satire from the pen of Thomas Love Peacock in *Headlong Hall* (1816):

> 'I perceive,' said Mr Milestone, after they had walked a few paces, 'these grounds have never been touched by the finger of taste.'
> 'The place is quite a wilderness,' said Squire Headlong…
> 'My dear Sir,' said Mr Milestone, 'accord me your permission to wave the wand of enchantment over your grounds. The rocks shall be blown up, the trees shall be cut down, the wilderness and all its goats shall vanish like mist. Pagodas and Chinese bridges, gravel walks and shrubberies, bowling-greens, canals, and clumps of larch, shall rise upon its ruins. One age, Sir, has brought to light the treasures of ancient learning; a second has

penetrated into the depths of metaphysics; a third has brought to
perfection the science of astronomy: but it was reserved for the
exclusive genius of the present times to invent the noble art of
picturesque gardening, which has given, as it were, a new tint to
the complexion of nature, and a new outline to the physiognomy
of the universe!'

'Give me leave,' said Sir Patrick O'Prism, 'to take an exception to that
same. Your system of levelling, and trimming, and clipping, and docking,
and clumping, and polishing, and cropping, and shaving, destroys all the
beautiful harmonies of light and shade, melting into one another, as you
see them on that rock over yonder. I never saw one of your improved
places, as you call them, and which are nothing but big bowling-greens,
like sheets of green paper, with a parcel of round clumps scattered over
them like so many spots of ink, flicked at random out of a pen, and a
solitary animal here and there looking as if it were lost, that I did not think
it was for all the world like Hounslow Heath, thinly sprinkled over with
bushes and highwaymen.'

'Sir,' said Mr Milestone, 'you will have the goodness to make a distinction
between the picturesque and the beautiful,'

Will I?' said Sir Patrick: 'Och! But I won't. For what is beautiful? That
what pleases the eye. And what pleases the eye? Tints variously broken
and blended. Now, tints variously broken and blended constitute the
picturesque.'

'Allow me,' said Mr Gall. 'I distinguish the picturesque and the beautiful,
and I add to them, in the layout out of grounds, a third and distinct
character, which I call unexpectedness.'

'Pray, Sir,' said Mr Milestone, 'by what name do you distinguish this
character, when a person walks round the grounds for the second time?'

Whichever side they took in the controversy, most observers agreed that landscapes and gardens should have a pictorial quality. To return to Catherine
Morland in *Northanger Abbey*, her young friends the Tilneys, of whom she was a
little in awe for their sophistication and culture, 'were viewing the country with
the eyes of persons accustomed to drawing, and deciding on its capability of
being formed into pictures, with all the eagerness of real taste,' much as, today,
many garden-lovers view their subject through the lens of a camera.

William Shenstone, writing at his *ferme ornée* at The Leasowes in about 1755, was
one of the first to formulate the principle that garden making was a matter of

making pictures. Shenstone set out his ideas on landscape design in *Unconnected thoughts on Gardening*, published in 1764:

> Gardening may be divided into three species – kitchen gardening –
> parterre-gardening – and landskip, or picturesque gardening: which
> latter consists in pleasing the imagination by scenes of grandeur, beauty,
> or variety....
> A ruin may...afford that pleasing melancholy which proceeds from
> a reflexion on decayed magnificence...A rural scene to me is never
> perfect without the addition of some kind of building.
> Landskip should contain variety enough to form a picture upon canvas;
> and this is no bad test, as I think the landskip painter is the gardener's best
> designer...
> The eye should always look rather down upon water... Water should
> ever appear as an irregular shape or winding stream. Islands give
> beauty...The fall of water is Nature's province – only the vulgar
> citizen... squirts up his rivulets in jettaux.
> The side-trees in vistas should be so circumstanced as to afford a
> probability that they grew by nature... Hedges... are universally
> bad... There is no more sudden, and obvious improvement, than an
> hedge removed, and the trees remaining.

'The pleasures of a garden have of late been very much neglected': Repton

At the time, the Picturesque controversy had everything to do with landscape but less to do with gardens. Nevertheless, the theory that garden design, like landscape design, was a matter of making a series of pictures, was to become entrenched for the next 200 years.

Humphrey Repton followed 'Capability' Brown as the most fashionable landscape designer of his generation. The famous Red Books he prepared for his clients, showing 'before' and 'after' watercolour drawings of his proposals, were the ultimate in pictorial presentation to tempt the client. Repton modified and softened the austerity of Brown's landscapes, and revived the art of garden design. He regretted 'The prevailing custom of placing a House in the middle of a Park, detached from all objects, whether of convenience or magnificence, and thus making a country residence as solitary and unconnected as the Prison on Dartmoor.' Such isolation accorded with Brown's vision of the house in the landscape untrammelled by parterres and shrubberies, but Repton saw the house in a garden setting, which blended into the landscape beyond.

He differed from Uvedale Price and Richard Payne Knight, the champions of the Picturesque, in his practical approach. His aim was to combine beauty with utility, stating that 'While mouldering abbeys and the antiquated cottage with its chimney smothered in ivy may be eminently appealing to the painter, in whatever relates to man, propriety and convenience are not less objectives of good taste than picturesque effects.'

Repton's pictorial ideas for gardens were inventive and varied. He was not afraid to design gardens that were as pretty as a picture, and his own drawings of, for example, the Rosary at Ashridge in Hertfordshire, were enticing. When presented with a large site attached to a grand house, he proposed a series of separate gardens each with its own theme. At Ashridge, besides the Rosary, he planned 14 other gardens, including a Monk's Garden, a Mount Garden and an American Garden, though not all were executed.

Repton's designs were characterized by a lightness of touch, with airy trelliswork, rose arches, and filigree baskets of flowers on the lawn. He sometimes became involved with the architecture of the house as well as the design of the garden, and had a fruitful partnership with the architect Jeffry Wyatt at Endsleigh in Devon, where the garden was planned to take full advantage of fine views. There was a Terrace Walk and a Children's Garden with a covered walk, formal flowerbeds, a splashy fountain and a shallow canal where the children could sail their toy boats.

Repton also worked with John Nash on several projects, and both his sons worked in Nash's office. First Humphrey Repton, and then his son George, collaborated with Nash at Blaise Castle near Bristol. Their client was John Harford, a Bristol Quaker (like Thomas Goldney), with banking and industrial interests. Harford employed a Bristol architect, William Paty, to build a new house, and Repton advised on its site. Blaise Castle, a gothic folly built in 1766 on top of a hill above a dramatic gorge, was the epitome of Picturesque, and Repton manipulated the woodland planting, opening up a clearing with a cheerful woodman's cottage to contrast with the brooding castle 'embosm'd high in tufted trees'. He designed a new approach to the main house, taking advantage of the spectacular scenery along the Hazel Brook Gorge.

Nearer the house, Nash built a ridiculously pretty thatched dairy, and elsewhere on the estate, he and George Repton designed Blaise Hamlet, consisting of nine fantasy cottages grouped around a village green with a pillared pump at its centre. Following the Picturesque principles of irregularity, each cottage was built to a different design, but all were made of the same stone, with steep, thatched roofs, and they all had massive ornamental chimneys. The facilities provided for the tenants were in advance of their time, each cottage being equipped with a privy, an oven and a washing copper.

Work for the Duke of Bedford at Woburn Abbey allowed Repton to indulge his taste for fantasy in other directions too: the Thornery, built as a picnic house in a woodland clearing using different sorts of thorn trees, consisted of a room painted with flowers and treillage, with a basement kitchen. Also for Woburn, he designed a large, elaborate dairy in the Chinese style, with a pagoda turret and fretwork verandah, all reflected in a large lily pond, and viewed from a Chinese summer pavilion opposite. For the Prince Regent, he drew up plans for reconstructing the Royal Pavilion in the Indian style, including proposals for the gardens. To his bitter disappointment the Prince, having at first shown great enthusiasm, turned his plans down in favour of the ambitious and manipulative Nash's scheme.

Repton was not the first to revive an interest in flower gardens among fashionable people (the interest among those with no pretensions to fashion had never waned). In the 1770s, Lord Nuneham, the son of the 1st Earl Harcourt, asked William Mason, professor of poetry at Oxford and author of a long poem 'The English Garden', to make a two-acre flower garden in his grounds at Nuneham Courtenay. Its inspiration was 'Julie's Garden' in Rousseau's novel *La Nouvelle Heloise* (1761). Julie's garden, the idealized '*Elysée*', was a secret garden, hidden by dense trees and shrubs. The garden appeared as if nature, not man, had made it: a garden where, to take Bishop Heber's words out of context and out of their chronological place, 'every prospect pleases and only man is vile'.

We know how the Nuneham Courtenay garden looked from Paul Sandby's watercolours, painted in 1777. They show vistas to and from a classical temple, framed by curving, irregularly shaped flowerbeds with serpentine box edging. In the beds, herbaceous plants are arranged with the tallest at the centre, the smallest in front. Beyond the flowerbeds are informal screens of flowering shrubs and mixed deciduous and coniferous trees. In the garden, as well as the Temple of Flora, the Roman goddess of flowers, there was an orangery, a grotto, a well, and various urns and statues.

'An earth house in the melon ground'

The latter part of the eighteenth century also saw changes in modest country gardens. The Reverend Gilbert White's was a fairly typical village garden, but White himself was anything but typical. He was not, as is sometimes assumed, the vicar of Selborne. He was born in the vicarage at Selborne (his grandfather was the vicar) and, except when travelling, lived all his life there, acting as a temporary curate on three separate occasions. But the curacy he held for 24 years was in the nearby parish of Farringdon. In 1784 he became curate of Selborne again, retaining the post until his death in 1793 at the age of 72.

The Wakes, White's house in Selborne, had about an acre of garden and a couple of fields serving as a miniature park. Fortunately for us, he kept his Garden Kalendar with the same enthusiasm and meticulous attention to detail as is shown in the Journals, which formed the basis of his classic book, *Natural History & Antiquities of Selborne*. The latter has never been out of print since it was published in 1789.

White was conscious of changing fashion in gardening and landscape design. He built a ha-ha to open up his lawn to the fields beyond and combined the formality of a quincunx of cypress trees planted on a small mound, with carefully contrived views across his small park, and a planned route around it. The quincunx is reached from the house by a walk through the orchard, replanted today with fruit varieties mentioned in White's Kalendar. There is a choice between a straight or zigzag path up the slope. The centre of the quincunx is marked by a large terracotta oil jar. From here, White contrived a view across the field to a mound supporting a thatched wine barrel fitted out with a seat and set on a revolving base, from which one can survey the view in all directions. There is also an eye-catcher in the park in the form of a 3.8m (12ft 6in) tall wooden cut-out silhouette of the Hesperian Hercules, a scaled-down version of the 9m (30ft) high statues at Caserta and Vaux-le-Vicomte.

As well as making his small landscaped park, complete with its circuit walk and classical references, White worked busily and happily in his kitchen garden. In the Kalendar he records the sowing and harvesting of all kinds of vegetables and fruit:

31.8.1789 Cucumber, green: gather 238 Well Grown. [What on earth did he do with such a huge quantity?]

24. 6. 1777: Kidney Beans: Miserable.
28.9.1779: Black Grapes rich & sweet

White also records the methods by which he nurtured his beloved melons:

1755 March 31. Sowed one pot of Mr Garniers Cantalupe 1753, one pot of Lincolns Green Cantalupe 1751. One pot of Mr Hunters yellow cantalupe 1752, and one pot of Millers very fine old seeds.

1757 March 11. Made a melon paper House 8 feet long and 5 feet wide: to be covered with the best writing paper.

1758 Jan: 17. Finished an earth-house in the melon ground. It is worked in a circular shape with rods and coped over with the same, & then well thatched: is nine feet over and eight feet high: & has room to hold a good Quantity of mould, & a man at work without any inconvenience.

Gilbert White was immensely proud of his melons, and, when they were at their peak of ripe, sweet, aromatic perfection, he would share them with his friends and neighbours by holding a melon party.

Thanks to the Kalendar, and to generous donations from various charities, it has been possible to reconstruct Gilbert White's garden, including such features as the paper melon house. It is open to visitors, as is the house, with some rooms furnished as they were in White's day. The rest houses the Oates Museum, which is devoted to explorers Frank Oates and Captain Lawrence Oates.

'Equal parts of blood and common garden mould'
It is possible that Gilbert White knew or corresponded with another genial scientist and naturalist of his day, Dr Edward Jenner of Berkeley, Gloucestershire. But Jenner was 30 years younger than White and there is no evidence that they knew each other. However, Jenner would probably have read White's *Natural History*. The book was a success from its publication in 1789, when Dr Jenner was 40 years old, had been married for a year, and had lived at the Chantry in Berkeley for four years.

Like Gilbert White, Jenner lived most of his life in the village where he was born. Like White, he was born into a family of clergy: his father was vicar of Berkeley and both his brothers became clergymen. White and Jenner also shared a love of nature, acute observation and a spirit of analytical enquiry into the ways of animals, birds and plants.

Jenner made new discoveries about the effect of hibernation on dormice and hedgehogs, and about the physical attributes of young cuckoos that enable them to oust eggs or other baby birds from their adopted nest. He also studied bird migration, a favourite interest of White's. White would also have been interested by experiments carried out by Jenner in his garden to discover how effective blood was as a fertilizer, and in what dilution it should be used. Being a doctor, he had access to plentiful supplies of human blood, and this is what he used, either fresh or in the form of serum.

Jenner described one of his experiments to his friend Sir Joseph Banks, President of the Royal Society and one of the founders of the Royal Horticultural Society:

April 20th 1782. – I took four young currant trees… planted in large garden pots of an equal size, in the following different substances.
No.1. was planted in the coagulated part of fresh blood, the surface of the pot only being covered with garden mould [compost].
No.2. was planted in equal parts of blood and common garden mould mixed together, and the surface being covered with plain mould.
No.3. was planted in common garden mould, without a mixture of any other substance; but this plant will, from time to time, be moistened with the serum of blood, marking the quantity made use of each time.
No.4. was planted in garden mould, and is to remain as a standard without the addition of any animal substance, to point out the indifference of vegetation.
The four pots were placed under an east wall in the open air.
April 26. – A pint of serum was poured on no.3.
May 3. – the serum in the same quantity applied again.
June 6. – No.1. dead.
No 2. nearly so.
No.3. sickly – though it vegetates in a small degree.
No. 4. healthy.
July 20. - No. 3 recovered – shoots, and looks healthy.

Doctor Jenner about to Vaccinate a Child. Doctor Jenner was below the middle stature, his hair dark and a little inclining to curl and it was observed at his death he was not the least gray. He was rather near sighted but never made use of Glasses, his dress was black, a large collar to the coat and loose low trowsers the dress of the day

Unlike White, Jenner chose medicine rather than the Church for his own career, a choice which turned out to be of immense benefit to mankind. It led to his work on the smallpox vaccine, which resulted eventually in the World Health Organization's announcement in 1980 that smallpox had been eradicated

from the world. Dr Jenner established a routine of inoculating the poor people of his neighbourhood free of charge on certain days in a modest garden hut known as the Temple of Vaccinia. The Reverend Mr Ferryman, a neighbour of the Jenners, built it for them. Thomas Dudley Fosbroke in *Biographical Anecdotes of Dr Jenner* (1821) described Ferryman as 'a Clergyman of very original and surpassing taste in two particular departments of picturesque gardening... exquisite informal primrose tumps and perfect rustic work'. Both can still be seen in the garden of The Chantry, Jenner's house, today. Here is Fosbroke's description of the fashionably rustic building:

> The open side of it is covered by an irregular primrosed tump,
> surmounted by a branchy decayed stump, like a classical trophy,
> supporting a flaunting honeysuckle. The dead wall is further broken
> by a rose or two, growing wildly. The roof is overshadowed by the forest
> trees. The entrance is darkened on the sides, but commands, when a
> person stands under it, a fine distant view of Stinchcombe Hill, a giant
> reclining. The jambs of the doorway consist of pollard trees, meeting, with
> their jagged heads, in a Gothic arch.... One might suppose it the residence
> of a Faun or a dryad, or an Arcadian Deity.

'A prettyish kind of a little wilderness'
The hermitage in the Bennets' garden in Jane Austen's *Pride and Prejudice* must have been in rather the same style as the Temple of Vaccinia. Mrs Bennet boasted of it to Lady Catherine de Bourgh to show that her garden was up to the minute.

Above: *The Temple of Vaccinia in Dr Jenner's garden at The Chantry, Gloucestershire. The doctor used to vaccinate local people against smallpox in this rustic summerhouse.* Above left: *'Dr Jenner About to Vaccinate a Child', by Dr Jenner's great-nephew Stephen Jenner, 1820s.*

The overbearing, proud and snobbish Lady Catherine swept into the Bennet house to tick Elizabeth Bennet off for her presumption in being loved by Lady Catherine's nephew, Mr Darcy. Wishing to speak privately to Elizabeth, Lady Catherine said, 'Miss Bennet, there seemed to be a prettyish kind of a little wilderness on one side of your lawn. I should be glad to take a turn in it, if you will favour me with your company.'

'Go, my dear,' cried her mother, 'and shew her ladyship about the different walks. I think she will be pleased with the hermitage.'

Mrs Bennet's wilderness would have been quite tame in comparison with twentieth-century wild gardens. It would have been planted with neatly trimmed flowering shrubs, with a ground layer, perhaps, of bulbs and her-baceous perennials in tidy beds. 'The different walks' would have been surfaced with gravel so that the ladies could walk in all weathers without getting their feet wet. The Bennet girls did some work in the garden, but Elizabeth's friend Charlotte left her husband Mr Collins to tend the garden of what he describes as '…our humble abode. Our plain manner of living, our small rooms, and few domestics.' The garden, we learn, was large and well laid out. For Mr Collins, 'to work in his garden was one of his most respectable pleasures'. It gave Charlotte pleasure too, as it kept him out of her way.

'…strait canals have been for some time very properly exploded'

No doubt the walks in Mrs Bennet's garden twisted and turned in the fashion of the day. 'Serpentine', 'meander', 'crinkle-crankle', 'zigzag' were words with which to impress your acquaintance, and an ability to express your admiration for 'the waving line' in verse would guarantee a reputation for good taste and sensibility. These lines were composed by an anonymous visitor to William Shenstone's garden at The Leasowes:

> The spiral wood, the winding vale,
> Yon stream that wanders down the dale,
> The path which, wrought with hidden skill,
> Slow twining scales yon distant hill
> With fir invested – all combine
> To recommend the waving line.

James Gillray's etching 'Delicious Weather', 1808, mocks the middle-class villa owner, satirized elsewhere as the newly rich 'Squire Mushroom', for his attempts to make an elegant landscape in a 2-acre garden

But it never takes long for those who have clambered to the pinnacle of fashion to look down at those still struggling on the nursery slopes and mock their efforts to rise higher. The zigzag line comes in for a sneer from David Garrick and George Colman in their play *The Clandestine Marriage* (1763). Mr Sterling, a character anxious to demonstrate how *au fait* he is with the fashionable gardening style, asks Lord Ogleby's opinion of the walks in his garden:

> *Lord Ogleby*   A most excellent serpentine! It forms a perfect maze and winds like a true lovers' knot.
> *Sterling*   Ay — here's none of your strait lines here — but all taste — zig-zag — crinkum-crankum — in and out — right and left — to and again — twisting and turning like a worm, my lord!
> *Lord Ogleby*   Admirably laid out indeed, Mr Sterling! One can hardly see an inch beyond one's nose anywhere in these walks. — You are a most excellent oeconomist of your land, and make a little go a great way.

Robert Dodsley's weekly magazine *The World* declared in 1753,

> Clipt hedges, avenues, regular platforms, strait canals have been for some time very properly exploded. There is not a citizen who does not take more pains to torture his acre and half into irregularities, than he formerly would have employed to make it as formal as his cravat.

Francis Coventry, writing for *The World*, mocked newly rich 'Squire Mushroom' and others like him. Their 'grotesque little villas which grow up every summer within a certain distance of London, are fatal proofs of the degeneracy of our national taste…' In less than two acres ,

> the eye is saluted with a yellow serpentine river stagnating through a beautiful valley, which extends near twenty yards in length. Over the river is thrown a bridge, partly in the Chinese manner, and a little ship, with sails spread and streamers flying, floats in the midst of it.

The path twists to and fro in a grove 'perplexed with errors and crooked walks…' via an old hermitage built with tree roots to 'a pompous clumsy and gilded building, said to be a Temple and consecrated to Venus; for no other reason, which I could learn, but because the squire riots here sometimes in vulgar love with a couple of orange-wenches taken from the purlieus of the

Playhouse.' Yet many of the ridiculed features could be used charmingly in small gardens, though perhaps not all in the same garden. In any garden even slightly bigger than Squire Mushroom's 'two acres', the temples and hermitages served two useful purposes: they acted as 'eye-catchers', providing focal points in what otherwise might be a dull landscape; and, in England's uncertain climate, they provided shelter from sudden storms and showers and somewhere for visitors to sit and rest.

But snobs among the gentry have always enjoyed sneering at the nouveaux riches and no doubt they also enjoyed Robert Lloyd's poem teasing those who put together their new gardens from such popular pattern-books as that of William Halfpenny, author of *Practical Architecture, Useful Architecture* (1751).

> The trav'ler with amazement sees
> A temple, Gothic or Chinese,
> With many a bell and tawdry rag on
> And created with a sprawling dragon;
> A wooden arch is bent astride
> A ditch of water four feet wide,
> With angles, curves and zig-zag lines
> From Halfpenny's exact designs.
>
> *The Cit's Country Box*, Robert Lloyd, 1767

There are gardens in almost all the streets

In 1830 a French traveller, François Philippar, noted in his *Voyage agronomique en Angleterre*:

> The Taste for Gardens in England is so pronounced that one finds them before almost every house. In towns and villages and in London too, there are gardens in almost all the streets. These small plots are generally the same width as the individual houses, and are as long as they are wide. The Garden layouts vary – simple and regular in small spaces, and irregular in larger grounds.

Philippar's surprise at finding so many gardens is a reminder of how different England was from other European countries in this respect. He also found a greater variety of plant species than in French gardens. Evergreen shrubs such as laurustinus, Portugal laurel, yew, holly and rhododendron were already familiar to him, but he was very taken with a beautiful white broom, and 'new and

unusual herbaceous plants. The gardens are separated from one another by hedges; and when there are walls they are often covered with climbers and sometimes figs or currants.'

Many of the village gardens noticed by Philippar were attached to newly built cottages. Gilbert White noted that, in Selborne, by the end of the eighteenth century all the mud cottages had disappeared and even the poorest people now lived in brick or stone cottages, which had upstairs bedrooms and glass in the windows.

Urban development also made provision for gardens. In Ralph Allen's Bath, there are no front gardens like those in other towns and villages; the elegant stone facades of the new terraces, crescents and parades meet stone pavements in uninterrupted harmony. But there were invariably back gardens where tenants could take the air when they were not taking the waters. Behind no.4

In this painting, 'St James's Square, Bristol', c.1806, by Pole, gardeners tend a typical back garden of a town house, pruning and tying in climbing plants against the boundary wall, and weeding the gravel path. A neat grass verge divides the path from the bed on the right.

The Circus, meticulous archaeological investigation has uncovered a garden made soon after the Circus was built in 1760, and yielded enough information for the Bath Preservation Trust to restore it. The plot is southwest facing and wedge-shaped, 31.75m (104ft) long, and 9m (30ft) wide at the house end, widening to 14.25m (47ft) at the far boundary. The original layout consisted of borders along each side of the garden, and a wide flowerbed at the far end. A flagstone path ran down each side, separating the borders from a central area of gravel, and three flowerbeds were set into the gravel, an oval bed at the centre and smaller, round beds on each side of it. In the large bed at the end the excavations uncovered two post holes, which may have supported a pergola or screen.

So it was a formal garden of simple structure, the main area being surfaced with gravel (no lawn). There is, disappointingly, no evidence of the plants in this eighteenth-century garden, but holes at regular intervals around the central, oval bed indicate that there may have been clipped evergreen shrubs, and the beds themselves were probably edged with box. The plants used in the restored garden are those that were available and fashionable at the time.

Towns and villages were expanding all the time, and the majority of new houses were provided with gardens. Many owners sought advice on how to lay out and plant their new gardens. The advice might be forthcoming from builders, from local nurserymen, from a jobbing gardener, from neighbours, from books or magazines or, for the wealthy, from a professional designer. In the next century, all these sources of information would proliferate.

The most successful garden designer in the first part of the nineteenth century was John Claudius Loudon (not to be confused with George London whose brilliant and profitable career in partnership with Henry Wise, was at its peak 100 years earlier). He made his expertise available to the widest possible audience by publishing, in 1822, *An Encyclopaedia of Gardening* and followed up by founding *The Gardener's Magazine* in 1826. In *The Suburban Gardener and Villa Companion* (1838) Loudon deals with town as well as suburban gardens, explaining that 'It must be obvious that, in gardens of so regular a shape, whether large or small, there can be very little variety produced in laying them out; that the style adopted must be regular, as indicated by the shape and the boundaries of the house; and that the chief interest must depend on the trees and plants introduced and their culture.'

The development of suburbs would be partly a result of the English passion for gardening. It would also serve to nourish that passion.

7

THE NINETEENTH
CENTURY I

Celebrating Nature

I N HIS BOOKS and his periodical *The Gardener's Magazine*, John Claudius Loudon offered meticulously detailed advice on garden making and gardening, at first under his name alone, and then, after their marriage in 1830, in close collaboration with his wife Jane. Their advice was directed mainly towards a new and receptive audience: a prosperous and rapidly increasing middle class. Their  prosperity was generated by new industries such as coal mining, iron and steel, and manufacturing goods for which the expanding empire supplied both the raw materials and a ready market. To provide workers for the new industries, towns grew at a rapid rate and domestic industries followed, to service the new urban population.

Some of the newly rich factory owners became landowners, acquiring large houses on country estates. But there were many prosperous families who required a different kind of domestic establishment. The breadwinner might own a successful business or be a professional man: a doctor or lawyer. Some occupied town houses, especially in places where there was already an established pattern of occupation by the gentry, as in the spas of Bath, Cheltenham, and Leamington. Many others preferred to be close to the town but not in it; with

The laurel (Prunus laurocerasus) maze planted in 1833 on a steep slope at Glendurgan, one of the great Cornish valley gardens of the early nineteenth century, made by Alfred Fox.

easy access to the factory, but with green space around them; able to breath salubrious country air rather than the increasingly polluted air of industry. For them, the suburb was created, and in it a new kind of house, a villa.

'The scarring, lining and wrinkling of Britain's face'

Initially, not all industrial towns were dark, satanic and unhealthy. In Birmingham, the population doubled in the last 40 years of the eighteenth century, causing one commentator to remark, 'The traveler who visits [Birmingham] once in six months… may chance to find a street of houses in the autumn, where he saw his horse at grass in the spring.' In spite of such rapid development, middle-class streets still had views of open countryside and working-class houses had gardens. It was the coming of steam in the nineteenth century that made cities dirty, overcrowded and diseased, and those who could afford to do so, put themselves at a safe distance from such conditions. Where there had formerly been substantial houses with large gardens in town centres, and orchards, the green spaces were built over until no space was left to infill.

Edward Hyams in *The Changing Face of Britain* (1974) described the relentless changes as, '…the scarring, lining and wrinkling of Britain's face, the premature ageing and disfigurement of great areas of land…' And this is how Wordsworth saw the change:

> Meanwhile, at social Industry's command,
> How quick, how vast an increase! From the germ
> Of some poor hamlet, rapidly produced
> Here a huge town, continuous and compact,
> Hiding the face of earth for leagues – and there,
> Where not a habitation stood before,
> Abodes of men irregularly massed
> Like trees in forests, – spread through spacious tracts,
> O'er which the smoke of unremitting fires
> Hangs permanent, and plentiful as wreaths
> Of vapour glittering in the morning sun.
> And, wheresoe'er the traveller turns his steps,
> He sees the barren wilderness erased,
> Or disappearing; triumph that proclaims
> How much the mild Directress of the plough
> Owes to alliance with these new-born arts!…
>
> *The Excursion*, 1814

There were more and more people and less and less land. Between 1801 and 1831 the population of England increased from nearly 9 million to just under 16 million. In many parts of the country urban expansion was accompanied by rural decay. According to angry William Cobbett, whose *Rural Rides* in 1822 took him all over the south of England, taxation and enclosure for suburban development must bear the blame. He described what was then becoming, and still is, the Stockbroker Belt, within commuting distance of London:

> …this rascally heath… is not far distant from the Stock-Jobbing crew. The roads to it are level. They are smooth. The wretches can go to it from 'Change without any danger to their worthless necks. And thus it is '*Vastly improved, ma'am!*' …You come (on the road to Egham) to a little place called *Sunning Hill*… a spot all made into '*grounds*' and gardens by *tax-eaters*. The inhabitants of it have beggared twenty agricultural villages and hamlets.

In Hampshire, Cobbett reported, 'The villages are all in a state of decay. The farm-buildings dropping down, bit by bit. The produce is, by a few great farmers, dragged to a few spots, and all the rest is falling into decay.' The agricultural depression meant that many landowners were having problems keeping their land in good heart. As a result, the tenants who had laboured for them in better circumstances came close to starvation. Charles Fetherston-Dilke of Packwood House in Warwickshire was perhaps not typical of his kind, but, even if it did not solve the problem, he set other landowners a good example in difficult times. He was described in 1815 as

> …living in the true style of an English gentleman, who seems to feel a patriotic pride in being clad in the produce of his own estate. His hat, coat and under apparel, stockings, etc, and even his shoes, are the produce of his own lands, herds, etc and are manufactured and made within his own walls.

The owners of great estates were certainly not constructing new gardens at this time, and some had difficulty maintaining those they already had to a reasonable standard. John Claudius Loudon said he had never seen country seats in a worse state. Blenheim, among others, was going rapidly to decay. 'Almost the only highly kept gardens which we saw were those of small proprietors, professional men, merchants, or bankers.' The new money, the money for making gardens, was no longer in the countryside – it was in suburbia.

'…a perfect model of order and neatness'

John Claudius Loudon is frank about the purpose of a garden, stating, with no hint of irony that gardens are '…intended to show that they are works of art, and to display the taste and wealth of the owner.'

One of the gardens Loudon admired and described in his magazine was a 'small villa', Stroud House near Haslemere, the home of Miss Perry and her four sisters, three of whom were 'acute systematic botanists'. It was

A perfect model of order and neatness in the house and grounds, and quiet, elegant, rural retirement in the family… Stroud House is built in a glade in the skirt of an extensive natural oak copse near the road, with a lawn in front and behind, the kitchen-garden and offices at one side, and an orchard and gardener's cottage at the other… The keeping of the lawn, and every thing about the house, is as high and perfect as any thing we have ever seen; and the walks in the copse are kept as clean, dry and open as copse walks can be.

It was in the style of a small *ferme ornée,* with a circuitous walk giving glimpses of paddocks and winding brooks crossed by several bridges. Loudon was delighted by the 'numerous wild plants, abundance of pheasants, singing birds, butterflies, dragon flies in their season, owls in the evening, &c.' It was the Misses Perry who first introduced archery into their part of the country, about 15 years earlier, 'and it is now become general in the neighbourhood among ladies.'

Loudon went on to praise the Perrys' gardener, Arthur Morrey. Since his visit to Stroud House he had sent Morrey's four children each a school-book, and Morrey himself a pair of French *sabots* to keep his feet warm and dry when standing on wet ground pruning trees in the winter and spring. Loudon makes an offer to the readers of *The Gardener's Magazine* of a copy of *Hortus Britannicus* 'to the first head-gardener in England who shall, with the consent of his employer, procure 20 pairs of *sabots* from a London nurseryman for the use of his men.' One of Loudon's endearing characteristics is his desire to do good and improve other men's lot.

On his garden visits he always comments, favourably or critically, on the standard of maintenance, and mentions anything he thinks may interest his readers, such as, in the Pulborough churchyard 'four children of one birth in one grave'; Lord Egremont's tortoise at Petworth; and a laburnum tunnel at Westdean House, which 'in the flowering season has a remarkably fine aspect, few colours looking so well in the shade as yellow.'

He was prepared to criticize as well as to praise. 'We were rather surprised,' he wrote of Eaton Hall, 'to find this pleasure ground in very bad order.' Virginia Water 'like most of the other garden scenes of George the Fourth, ...entirely disappointed us... with the cascade and rockwork we have no fault to find; and little with the Grecian fragments, which are put together with considerable taste; but all the rest we consider bad.' He did not pull his punches at Windsor Castle, either. 'In some of the vases there were a few shabby half-starved fuchsias and other greenhouse plants, which would be considered a disgrace in a cottager's window.'

He also offers his readers severe general criticism of villa gardens as well as more positive advice on their design:

> The faults of the villa residences which we have seen are, to a certain
> extent, those of the mansion residences...We shall pass over the ridiculous
> twisting and turning of walks, without real or apparent reason, which is so
> frequently met with, and rather dwell on the bad shapes and improper
> places of groups of shrubs and flowers on lawns. In several parts of this
> Magazine we have laid down the fundamental principles which ought to
> guide the placing of groups, viz. to arrange them so as to render them
> cooperating parts, with those which surround them, in the formation of
> one whole. It is not very easy to convey this principle to a mind that has
> not been a good deal cultivated in respect to the beauty of lines and forms;
> or to a person who has not had some practice in sketching landscape.

His aims were high: 'to disseminate new and important information on all topics connected with horticulture, and to raise the intellect and the character of those engaged in this art.' In *The Suburban Gardener and Villa Companion* he offers numerous garden plans 'for grounds from 1 perch [just over 25sq m/30sq yds] to 50 acres... more particularly for the Use of Ladies.' His plant lists are set out in a practical way, for different purposes and are useful to gardeners in any century:

> for covering naked Walls, or other upright Deformities, and for
> shutting out distant Objects which it is desirable to exclude... for
> concealing Defects on horizontal Surfaces; as naked sub-barren Spots,
> unsightly Banks &c; Flowers which will grow under the Shade and
> Drip of Trees; Flowers for Ornamenting Rocks, or Aggregations of Stone,
> Flints, &c; Evergreen-leaved Plants, Edgings to Beds or Borders, Highly
> Odoriferous Plants.

'Economy of management and neatness of appearance'

One category of garden described by Loudon as 'detached from their houses' and 'situated in the suburbs of towns, generally collected together, and separated by hedges' were presumably what we now know as allotments. There were up-wards of 2000 such gardens around Birmingham, cultivated in the evenings by single men, such as clerks and journeymen. A Mr Clarke of Birmingham, a chemist and druggist who invented Clarke's Marking Ink, had a selection of hardy shrubs and plants which 'quite astonished' the Loudons. And cottages, genuine or fake, still had the power to charm:

> Nothing gives more general satisfaction than a neat and comfortable picturesque cottage, fig. 259, with a good garden, in neat order and cultivation; and such buildings may always be applied to some useful purpose, even in the grounds of small villas, or *fermes ornées*. In more extensive scenes, cottages of different styles may be introduced, from that of the Greenlander or Norwegian to the Hindoo; and there can be no reason why a proprietor, if he chooses to go to the expense, and will attend to the comfort of the interior, should not ornament the dwelling of an upper servant in any style he pleases, even that of a Chinese mandarin.
>
> *An Encyclopaedia of Gardening*, 1822

Alas, Loudon's ideas of a Norwegian or Hindoo cottage were not described or illustrated.

He dealt in his books and magazine with gardens of all sizes, from those of terraced town houses, which he calls 'fourth rate', a term descriptive of size rather than quality, to those of a country estate. In a fourth-rate garden he took the 'Great objects' to be 'economy of management and neatness of appearance'. The plans illustrating his recommendations are sensibly simple, consisting of not much more than a few trees and shrubs set in grass. He is realistic about the problems of air pollution in cities, recommending, for front gardens, *Aucuba japonica* and 'common purple lilac' as able to withstand it, and for back gardens, double flowered and scarlet hawthorn, laburnum, almond, mulberry, weeping cherry and all kinds of ivy. He recognized that getting grass to grow is a problem; *Poa annua*, he wrote, is 'greener than any other grass that will grow in a town'. Worn lawns could be quickly revived at any season by seeding with this grass, which would give results in a few days.

For a bigger garden, Loudon suggested keeping an open space, about 30m (100ft) long, at the centre , 'well adapted for a party walking backwards and forwards on in the summer season, for a dance or for placing a tent on.' He put the yearly cost of mowing the lawns at 2s.6d a time, and recommended that there be six cuts a year.

A few years before Loudon arrived at this figure, in 1832, a revolutionary invention was patented by Edward Budding, an engineer in a textile factory: the first mechanical lawnmower. Loudon strongly approved and recommended the machine to his readers, and Budding himself suggested that 'Country gentlemen may find, in using my machine themselves, an amusing, useful, and healthy exercise.' In large gardens, a bigger, heavier version of the machine was pulled by a horse wearing leather boots to protect the sward. Gentlemen did take to the new machine; it provided a new interest and occupation for the enthusiastic amateur gardener and, being men's work, reinforced the idea which has not changed much in 200 years, that in general lawns and vegetables are the husband's concern, and flowers that of the wife.

Jane Loudon also held a view, still shared by many people, that the creative aspects of gardening are the province of the woman of the household. Only a female's artistic eye would do when it came to arranging flowers and shrubs. After her husband's death in 1843, Jane published several successful books of her own, based on this premise. They included *Gardening for Ladies* and *The Ladies' Flower Garden* in four volumes. Her confident, authoritative style paved the way for future female experts, assuring success, in due course, for Gertrude Jekyll, Vita Sackville-West, Margery Fish and Rosemary Verey.

The garden of Reading Gaol

In his magazine, Loudon included descriptions of places and gardens he and his wife had visited on several tours they took of the British Isles. These are an invaluable source of information on all sorts of topics as well as the nature of the gardens themselves. In Reading, Berkshire, he notes that 'flowers, both cut and in pots, are brought to market on Saturdays, both from market-gardens and private gardens. Great quantities of green-house plants in pots have been exposed for sale in the market-place, from the gardens of private gentlemen, and also hawked round the town in carts.' He goes on to describe

> The garden of the Reading Gaol
> [It] well deserves notice in a work, the great object of which is to promote a taste for this art. It is, as may be supposed, small; but the governor has a taste not only for gardening, but for natural history. He has, on his lawn or grass plot, a beautiful piece of rockwork, composed of flints and fragments

of mural antiquities. He has, also, a variety of plants of the choicest kinds, such as Wistaria, double furze, Ribes several species, Petunia phoenicea, and numerous pelargoniums, the whole mixed with fruit trees. Every advantage was taken of the high brick walls of the gaol for training vines and fruit trees. The governor had also a collection of fancy rabbits, a beautiful cockatoo, &c. The prisoners were watering the plants; and we can only account for the neatness of the whole from the abundance of hands at the command of the master. On looking through the prison we felt, as we did at Aylesbury, in 1831, the deepest regret at seeing so many persons imprisoned for mere trifles, without any reference to their reformation; which imprisonment, as the gaoler himself remarked, could only have the effect of making them worse.

It is interesting to compare this with a scene in another prison 20 years earlier. In *The Life and Times of William Hazlitt* (2001), A.C. Grayling describes Leigh Hunt's life in Horse-monger Lane Gaol, where he was serving two years for libelling the Prince Regent. He was allowed to continue editing the *Examiner*, in which the libel had appeared, from his cell.

He had papered his cell with roses on the walls and painted a blue sky on the ceiling. His door stood open and visitors walked in as if he was in the drawing room of his own home. His cell was in the part of the prison that housed the Governor and there was a little garden outside which Hunt fenced with green palings and adorned with a trellis. He planted a small lawn and bordered it 'with a thick bed from a nursery'. He wrote 'the earth I filled with flowers and young trees. There was an apple tree from which we managed to get a pudding in the second year.' The 'we' refers to his wife and son, who lived with him in his cell. Thomas Moore and Lord Byron called and admired his snug corner.

The Lake District, Loudon thought, was, 'by its varied surface, rocks and waters, admirably suited for the summer residences of persons engaged in business in towns.' He looked forward to the day, perhaps just ten years away, when the

'My Front Garden' by Frederick Walker, 1864, shows the artist and illustrator's own London garden, painted at a time when John and Jane Loudon's ideas about the layout and planting of gardens were well established.

railway would make this possible and the hills would be 'thickly studded with villas and cottages.' He wanted the landscape for 'human use and enjoyment' and, although he was aware that his views would shock existing residents in the area, he could not 'sympathise with exclusiveness, even in natural scenery'.

'…a pastoral cottage'
The colonization Loudon hoped for had already begun when he visited the village of Bowness on Lake Windermere. He described a garden belonging to a Manchester manufacturer and his wife, Mr and Mrs Starkey. Their house had a long frontage on the village street with a trellised verandah covered in hardy, woody climbing plants with an additional summer display of pelargoniums, maurandyas and lithospermums. The Starkeys' flower garden was across the street, enclosed by more trellis covered with purple and white clematis, sweet peas, nasturtiums, and pelargoniums. Not content with making their own

charming cottage garden, Mr and Mrs Starkey had colonized the road verge with evergreens and flowers, and covered the churchyard wall with laurels, box and holly. The Starkeys' enthusiasm may have sparked off the spirit of rivalry sometimes found among village gardeners, for the Loudons praised the villagers in general for growing kerria, *Cydonia japonica*, different sorts of China roses and clematis against their cottage walls, and 'many of the new potentillas, geums, lupines, clarkia &c.' in their gardens.

John and Jane Loudon classified The Starkeys' house as a 'Villa Residence' and put Wordsworth's house at Rydal Mount in the same category. But the Wordsworths' house was not one of the new villas John Loudon hoped to see covering the hills of the Lake District. It was a sixteenth-century cottage, which had been enlarged in the mid-eighteenth century. The Loudons gave only a brief description of Rydal Mount in their magazine, as:

> …a pastoral cottage, many of the walks being of turf. There is a terrace
> walk, with some scraps of natural rockwork planted by art; and displaying

*In their garden at Dove Cottage, Grasmere, William Wordsworth and his sister Dorothy grew a
combination of traditional cottage-garden flowers and plants brought in from the wild,
like these snake's head fritillaries and daffodils.*

at the same time the taste of the painter in the arrangement of the colours, and the science of the botanist in choosing the plants.

Perennial bowers and murmuring pines

If only the Loudons had told us more. Fortunately, the garden's structure as we see it today, is still much as Wordsworth laid it out. The garden occupies a steep 4-acre site. There is a lawn in front of the house with steps leading from it to an ancient mound, a vantage point from which Lake Windermere and Rydal Water can be seen. But the visitor is drawn to an upper level with a terrace walk, known as the Sloping Terrace, leading from the house to a rustic wooden summerhouse. From there to the end of the garden the Far Terrace extends, where Wordsworth is said to have paced to and fro, writing poetry in his head and testing lines by declaiming them aloud. Steep, slippery steps lead to a lower terrace built for Isabella Fenwick, whom Wordsworth called 'The star that came at close of day to shine.' Down the hillside a stream tumbles over rocks and creeps under ferns and through pools. The wild, natural landscape was Wordsworth's passion and his inspiration, but he also cared greatly for his garden. He was 43 when he came to Rydal Mount in 1813 and he remained there until his death in 1850.

By the time he came to Rydal Mount, the death of his brother and two of his children had darkened Wordsworth's life, and no doubt his pleasure in gardening was touched with sadness. In contrast, his first garden, made with his sister Dorothy at Dove Cottage, Grasmere, seems to have been unalloyed delight. They started from scratch, and made a practical garden with an orchard of fruit trees planted in a meadow full of primroses, celandines, violets, stitchwort and vetches. They kept bees to help with pollination and supply them with honey. William dug beds, raked out the stones, and cut pea-sticks. He constructed steps and a bower, made a bench, and pulled away and hacked out brambles to reveal an old rock seat. Dorothy grew vegetables from seed, grew a hedge from cuttings, planted, pruned, hoed and weeded. They grew flowers, too, buying shrubs from a local nursery, and receiving presents from the vicar and from local farmers' wives, including yellow and white lilies, sunflowers, bachelor's buttons and periwinkle.

Above all, the Wordsworths brought wild flowers into the garden: globeflowers, snowdrops, orchises, strawberries, thyme, columbines, foxgloves, honeysuckle, buttercups and daisies. In her diary, Dorothy recorded a happy day in the orchard when they sowed runner beans, read *Henry V* aloud and built a new step. No wonder Wordsworth put up a staunch defence against the invasion of his wild places by the railway and all it brought with it. He argued against a proposal in 1844 to construct a railway from Kendal to Lake Windermere:

> Is then no nook of English ground secure
> From rash assault?

In two long letters to the *Morning Post* he put forward the arguments against the proposal, concluding,

> We have too much hurrying about in these islands; much for idle pleasure, and more from over activity in the pursuit of wealth, without regard to the good or happiness of others.

Some of the Wordsworths' neighbours were almost as great a threat as the railway. They scorned Samuel Barber for slavish adherence to Loudon's advice in making his garden at Grasmere. Mary Wordsworth wrote:

> …he has his arched stone bridge, his waterfall, and is to have his Swiss bridge over the rocks to the alcove, that is to be, in the neighbourhood of the Fairy Chapel, and ten thousand other things – all found in the mass of wisdom contained in this said new book.

A spot where winter cannot touch

Wordsworth's advice about landscape and garden design was sought by his friends Sir George and Lady Beaumont, who were building a house and planning its surroundings at Beaumont's family estate, Coleorton in Leicestershire. Beaumont was a connoisseur, collector and competent practitioner of landscape painting, and so naturally viewed his estate from a Picturesque point of view. In 1805 Wordsworth wrote to him from Grasmere:

> With respect to the grounds, you have there the advantage of being in good hands, namely, those of Nature… Setting out from the distinction made by Coleridge which you mentioned, that your House will belong to the Country, and not the Country be an appendage to your House, you

---

The sight of a meadow full of wild flowers was a commonplace pleasure in nineteenth-century England. In the twenty-first century, people go to a great deal of trouble to achieve the same effect by growing wild flowers from seed in their gardens.

cannot be wrong… It was a misconception of the meaning and principles of poets and painters which gave countenance to the modern system of gardening which is now, I hope on the decline.

So Wordsworth is firm that there should be minimum interference with the natural landscape, and that literary and artistic references should be considered. His hope that 'modern' gardening, by which he presumably meant Loudon's 'Gardenesque' style, was on the decline was wide of the mark.

His letter to Sir George makes Wordsworth's ideas about garden design seem austere, but they were not. We have seen that at Dove Cottage he and Dorothy gardened in a happy, cottagey style, and as well as native plants, they grew exotics as flamboyant as sunflowers and lilies. The main project that the Beaumonts involved Wordsworth in at Coleorton was far from naturalistic. He pointed out to them an article in the *Spectator* by Joseph Addison, suggesting a winter garden planted entirely with evergreens, 'a Spot of Ground which is covered with Trees that smile amidst all the Rigours of winter and give us a View of the most gay Season in the Midst of that which is the most dead and melancholy.' Lady Beaumont asked Wordsworth to design such a garden for Coleorton, and he took up the project with great enthusiasm. He saw the garden as a 'spot where winter cannot touch, which should present no image of chillness, decay or desolation, when the face of Nature everywhere else is cold, decayed and desolate.'

The winter garden was near the house, in the shelter of an old quarry. A belt of evergreen shrubs (juniper, box and holly) mixed among cypresses and firs, surrounded it and against the walls were ivies and pyracanthas. There were also plants which flower early, such as *Daphne mezereum*, winter cherries, Christmas roses, polyanthuses, auriculas, and masses of bulbs: snowdrops, crocuses, hyacinths, jonquils. In true Picturesque style, there were two ruined cottages, a bower paved with a pebble mosaic, and a small pool for gold or silver fish. Lady Beaumont called it 'a monument to his taste for the picturesque'. The poet wrote a sonnet for the lady:

> Lady! The songs of Spring were in the grove
> While I was framing beds for winter flowers;
> While I was planting green unfading bowers,
> And shrubs to hang upon the warm alcove,
> And sheltering wall; and still, as fancy wove
> The dream, to time and nature's blended powers

I gave this paradise for winter hours,
A labyrinth Lady! which your feet shall rove.
Yes! When the sun of life more feebly shines,
Becoming thoughts, I trust, of solemn gloom
Or of high gladness you shall hither bring;
And these perennial bowers and murmuring pines
Be gracious as the music and the bloom
And all the mighty ravishment of Spring.

It is worth noting that Wordsworth thought the art of gardening should inspire thoughts of 'solemn gloom' as well as 'high gladness'.

Lady Beaumont was such a passionately keen gardener that Sir George teased her by saying she would take root herself. At Coleorton she made a formal flower garden with just the sort of complex geometric design that the Loudons advocated.

'The proper display of good plants'

Loudon was certainly an immensely gifted communicator, but it may be questioned whether his contribution to garden design was entirely beneficial. The Loudons coined the word 'gardenesque' to describe the style they approved. It was the picturesque style writ small, with diverse elements crammed into a few acres: 'Grottos and mosshouses are very agreeable additions to pleasure ground scenery.' Neatness and immaculate maintenance were considered important, and there was not room for Wordsworth's 'solemn gloom'.

But above all, John Claudius Loudon's stated purpose was 'To display the individual beauty of trees, shrubs and plants'. Edward Hyams later blamed this purpose, at least partly, for

> the English fault of putting garden design well below love of flowers, for
> in his so-called 'gardenesque' style he conceived of good gardening as the
> proper display of good plants, and not as the creation of a supplementary
> living-room out of doors.

The standard designs for small gardens published by the Loudons were followed slavishly, and as a result rows of identical houses in the suburbs acquired nearly identical gardens with a patch of lawn, gravel paths and flower beds filled with identical flowers. Each garden would be separated from the next by a hedge of privet or spotty laurel. Owners with ambitions to outdo their neighbours would plant a monkey puzzle tree (*Araucaria araucana*), newly arrived from Chile, in the middle of their lawn. The strangeness of this evergreen conifer had great appeal. In due course, in 1844, a complete avenue was planted at Bicton in Devon where the warm, damp climate suits it well. The avenue is still there.

From Greenland's icy mountains, from India's coral strand

The monkey puzzle came to Britain by a happy accident in 1795. Archibald Menzies, a botanist and surgeon, travelled as botanist and ship's surgeon on the

Discovery with Captain George Vancouver's survey expedition of the Pacific coast of North America. At Santiago, in Chile, the Governor entertained the ship's officers to dinner, and Menzies pocketed some nuts that were served as dessert. Back on board, he sowed them, and, on his return to England, had five live plants. Menzies was a good botanist, trained at Edinburgh University and Botanic Gardens, and a good surgeon. On the *Discovery*'s five-year voyage not a single man died of ill health.

Menzies owed his presence on that voyage to Sir Joseph Banks, who was himself a plant collector and did more than anyone to encourage other collectors and provide them with sponsorship. Banks was 18 when his father died leaving him a substantial fortune. He was already passionately interested in botany and unusually knowledgeable. In 1766, when he was only 23, he was elected a Fellow of the Royal Society, of which he was to become President from 1778 to 1820. He had a wide circle of friends, including Dr Edward Jenner, with whom he corresponded not only on horticultural matters but also on such subjects as the anatomy of the cuckoo (Jenner discovered that cuckoos have unusually developed shoulders for ousting other birds from their nests) and the crossing of a Jack Russell terrier with a fox. Jenner wrote to Banks in 1787, 'The bitch did not seem very desirous of receiving the fox at his first approaching her; but after a little amorous dalliance she soon came to… It did not appear in consequence of this union that the bitch showed any signs of pregnancy.

Above: *Rhododendrons flowering in the snow, illustrated in the 'Himalayan Journals' of Joseph Hooker, 1854.* Right: *Rhododendron barbatum, perhaps the plant shown above, from 'The Rhododendrons of Sikkim-Himalaya' by Joseph Hooker, 1849–50.*

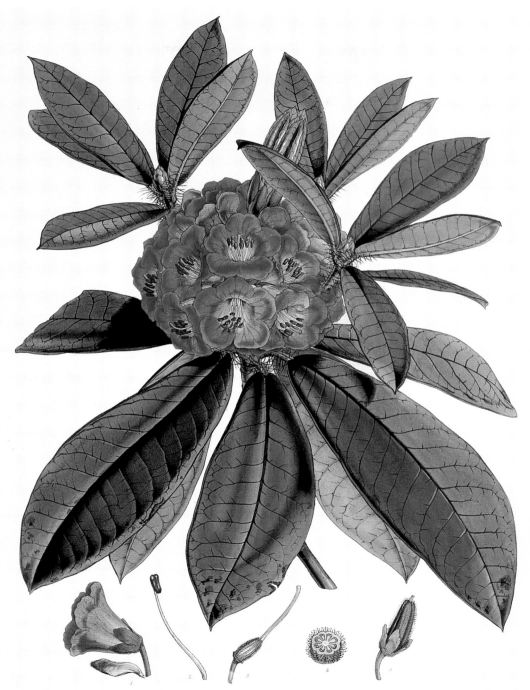

Banks, who was later to become one of the seven founder members of what is now the Royal Horticultural Society, went on Captain Cook's expedition in the *Endeavour* in 1768 to Tahiti via Cape Horn, New Zealand, Australia and New Guinea. On his return, Jenner catalogued a number of his botanical specimens for him. Banks was put more or less in charge of Kew by King George III, and set about building up Kew's collection of exotic plants with great energy.

In 1772, Banks sent Francis Masson, the first of the great Kew plant hunters, to the Cape in South Africa. It would be difficult to exaggerate the romance, excitement and danger of early plant-hunting expeditions. Masson travelled 650km (400 miles) by ox-drawn trekking wagon through rugged, almost impassable territory. He found much to interest him, and returned a year later with the Swedish botanist Thunberg. They had to fend off attacks by hyenas, leopards and lions, they nearly ran out of food and water, their wagon almost fell apart and their oxen fell sick. Nevertheless Masson was able to add more than 400 species to Kew's collection. They included ixias, gladioli, gazanias, chincherinchees, irises, stapelias, and Cape jasmine (*Gardenia stellata*). Masson seldom stayed put in England for long. Later expeditions took him to Madeira, the Canaries, the Azores and the West Indies; in Grenada he was captured by the French and in St Lucia he lost all his specimens during a hurricane. One specimen he did bring home was the ever-popular house-plant, cinerarea, now called *Pericallis* x *hybrida*.

Another protégé of Sir Joseph Banks, William Hooker, was Professor of Botany at Glasgow University and director of the university's botanical garden. After 21 years there he became Director of Kew Gardens and took the major step of opening the gardens to the public. They became an immensely popular attraction. Hooker was a brilliant botanist and a brilliant administrator, building up the herbarium collection and the collection of live plants by sending out expeditions to remote parts of the world. His second son, Joseph Hooker, inherited his father's talents, becoming a skilful botanist and botanical artist, a diligent and adventurous plant explorer (he wrote of some of his adventures in his book *Himalayan Journals*), and, like his father, Director of Kew.

All these explorers came safely home. Poor David Douglas did not. His story illustrates the terrible hardships explorers encountered. In 1824 he went, for the Royal Horticultural Society, to follow up Vancouver's exploratory work on the west coast of North America, of special interest because its climate was thought to be similar to that of Britain. At the aptly named Cape Foulweather, he and his companions sent their porters home because their rations had run out. They then endured a hurricane bringing sleet and hail. They had no protection other than wet blankets and spent days with nothing to eat but the roots of the aquatic plant *Sagittaria* and the berries they had collected for their seeds. On a later expedition, descending the Fraser River, Douglas's canoe was wrecked and his journal, equipment and 400 plant specimens were lost. But he was undaunted. He was captivated by the scenery and by the huge conifers, the like of which had not been seen before. He wrote:

> The high mountains in the neighbourhood, which are for the most part covered with pines of several species, some of which grow to an enormous size, are all loaded with snow; the rainbow from the vapour of the agitated waters, which rushes with furious rapidity over shattered rocks and deep caverns, producing an agreeable although at the same time a somewhat melancholy echo through the thick wooded valley; the reflections from the snow on the mountains, together with the vivid green of the gigantic pines, form a contrast of rural grandeur that can scarcely be surpassed.

The redwood tree (*Sequoia sempervirens*) amazed Douglas. He described it as 'the great beauty of Californian vegetation… which gives the mountains a most peculiar, I was almost going to say awful, appearance, something that plainly tells us we are not in Europe.' His last expedition in 1833–34 took him to Hawaii where 'one day… is worth one year of common existence'. Alas, it was in Hawaii that he died alone, aged 35, in a pit dug to trap wild cattle, into which a bull had already fallen. David Douglas's plant introductions were his legacy. The use of some of his conifers in forestry, including the Douglas fir (*Pseudotsuga menziesii*), has changed the British landscape. Shrubs such as vine maple (*Acer circinatum*), *Garrya elliptica*, Oregon grape (*Mahonia aquifolium*) and flowering currant (*Ribes sanguineum*) have become indispensable in our gardens. And the obliging, self-seeding little poached egg flower, *Limnanthes douglasii*, bears his name.

Nurseries and seed merchants lost no time in marketing the new plants and gardeners greeted them ecstatically. In the early nineteenth century there were comparatively few plants available, so anyone seeing a yellow rose, a wisteria, a rhododendron, or a tree peony in flower for the first time, would find it irresistible. No wonder the Gardenesque style, which gave individual plants the starring roles, was first in fashion and the precious rarities were displayed with pride. The shapes of beds became freer and less symmetrical. One gardener who was not impressed by the latest style was T. James, who wrote in the *Gardener's Magazine* in May 1939, '…Scores of unmeaning flower beds in the shape of kidneys and tadpoles and sausages and leeches and commas now disfigure the lawn.' But others were finding new ways to display the new plants.

The Cornish Himalayas

The scope of gardening was always limited by local conditions. Where there was thin, acid soil over impermeable rock, only a small range of plants would grow. This applied particularly to the coastal areas of Cornwall. With the advent of the new plant discoveries of the nineteenth century, it was soon realized that these geological and climatic conditions could be an advantage rather than a handicap. Similar to conditions in the Himalayas, parts of North America and other recently explored places, they were ideal for rhododendrons, camellias, a number of fine coniferous trees, and other plants requiring specialized treatment. This was the beginning of a gardening style which would lead, in due course, to the creation of matchless woodland gardens and exotic landscape gardens in the home counties, at Bodnant near Conway in North Wales, in Devon and in Cornwall, where the terrain was perfectly suited to the creation of Himalayan ravines in miniature.

In one small part of West Cornwall, near Falmouth, several adjacent valleys descending to the estuary of the Helford River offer just these conditions.

First off the mark was Alfred Fox at Glendurgan. He was born in 1794 into a prosperous family of shipping agents, based at Falmouth. A devout Quaker, he was described in the *West Briton* newspaper as an 'upright, conscientious man of business'. His connection with Glendurgan began when he rented cellars at Durgan village, a sheltered harbour on the Helford estuary. He also rented orchards in the three valleys above the village. In 1826, Fox and his wife Sarah built a thatched cottage at the top of the main valley. They cleared the valley, extending the orchards and planting lime, beech, sycamore, oak and ash for shelter, and a high proportion of evergreens: holm oaks, and the new North American conifers.

Fox's shipping connections gave him early knowledge of, and access to, plants imported from abroad. In the centre of the main valley, he made a pond and stocked it with trout, and in 1833 planted a maze of cherry laurel (*Prunus laurocerasus*) just above the pond, with a modest thatched summerhouse at the centre. Its design was based on a maze at Sydney Gardens in Bath and is unusual in that it is not symmetrical, but has serpentine and flowing lines. Cherry laurel is also an unusual choice. Perhaps the Foxes wanted quick results, but its fast growth causes maintenance problems: it needs trimming four times a year to keep it under control.

In 1837, the Foxes' cottage burnt down. Alfred was having lunch in Falmouth when he heard the news, and is said to have laughed heartily at it, since his family had outgrown the cottage (he and Sarah had 12 children) and he was now ready to build something larger. The new house, modest enough, was later extended by his son George, who took over in the 1890s and continued to add to his father's plant collection.

George's special interest was the cultivation of fruit, and one citrus fruit grown on the estate in 1897 was recorded as being almost as big as his head: 'It would just squeeze into my hat endways but would not go in the long way.' Today, the garden is maintained in immaculate condition by The National Trust. When planting needs renewing, it is done very much in the spirit of Alfred Fox's original intentions, with trees and shrubs planted individually or in informal groups separated by banks and glades sparkling with wild flowers and spring bulbs. The original, carefully planned views to the estuary are kept open. A few plants still remain from Alfred Fox's day, including two vast and magnificent tulip trees (*Liriodendron tulipifera*) just above his cherry orchard, replanted today with a collection of white-flowered cherry trees.

At the top of the garden is a small area called the Holy Bank, with plants to remind this Quaker family of their Christian faith, including the tree of heaven (*Ailanthus altissima*), the Judas tree (*Cercis siliquastrum*), the crown of thorns (*Paliurus spina-christi*) and a Glastonbury thorn (*Crataegus monogyna* 'Biflora').

Alfred Fox was one of four brothers. Charles Fox made an equally celebrated garden in the 1840s in the next valley, at Trebah. A 'literary man, with a vast fund of diligently accumulated learning and information' (*West Briton*), he bought his house in 1826 and immediately assured shelter for his future garden by making extensive plantations of maritime pine (*Pinus pinaster*). The ravine occupied by the garden is 500m (1640ft) long and drops 70m (230ft) down to the Helford River. Charles Fox harnessed the streams and springs of the valley to make a series of watercourses and pools, some of which, today, are home to huge Koi carp. His tree planting was directed from a top-floor window. With the aid of a telescope and megaphone, he communicated with a team of gardeners who constructed scaffold towers to show how each plant would look at maturity.

Although, like Glendurgan, Trebah is planted in a naturalistic style, the result is very different. Water plays a greater part and the planting is denser, more jungly and mysterious. Today, there are a great many tree ferns and a dark tunnel formed by the giant leaves of giant rhubarb (*Gunnera manicata*). Combined with some fine Chusan palms, these give a tropical effect.

Previous page: *The garden at Overbecks, Devon, looking across the estuary at Salcombe, shares with other gardens in Cornwall and Devon a mild, maritime climate that enables collections of exotic plants, many of them rare and tender, to thrive.*

Charles Fox bequeathed the property to his son-in-law Edmund Backhouse, and his son, Sir Jonathan Backhouse sold it in 1906 to Charles Hext, a member of a distinguished old Cornish family. The Hexts added one of the garden's most unusual features, building the lower pool at the bottom of the garden, and stocking it with pink flamingos. Today the pool is fringed with 2 acres of blue and white hydrangeas, a spectacular sight in late summer and early autumn.

A third adjacent valley was transformed into a 12-acre garden in the 1800s, at Carwinion, by the Rogers family, connections of the Backhouses. It has a remarkable collection of bamboos. These Cornish gardens can convince visitors they are in a separate world because the unique geology and climate of the region limits the plants that can be grown there. At the same time, it provides an opportunity to grow plants that can only be grown with great difficulty in other regions of Britain. The result is a satisfying harmony between the plants and Pope's 'Genius of the Place'.

Mexico, Egypt and China in Staffordshire

In a few other gardens, the opportunities presented by the introduction of new plants were seized in a very different spirit. One of the most spectacular was the garden made by James and Maria Bateman at Biddulph Grange in Staffordshire. James Bateman (1811–97) was not a brash industrialist creating a garden as a status symbol. He was rich and was considered a dandy at Magdalen College, Oxford, but he was also a knowledgeable gardener and a passionate orchid-fancier (a dandy's taste, perhaps). He made a fine orchid collection in his father's glasshouses, and published an illustrated account of *The Orchidaceae of Mexico and Guatemala* in parts between 1837 and 1841, a huge book measuring 77 by 50cm (30 by 20in). He was only 26 when the first part came out. In 1838 he married Maria Warburton, whose brother Peter was an explorer in Australia. She, too, was a keen botanist and gardener, and developed in her husband an interest in hardy plants as well as orchids. Between 1842, when they bought Biddulph Grange, and 1856 they built a mansion and made an extraordinary garden, now completely restored by The National Trust.

They wanted everything, and within their 22 acres, they got it. The design was entirely their own and included a Rainbow Garden (a stepped amphitheatre planted with bands of massed azaleas and rhododendrons), terraces, parterres, a

In the Batemans' garden at Biddulph Grange in Staffordshire, designed to display their extensive collection of plants, a gilded water buffalo presides over a typical Victorian parterre decorated with Chinese dragons cut out of the turf.

rose garden, a dahlia walk backed by sober yew hedges, a pinetum, a Cheshire cottage, 'Little Egypt', a grotto approached via a rock garden, a stumpery, a bog garden and a fernery. There was also a bowling green and quoit ground surrounded by Mexican pines, a cherry orchard, an arboretum and a spectacular avenue of wellingtonias. But the high point was the Chinese garden, complete with a section of ruined Great Wall, a joss house, a giant frog and a red dragon.

Sadly, the Batemans did not enjoy their garden, created with such gusto, for long. Although their skilful manipulation of the site enabled them to grow all sorts of fragile plants, Maria Bateman found the chill Staffordshire climate too much for her and in 1860 they moved to Worthing in salubrious Sussex, where they grew and studied alpines in a small rock garden.

'Little paradises of cultivated life'

Some of the new plants were already finding their way into cottage gardens. We know this from descriptions by William Howitt of 'Little paradises of cultivated life' in his book *The Rural Life of England* (1838). Howitt, like William Cobbett whom he much admired, travelled through England and Scotland observing country life. Mary Russell Mitford's *Our Village* also described country life in an amalgam of Hampshire villages including her own of Three Mile Cross. *Our Village* first appeared as a series of sketches in the *Lady's Magazine* between 1824 and 1832.

The choice of plants available to cottage gardeners had greatly increased. Miss Mitford described well-kept gardens with clematis, jasmine and passion flowers, as well as roses and honeysuckle round the door, and chrysanthemums (introduced in 1795 from China) and dahlias (1798 from Mexico) of prize quality fronting the village street, and geraniums in pots on the doorstep. In the flowerbeds there might be roses, mignonette, stocks and sweet peas for scent, larkspurs, Michaelmas daisies (early eighteenth century, from America) and tiger lilies (1804 from China).

'Florists' flowers', usually grown by city-dwellers for the show benches of specialist florists' societies, were also sometimes grown in cottages and other country gardens. Miss Mitford in *Our Village* described a farmer's wife as:

A gilded dragon on the roof of the Chinese Temple at Biddulph Grange carried a chiming bell in its mouth. The temple is also decorated with seahorses and carved birds.

A real, genuine florist: valued pinks, tulips and auriculas for certain qualities of shape and colour, with which beauty has nothing to do; preferred black ranunculuses, and gave in to all those obliquities of a triple-refined taste by which the professed florist contrives to keep pace with the vagaries of the bibliomaniac. Of all odd fashions, that of dark, gloomy, dingy flowers appears to me the oddest. Your true connoisseurs now shall prefer a deep puce hollyhock to the gay pink blossoms which cluster round that splendid plant like a pyramid of roses!

Because there were more plants to choose from, with bigger, brighter flowers, cottage gardens were beginning to produce the 'riot of colour' that would have such appeal in Victorian paintings of idyllic cottages on calendars and postcards. But the practical matters of fruit, vegetables, bees and hens, and perhaps the pig, had still to be attended to. The normal layout for a cottage garden was still a rectangle with a path up the middle, although the path was now likely to be lined with a succession of colourful flowers to hide the rows of potatoes, cabbages, peas and beans beyond. Certainly the impression John Clare's poetry gives of the Northamptonshire gardens he knew and loved is one of delicious floweriness:

The timid maid

Pleased to be praised, and yet of praise afraid,
Seeks the best flowers; not those of wood and fields,
But such as every farmer's garden yields –
Fine cabbage-roses, painted like her face,
The shining pansy, trimm'd with golden lace,
The tall-topped larkheels, feather'd thick with flowers,
The woodbine, climbing o'er the door in bowers,
The London tufts, of many a mottled hue,
The pale pink pea, and monskhood darkly blue,
The white and purple gillyflowers, that stay
Ling'ring, in blossom, summer half away,
The single blood-walls, of a luscious smell,
Old-fashion'd flowers which housewives love so well,
The columbines, stone-blue, or deep night-brown,
Their honeycomb-like blossoms hanging down
Each cottage-garden's fond adopted child,
Though heaths still claim them, where they yet grow wild.

The Shepherd's Calendar, John Clare, 1827

8

THE NINETEENTH CENTURY II

Controlling Nature

THERE ARE PARALLELS to be drawn between the cultures of Victorian and Elizabethan Britain. Queen Elizabeth I ruled alone for 45 years and Queen Victoria was alone for 40 years of her 68-year reign (Prince Albert died when they had been happily married for nearly 30 years). Both women presided over the development of a prosperous and confident middle class, both saw the expansion of the British Empire and the resulting introduction of diverse goods, including new plants, useful and ornamental, from distant places. Rich and successful Victorian women loved to dress in richly coloured and elaborately decorated clothes in sumptuous fabrics, as did women in the Elizabethan period. In both instances, women's clothes were tight, restrictive and uncomfortable: starched and goffered ruffs and rigid stomachers for the Tudors; boned bodices, long pantaloons, petticoats and ruched crinolines for the Victorians.

Houses as well as persons were formal and elaborately adorned, with ceilings intricately plastered, panelling cunningly carved and doors and windows draped with heavy velvet and brocade hangings, which themselves were braided and fringed. How were these themes expressed in the garden?

Francis H. Bate's painting 'Cottage Garden, Summer', 1892, typifies the Victorian gardener's love of brilliantly coloured flowers.

Domination over nature was celebrated triumphantly and a rigid geometric structure was imposed on the garden landscape. Undulating ground was made level to form rectangular enclosures, walled or surrounded by immaculately trimmed hedges. On sloping ground, elaborate terraces and waterworks were built in the Italian style. Plants were controlled and manipulated to form arbitrary, manmade shapes and patterns, emulating those found indoors on ceilings, panelling and fabrics.

Both Tudor and Victorian gardeners had a passion for elaborate pattern, but for the Tudors, opportunities for expressing their love of colour were limited. As we have seen, lacking a wide choice of colourful flowers for all seasons, they resorted to filling knots and parterres with crushed red clay bricks, glittering black coal dust, dazzling white chalk and bright gravels. The Victorians, on the other hand, were able to indulge to the full a taste for vivid, rich colours in flowers and foliage. An enormous range of trees, shrubs, climbing plants, perennials, bulbs and annuals from every continent and climate had become available. Other assets not available in Tudor times included the technology for growing tender plants in greenhouses and conservatories, and a knowledge of the science of plant breeding. Up-to-date methods of cross-pollination led to the development of plants with larger and more brilliant (or gaudy, depending on the observer's taste) flowers. If Tudor gardeners had been able to grow the same plants as the Victorians, their parterres might also have blazed with colour. They, too, might have invented carpet bedding and ribbon borders.

Whether you care for the formal Victorian style or not, there is no doubting its vigour and confidence. It can be seen and marvelled at today in gardens where nineteenth-century plans have been meticulously restored. At Lyme Park in Cheshire, The National Trust's foremost example of high-Victorian bedding forms part of the 17-acre garden of a Palladian mansion with many historically important features from other periods. Sloping ground at Cragside in Northumberland, another National Trust garden, was terraced to make diverse gardens, including elaborate formal beds where 6000 tulips are still planted each year, and a literal interpretation of carpet bedding is based on a floor covering inside the Norman Shaw house. At the château built by Baron Ferdinand de Rothschild between 1874 and 1889 at Waddesdon Manor in Buckinghamshire, the Victorian parterre gobbles up 100,000 plants in its summer display.

Such grandiose schemes were indicators of the owners' status. A Rothschild head gardener declared that a squire's garden would need 10,000 bedding plants; a baronet's, 20,000; an earl's, 30,000 and a duke's garden, 50,000. Only a Rothschild would use more plants than that.

Taste in design and planting has moved a long way away from formal bedding, partly because of the enormous expense involved: at Waddesdon it takes 12 gardeners two weeks to make the changeover from the spring to the summer display. But it is a style kept alive by a few urban parks departments, the cost being justified as a tourist attraction – the bedding schemes in the squares and parks of Cheltenham, for example, are outstanding. Many public parks and pleasure gardens had their origin in the Victorian era. In those days, public parks bridged the chasm between the staggeringly complex and expensive bedding schemes laid out for great landowners and industrial magnates for their private enjoyment, and the small plots gardened by the rest of the population. It was by visiting parks that ordinary gardeners were able to see all the possibilities and adapt them for their own use.

People who gardened on a small scale in city, suburban and cottage gardens might take their cue from the gardens of the Astors or the Rothschilds, with their local park as intermediary, but their own schemes were limited by how many plants could be got from a few penny packets of seeds. Their triumphs

The elaborate bedding schemes devised for the mansions of industrialists used many thousands of plants and epitomized the owners' taste for ostentatious display. This painting of Aston Hall, Birmingham, 1906, is by Elizabeth M. Chettle.

were achieved for a few pence plus those priceless assets, enthusiasm, time and skill. Imposing order on nature's chaos is one of the great pleasures of gardening, and there is nothing more orderly than symmetrical beds carved out of turf as if with pastry cutters, and planted with neat rows and blocks of bright colour, particularly when the colour shines out against the soot-stained buildings and smog-laden or drizzle-filled grey skies of an English industrial landscape. No doubt, in the year of Queen Victoria's Diamond Jubilee a rash of patriotic beds appeared, planted with red salvias, white alyssum and blue lobelias in the shape of the Union Jack. They certainly did when Queen Elizabeth II's 50 years on the throne was celebrated in 2002.

Until quite recently, the tradition of Victorian bedding was still alive in small gardens. Twenty years ago its vivid impact could be seen in villages and towns like Wotton-under-Edge in Gloucestershire, a small country town with a long history. In one fairly typical street of semidetached council houses with small front gardens, the owners would vie with each other to produce the healthiest plants with the biggest flowers, the greenest, most weed-free turf and the sharpest edges to their beds. The spring display might show hyacinths and pansies in one garden, wallflowers and tulips in another. In summer there were patterns of marigolds and begonias, and mixed tapestries of petunias, geraniums and busy lizzies. These twentieth-century gardeners were fulfilling a strong tradition. They might have been following to the letter the advice given in Gervase Markham's *The English Husbandman* in 1613, to

> Plant in every several thread flowers of one kinde and colour, as thus for example; in one thread plant your carnation gillyflower, in another your great white gillyflower, in another your mingle coloured gillyflower, and in another your blood-red gillyflower and so likewise… you may in this sort plant your several coloured hyacinths, your several coloured Dulippos [tulips] and many other Italian and French flowers. It shall appear like a knot made of divers coloured ribbons, most pleasing and most rare.

Today only one garden in the terrace in Wotton-under-Edge retains its seasonal colour. The rest have been gravelled over to make parking spaces, and instead of the scent of hyacinths and wallflowers, petrol and diesel fumes fill the air. Nevertheless, bedding plants have not been completely ousted from small gardens. They have moved up in the world, into hanging baskets and window boxes, leaving room for cars below.

Bright and exuberant bedding schemes made nonsense of the Reverend Samuel Wesley's advice, to be 'Neat, but not gaudy'. Wesley's subject was literary style, in *An Epistle to a Friend concerning Poetry* (1700):

> Style is the dress of thought; a modest dress,
> Neat, but not gaudy, will true critics please.

But in a garden context, Charles Lamb, writing to Wordsworth 100 years later, reached for the same phrase to describe with approval 'A little thin, flowery border round, neat, not gaudy.'

'The chief business of Mrs Disraeli…'

The Victorians wanted their gardens to be both neat *and* gaudy, and there are gardeners who still love the style and practise it with skill. It enlivens the grey English climate, and is, perhaps, well suited to the English character.

But even in its nineteenth-century heyday, bedding, and particularly carpet bedding (the making of patterns using ground-hugging plants with coloured foliage), was not universally admired. Lord St Aldegonde, the aristocratic republican in Benjamin Disraeli's novel *Lothair* (1870), complains:

> 'How I hate modern gardens.' (looking out of the window) 'What a horrid thing this is! One might as well have a mosaic pavement there. Give me cabbage roses, sweet peas and wallflowers. That is my idea of a garden. Corisande's garden is the only sensible thing of the sort…huge bunches of honeysuckle and bowers of sweet pea and Jassamine clustering over the walls and gilly flowers scenting with their sweet breath the ancient bricks from which they seemed to spring. There were banks of violets which the southern breeze always stirred and mignonette filled every vacant nook…. It seemed a blaze of roses and carnations, though one recognized…the lily, the heliotrope and the stock.'

Disraeli's wife, however, was not immune to the current fashion. Visitors to Hughenden Manor, the Disraelis' country house in Buckinghamshire, commented on the blindingly bright colours of her bedding schemes. In August, 1858 Disraeli wrote in a letter:

> The chief business of Mrs Disraeli, during this residence, has been to adorn her terrace in the Italian style with a beautiful series of Vases, which come

from Florence, and which sparkle in the sun, their white and graceful forms contrasting well with the tall geraniums and blue agapanthus lilies, which they hold...

In the 5-acre garden there were also more restful elements, such as woodland walks, shrubberies and an old orchard, and beyond it, an exceptionally beautiful park where the prime minister enjoyed 'the sultry note of the cuckoo, the cooing of the wood pigeons and the blaze of rosy May' in spring and, in the

The Victorians loved and romanticized the Elizabethan age, enjoying and sometimes copying Tudor architecture and making flower gardens to enhance the mellow stone or brick buildings. 'The Gardens at Montacute House', Ernest Arthur Rowe, 1893.

autumn, he praises the beauty of the trees in the garden:

The limes all golden, the beeches ruddy brown, while the oaks and elms and pines are still dark and green, and contrast well with the brighter tints. But not a leaf has fallen; they want the first whisper of the frost, and then they will go out like the lamps when the dawn breaks on a long festival.

The National Trust has restored Mary Anne Disraeli's garden, complete with her blinding bedding: orange cosmos and royal-blue salvias with silver cineraria; lime-green nicotianas with violet verbenas and orange marigolds; purple heliotrope with salmon geraniums and blue-leaved melianthus.

His was the prize, and joy o'er-flowed his heart.
Dean Hole, the great Victorian rosarian, used to judge the annual flower show at Oundle in Northamptonshire and recalled, in *A Book about Roses*, a local butcher, Thorneycroft of Floore.

He told me that by rising early, sometimes at 3 a.m., and by working late, he not only carried on an extensive trade, but found time to put up three glass-houses of his own handiwork; and that, in addition to Rose-trees, most of which he had budded, and all of which he had pruned and cared for likewise with his own hands. From his houses he showed beautiful seedling Gloxinias, which won first prizes and special commendations; obtained prizes for specimen plants of recent introduction, as well as for those of a more ordinary kind; while from his Rose-garden he brought collections which often took first and second honours, and were always meritorious.

Dean Hole said he had never seen better specimens of cut roses grown under glass than those exhibited by the working-men of Nottingham. He described going with a group of exhibitors to see their gardens. They turned out to be 'tiny allotments on sunny slopes, just out of the town of Nottingham, separated by hedges or boards, in size about three to the rood [1/4 acre] – such An extent as a country squire in Lilliput might be expected to devote to horticulture.' Among the plants grown on the allotments were, in winter, Christmas roses, aconites, laurustinus, golden holly, wintersweet (*Chimonanthus fragrans*), yellow jasmine and winter violets, followed in spring by mezereon (*Daphne mezereum*), erica, berberis, snowdrops, hepatica, polyanthus, crocus and tulip. Later came lilac, syringa, laburnum, ribes, wistaria and, of course, roses.

According to the Dean, there were nearly 10,000 allotments on Hunger Hill outside Nottingham, many of them subdivided, so that nearly half the population were gardening. They grew cabbage, lettuce, rhubarb and celery, as well as flowers. The allotment-holders – bricklayers, twist-hands, textile workers, shoe-makers, tailors and mechanics – would visit their plots on the way to work, on the way home and in their dinner hour between twelve and one. One walked more than a mile each way, three times a day. Another sacrificed the second blanket from the matrimonial bed to protect his greenhouse from winter frost. As urban life became increasingly crowded and unpleasant, it became more and more important to be able to escape to an allotment whenever time permitted.

The traditional 'florists' flowers' grown for showing by the industrial workers of the North of England and the Midlands, were auricula, polyanthus, hyacinth, anemone, tulip, ranunculus, carnation and pink. Later, pansy, picotee and sweet William were added. What these flowers had in common was their almost end-less variation, with single, semidouble and double flowers composed of streaked, spotted, striped or otherwise patterned petals. They were grown for the perfec-tion of their individual flowers, and it was against carefully defined standards of perfection that they were judged on the show bench. You had to be a member of a florists' club to exhibit, and the shows were usually combined with a feast. Florists had their own literature, their earliest 'Bible' being James Maddock's *Florist's Directory* of 1792, followed by a *Practical Treatise on the Culture of the Carnation, Pink, Auricula, Polyanthus, Tulip and other Flowers* by Thomas Hogg, which went through six editions between 1820 and 1839. Periodicals were the *Floricultural Cabinet* and *Florist's Magazine*. Climatic differences and varying traditions led to local specialization, and Paisley became known for it pinks, Lancashire for auric-ulas, Staffordshire for polyanthus and Derbyshire for pansies.

Even workers without access to an allotment could be successful florists. The hobby needed time and skill rather than space, and could be practised in a small back yard or even on a windowsill. Many prizewinners had secret formulas for achieving success. An auricula grower, Isaac Emmerton, was persuaded in 1815 to part with his recipe for compost; it consisted of two parts of goose dung steeped in bullock's blood, two parts of baker's sugar scum, two parts of night-soil, three parts of yellow loam, preferably the soil cast up by moles, plus two pecks of sand per barrow-load.

George Crabbe, poet, parson and botanist, captures the excitement of the prizewinner in his description of a weaver-florist:

> In vain a rival tried his utmost art,
> His was the prize, and joy o'er-flowed his heart.
> 'This, this is beauty! Cast, I pray, your eyes
> On this my glory! See the grace – the size!
> Was ever stem so tall, so stout, so strong,
> Exact in breadth, in just proportion long;
> No kindred tint, no blending streaks between;
> This is no shaded, run-off, pin-eyed thing,
> A king of flowers, a flower for England's king!'

'This is where I propose to have an erection' Sir George Sitwell

No doubt there were keen florists among the coal miners and ironworkers at Renishaw in Derbyshire. If there were, Sir George Sitwell, whose income was derived from their labour, was unaware of them. Renishaw Hall, the seat of the Sitwell family, was poised above a Derbyshire valley rich in coal, on which, with the manufacture of iron, the family's fortune was based. In a memoir addressed to Sir George's son Osbert Sitwell, Evelyn Waugh describes his only meeting with Sir George. It was at Renishaw on a summer evening.

> We had all come out on the terrace to enjoy the beauty of the
> sunset which was breaking through the mist and was lighting up
> the opposing hills.
>
> Your father was wearing a long-tailed evening coat with a black waistcoat
> as though he had gone into mourning with the Court many years before,
> had taken a liking to the style and retained it in deference to some august
> and secret bereavement of his own. He seemed slightly estranged from the
> large party you and Sachie had invited and edged away to the extreme
> fringe of the group, where I was standing, and stood silently, gazing out
> across the valley....
>
> ...I think it was in his mind, then, that rather than being, as he was, a rare
> visitor at Renishaw, he lived there uninterruptedly all the year round and
> had in consequence lost touch with the life of fashion which was his
> birthright.

In the valley at our feet, still half hidden in mist, lay farms, cottages, villas, the railway, the colliery and the densely teeming streets of the men who worked there. They lay in shadow; the heights beyond were golden.

Your father had seldom addressed me directly during my visit. Now, since I was next to him, he turned and spoke in the wistful, nostalgic tones of a castaway, yet of a castaway who was reconciled to his solitude. 'You see,' he said, 'there is no one between us and the Locker-Lampsons'.

Sir George Sitwell's vision was of his park, and the still sunlit uplands beyond. His interest was in the play of light and shade on the woods and fields, and, although he knew his country-house neighbours were a long way off, he was apparently unaware of the sooty industrial landscape in the valley, the back-to-back terraces and the workers they housed.

A scholarly antiquarian, a baronet and an eccentric, Sir George inherited Renishaw in 1862 when he was still a baby, married in 1886 and in 1895 began to lay out new gardens and make a lake. He held strong, passionately expressed views about the design of gardens, and, of his prolific literary output, it is only *On the Making of Gardens* (1909) that is remembered still. 'If the world is to make great gardens again,' he wrote, 'we must discover and apply in the changed circumstances of modern life the principles which guided the garden makers of the Renaissance.' His other great passion was Italy, and by 'the Renaissance' he meant the Italian Renaissance. The garden he made at Renishaw was strongly influenced by his love of Italian gardens and after he bought Castello di Montegufoni in 1909 he spent over 15 years working on the gardens there.

At Renishaw, according to his son Osbert, 'He abolished small hills, created lakes, and particularly liked to alter the levels at which full grown trees were standing. Two old yew trees in front of the dining-room window… were regularly heightened and lowered; a process which I believe could have been shown to chart, like a thermometer, the temperature of his mood.' Sir George did all the planning himself, and could often be seen striding around with a measuring rod in one hand and binoculars in the other.

On one occasion, described in Osbert's autobiographical book *Laughter in the Next Room*, Constant Lambert, the composer and a friend of Osbert and Sacheverell, was staying at the house.

Constant was only eighteen, and, since this was his first large house-party, was very alert and rather nervous. In consequence, he was punctual to the

minute in coming down to breakfast at nine o'clock in the dining-room.
He found it empty, though the table was laid and the air was full of the
savour of breakfast dishes. A plume of steam hovered in the air from a
Viennese coffee machine on a sideboard. An almost electric tension
brooded in the emptiness, as if anything might occur at any moment.
The young musician, however, concentrated on eggs and bacon and
coffee, and sat down, with his back to the chimney, and facing the sash
windows… Suddenly, the strange happening for which subconsciously
he had been waiting occurred: for, looking towards the window opposite
him, he was amazed to see the distinguished, bearded, medieval face of an

Sir George Sitwell's garden at Renishaw Hall, Derbyshire, shown in this contemporary photograph,
is a classic composition of hedges, lawns, water and stone in the Italian style. Sir George
commissioned planting plans from Gertrude Jekyll but found them too colourful.

elderly gentleman, crowned with a large grey felt hat, pass just outside, in a horizontal position, – as if he had fallen prone and was about to raise himself – and holding a Malacca walking-stick in the mouth. The vision of this venerable figure proceeding on all fours was startling in its unexpectedness, and strongly recalled to the mind of him who beheld it Blake's picture of Nebuchadnezzar, though it is true that the Babylonish king was notably less spruce in appearance, and that his counterpart was plainly English and lacked those memorable nails shaped like the claws of birds. Constant hurried to the window, looked out – and realized what was happening. It was – it must be – my father, at work, and carrying his cane in this unusual manner in order to observe the views and measure from the new level – for he intended to drop the lawn three or four feet, and so, in his present position, was at the height of a man standing at the altitude he planned... But even though Constant knew in his heart who it must be, he was too bewildered to mention what he had seen to the other guests, who now came into the dining-room, filling it with their chatter.

Sir George's extravagant expenditure on the garden was a recurring worry to his agent who complained of having to employ 80 men, 21 horses, a traction engine and a steam wagon on one project, and, on another occasion, having to arrange for the turf of the main lawn to be lifted, the subsoil removed and 45cm (18in) of good topsoil put in its place.

In his memoirs, Osbert quoted from notes his father made to justify building a pavilion overlooking the lake:

> Purpose: for visitors to be able to bathe and breakfast there and if desired spend the whole day on the lake. As a place for afternoon tea. Occasionally for entertaining a large number at tea or for small luncheon parties. For the owner when the house is empty to be able to be there alone for study or business.

Sir George invariably had some new project afoot. Robert Heber Percy, another friend of Osbert's, remembered a walk in the park at Renishaw after lunch one Sunday. When they reached a grassy knoll, Sir George stood on it and embraced the view with an expansive gesture. 'And this,' he said, 'is where I propose to have an erection.'

Not all his projects came to fruition, but he did succeed in creating an elegant and beautiful garden at Renishaw. Terraces descend from the south front of the house, embraced and defined by sharply clipped yew hedges with strongly architectural buttresses and piers. The lake lies below and wooded slopes rise beyond it. There are fine stone statues, and broad borders of shrubs and herbaceous plants. Sir George commissioned planting plans from Miss Jekyll. She recommended blue, orange and lemon-yellow flowers in one area, and French eighteenth-century blues and pinks in another. Osbert Sitwell remembered that 'The heads of dahlias and zinnias and carnations and roses were heavier and more velvety than in the previous decade, while at dusk the fragrance of the tobacco plants and the stocks became overwhelming.'

Miss Jekyll's plans were considered too colourful by Sir George. They were not in tune with his visions of light and shade, nurtured in Italy. But today the planting is again very much in the Jekyll style. Above the terraced garden and at right angles to the house, the greater part of John Evelyn's lime avenue of 1625 is still there, as is the 1806 gothic temple, originally built as an aviary by Sir Sitwell Sitwell.

The garden at Renishaw was inspired by a cultivated and original creative mind, aware of, but not influenced by, the fashions of the day. But for garden makers who were receptive to them there were numerous new and fashionable ideas to choose from.

'That which is intended to imitate natural scenery'

Many of the alterations to gardens great and small at this time were undertaken in order to increase the opportunities for growing the ever-widening range of plants available. Serious gardeners realized that if, for example, alpine plants were to thrive, the right conditions must be provided for them. The passion for alpines was, initially, a by-product of the eighteenth-century interest in 'sublime' scenery.

As early as the 1780s, William Beckford started an 'Alpine garden' on a lakeside slope at his estate at Fonthill. At the age of 21 Beckford had visited Mount Edgcumbe in Cornwall and found the naturally rocky landscape inspiring: 'I have been up and down everywhere upon the Rocks... You would delight in the picturesque fragments — the crooked pines and luxuriant shrubs amongst which I have passed my day.' On a tour of the Cintra Mountains in Portugal, Beckford was fascinated by the alpine plants he saw:

Amidst the crevices of the mouldering walls... I noticed some capillaries and polypodiums of infinite delicacy; and on a little flat space before the convent a numerous tribe of pinks, gentians and other alpine plants,

fanned and invigorated by the pure mountain air. These refreshing
breezes, impregnated with the perfume of innumerable aromatic herbs
and flowers, seemed to infuse new life into my veins, and, with it, an
almost irresistible impulse to fall down and worship in this vast temple
of nature the source and cause of existence.

Beckford was ahead of his time: to most observers it was the awful grandeur of
the rocks themselves and any associated grottos and ruins that were the attraction, rather than the plants associated with rocky conditions.

In the nineteenth century, it was already recognized that a rockery was one of
the hardest things in the garden to do well. In 1831 '*An Essay on Rockwork in Garden
Scenery*' which appeared in *The Gardener's Magazine* gives a warning:

As the expense of collecting large stones is considerable, rockworks, in
general, are made on too small a scale, and more resemble heaps of stones,
with the interstices filled with weeds, than the protrusion from the soil of

*Lady Broughton's rockery was on a grand scale, representing 'the mountains of Savoy, with the valley
of Chamouni', including la Mer de Glace. It is depicted in this painting by George Pickering,
'The Rockery at Hoole House', c.1830.*

a portion of real rock, decorated with ornamental plants. In a grand place, every thing ought to be on a grand scale; and few objects produce a more striking effect than immense masses of stone, piled together in such a way as at once to give a particular character of rocky mass, and to form a proper nidus [nest] for valuable plants.

The grand difficulty in rockwork is to form and maintain a particular character or style in the disposition of the masses; and the only way to conquer this difficulty is to observe the manner in which masses of rock are disposed in nature, or rather in such natural scenes as are admired by men of taste, and specially painters. And here the study of geology will assist both the painter and gardener.

It is difficult to know whether the writer of this essay would have approved of the massive rockery built for Lady Broughton at Hoole House near Chester. Lady Broughton's intention, described by the Loudons who visited Hoole House in 1831, was certainly correct, to create 'a small model representing the mountains of Savoy, with the valley of Chamouni'. The description of what the Loudons referred to as the 'rock-fence' and the 'rock boundary' enclosing the flower garden, continued,

It has been the work of many years to complete it, the difficulty being to make it stand against the weather. Rain washed away the soil, and frost swelled the stones: several times the main wall failed from the weight put upon it. The walls and the foundation are built of the red sandstone of the country; and the other materials have been collected from various quarters, chiefly from Wales; but it is now so generally covered with creeping and alpine plants, that it all mingles together in one mass. The outline, however, is carefully preserved; and the part of the model that represents 'la Mer de Glace' is worked with grey limestone, quartz and spar. It has no cells for plants: the spaces are filled up with broken fragments of white marble, to look like snow; and the spar is intended for the glacier… There must be the eye of the artist presiding over every step… Lady Broughton was her own artist; and the work which she has produced evinces the most exquisite taste for this description of scenery.

The Loudons went on to describe how each plant was provided with its specific requirements as to soil, shelter and drainage. George Pickering's watercolour shows her ladyship directing planting operations.

There is a remarkable rockery at Lamport Hall in Northamptonshire, where, like Lady Broughton, Sir Charles Isham attempted in the 1850s a replica of part of the Alps. Constructed from local ironstone and hidden from the rest of the garden by a wall, the recently restored structure is 27m (88ft) long, 14m (46ft) wide and 7m (23ft) high. It faces north, towards the windows of the house. Sir Charles made his rockery into the Disneyland of his day, where gnomes, imported from Nuremberg in large numbers, could be seen mining crystal in miniature caves and canyons. In Sir Charles's day large numbers of tourists came in charabancs from London to see the gnomes. It is still a place of pilgrimage for gnome connoisseurs who come to see the one remaining gnome, displayed in the house. Sir Charles was a spiritualist and was convinced that 'Seeing and hearing gnomes is not mental delusion, but extension of faculty.' He believed that other gnomes besides those purchased at Nuremberg were at work in his rockery, and published an article entitled *Visions of Fairy Blacksmiths at Work*.

Jane Loudon in the *Ladies' Companion* distinguished between rock-work 'which is intended to imitate natural scenery… and that which is intended to serve merely as a receptacle for plants.'

For the imitation of natural scenery in areas where there was no natural rock the Pulhams, father and son, came to the rescue. From the 1830s on, they invented, manufactured and marketed Pulhamite, a composite material made from clinker and Portland cement. Their structures can still be seen at Highnam Court, Gloucestershire and at Battersea Park in London.

By the end of the nineteenth century most self-respecting owners of large gardens could boast a rockery. But small gardens and even tiny gardens could also accommodate enough small rocks or large stones to provide Jane Loudon's 'receptacle for plants.' Moreover, many alpine plants were on exactly the right scale for a small garden. With this kind of gardening, it was not the overall effect that mattered, it was the close-up detail of plants and flowers, and a taste for enjoying plants in close-up was encouraged by botanizing, a leisure pursuit especially popular among women.

With the advent of Thomas Cook's organized tours, promising safe, comfortable travel, botanizing in the French, Austrian, Swiss and Italian Alps became a possibility for all but the most timid traveller. Who could fail to be moved by the jewel-box colours of the little irises, gentians, alpine phlox and dianthus? In the hearts of most gardeners, the sight of such plants growing in the wild, kindles a collector's spark, a covetous urge to possess. And enterprising nurserymen made sure the urge could be satisfied when the traveller returned home.

Although the Alpine Garden Society was not founded until 1929, there was plenty of written advice available for nineteenth-century gardeners. William Robinson, who we will get to know better in the next chapter, was inspired by a visit to France and Switzerland to write *Alpine Flowers for English Gardens* in 1870. David Fish and Edward Badger both wrote on the subject in *Cassell's Popular Gardening* under the general title of *Rock, Alpine, Fern, and Wild Gardening*. Fish, who edited *Cassell's Popular Gardening* from 1866 to 1884, began:

> To imitate nature so closely as to be mistaken for it, while providing all the most fostering growing conditions possible to the highest art, may be described as the perfection of rock building and furnishing.

He goes on to explain that it is almost impossible to get it right. In any event, his design advice is slightly suspect: 'If a rustic alcove arch could be worked into the rockery,' he wrote, 'so much the better.' His most interesting suggestion is to 'make a moat (a few inches wide is enough) to keep slugs out. They can neither swim nor fly.'

'Wallflowers and tulips, lavender and sweet william'

The cottage garden, as opposed to the garden of the *cottage orné,* began to attract admiration for its artless charm, and enthusiastic attempts were made at imitation, that most sincere form of flattery. We have already seen the d'Arblays and the Wordsworths getting a great deal of pleasure and a certain amount of produce from their own cottage gardens. The romantic idea of the simple, wholesome rural life was enhanced by comparison with the dirt, squalor and disease of industrial urban life. The disciplined but natural appearance of a well-kept cottage garden, its fitness for purpose, was an antidote, too, to the tight, over-elaborate, gardenesque style that was fashionable in the first half of the nineteenth century.

By the 1860s and 1870s, painters had begun to show pictures of happy families in cottage gardens. By the end of the century, as Anne Scott-James tells us in *The Cottage Garden*:

> Every county in England could now boast of picture-postcard villages with gardens with apple-trees, hollyhocks, sunflowers, mignonette and the other cottage favourites. They were cultivated by clergymen, doctors, minor civil servants, retired gentry, craftsmen, small farmers, labourers and independent gentlewomen, and all the other people who make up village society.

The planting in cottage gardens was becoming more self-conscious, more artfully cottagey, and more complex. Alongside the familiar cottage flowers, the sweet williams, pansies, poppies, wallflowers, columbines, snowdrops, daffodils, forget-me-nots, love-lies-bleeding and Michaelmas daisies (the list could fill a page), there were now plants too novel to have English country names: plants like wisteria, fuchsias, chrysanthemums, dahlias, hydrangeas, and tender begonias. The balance between flowers and fruit and vegetables had changed in many village gardens. Those who were not forced by necessity to grow their own food preferred growing flowers to potatoes.

And yet, in many of the more remote villages, the reality was still poverty, though not starvation. The best account of village life in the 1880s is Flora Thompson's in *Lark Rise to Candleford*. She wrote it in three separate volumes published in 1939, 1941 and 1943 respectively. She was born in 1876 and the books describe her childhood on the Oxfordshire-Northamptonhire border in the hamlet of Lark Rise where she was born, the nearby village of Candleford Green and the nearest small town, Candleford. They are fictional names for real places. The inhabitants of hamlet and village were labouring people. The professional and retired people Anne Scott-James referred to above had not yet arrived.

> The community was largely self-supporting. Every household grew its own vegetables, produced its new-laid eggs and cured its own bacon. Jams and jellies, wines and pickles, were made at home as a matter of course. Most gardens had a row of beehives. In the houses of the well-to-do there was an abundance of such foods, and even the poor enjoyed a rough plenty.

Most of the men worked on the land, but Laura's (as Flora Thompson called herself in the books) father was a stonemason and walked the few miles to and from Candleford to work each day. The vegetable plot was of vital importance, and was men's work.

> … all vegetables, including potatoes, were home-grown and grown in abundance. The men took great pride in their gardens and allotments and there was always competition amongst them as to who should have the earliest and choicest of each kind. Fat green peas, broad beans as big as a halfpenny, cauliflowers a child could make an armchair of, runner beans and cabbage and kale, all in their seasons went into the pot with the roly-poly and slip of bacon.

Then they ate plenty of green food, all home-grown and freshly pulled; lettuce and radishes and young onions with pearly heads and leaves like fine grass. A few slices of bread and home-made lard, flavoured with rosemary, and plenty of green food 'went down good' as they used to say.

The time available to the men for working in their gardens or on their allotments was limited to evenings after tea when there was enough light. The soil was good and there was plenty of manure from the pigs. But they were also conscientious about hoeing out the weeds between the rows of vegetables, and watering in dry weather. As the water had to be carried from the brook a quarter of a mile away, this was quite a chore. The gardens were for vegetables, the allotments for potatoes and wheat or barley, half-and-half. Most vegetable seeds and the seed potatoes were saved from the previous year. Flora Thompson noted that most of the men sang or whistled as they dug or hoed.

There was a ready market for paintings of idealized cottage gardens, but rural life was harsh, and pretty flower gardens were the exception rather than the rule. 'The Flower Garden', Abbot Fuller Graves, c.1900

Old Sally's was the prettiest garden. She was over 80, and remembered more prosperous times for country people.

> The garden was a large one, tailing off at the bottom into a little field where Dick grew his corn crop. Nearer the cottage were fruit trees, then the yew hedge, close and solid as a wall, which sheltered the beehives and enclosed the flower garden. Sally had such flowers, and so many of them, and nearly all of them sweet-scented! Wallflowers and tulips, lavender and sweet william, and pinks and old-world roses with enchanting names – Seven Sisters, Maiden's Blush, moss rose, monthly rose, cabbage rose, blood rose, and, most thrilling of all to the children, a big bush of the York and Lancaster rose, in the blooms of which the rival roses mingled in a pied white and red. It seemed as though all the roses in Lark Rise had gathered together in that one garden. Most of the gardens had only one poor starveling bush or none.

The same flowers were repeated in gardens throughout Lark Rise, for nobody could afford to buy plants; neighbours would pass on cuttings and roots to each other. Most houses had a narrow flower border along the path, and some gave over more space to flowers. As well as the flowers mentioned in Old Sally's garden, there were love-in-a-mist, forget-me-nots and hollyhocks; old man (southernwood) and sweetbrier. There was always a herb patch of thyme, sage, parsley and rosemary for cooking, and peppermint, pennyroyal, horehound, chamomile, tansy, balm and rue for medicine. Large quantities of camomile tea were drunk to ward off colds and soothe the nerves; horehound, mixed with honey, was for sore throats and chesty colds.

Another garden from an earlier generation was that of Laura's grandparents

William Morris (1834–98) loved gardens and was attracted by the unpretentious English cottage style. He loathed the more formal look and harsh colours of Victorian bedding plants, such as red geraniums and yellow calceolarias.

who lived in a funny little round house out in the fields. The garden, on the other side of a cart track, was full of currant and gooseberry bushes and raspberry canes. The grandfather had grown too stiff in the joints to prune or trim the garden, so the old flowers had run wild. Laura had a secret corner overhung by a damson tree and walled in with bushes and flowers.

Flora Thompson wrote from experience and without sentimentality, and was still able to say, 'People were poorer and had not the comforts, amusements, or knowledge we have today; but they were happier. Which seems to suggest that happiness depends more upon the state of mind – and body, perhaps – than upon circumstances and events.' It was probably the state of mind in country villages as much as the way of life that many artists and writers found so attractive and enviable.

'It should look both orderly and rich' Willam Morris

William Morris, artist, poet and craftsman, loved gardens all his life. According to his biographer, Fiona MacCarthy,

> The small boy had his own garden, first of many. All his gardens were beautiful, wrote the old friend who had seen most of them…. At Woodford Hall he studied the family copy of John Gerard's *Herball* (1597), an encyclopaedic study with meticulous drawings of plant forms. As a child he was already developing his sense of floral colours, textures, scents, structures and life cycles.
>
> …The making and nurturing of gardens satisfied his organsing powers and his most private urges. The gardens he created were a strange and lovely mixture of formality and wildness, reflecting quite uncannily the tension between the conservative and radical in Morris's own temperament. In so much of his writing, both poetry and prose, a garden is set right at the emotional centre, the place of discovery, the end of the long journey, where lovers meet and linger, on a carved primeval bench, by a swiftly flowing fountain, by a medieval trellis. There are always scents and blossoms.

It is not surprising that Morris, with his emotional and mystical feeling for gardens, had nothing good to say about Victorian garden fashions. He complained that suburban London gardeners 'oftenest wind about their little bit of gravel walk in ridiculous imitation of an ugly big garden of the landscape-gardening style, and then with a strange perversity fill up the spaces with the most formal plants they can get.' His own vision of a town garden was one laid out in the simplest way, fenced off from the road, and internally divided if the garden was big enough. The flower-growing space should be filled with 'things that are free and interesting in their growth, leaving Nature to do the desired complexity.' And there should be trees. The felling of trees in town gardens appalled him: 'one trembles at the very sound of an axe as one sits at one's work at home.' When it came to choosing a London house, one of the attractions of Kelmscott House, on the Thames at Hammersmith, where the Morrises lived between 1879 and 1881 was its trees. Morris listed them in a letter to his wife Janey: '1st a walnut by the stable; 2nd a very fine tulip-tree halfway down the lawn, 3rd 2 horse chestnuts at the end of the lawn.' There was a small orchard beyond, a greenhouse and a kitchen garden with fruit trees trained against the walls. But he found the problems of a town garden, with soil composed of 'old shoes and soot' and cats using it 'as a pleasure ground', depressing.

Morris knew as much as anyone can ever know about colour, and could not bear to see it brashly misused in the garden. In 1882 he wrote:

> Flowers in masses are mighty strong colour, and if not used with a great deal of caution are very destructive to pleasure in gardening. On the whole, I think the best and safest plan is to mix up your flowers, and rather eschew great masses of colour – in combination I mean. But there are some flowers (inventions of men, i.e.. florists) which are bad colours altogether, and not to be used at all. Scarlet geraniums, for instance, or the yellow calceolaria, which indeed are not uncommonly grown together profusely, in order, I suppose, to show that even flowers can be thoroughly ugly.
>
> Another thing also much too commonly seen is an aberration of the human mind, which otherwise I should have been ashamed to warn you of. It is technically called carpet-gardening. Need I explain it further? I had rather not, for when I think of it even when I am quite alone I blush with shame at the thought.

It was not that Morris was afraid of colour, just that he hated to see it used carelessly. He planted a vibrant combination of blue larkspurs with orange lilies in

Part of William and Janey Morris's garden at Kelmscott Manor, beside the River Thames near Lechlade, Gloucestershire. Frontispiece of William Morris's 'News from Nowhere' by Charles March Gere, engraved by W.H. Hooper, 1892.

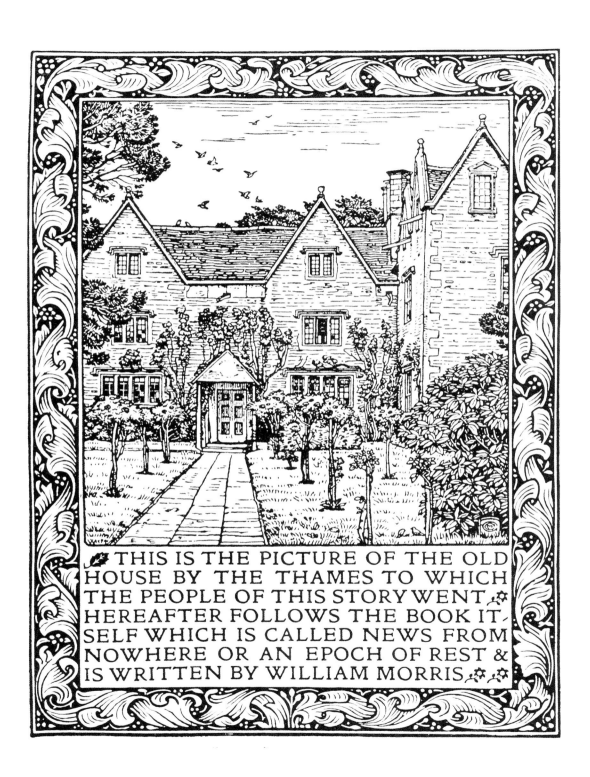

THIS IS THE PICTURE OF THE OLD
HOUSE BY THE THAMES TO WHICH
THE PEOPLE OF THIS STORY WENT.
HEREAFTER FOLLOWS THE BOOK IT
SELF WHICH IS CALLED NEWS FROM
NOWHERE OR AN EPOCH OF REST &
IS WRITTEN BY WILLIAM MORRIS.

one of the flower borders at Merton Abbey, a former silk-weaving factory which Morris revived as a factory and workshop.

William Morris's own gardens reflected the views he expressed in a lecture on 'Making the Best of It' in 1879:

> ...large and small, it should look both orderly and rich. It should be well fenced from the outside world. It should by no means imitate either the willfulness or wildness of nature, but should look like a thing never to be seen except near a house. It should in fact look like part of a house.

Red House, designed for William and Janey Morris by Philip Webb, was built in a Kent apple and cherry orchard in a carefully chosen setting of picturesquely gnarled old fruit trees, with, in those days, distant rural views. The Morrises moved there in 1860. The house and garden were planned together, to satisfy Morris's craving for the romance and craftsmanship of medieval life, and to be 'the beautifullest place on earth'. They and their friends of the Pre-Raphaelite Brotherhood took their medieval philosophy and alternative lifestyle seriously. The women of the household dressed in flowing robes in rich, sometimes sombre, colours. Agnes, the more conventional sister of Georgiana Burne-Jones, complained that she could hardly manage to get through the doors at Red House in her crinoline.

The inner garden was a courtyard, planned by Webb to be integral with the house. It was in the medieval tradition, laid out as a quartered square, enclosed on two sides by the L-shaped house, and on the other two by wattle fences covered densely with roses. Each quarter formed a separate, enclosed *hortus conclusus*, and led into the next. At the centre was a turreted wellhouse. Among the flowers grown in beds edged with lavender and rosemary, were lilies, sunflowers, peonies and poppies, and against the house walls there were white jasmine, roses, honeysuckle and the passion flower. All of them would appear in Morris's designs for textiles and wall-coverings. Beyond the inner garden there was a bowling green, and sweetbriar scented walks through the orchard.

The garden Morris probably loved the most was at Kelmscott Manor, his Elizabethan house in the Oxfordshire Cotswolds, built from the mellow local stone at a time when domestic architecture on a modest scale was at its finest. The river at the bottom of the garden, 'the baby Thames' was a joy to him. All his life he had a passion for fishing, and at Kelmscott he could indulge it at will. The curtains of willow overhanging his stretch of river inspired one of his most popular designs. He also loved the rightness of the Cotswold villages and country-side, though he despised the 'hunters of the picturesque'. In his socialist paper *The Commonweal* he wrote:

> Midsummer in the country: here you may walk between the fields and hedges that are as it were one huge nosegay for you, redolent of bean-flowers and clover and sweet hay and elder-blossom. The cottage-gardens are bright with flowers, the cottages themselves mostly models of architecture in their way. Above them towers here and there the architecture proper of days bygone, when every craftsman was an artist and brought definite intelligence to bear upon his work. Man in the past, nature in the present, seem to be bent on pleasing you and making all things delightful to your senses.

The gardens of nostalgia

In the later part of the nineteenth century and the early part of the twentieth, a change was taking place. Garden makers stopped testing new ideas, and started looking back, seeking inspiration in gardens of the past. Different designers had different ideas. For William Morris and his admirers, it was an Arthurian dream of a garden where knights courted languid ladies or suitors battled through cruel briars to the Sleeping Beauty's bower. Others dreamed of the Italian Renaissance, of balustraded terraces descending to sunken fountain courts; their champions were George Sitwell, Reginald Blomfield, whose book *The Formal Garden in England* was published in 1892, and Harold Peto who, in his own garden at Iford Manor, Wiltshire, looked back beyond Renaissance Italy to Classical Rome.

The most beautiful and moving exercise in nostalgia is to be seen in Dorset at Athelhampton House. The house is a perfect example of domestic architecture of the fifteenth and sixteenth centuries. The dream of Alfred Cart de Lafontaine, the owner between 1891 and 1918, was to create gardens that would seem as if they had always belonged to the house. He laid out the gardens with help from Francis Inigo Thomas, an architect and garden designer who also drew the illustrations for Blomfield's book. They form a series of linked courts presided over by a raised terrace with a pavilion at each end, the House of Joy and Summer to the west and the House of Sorrow and Winter at the east end. At the heart of the garden is the Corona, a courtyard enclosed by a circular wall decorated with tall obelisks, a fountain in a lead urn at its centre. The terraces, steps and walls are all made of golden Ham stone, which seems sun-warmed even on the dullest day. Each part of the garden has its fountain or canal; the sound of falling water is always in the visitor's ears.

9

THE TWENTIETH CENTURY

Understanding Nature

WHILE STILL AN undergraduate at Oxford, William Morris was a great admirer of John Ruskin and was strongly influenced by his books, especially Ruskin's revelatory chapter 'On the Nature of Gothic' in *The Stones of Venice*, which much later was published by Morris's own Kelmscott Press. When he heard that Ruskin had said 'Morris is beaten gold' and described him as 'the ablest man of his time' Morris was overjoyed.

Besides a passion for medieval gothic architecture and all that went with it, the two men shared other important ideas. In 1877, Morris and his friends set up the Society for the Protection of Ancient Buildings (SPAB), and Morris was its leading light. He persuaded Ruskin to become involved following a row about proposed restoration work to St Mark's in Venice. Both men were far in advance of their time in their recognition that urban and industrial development and pollution seriously threatened the English landscape. Ruskin was present (in the chair) in 1883 when Morris gave the angry lecture on 'Art and Democracy' at University College, Oxford, in which he publicly declared himself as a Socialist. He pointed out that change in society would definitely come and he also set out his agenda for the environment:

The rill garden at Hestercombe, Somerset, designed by Edwin Lutyens and Gertrude Jekyll: the rill itself and the round pool under the arched alcove are favourite devices of the partnership.

To keep the air pure and the rivers clean, to take some pains to keep the meadows and tillage as pleasant as reasonable use will allow them to be; to allow peaceable citizens freedom to wander where they will, so they do no hurt to garden or cornfield; nay, even to leave here and there some piece of waste or mountain sacredly free from fence or tillage as a memory of man's ruder struggles with nature in his earlier days; is it too much to ask civilization to be so far thoughtful of man's pleasure and rest, and to help so far as this her children to whom she has most often set such heavy tasks of grinding labour? Surely not an unreasonable asking.

This early plea for the 'right to roam' must have seemed radical and perhaps hopelessly idealistic. It will finally be achieved by Government legislation in the year 2005, when public access rights will be granted to areas currently being mapped and agreed. Morris's ideas were shared by John Ruskin who railed against industrial pollution:

Manchester has become the funnel of a volcano, which, not content in vomiting pestilence, gorges the whole rain of heaven, that falls over a district as distant as the ancient Scottish border.

Although he was not directly involved, Ruskin was instrumental in the foundation of The National Trust. It is easy to forget that the Trust was originally formed to preserve and give access to the countryside rather than to great houses and their gardens. Two of the three founders, Octavia Hill and Canon Hardwicke Rawnsley, were Ruskin's students and Rawnsley stated '…it was Ruskin's teaching which was the fountain head of the teaching which set forward this National Trust.' The greater the threat of pollution, the more highly valued unspoiled landscapes became. A garden was a precious retreat.

'Wild nature tamed but not degraded'

Ruskin made his own garden at Brantwood, Coniston, according to deeply felt principles. His diary for 15 September 1871, a year before he moved into the house, read 'First day's work clearing garden. See weeds burnt in twilight.' He organized the construction of a small harbour at the lakeside to make Brantwood more accessible to visitors arriving by water, and an ice house. Apart from these practical projects, his aim was to 'Go to nature, in all singleness of heart,' in the hope of achieving 'Wild nature tamed but not degraded under the hand of Man, neither overpowering him nor overpowered, but fitted for his house.'

Ruskin believed in the dignity of labour, regarding work as '…at once a luxury and a necessity; no man can retain health of mind or of body without it.' He involved himself and his friends in the manual labour of constructing his lake-side harbour, and set himself to work with an axe in the woods around the house, clearing paths and coppicing trees. With his own hands he shifted rocks to improve the watercourses tumbling down the hillside. He sowed and planted in the belief that

> Your garden is to enable you to obtain such knowledge of plants as you may best use in the country in which you live by communicating it to others; and teaching them to take pleasure in the green herb, given for meat, and the coloured flower given for joy.

He wanted children to be taught about local natural history so that they might understand 'the nature and uses of the herbs that grow in the meadows…'.

Ruskin's respect for nature and for the native flowers of England was apparent in his garden as well as in his paintings, such as this watercolour study of rocks and ferns in a wood at Crossmount, Perthshire, 1843.

Ruskin's goal was a return to a medieval respect for the properties of plants. He wrote that

> happiness is increased not by the enlargement of the possessions, but of the heart; and days lengthened, not by the crowding of emotions, but the economy of them… No manner of temperance in pleasure would be better rewarded than that of making our gardens gay only with common flowers.

Like William Morris, he abhorred gaudy hybrid flowers of excessive size, scent or colour, an opinion shared, and expressed with less earnestness, by the novelist George Gissing, an acquaintance of the Morrises, in 1903

> The only garden flowers I care for are the quite old-fashioned roses, sunflowers, hollyhocks, lilies and so on, and these I like to see growing as much as possible as if they were wild. Trim and symmetrical beds are my abhorrence, and most of the flowers which are put into them – hybrids with some grotesque name – Jonesia, Snooksia, – hurt my eyes. On the other hand, a garden is a garden, and I would not try to introduce into it the flowers which are my solace in lanes and fields. Foxgloves, for instance – it would pain me to see them thus transplanted.
>
> *The Private Papers of Henry Ryecroft*, George Gissing, 1903

Ruskin had no such reservations about planting native flowers in his garden. On the contrary, wild flowers were his delight and he brought them into various parts of the garden, notably his own special plot known as 'the Professor's Garden', where he liked to get to know his plants intimately. A small meadow by the Harbour Walk was planted with wild daffodils (*Narcissus pseudonarcissus*). Ruskin planted them to remind himself of a colony of the same flowers at Vevay on Lake Geneva, but today they also seem like a link with Wordsworth, not far away at Rydal Mount. After Ruskin died, his garden in due course reverted to a tangled wilderness, thereby proving that nature, unaided, cannot make a garden; a restraining hand, albeit a gentle one, is needed. The garden is in the process of being restored.

The ideals expressed in Ruskin's garden were both radical and traditional. His respect for the existing landscape and his sensitive enhancement of it were quite new. But his pleasure in plants went back to the days when Adam dug and Eve span. It is the reason why men have always made gardens:

To own a bit of ground, to scratch it with a hoe, to plant seeds, and watch their renewal of life, – this is the commonest delight of the race, the most satisfactory thing a man can do.

My Summer in a Garden, Charles Dudley Warner, 1876

'Ways of escape from the death-note of the pastry-cook's garden'
The first edition of William Robinson's book *The Wild Garden* came out in 1870, the year before Ruskin acquired Brantwood, so it is possible Ruskin had read the book and was influenced by Robinson's ideas. It is also possible that, before he wrote the book, Robinson was aware of the feeling for nature and for wild plants, and the general climate of opinion generated by Ruskin, Morris and others involved in the Arts and Crafts movement. Or perhaps they both happened to be in tune with the time. Today, we know what is meant by a wild garden, but to Robinson's readers this was a new and startling phrase and he had to explain it:

> My object in the *Wild Garden* is now to show how we may have more of the
> varied beauty of hardy flowers than the most ardent admirer of the old
> style of garden ever dreams of, by naturalizing many beautiful plants of
> many regions of the earth in our fields, woods and copses, outer parts of
> pleasure grounds, and in neglected places in almost every kind of garden.

Unusual as this idea was, it was not intended to supplant the prevailing fashion of formal flowerbeds around the house. It was a way of dealing with the perimeter of the garden, the shrubberies and other places where the garden ends or merges into the countryside. The fashion for tender, exotic plants had reached a stage where very few hardy herbaceous plants were grown, and the cost of producing a fresh crop of bedding plants under glass twice a year was extortionate. The beds near the house should be filled with 'rare or tender plants or choice garden flowers like the Tea Rose and Carnation – plants which often depend for their beauty on their double states, and for which rich soil and care and often protection are essential.' Robinson wrote:

> The Wild Garden is to be kept distinct in the mind from the various sorts
> of hardy plant cultivation in groups, beds, and borders, in which good
> gardening and good taste may produce many happy effects; distinct from
> the rock garden in its many aspects – all asking for skill and care; for the
> borders reserved for choice hardy flowers of all kinds…

Robinson's intention is to emulate the

Innumerable and infinitely varied scenes [which] occur in all northern and temperate regions, at many different elevations, the loveliness of which it is impossible to portray; the essential thing to bear in mind is that the plants that go to form them are hardy, and will thrive in our climate as well as native plants....

To some a plant in a free state is more charming than any garden denizen. It is taking care of itself; and, moreover, it is usually surrounded by some degree of graceful wild spray – the green above, and the moss or grass around.

Numbers of plants of the highest order of beauty may be at home in the spaces now devoted to rank grass and weeds, and by wood walks in our shrubberies.

There is a section in *The Wild Garden* on British wild flowers and trees, and how to use them in the garden. But Robinson's real interest was in naturalizing foreign plants so that they could take care of themselves. The chapter headings tell part of the story: 'Example from Hardy Bulbs in Grass of Lawns or Meadows', 'Example from the Globe Flower Order', 'Ditches, Shady Lanes, Copses, and Hedgerows', 'Shrubbery, Plantation and Wood' and 'Wild and other Roses in the Wild Garden'. His approach was practical, and he emphasized the importance of matching the plants to the soil, giving lists for moist rich soils, peat soil, calcareous soil, dry and gravelly soil, and old walls, ruins or rocky slopes.

Rabbits are recognized as a problem (a warren is no longer regarded as a productive asset as it was in medieval and Tudor times). Robinson says 'Hungry rabbits, like hungry dogs or starving men, will eat almost anything that can be got.' He recommends a couple of seasons shooting and ferreting to control them, but also passes on tips from a correspondent who says 'Most of the Lily family are rejected by them, including Daffodils, Tulips, Snowdrops, Snowflakes, Lilies, Day Lilies, Asphodels, and others, and they cannot be too extensively planted; but even in that tribe the Crocus is greedily devoured.' Among shrubs recommended as immune to rabbits are southernwood (*Artemisia abrotanum*), barberry (*Berberis darwinii*), *Deutzia scabra*, elder, euonymus, fuchsia, *Hibiscus syriacus*, honeysuckle (*Lonicera*), Oregon grape (*Mahonia aquifolium*), butcher's broom (*Ruscus*), snowberry, lilac, *Weigela rosea* and *Yucca gloriosa*. Herbaceous survivors are *Anemone japonica*, aubrieta, Canterbury bells, columbine, honesty, iris, monkshood, phlox, poppies, lamb's tongue (*Stachys lanata*), pansies, periwinkle,

primroses and violets. A memorable example of Robinsonian wild gardening can be seen at Spetchley Park in Worcestershire, where great drifts of martagon lilies flower and seed themselves in grass under trees.

Robinson was abrasive and opinionated, not an easy man to get on with. He is said to have quarrelled with his first employer in Ireland, and allegedly walked out one frosty night never to return, leaving all the greenhouses open. In due course he was engaged by Robert Marnock to look after the hardy herbaceous plants at the Royal Botanic Gardens in Regent's Park, a job after his own heart. However, he found his true vocation when he became horticultural correspondent to *The Times*. He was a natural writer with a distinctive, straightforward style, and had a successful and lucrative career. A year after *The Wild Garden* came out he started a weekly magazine, *The Garden*, which became a huge success. Another very influential and best-selling book followed in 1883: *The English Flower Garden*, full of sound technical advice on growing plants, and design advice on how to arrange them in the garden. It went through 15 editions and many reprints during his lifetime. His own garden at Gravetye Manor in Sussex

In 'The Wild Garden', 1870, as well as recommending hardy garden plants to naturalize in wilder areas, William Robinson advocated bringing native plants, such as primroses and violets, into the garden. Both featured on his list of rabbit-proof plants.

remained resolutely formal, but the layout was simple, with numerous plain rectangular beds, containing informally mixed hardy plants.

'The best kind of pictorial beauty of flower and foliage'

Gertrude Jekyll first met William Robinson in 1875, when his success was already well established. They seem to have found an instant rapport, which is hardly surprising since they shared so many ideas about plants and gardens. Miss Jekyll was well connected in the avant-garde art world and knew William Morris and John Ruskin. She trained at the School of Art in South Kensington at a time when women students were in a tiny minority, became an immensely skilled embroiderer and also worked in wood and metal. Her designs were very much in the Morris Arts and Crafts style. Poor eyesight forced her to switch her talents away from close, detailed work, and the direction she chose was gardening and garden design. Miss Jekyll wrote for William Robinson's magazine *The Garden* and together they developed each other's creative skills at designing with plants.

Much of her talent went into her nine books. They are still read, and are still relevant – more so than Robinson's – and her most Robinsonian book *Wood and Garden* is probably less popular today than the others. Gardening, for Miss Jekyll, came very close to religion. Her creed was

> I hold the firm belief that the purpose of a garden is to give happiness and repose of mind, firstly and above all other considerations, and to give it through the representation of the best kind of pictorial beauty of flower and foliage that can be combined or invented.

She believed it was a waste of time having a garden unless you took the trouble to understand how to make it beautiful:

> Just as an un-assorted assemblage of mere words, though they may be the best words in our language, will express no thought, or as the purest colours on an artist's palette – so long as they remain on the palette – do not form a picture, so our garden plants, placed without due consideration or definite intention, cannot show what they can best do for us.
>
> 'A Definite Purpose in Gardening', The World, 1905

She offered advice in a clear, straightforward and sometimes entertaining style. *Colour in the Flower Garden* was her most innovative book, and the one which has been followed most closely since she was rediscovered towards the end of the twentieth century. She was the first writer to discuss flower colour and its use to compose pleasing pictures. Before Jekyll, gardeners did not think in terms of hot borders and cool borders, of complementary colours or harmonious shades. After Jekyll they are matters almost every gardener has considered.

Miss Jekyll was completely unpretentious. She learned (and urged her readers to learn) much from cottage gardens, particularly those in the villages around Munstead, in Surrey where she lived. She wrote,

> Not infrequently in passing along a country road, with eye alert to note the beauties that are so often presented by little wayside cottage gardens, something is seen that may well serve as a lesson in better planting. The lesson is generally one that teaches greater simplicity – the doing of one thing at a time; the avoidance of overmuch detail.
>
> *Home and Garden*, 1900

> One can hardly go into the smallest cottage garden without learning or observing something new. It may be some two plants growing beautifully together by some happy chance, or a pretty tangle of mixed creepers, or something that one has always thought must have a south wall doing better on an east one.   *Wood and Garden*, 1899

Miss Jekyll was famous for her herbaceous borders, where she was able to put her colour theories into practice, but her woodland garden was just as important to her. 'Woodland is always charming and restful and enduringly beautiful.'

'The best hybrid rhododendron ever raised': Gardening dynasties

Gertrude Jekyll's idea of woodland was to enhance nature with restraint and discretion. The effects her woodland planting created were intended to seem like happy accident. But for other garden makers, woodland presented thrilling opportunities for exotic, alien landscapes. They wanted to grow the exciting plants that were being imported, and they found the perfect habitat for them in the lightly shaded, sheltered conditions provided by a carefully managed wood. Very often acid or at any rate neutral soil went with the woodland environment, making it perfect for azaleas, rhododendrons, magnolias and camellias.

In some parts of the country this kind of woodland garden had been created some time before Robinson and Jekyll wrote about the wild garden. We have already looked briefly at the great Cornish ravine gardens of the mid-nineteenth century (see page 204). At the end of the century, enthusiasm grew for those difficult plants that would not thrive unless their requirements were met absolutely. A few plant connoisseurs, with the means to indulge their tastes, caught the incurable disease of rhododendromania. There were two strains of the disease: the collector's and the equally incurable hybridizer's; some garden makers suffered from both at the same time. The main symptom was a hunger that could never be assuaged for new species and varieties.

In some families, rhododendromania turned out to be hereditary. The Loders were such a family. *Rhododendron loderi* was called after Sir Edmund. It is 'generally considered,' according to Hillier & Sons *Manual of Trees and Shrubs*, 'to be the finest rhododendron hybrid.' There are more than a dozen variations of Loder's spectacular hybrid, all with huge trusses of large, richly scented flowers in a colour range from white and cream to soft pink. Sir Edmund grew them at Leonardslee in Sussex, a woodland garden on a vast scale (240 acres, seven lakes). J.G. Millais, author of *Rhododendrons and the various Hybrids* (1917) wrote of another outstanding rhododendron hybrid, 'Loder's White', 'Cornish gardeners, who enjoy a galaxy of fine things, and are not superabundant in their praises, consider Loder's White the best hybrid rhododendron ever raised, not even excepting Loderi, and no doubt many agree with them.' The original 'Loder's White' scions grafted by Sir Edmund are said to have come from the nursery of Mr J.H. Mangles, in whose Surrey garden the legendary partnership between Gertrude Jekyll and Edwin Lutyens began.

Sir Edmund Loder's younger brother Wilfred gardened a mere 20 acres nearby at High Beeches, and Gerald Loder had Wakehurst Place, now owned by The National Trust and looked after by the Royal Botanic Gardens at Kew. There is much more to all these gardens than 'just' rhododendrons. They are all distinguished collections of trees and shrubs, and a joy to visit, particularly in spring and autumn.

Nothing is so infectious as gardening, or so competitive. The Messel family made equally spectacular gardens at Nymans nearby, and at Exbury, Lionel de Rothschild, of the great banking and gardening dynasty, grew and bred rhododendrons and azaleas in spectacular 200-acre gardens.

These and other great plant collections, like that of the Cavendish family at Holker Hall in Cumbria or the Queen's Savill Garden at Windsor, are not what Robinson and Jekyll meant by wild gardens or woodland gardens. In their way they were as labour-intensive as more formal garden. Mrs C.W. Earle, who wrote about her own garden in *Pot-pourri from a Surrey Garden*, noted in 1897: 'I live near one of the most beautiful so-called wild gardens in England, but it requires endless care, and is always extending in all directions in search of fresh soil.'

'Why should we imitate wild nature?'

The Robinson/Jekyll vision of a wild garden was never quite so romantically dishevelled as the one in Frances Hodgson Burnett's *The Secret Garden*, the book that has entranced so many generations of children and grownups since she wrote it in 1911, or this garden imagined by Robert Louis Stevenson:

> The old flowers are the best and should grow carelessly in corners.
> Indeed the ideal fortune is to find an old garden, once very richly cared
> for, since sunk into neglect, and to tend, not repair, that neglect; it will
> thus have a smack of nature and wilderness which skilful dispositions
> cannot overtake…. It is a golden maxim to cultivate the garden for the
> nose, and the eyes will take care of themselves. Nor must the ear be
> forgotten; without birds a garden is a prison-yard.
>
> Essays of Travel, Robert Louis Stevenson, 1905

Although they would have agreed wholeheartedly about the need for scent and the sound of birdsong in a garden, neither Robinson nor Jekyll would have countenanced untidiness. Their ideas for a natural style of planting related only to shrubberies, orchards and the areas where the garden meets the woods and fields, not to the formal terraces and lawns around the house.

Their innovative ideas generated controversy. S. Baring-Gould, the novelist who also wrote the hymn 'Onward Christian Soldiers', wrote in *Old Country Life*, 1890:

> Why should we imitate wild nature? The garden is a product of civilization.
> Why any more make of our gardens imitation of wild nature, than paint
> our children with woad, and make them run about naked in an effort to
> imitate nature unadorned? The very charm of a garden is that it is taken
> out of savagery, trimmed, clothed and disciplined.

Eden Phillpotts, another novelist of about the same vintage, shared Baring-Gould's opinion and in his book *My Garden*, 1906, wrote:

> I am frankly and absolutely for a formal garden… [In my garden] there
> is not the least attempt to imitate natural scenery. There are no winding
> walks, no boskages, no sylvan dells, no grottoes stuck with stones and
> stalactites. My garden is simply an artificial, but none the less beautiful,
> arrangement of all the best plants that I can contrive to collect.

Gertrude Jekyll would have done her best to persuade Phillpotts that a winding walk through a sylvan dell was not only permissible but desirable. She would also have happily catered for more formal tastes, changing the style of the garden by simplifying the layout of beds and borders and introducing her own generous and relaxed way of planting.

'A Lutyens house in a Jekyll Garden'

The famous Lutyens-Jekyll partnership began in 1889 when Edwin Lutyens the architect met Gertrude Jekyll the gardener at a tea table in Mr Mangles' rhododendron garden. She was 45 and he was 20. They became friends immediately, and she commissioned him to build her a house at Munstead Wood, next to her mother's house, which would in due course become famous for its garden. 'A Lutyens house in a Jekyll Garden' as a recipe for success has become something of a cliché, and the phrase is a little misleading, for there was Jekyll in the architecture of the house, and Lutyens in the layout of the garden.

The brilliance of their partnership depended to a great extent on Lutyens's genius for getting the garden layout right. His skill lay in setting the house in the ideal position in its site, and in planning the garden so that it was completely integrated with the house. The arrangement was always formal, but usually not symmetrical. Changes of level, and ways of getting from one terrace to another, were managed with great skill. Local materials, including brick, timber and stone, were chosen with care and the hard landscape was constructed with skilful craftsmanship, very much in the William Morris Arts and Crafts tradition. Miss Jekyll influenced Lutyens's architecture from the start, by infecting him with her love of vernacular building styles.

She was not always involved with the layout of the gardens they worked on together. Sometimes they met to discuss it, and at other times would correspond, sending drawings to and fro. Sometimes Lutyens would just send the plans and she would add the plants to them. Her planting plans were her great contribution, and her great legacy to us. By great good fortune many of her drawings have survived, so it is possible to reconstruct her beds and borders. The formality of Lutyens's terraces, plats, rills and pools was modified and softened by Jekyll's planting with its carefully planned harmonies and contrasts of foliage form and texture as well as flower colour. 'It seems desirable', she wrote, 'to

The restored gardens at Hestercombe, with their terraces, rills, formal planting and pergola, are an outstanding example of the Lutyens/Jekyll design partnership which has contributed so much to English gardening.

have, next to grass, some foliage of rather distinct and important size and form. For this the Meagaseas [now called Bergenias] are invaluable'.

'We are growing impatient of the usual Rose garden'

As plant hunters and plant breeders supplied more and more plants with different habits and requirements, the vogue for specialized gardens increased. There were rock gardens, ferneries, stumperies, water gardens, bog gardens, winter gardens and spring gardens. Some plant connoisseurs made American gardens for American plants, others made New Zealand gardens. Rose gardens were perennially popular. Almost any garden bigger than a postage stamp had a separate, formal rose garden to display the exciting new Hybrid Tea roses 'decidedly the most in vogue now.' Gertrude Jekyll was critical of the design of most rose gardens. In *Roses for English Gardens* she wrote:

We are growing impatient of the usual Rose garden, generally a sort of

A rustic pergola in the Rose Garden at Polesden Lacey in Surrey. Now owned by The National Trust, the garden was originally developed by the Edwardian hostess the Honourable Mrs Ronald Greville around an earlier Greek Revival house.

target of concentric rings of beds placed upon turf, often with no special aim at connected design with the portions of the garden immediately about it, and filled with plants without a thought of their colour effect or any other worthy intention.

She felt that 'In this, as in so much other gardening, it is much to be desired that the formal and free ways should both be used.'

In her book she offers two plans for rose gardens, one for a long, narrow, sloping site and the other for a level, more or less square site. She emphasizes the importance of enclosure to provide a background for the roses; the first garden is 'embowered in native woodland', the second 'enclosed by yew hedges, beyond which are tall evergreens, such as ilex or cypress.' Drawings of both plans are shown in her book, and the square garden has a very similar layout to the rose garden made at Warwick Castle by Robert Marnock, William Robinson's employer at Regent's Park. The Victorian Rose Garden at Warwick Castle has been reconstructed and can be seen today.

A favourite way of displaying climbing and rambling roses, advocated by both Robinson and Jekyll, was on a pergola, not a new device, but an Edwardian adaptation of the medieval arbour. Pergolas were constructed in a wide variety of styles, using different materials. There were classical stone columns supporting sturdy oak beams, slender metal arches, or pillars constructed from brick, dry-stone, criss-cross wooden trellis, or rustic larch. The rustic look was popular in even quite grand gardens: it added to the fashionable cottagey look. There is an example at Polesden Lacey in Surrey, in the garden where the Honourable Mrs Ronald Greville, the fashionable Edwardian hostess, entertained house parties in which Edward VII was often included. On the pergola are those quintessentially Edwardian roses, 'American Pillar' and 'Dorothy Perkins'.

Anyone planning a rose garden at that time might have turned to Miss Jekyll's book, first published in 1902, for advice. They would find her strict. She did not care, for example, for opulence in roses and avoided those of magenta-purple colouring: '…a Rose garden can never be called gorgeous; the term is quite unfitting.' She urged her readers to use roses in all sorts of positions outside the rose garden proper, offering advice on growing roses up trees in a chapter on 'Roses as Fountains and Growing Free'. In another useful chapter, 'Roses for Converting Ugliness to Beauty' she suggests covering an ordinary off-the-peg wooden summerhouse with a frame supporting rambler roses. Redundant farm buildings could also be disguised with roses, for 'Many an old farmhouse,' she wrote, 'is now being converted into a dwelling-house for another class of resident.' The back-door region of small houses would also benefit:

> [It] may be a model of tidy dullness, or it may be a warning example of sordid neglect; but a cataract of Rose bloom will in the one case give added happiness to the well-trained servants of the good housewife, and in the other may redeem the squalor by its gracious presence, and even by its clean, fresh beauty put better thoughts and desires into the minds of slatternly people.

'We have nothing like it in Japan'

From 1868 onwards, Japan became accessible to the West for the first time. There was a general, if superficial, interest in Japanese culture, made manifest in Gilbert and Sullivan's opera *The Mikado* (1885) and Puccini's *Madame Butterfly* (1904). Fashionable ladies took to wearing silk kimonos when en deshabille, and protecting themselves from draughts with folding lacquer screens. French impressionist painters became fascinated by Japanese prints and woodcuts; in England, Aubrey Beardsley's work reflected their style, and in 1910 the fashionable world flocked to the Japanese-British exhibition.

As far as gardens were concerned, in 1891 Josiah Conder published *Flowers of Japan and the Art of Floral Arrangement*, followed by *Landscape Gardening in Japan* in 1893. These books greatly increased the demand for acers, flowering cherries, bamboos, peonies and chrysanthemums. *The Flowers and Gardens of Japan* by Florence and Ella Du Cane came out in 1908. There was no shortage of plants to satisfy demand; collectors had been sending material back from Japan for some time, and *japonica* as a species description was quite familiar to gardeners. *Acer japonicum* had been introduced in 1864, *Prunus sargentii*, one of the loveliest Japanese cherries, in 1890. Many others soon followed.

'Japanese' gardens were created with little understanding of the culture and philosophy behind the genuine article, and the symbolism employed in its construction, but there were a few enthusiasts who did their best to ensure authenticity by importing Japanese gardeners to make the gardens. Louis Greville did this at Heale House, Wiltshire in 1901. He had spent some time in the diplomatic service in Tokyo, and brought four Japanese gardeners to England to make a garden beside the very English River Avon, spanning it with a small version of the famous Nikko Bridge, painted brilliant scarlet. The river divides into little streams and where two intersect, a thatched teahouse, with a fretted balcony and sliding rice-paper shutters, was built across them. There is a massive stone temple lantern and a gnarled walnut tree like a giant bonsai specimen. In the hundred years since the garden was made, much of the rockwork has gone and the planting has become anglicized, with roses cascading out of trees and water-side plants growing with luxuriant abandon. But there are still magnolias and acers to give an oriental feel to the garden, and the fact that it has adapted to the lush water meadows surrounding it adds to its charm.

The Japanese garden at Tatton Park in Cheshire was also made the traditional way by Japanese workmen in 1910. A Shinto temple overlooks the Golden Brook with a background of majestic swamp cypresses and a foreground of irises and water lilies. From the temple there are carefully contrived views, taking in a miniature Mount Fuji, a pagoda, and various stone lanterns of different shapes and significance. There are meandering streams crossed by stone slab bridges, and all the plants are Japanese. The tranquillity intended as an aid to contemplation, so important in 'real' Japanese gardens, has been achieved here. But Lionel de Rothschild's Japanese garden at Gunnersbury, West London, was rather different. The Japanese ambassador attended the opening and, when asked what he thought of the garden, said, as if paying a great compliment, 'We have nothing like it in Japan.'

Although Japanese plants have become an essential component of the English garden, Japanese gardens turned out to be a temporary craze. There are not many examples today, perhaps because the Japanese tradition is too austere for the English passion for colourful flowers. Rose gardens, however, so well suited to the English climate and to the temperament of the English gardener, are still being made in the twenty-first century, often to exactly the pattern that Miss Jekyll abhorred.

'Great ladies were taking up gardening'

The books of William Robinson and Gertrude Jekyll were aimed at an upper-middle-class readership and at middle-class householders with upwardly mobile aspirations: the garden-owning and book-buying classes. Gertrude Jekyll's *Gardens for Small Country Houses*, a joint venture with Sir Laurence Weaver, went through five editions between 1912 and 1924. Many of the 'small country houses' illustrated were substantial by today's standards, and the gardens were spacious, some of them able to accommodate a tennis lawn, croquet lawn, rose garden and kitchen garden, as well as several areas for different kinds of plants. These gardens needed gardeners, in the plural, to look after them. The involvement of the owners varied. Not all of them were interested in what their gardeners were doing. Some were happy to leave the design of the garden and the choice of the plants to the head gardener, and would not interfere as long as the

garden looked tidy and colourful, and supplied flowers and hothouse plants to decorate the house.

But gardening had become a fashionable occupation. Ladies liked to put on a becoming shady hat, take their basket and secateurs, and deadhead the roses. They also liked to show off their knowledge to each other at flower shows – soon after its inception in 1913 the Royal Horticultural Society's annual Chelsea Show became an essential part of 'the season' – or play the name-dropping game in each other's gardens, letting fall, not the names of aristocrats, statesmen and other scions of fashionable society, but names such as *Liriodendron tulipifera*, *Agapanthus campanulatus* or *Ceanothus veitchianus*. In the rose garden, social and horticultural ambitions could be merged by showing an acquaintance with 'Princesse de Nassau', 'Baroness Rothschild' or the dashing 'Commandant Beaurepaire'. A knowledge of gardening could also be the means of climbing the social

The traditional Japanese garden at Tatton Park, Cheshire, restored by The National Trust in 2001, was made by a team of Japanese workmen in 1910. The arched bridge leads to a Shinto Temple built on a small island.

ladder. Angela Thirkell, who wrote popular novels about upper-middle-class country life in the 1930s, described in *Wild Strawberries* the progress of Mr Holt – a middle-aged solicitor, a bachelor who was almost, but not quite, out of the top drawer, and whose skill as a gossip meant you could 'ask him to dinner at a pinch'.

'To get a footing among the wives was more difficult in those late Victorian and Edwardian days. After some thought he decided to enter the charmed world of his ambition by the garden gate. Great ladies were taking up gardening. Mr Holt applied him-self to the science, read copiously, neglected no opportunity of picking up information, and in a few years made himself a first-rate authority on shrubs and flowers, from the wild flowers of a particular county or England to the rarest bulbs or slips from the Himalayas or the Andes…

To do him justice it must be said that the pursuit which he had taken up as a means to social improvement had finished by winning what heart he had. In spite of his snobbery, his pedantism, his insufferable egotism, a new blossom, a rare bulb would thrill him with a lover's emotion. As he had no garden of his own there was no fear of his competition. Great ladies rivalled each other in their efforts to get him for week-ends, for summer and Easter visits, for Christmas house-parties. Here he moved in complete happiness, amusing such guests as he did not irritate to madness, and making himself really useful in the garden, to the ill-concealed fury of the good Scotch head-gardeners.'

In *Wild Strawberries*, Lady Emily Leslie invited Mr Holt to come and stay, much to the annoyance of her children. To their double annoyance, another of his patronesses, Lady Norton, came to lunch. Lady Emily remembered meeting her 'at Chelsea, I think, or perhaps at Vincent Square, but I know it was the year the blue Meconopsis came out… She knows a great deal about poppies and is going to send me some seed.'

> She and Lady Emily spent some of the afternoon in the garden, exchanging names of flowers and promises of bulbs and seedlings. Mr Banister [the vicar] who came in to tea, was admitted as a fellow-gardener on the strength of some seeds which he had once brought back from the Holy Land.

Gardeners like Lady Emily were clearly interested in being part of an elite among whom rarities were discussed and exchanged. Not all of them were interested in arranging their plants in an aesthetically pleasing way. Harold Acton, attending a charity bazaar in Lady Battersea's garden sometime before 1914, was displeased. In *Memoirs of an Aesthete* (1948) he remembers:

> The flowers were superb, the lawns like carpets, yet I was disappointed. Evidently flowers alone make a garden in England. This was my first sight of herbaceous borders, a riot of colour which I failed to appreciate; they seemed to be stacked higgledy-piggledy, like counters at a country fair. One wandered beside them, attracted by a lupin here, a lobelia there, feeling more of a bee than a human being. It was appropriate enough for a bazaar, a thing of gaudy shreds and patches, but what would become of it in winter when the bazaar was over?

A new kind of house, a new kind of garden

The turn of the century was a good time for the fairly new profession of garden designer. Earlier, most large gardens had evolved gradually, with radical changes being made only at times when the house itself was altered. When a new generation inherited or bought the house, the new owners might ask their architect to modernize the garden along with the house. At other times, the head gardener, in consultation with the lady of the house, would be entrusted with making the alterations.

But in the late Victorian and Edwardian era, a new kind of house, built to suit the lifestyle of new industrialists and entrepreneurs, demanded a new kind of garden, and several designers turned their talents in this direction. Some were architects with a special interest in garden design. Sir Reginald Blomfield, Harold Peto and of course Sir Edwin Lutyens were in this category. Others became sought-after for their advice as a result of publishing books on the subject.

They included H. Avray Tipping, garden correspondent of *The Morning Post*, and Thomas Mawson, author of *The Art and Craft of Garden Making* (1900).

Mawson was largely self-educated, having left school at the age of 12 to work as office boy for an uncle who was a builder in Lancaster. He was a naturally skilled draughtsman, and was soon making working drawings for his uncle's business. Later, after a spell working as a landscape gardener in London, Thomas and his two brothers started the Lakeland Nurseries at Windermere in 1885, a business which gradually developed into a successful design, build and plant enterprise. Much of Mawson's work was local and a few examples can still be seen.

Much has been made of the argument that raged between advocates of a formal, architectural garden style and those who favoured the naturalistic style. Thomas Mawson had no difficulty in resolving the conflict. Most of his gardens are treated formally around the house and are designed to become progressively less formal until they merge with the surrounding landscape. This can be seen at Brockhole, Windermere, where the garden falls in a series of terraces with rose beds and herbaceous borders, to a wild flower meadow flanked by mature woodland. As the visitor progresses through the garden, fresh views open up to the lake and the Langdale Pikes, a range of hills. At nearby Graythwaite Hall Mawson used topiary to contrast with informal woodland and shrub planting. Of his work for the Cavendish family at Holker Hall in Cumbria, a pergola and balustrade survive.

Some of Mawson's clients were immensely successful industrialists and manufacturers, like Lord Leverhulme (soap) for whom Mawson made gardens at Rivington near Manchester, and at Thornton Manor, Cheshire, where his brief was to make 'a garden for promenading and walking'. Mawson's gardens for Reginald Cory (coal and shipping) at Dyffryn near Cardiff are currently being restored. They were, and still are, extensive, spacious, imposing and elaborately complex. There were paved terraces, a tennis lawn, a croquet lawn, a walled kitchen garden, a rose garden and a lake: almost obligatory features in a rich man's large garden of the period. But in this instance, designer and client seem to have enjoyed a fertile creative relationship, and to have had fun thinking up ideas. To the list they added a Pompeian garden in the Roman style, an Italian terrace, a cloister, a lavender court, heart garden, theatre garden, bathing-pool garden, dahlia garden and a large lily canal.

In fitting these diverse elements into a logical sequence within a coherent whole, Mawson showed his skill, dividing each enclosure from the next with yew hedges, contrasting open with enclosed, formal with informal, straight with serpentine. Reginald Cory was a keen and knowledgeable plantsman, and the gardens at Dyffryn are full of rare trees and shrubs. Not all their joint plans were executed. An observation tower was built, but ideas for a water pavilion and an underwater room for watching the fish in the lake were abandoned for practical reasons.

'The further …from the house the freer… the garden scheme.'

Mawson was also the choice as garden designer of the Mander family (paint) at Wightwick Manor in the West Midlands, now owned by The National Trust. Theodore Mander and his son Geoffrey both epitomized the philanthropic industrialist of their day. They were Liberal in their politics, devoutly Protestant in their religion, active in local government (Theodore became mayor of Wolverhampton), charitable, and interested in the arts. Theodore, born in 1853, ran a successful family business making paints and varnishes. He was a lay preacher and a member of the temperance movement, and also skilled in the gentlemanly pursuits of hunting, shooting and fishing.

Mander was also an admirer of Ruskin and Morris, and, in building and decorating his house, set out to put their ideas into practice. The Cheshire architect Edward Ould designed Wightwick Manor in the half-timbered 'Old English' style, taking late medieval architecture and craftsmanship as his model. Inside the house, Theodore and his wife Flora used the best examples they could find of modern design: wall coverings and fabrics by William Morris, ceramics by William de Morgan, stained glass by Charles Kempe. Theodore died in 1900 aged 47 and his son Geoffrey inherited the business, the house, and many of his father's sterling qualities, becoming a magistrate at the age of 24, and a Liberal MP in 1929. His wife Rosalie Glynn Grylls was a scholar of English literature. Together they collected Pre-Raphaelite paintings for the house, and it was they who developed the gardens as they are today.

Mawson drew up plans for the garden in 1904 and 1910 and, although they were never implemented in their entirety, much of the layout is as planned by Mawson. Sir Geoffrey and Lady Mander continued to clothe the bones of the garden, and alter it here and there, for 50 years. Mawson assigned equal importance to the views from the house across the garden and beyond, and to the views back towards the house from various parts of the garden, which is small scale and intimate compared to Mawson's work for Lord Leverhulme and Reginald Cory. Generous flights of steps descend from a paved, balustraded terrace across the main front of the house, to lawns with long vistas marked out with clipped yew cylinders or evergreen hedges.

Several principles that Mawson liked to follow are expressed at Wightwick: he wrote, 'the further we proceed from the house the freer should be the treatment of the details of the garden scheme.' And so it is here. Terraces and formal lawns provide an architectural setting for the house and orchards, watercourses and shrub groups in rough grass take the garden 'by easy gradation into the landscape beyond.'

In gardens 'of moderate dimensions' Mawson liked to make a yew alley or walk. At Wightwick there are two: the Long Walk between clipped yew hedges, with a seat made to Mawson's design at the end, and the Yew and Holly Walk, where Irish yews alternate with 'Golden Queen' variegated holly trees. This walk leads to the Grigg House, a rustic summerhouse thatched with heather from the Long Mynd in Shropshire. Sir Geoffrey Mander liked to refer to the Yew and Holly Walk as the Addison Walk. He enjoyed literary references, and made Poets' Gardens below the terrace, with beds of acanthus and astrantia for Shelley, plants from Kelmscott given by William Morris's daughter May, and beds of plants from Dickens's garden at Gad's Hill in Kent, and Tennyson's at Farringford on the Isle of Wight.

'Even the hens were fed to time': Rachel Morris (née Lander)

Before the Manders built Wightwick Manor they had lived in a large semi-detached house in Wolverhampton where their business was situated. It must have had much in common with 'Sunnycroft', a suburban villa, also now owned by The National Trust, on the outskirts of the market town of Wellington in Shropshire. Sunnycroft was built in 1880 for a local brewer, and acquired in the early 1890s by Mary Slaney, the widow of a wine merchant. She extended the house and on her death it went to her brother in law, J.V.T. Lander, a mildly eccentric Wellington solicitor sporting a large white moustache and a white bowler hat. The Landers remained at 'Sunnycroft' for three generations and J.V.T.'s granddaughter Joan Lander left it to The National Trust with a generous endowment; they received it on her death in 1997.

The 5-acre garden at 'Sunnycroft' is remarkable for its well-preserved ordinariness. Until the end of World War II there were many such houses around every market town. But their position on the edge of town meant that their sites were highly desirable for development, and in most places they are now occupied by housing estates or light industry. So the garden at 'Sunnycroft', for all its ordinariness, is a rare survival.

From photographs and the memories of Joan Lander's sister Rachel, a picture of life at 'Sunnycroft', changing very little over the generations, can be built up. On weekdays J.V.T. walked to his office wearing his white bowler hat, with a carnation from his conservatory in his buttonhole. Sundays were very strictly observed: church, perhaps a drive after lunch (which often consisted of sheep's head in parsley sauce), and hymn singing around the piano in the evening. The women of the family were not allowed to knit on a Sunday except during wartime. If the weather was suitable, the children were able to escape into the garden, where their grandfather might help them find birds' nests; there was always a robin's nest in a cannon parked under a group of lime trees.

Another favourite outdoor occupation was feeding the hens and collecting the eggs. For chicken food, leftovers were boiled up in a big iron pot on the kitchen range. Nothing was wasted; as well as the hens there were pigs in their sties beside the stables to take care of food scraps. Much of the garden was useful rather than ornamental. The chicken run and orchards were out of sight behind a row of limes and a laurel hedge. There were kitchen-garden plots for vegetables and soft fruit beyond the Wellingtonia trees that formed an avenue up the drive. Besides the stables and coach house there were a gardener's cottage next to the pigsties; a range of buildings incorporating a boilerhouse, cold store and log shed; dog kennels; and a lodge at the end of the drive. All contributed to a household that was close to being self-sufficient in food. At times of glut, eggs would be preserved in crocks of water glass (sodium silicate in water), beans would be salted, and other fruit and vegetables bottled in toughened glass Kilner jars, or made into jam and pickles. Apples from the orchard would be harvested and stored in the cellar on trays labelled 'Epicure', 'Lady Sudeley', 'Laxton's Superb', 'Edward VII' and 'Bramley'.

There was a tomato house, a vinery and a splendid conservatory designed by R. Halliday & Sons who also made the Rothschilds' glasshouses at Waddesdon Manor. The conservatory had rockwork and ferns planted around its perimeter and staging above this for camellias, carnations, geraniums and arum lilies. The 'Sunnycroft' garden was protected from the road by a belt of trees and a long paddock where two Jersey cows, Molly and Isobel, grazed. Between the paddock and the verandah fronting the south side of the house was a large lawn with space for croquet near the house and two tennis courts beyond. West of the house, in front of the conservatory, was a formal rose garden. During the summer there would be other sports and games as well as tennis and croquet, tea parties and, as family photographs show, learning to ride a bicycle. But presumably, none of these recreations was allowed on a Sunday.

Sundays apart, a time had arrived when a garden of a reasonable size might be considered to be all things to all men. Dean Hole, the genial rosarian, lists some of the possibilities in *Our Gardens* in 1899:

I asked a schoolboy, in the sweet summer-tide 'what he thought a garden
was for?' and he said *Strawberries*. His younger sister suggested *Croquet*
and the elder *Garden-parties*. The brother from Oxford made a prompt
declaration in favour of *Lawn Tennis and Cigarettes*, but he was rebuked by
a solemn senior, who wore spectacles, and more back hair than is usual
with males, and was told that 'a garden was designed for botanical
research, and for the classification of plants.' He was about to demonstrate
the differences between the *Acoty-* and the *Monocoty-ledonous* divisions, when
the collegian remembered an engagement elsewhere.
I repeated my question to a middle-aged nymph, who wore a feathered hat
of noble proportions over a loose green tunic with a silver belt, and she
replied with a rapturous disdain of the ignorance which presumed to ask

*Herbaceous borders flanking a gravel walk in the garden of 'Sunnycroft', Shropshire, a typical
suburban house occupied by a prosperous middle-class family. The garden and the house,
built in 1880, are now owned by The National Trust.*

'What is a garden for? For the soul, sir, for the soul of the poet! For visions of the invisible, for grasping the intangible, for hearing the inaudible, for exaltations… above the miserable dullness of common life into the splendid regions of imagination and romance.'

A capacious gentleman informed me that nothing in horticulture touched him so sensibly as green peas and new potatoes, and he spoke with so much cheerful candour that I could not be angry…

I met with many who held flowers in high estimation, not for their own sake, not for the loveliness and perfect beauty of their colour, their fragrance, and their form, not because even Solomon in all his glory was not arrayed like one of these, but because they were the most effective decorations of their window-sills, apartments, and tables, and the most becoming embellishments for their own personal display.

Not every family had a garden, but, a little further down the social and income scale from the owners of 'Sunnycroft', residents without gardens of their own were able, in some towns, to own or rent pleasure gardens separate from their houses. The garden need only be modest in size to provide fulfillment:

… let no one suppose that the beauty of a garden depends on its acreage, or on the amount of money spent upon it. Nay, one would almost prefer a small garden plot, so as to ensure that ample justice shall be done to it. In a small garden there is less fear of dissipated effort, more chance of making friends with its inmates, more time to spare to heighten the beauty of its effects.

Garden-craft Old and New, John Sedding, 1890

Hill Close Gardens in Linen Street, Warwick, are a rare survival of such gardens. They are being gradually cleared of a century of rubbish, brambles and other scrub, and restored. There were about 20 plots on a site of about 2.5 acres, each up to 27 x 24m (90 x 80ft), surrounded with high hedges, and entered by a lockable gate. They could be rented or bought. Each was laid out differently, in a way fairly similar to the conventional back garden of a terraced house, with lawns, paths, terraces and flower beds. Many had substantial brick-built summer-houses with tiled roofs, some of which had a basement or cellar, and a fireplace and chimney, so tea could be brewed, and simple meals cooked for picnics and parties. Fruit and vegetables were grown, as well as flowers, and several rare old fruit trees have survived. These little plots must have given great pleasure on

Sundays and on summer evenings to shopkeepers and other urban business people who perhaps lived above their trade premises, but had no garden attached to their dwelling.

'a nice little back garden which runs down to the railway'
The Pooter family in George and Weedon Grossmith's *The Diary of a Nobody* (1892) could have done with such a garden. Charles and Carrie Pooter's house, 'The Laurels', Brickfield Terrace, Holloway was

> A nice six-roomed residence, not counting basement, with a front
> breakfast-parlour. We have a little front garden and there is a flight
> of ten steps up to the front door… We have a nice little back garden
> which runs down to the railway. We were rather afraid of the noise of the
> trains at first, but the landlord said we should not notice them after a bit,
> and took £2 off the rent. He was certainly right; and beyond the cracking
> of the garden wall at the bottom, we have suffered no inconvenience.

After this initial description, the garden at 'The Laurels' doesn't get mentioned much. On 8 April Mr Pooter took a walk round the garden and discovered a beautiful spot for sowing mustard-and-cress and radishes, and a week later he

> Spent the whole of the afternoon in the garden, having this morning
> picked up at a bookstall for five-pence a capital little book, in good
> condition, on *Gardening*. I procured and sowed some half-hardy annuals in
> what I fancy will be a warm, sunny border. I thought of a joke, and called
> out Carrie. Carrie came out rather testy, I thought. I said: 'I have just
> discovered we have got a lodging-house.' She replied 'How do you mean?'
> I said: 'look at the *boarders*.' Carrie said: 'Is that all you wanted me for?' I said:
> 'Any other time you would have laughed at my little pleasantry.'

Things began to go wrong in August, when new neighbours moved in. Mr Pooter recorded on Sunday the 26th, 'while walking round the garden in my tall hat this afternoon a "throw-down" cracker was deliberately aimed at my hat, and exploded on it like a percussion cap.' On 28 August he 'found a large brick in the middle bed of geraniums, evidently come from next door.'

This persecution by his neighbours must have robbed Mr Pooter of any pleasure he might have had in harvesting his mustard-and-cress and radishes, and contemplating his half-hardy annuals.

10 BETWEEN THE WARS

Adapting Nature 265

T HE ENGLISH LOVE AFFAIR with gardens often begins in childhood. Frances Hodgson Burnett's much-loved classic *The Secret Garden*, written in 1911, tells of the love of three children for a particular garden. The story, provoking both laughter and tears, is told in film and television versions as well as on the printed page, and offers comfort to every lonely, disaffected child. Its hero-ine is Mary, a spoilt, bad-tempered, unloved orphan. She finds her way into an abandoned walled garden:

> It was the sweetest, most mysterious-looking place anyone could imagine.
> The high walls which shut it in were covered with the leafless stems of
> climbing roses, which were so thick that they were matted together...
> Everything was strange and silent, and she seemed to be hundreds of miles
> away from anyone, but somehow she did not feel lonely at all.

Mary sets about reviving the garden with the help of Colin, her chronically weak and sickly cousin, and Dickon, a robust, sensible country boy who under-stands plants. The three children tend the plants, sow seeds and watch the

---

Even an overgrown plot with a semi-derelict shelter may provide a peaceful retreat from the cares of everyday life, blurring the distinction between weeds and garden flowers

miracle of growth. By the end of the story, thanks to the garden's magic, the children have become fast friends; Mary is nice; Colin is healthy; and their gruff, austere grandfather has grown fond of them and they of him.

In real life, many distinguished gardeners have traced the origin of their passion back to early childhood years. Gertrude Jekyll's Damascene revelation came from a dandelion seen close up in Kensington Gardens at the age of four. Russell Page's imagination was first fired by a visit to the flower tent at a local agricultural show. But a taste for gardening is not always formed so early in life, and it is a mistake to think that children have an innate desire to grow plants. It is worth pointing them in the right direction by providing packets of mustard and cress to sow on a damp face flannel, or a broad bean in a jam jar where the roots and shoots can be seen increasing daily, but grownups should not be disappointed if these measures fail to produce results.

One or two generations ago, all country children had a first-hand knowledge of plants. There was always a jam jar of sticky chestnut buds or wild flowers on the nature table in their classroom. Before the advent of school buses, the journey to school was on foot through country lanes fringed with chin-high cow parsley in summer and with dry, frost-rimed grasses in winter. There was time, on the way home, to pull the petals off a daisy ('loves me, loves me not'), to hold a buttercup under your chin to see if you liked butter, to cram a few blackberries into your mouth, or to pop snowberries between finger and thumb.

To most children in town or country, the pleasure of a garden lay simply in being out of doors. However small the garden might be, it still represented greater space and freedom than indoor rooms where children were often in the way, and under the feet of grownups. 'Go and play outside' offered a chance to

*An illustration by Charles Robinson from Frances Hodgson Burnett's 'The Secret Garden', 1911,
an enduring story of three children and their love for a neglected garden: 'He would lie
on the grass "watching things growing"'.*

escape into a world where adults were temporarily excluded. Small children are closer to the ground than grownups, and it is the floor of the garden that appeals to them most. In *The Secret Garden*, when Mary first unlocked the door and found herself inside the walled garden, neglected for ten years, she saw sharp little pale green points sticking out of the black earth: 'She bent very close to them and sniffed the fresh scent of the damp earth. She liked it very much.'

Children like to be in close contact with the earth, squatting down to make mud pies, mixing, if there is no handy pool or puddle, spit with dust. Pebbles, snail shells and twigs can be arranged to make miniature landscapes. There are ants to be watched and poked with twigs to divert them from their course as they scurry purposefully about; beetles crawl through a forest of grass stalks. There are worms to be dissected and daisy chains to be made. Daisies also serve as doll-sized poached eggs, and cow parsley stalks as rhubarb. Children soon learn that the caterpillars of cabbage white butterflies are found on cabbages, and box edging is the place to look for big, Roman snails. Chanting the mantra

Snail, snail, come out of your hole
Or else I will beat you as black as a coal

might have the desired result, causing the creature to expand and unfurl, swivelling first one and then the other eye on its telescopic stalk.

For children, the point of a garden was never that it should look attractive and well-cared for. Quite the reverse. Children prefer the unkempt mystery of Mary Lennox's Secret Garden, or the Sleeping Beauty's bower. As they grow beyond the toddler stage and become more adventurous, what pleases them most is an overgrown area of shrubs where a secret den can become the background to games of fantasy and make-believe. A neglected corner of the garden can be a treasure island, a pirates' ship or Never-Never Land. From 1904 onwards J.M. Barrie's play *Peter Pan* was performed every year, and an increasingly wide and varied stream of literature written specially for children flowed out to water their fertile young imaginations.

If there were enough children, a game of tag could be organized, one child being chosen as 'it' by an eliminating rhyme like 'Eeny meeny miny mo', 'one potato, two potato' or 'ip, dip'. There were variations on the tag theme, like 'off-ground tag' or 'colour tag' when 'it' would call out a colour and run to catch any player who was unable to touch the colour in time. 'Touch blue!'- anchusa, per-haps, or love-in-a-mist; pink, yellow, red or white were easy flower colours to find in granny's flowerbeds. When 'it' became desperate, he might call 'Touch sky-blue pink with a rainbow border,' answered by an indignant chorus of 'Cheat! Cheat! Cheat!' Through such games, familiarity with plants seeped into children's subconscious.

As we have already seen, gardens were also the setting for organized games for adults, and where there was enough space, lawns were levelled for tennis, badminton and croquet. Provision was also made for children's recreation. There might be a Wendy house beyond the lawn under a tree, and a swing hung nearby from ropes attached to a sturdy horizontal branch. A plank balanced across a stout log served as a seesaw. In well-off families, scooters and tricycles were given as Christmas and birthday presents. Child-sized wheelbarrows and garden tools might also be given by parents, grandparents or godparents anxious to inculcate a love of gardening at an early age, and each child might have his or her own little plot of ground, their own garden.

Most children's enthusiasm for cultivating their garden was short-lived. Keeping it weeded and tidy was a tiresome chore and grownups had to offer bribes to get the work done. But for a few it became a real passion. Packets of seeds could be bought at Woolworths for a few pence each, with colourful pictures of flowers on the outside and names like Sweet sultan, Love-lies-bleeding, Love-in-a-mist and Bells of Ireland. The results were nearly always disappointing, but the pleasure was in the anticipation, and the lack of success invariably forgotten when seed-sowing time came round again.

'… those Fresh Air London children'

Not all children had access to a garden, although charitable organizations sometimes provided for some of the poorest from city slums to spend a few days in the country. Under such a scheme Gladys, the 'girlfriend' in P.G. Wodehouse's story 'Lord Emsworth and the Girlfriend' (1935), came to Blandings village.

Lord Emsworth's sister, Lady Constance, had spoilt his breakfast kipper for him by reminding him that it was August Bank Holiday, the day of the village fête, when 'he was not allowed to potter pleasantly about his gardens in an old coat; forces beyond his control shoved him into a stiff collar and a top hat and told him to go out and be genial.' Lady Constance reminded him,

> … you have to go to the village this morning to judge the cottage
> gardens… I think I will come to the village with you. There are a number
> of those Fresh Air London children staying there now, and I must warn
> them to behave properly when they come to the Fête this afternoon…
> McAllister says he found one of them in the gardens the other day, picking

his flowers... By the way, McAllister was speaking to me again last night about that gravel path through the yew alley. He seems very keen on it.'
'Gravel path!' Lord Emsworth stiffened through the whole length of his stringy body. Nature, he had always maintained, intended a yew alley to be carpeted with a mossy growth... he personally was dashed if he was going to have men with Clydeside accents and faces like dissipated potatoes coming along and mutilating that lovely expanse of green velvet.
'Gravel path, indeed! Why not asphalt? Why not a few hoardings with advertisements of liver pills and a filling-station? That's what the man would really like.'
...[But] except for that kink about gravel paths, Angus McAllister was a head gardener in a thousand, and he needed him.
The task of judging the floral displays in the cottage gardens of the little village of Blandings Parva was one to which Lord Emsworth had looked forward with pleasurable anticipation... But now... he judged the cottage gardens with a distrait eye. It was only when he came to the last on his list that anything like animation crept into his demeanour. This, he perceived, peering over its rickety fence, was not at all a bad little garden. It demanded closer inspection. He unlatched the gate and pottered in.

As Lord Emsworth bent to smell the wallflowers in the little garden, a mongrel dog attacked him. It only desisted when Gladys, a small girl of about 12, came out of the cottage and cried 'Hoy!' They conversed, and the friendship between the peer and the small girl was cemented when he discovered that she had picked a bunch of flowers in the garden of Blandings Castle that morning, been chased by McAllister and 'copped 'im on the shin wiv a stone.'

That afternoon, Lord Emsworth sought sanctuary from the fête in a cowshed, where he found Gladys snivelling in a corner, having been shut up there by Lady Constance for pinching 'two buns, two jem-sengwiches, two apples and a slicer cake.' They were for her brother Ern who had bitten Lady Constance on the leg that morning and was therefore forbidden to come to the fête. Lord Emsworth rewarded Gladys with tea in the castle library, and got Beach, the butler, to put together a bag of goodies for her to take home to her brother Ern. He then asked if there was anything else Ern might like.

A wistful look came into Gladys's eyes.
'Could he 'ave some flarze?'

'Certainly,' said Lord Emsworth. 'Certainly, certainly, certainly. By all means. Just what I was about to suggest my – er – what is flarze?'
Beach, the linguist, interpreted.
'I think the young lady means flowers, your lordship.'
'Yes, sir. Thank you, sir. Flarze.'
Flarze! It would be idle to deny that those gardens contained flarze in full measure. They were bright with Achillea, Bignonia Radicans, Campanula, Digitalis, Euphorbia, Funkia, Gypsophila, Helianthus, Iris, Liatris, Monarda, Phlox Drummondi, Salvia, Thalictrum, Vinca and Yucca. But the devil of it was that Angus McAllister would have a fit if they were picked…
As a general rule, the procedure for getting flowers out of Angus McAllister was as follows. You waited till he was in one of his rare moods of complaisance, then you led the conversation gently round to the subject of interior decoration, and then choosing your moment, you asked if he could possible spare a few to be put in vases. The last thing you thought of doing was to charge in and start helping yourself.

For a moment, discretion seemed the better part of valour to Lord Emsworth, but he pulled himself together and bravely asserted his right to do what he liked with his own flowers,

Oh, and by the way, McAllister… that matter of the gravel path through the yew alley… I won't have it. Not on any account. Mutilate my beautiful moss with a beastly gravel path? Make an eyesore of the loveliest spot in one of the finest and oldest gardens in the United Kingdom… Try to remember, McAllister, as you work in the gardens of Blandings Castle, that you are not back in Glasgow, laying out recreation grounds.

Blandings Castle and its garden are fictional, but have the ring of truth about them. Scottish head gardeners really were considered the best, and their employers really were afraid of thwarting them in case they should leave and go to work for a rival. McAllister was as important to Lord Emsworth in his garden as Anatole was to Aunt Dahlia in her kitchen.

The self-sufficient way of life in large country houses lingered on after World War I. Peter Dryden remembers that at Canon's Ashby, his family home in Northamptonshire: 'Venison came to the table whenever deer were killed, the Drydens liked theirs hung to ripen, the maids ate theirs fresh. As far as possible the household lived on their own produce, cows were kept to provide milk and butter; the pigs killed for bacon and hams, then the kitchen garden provided an abundant supply of all sorts of fruit and vegetables.'

'…gloved hands grubbed in the rockeries'

But the pattern of land ownership was changing. Advances in farm machinery meant that fewer workers were needed on the land. Cottages formerly occupied by farm labourers were now owned by commuters with city jobs, or by week-enders. Their gardens were usually maintained in the traditional cottage-garden style, but self-consciousness crept in: difficult to define, and not necessarily un-desirable, but sometimes erring on the side of twee-ness. The gardens of village houses and medium-sized country houses were changing too. Evelyn Waugh describes the change, in *Put out More Flags* (1942), with sharp disapproval:

> Most of Mrs Sothill's Garden-Party-Only list were people of late middle age who, on retirement from work in the cities or abroad, had bought the smaller manor houses and the larger rectories; houses that once had been supported on the rent of a thousand acres and a dozen cottages now went with a paddock and a walled garden… the lawns were close mown, fertilized and weeded, and from their splendid surface rose clumps of pampas grass and yucca; year in, year out, gloved hands grubbed in the rockeries, gloved hands snipped in the herbaceous border… in the dead depths of winter… ice stood thick on the lily ponds, and the kitchen gardens at night were a litter of sacking.

It was Waugh's stock in trade to sneer, and no doubt many gardens did display the uniformity and lack of taste of which he complains. But at the same time, a brilliant new age of gardening was dawning. Among the manor houses and rectories changing hands were houses such as Sissinghurst Castle in Kent and Hidcote Manor in Gloucestershire, where wonderful gardens were being made. At Sissinghurst, Harold Nicolson and his wife Vita Sackville-West owned rather more than 'a paddock and a walled garden': 250 acres of farmland to be precise, as well as 10 acres of garden and grounds around the house. Lawrence Johnston's garden at Hidcote covered about the same area, and was also at the heart of a home farm. These two gardens, with Christopher Lloyd's garden at Great Dixter, East Sussex, are probably the three most famous gardens made in the twentieth century, and are still top of the garden-visiting league.

Each of these gardens was made with the primary objective of satisfying the owners' love of plants in general and flowering plants in particular. A broad and deep knowledge of plants, how and when they perform, and what their cultural requirements are, were essential to this kind of garden making. To make gardens of such quality, the owners also needed a strongly creative imagination and impeccable taste in arranging their plants to provide effective harmonies and contrasts of colour, form and texture. Vita Sackville-West, Lawrence Johnson and Christopher Lloyd had all these qualities and made gardens that, at some deep level difficult to analyse, appeal to the heart and emotions as well as to the senses. They have been tremendously influential, elements from them being copied in smaller gardens with great enthusiasm for over half a century.

These three gardens and a few others like them (Rodmarton Manor in Gloucestershire comes to mind, developed in the Cotswolds Arts and Crafts style by the Biddulphs from 1909 onwards; Kiftsgate Court next door to Hidcote; Cothay Manor in Somerset) ushered in an age of hands-on owner-gardeners and owner-designers, each with their individual and idiosyncratic style. Hidcote and Sissinghurst tend to be bracketed together. Superficially, they have much in common, being laid out as a series of separate enclosures, for which the phrase 'garden rooms' has been coined. The Nicolsons planned Sissinghurst as a series of gardens connected by walks 'as the rooms of an enormous house would open off the arterial corridors'. In style, both Sissinghurst and Hidcote adhere to Vita Sackville-West's principle, expressed in her poem 'The Garden':

> Gardens should be romantic, but severe.
> Strike your strong lines, and take no further care
> Of such extravagance as pours the rose
> In wind-blown fountains down the broken walls,
> In gouts of blood, in dripping flower-falls,
> Or flings the jasmine where the walls enclose,
> Separate garths, a miniature surprise.

This principle, of luxuriant, informal planting within a strictly formal layout, has produced what may well endure as the classic English gardening style, adaptable for gardens of any size on any soil with any aspect. It is a style well suited to the English character and taste, and to our climate, at least until global warming takes full effect.

Hidcote and Sissinghurst also have in common the custodianship of The National Trust. A garden under the management of an institution can never have quite the same atmosphere as a garden still evolving under its owner's care,

no matter how much attention is given to preserving the former owner's ideas and style. The National Trust has the impossible task of setting a high standard of maintenance (both Sissinghurst and Hidcote are immaculate) and providing access and other facilities for the many thousands of visitors who flock there year after year, while preserving the character of the garden. Inevitably it is diminished a little. At both Sissinghurst and Hidcote the balance between formality and luxuriance is a little out of kilter, the rigid framework of the garden getting the better of the exuberant planting. Vita Sackville-West's roses no longer pour 'in wind-blown fountains down the broken walls'.

One of the garden 'rooms' at Hidcote Manor in Gloucestershire, a hugely influential garden of almost legendary status, made by Lawrence Johnston as 'a wild garden in a formal setting'. It has been in the ownership of The National Trust since 1948.

There is no such problem of institutionalization at Great Dixter, where the garden continues to evolve under the creative care of Christopher Lloyd, who was born there in 1921. Dixter shares with Hidcote and Sissinghurst a structure of linked enclosures, planned by that master of the art of laying out gardens, Edwin Lutyens, for Nathaniel Lloyd, Christopher's father. Lutyens also altered and extended the house, integrating it with a medieval hall moved from another site and linking it to outbuildings, thereby creating a characteristically integrated house and garden. The planting is all Christopher Lloyd's, and expresses an exuberant and uninhibited love of brilliant colours and strong forms. He writes in the guide book to Great Dixter, 'I have no segregated colour schemes. In fact, I take it as a challenge to combine every sort of colour effectively.'

Things are changing all the time in this garden, and it should really be described at the end of this book where the twentieth century meets the twenty-first. But because of its long-lasting heyday, it is here. Christopher Lloyd's most recent design adventure has been to turn Lutyens's rose garden into 'The Exotic Garden', full of lush, tropical-looking foliage and orange, scarlet and yellow dahlias and canna lilies. 'This has been a lot of fun' he writes, reminding us what gardening is all about.

It is our great good fortune that Vita Sackville-West was a writer and Christopher Lloyd still is, so we can not only visit and admire their gardens but also understand the ideas behind them. Vita, after earlier articles in the *Evening Standard*, *The Spectator* and the *New Statesman*, settled down postwar to writing a weekly column in *The Observer* for 15 years and also gave talks on the radio. She wrote with the authority of practical experience, but not in the didactic style of some experts. She described her experiments with pruning and feeding plants, her ideas for colour combinations, her close-up observations of flowers and scents, the poetic associations of plants and sometimes her own romantic feelings about them, in a direct, conversational style. Her rapport with readers was remarkable, generating sacks of letters and presents of seeds, roots and cuttings.

Sissinghurst was open to visitors, who were referred to by the Nicolsons as the 'shillingses'. They would often find Vita on hand to answer questions and discuss gardening matters with that instant camaraderie that gardeners can establish. She would garden in long earrings and a lacy shirt worn with a corduroy jacket, gamekeeper's breeches and top-boots laced up to the knee, with a dog at her heel: 'Lady Chatterley and her lover rolled into one.' The garden at Sissinghurst was large and complex, and the Nicolsons employed several gardeners. But Vita bitterly resented any suggestion that she was an 'armchair, library fireside gardener'. In one *Observer* article she assured a correspondent who implied as much, that, 'for the last forty years of my life I have broken my back, my finger-nails, and sometimes my heart, in the practical pursuit of my favourite occupation.' Such total commitment to gardening inspires confidence in readers and creates a bond between writer and reader.

Christopher Lloyd's books and his articles in *Country Life* and other magazines are shot through with the same urgent sense of shared enthusiasm. He has strong opinions, forcefully expressed, and is always ready to challenge received opinion. His style is straightforward and conversational. *The Well-Tempered Garden* (1970) is probably his best-known book. In its 'Preface' he expresses his feelings about gardening:

> There is room for many approaches to gardening and they give us the satisfaction of expressing ourselves. Ours, in its humble way, is an art as well as a craft. At the same time it keeps us in touch with the earth, the seasons, and with that complex of interrelated forces both animate and inanimate, which we call nature. It is a humanising occupation. Gardening has been the mainspring of my life and I have been lucky in my opportunities. In this book I have exploited most of the ingredients which, in my case, combine to make for happy gardening. Sometimes the reader may be incited to exclaim: 'what a lot of trouble!' or 'who wants to go through all that?' But however labour-saving you make your hobby, you will never get more out of it than you put in. Now and again it seems worth taking that extra bit of trouble that brings in its train some rather exciting result. You feel you have got somewhere. Effort is only trouble-some when you are bored. *The Well-Tempered Garden* is for gardeners who have not been dragged into this pursuit but are here because they love it.

Among the topics covered in the book are the pleasures of weeding on your hands and knees, described so persuasively that the reader is taken back to the blissful mud-pie stage of childhood. In this book, Christopher Lloyd also tackles the question of how to use the pampas grass so despised by Evelyn Waugh. His advice is to avoid self-conscious single specimens, and plant in triangular groups of three, filling in the foreground with lower-growing plants having contrasting foliage. '*Melianthus major* would be just right if you can be bothered with it, or the large-leaved annual tobacco plant, *Nicotiana sylvestris*.'

It is hard to analyse what makes the best of the owner-designed gardens so deeply satisfying. It may be the owner's singleness of purpose in working to-wards his or her vision. It may be the evolutionary nature of a design constantly under scrutiny from an eye in search of improvements. Continuity of care must surely be a factor. Professional designers, however skilful, seldom achieve such fine results. They come and look, draw the plans, implement them and go away again, returning initially once or twice a year to tweak the design. But the owner, on a daily, or almost daily basis, is able to develop an intimate knowledge of the garden in all its parts and at all seasons. The owner 'cares for' the garden in both senses of the phrase, and his care is absorbed into the earth and returned again in an invisible mist of wonder and contentment to envelope the visitor.

'The English Garden Style at its best'

Although it is difficult for The National Trust, English Heritage and other impersonal bodies to foster this atmosphere of contentment, it is not impossible. One National Trust garden where it can be strongly felt is that of The Courts, at Holt in Wiltshire.

The handsome stone Georgian house is on the site of former law courts in the village of Holt in the Avon valley east of Bath. It was built by John Phelps, a Quaker cloth merchant, in about 1720, with a cloth mill adjacent to it. The mill was powered by a stream running through the site, and produced fine West of England broadcloth. The mill no longer exists, but the stream and the ponds fed by it are important elements in the garden.

The 7-acre garden dates from 1900 when the architect Sir George Hastings bought the house. He laid out the bones of the garden, making paved paths and terraces, building the neo-Georgian conservatory and the classical garden temple, and planting hedges of yew, box and holly. The detailed planting of the garden only got under way after 1922 when Major Clarence Goff and his wife Lady Cecilie bought the house. She was the daughter of the Earl of Ancaster and grew up at Grimsthorpe Castle in Lincolnshire, where there were extensive formal gardens and a park designed by 'Capability' Brown. Her interest in plants and gardens may have been inspired by her childhood home. At any rate, she set about clothing Hastings's garden framework, concentrating on the harmonizing and contrasting effects of flower colour and texture. Today, the planting is adventurous and modern, but in sympathy with Lady Cecilie's intentions.

The garden is L-shaped but back to front, making the mirror-image of an L, with the house situated at the angle. The stream, contained in a rill crossed by

Christopher Lloyd's garden at Great Dixter in East Sussex: a strong framework of hedges and topiary is the background to borders of brilliant colour, with Aster 'Little Carlow', Plectranthus argentatus and Rudbeckia fulgida var. deamii.

narrow stone bridges, runs southeast from the house, along the short arm of the L, feeding a long, rectangular lily pond and a more or less kidney-shaped pond beyond, formerly the dye pool for the cloth mill. The garden is entered through a tunnel of closely planted pleached limes leading to the house. Hectic colour schemes include the Hot Bed planted in orange, red and yellow backed by *Cotinus coggyria* 'Foliis Purpureis', and bright astilbes beside the water. Open lawns and green topiary provide a cool contrast.

Throughout the garden, structure and secure anchorage are provided by yew and box clipped into billowing, organic shapes. Lady Cecilie's raised terrace, leading from the conservatory, has tall metal columns clothed with the striking foliage of *Vitis coignetiae* and *Vitis vinifera* 'Purpurea.' A parallel walk is flanked with tall cones of clipped yew. Elsewhere, there are secret, shady corners where ferns and hellebores arch over a small pond, or water drips from a spout in a wall. There is no visitor centre, no tearoom, no shop. The Courts does not suffer, as Sissinghurst and Hidcote do, from visitor fatigue, and so the atmosphere is retained intact.

'…the coming of steel and reinforced concrete'

The gardens we have looked at were created between the wars for period houses. Great Dixter was a medieval hall house, Sissinghurst Castle and Hidcote Manor were Tudor, and The Courts, Georgian. And the gardens, although full of new ideas, were appropriate to the houses. But what kind of gardens did modern houses have in the 1920s and 1930s, in the Jazz Age, the age of Art Deco?

The Modern Garden by G.C. Taylor, published by *Country Life* in 1936 with revised editions in 1937, 1946 and 1949, showed the gardens of substantial country and suburban houses, illustrated with black-and-white photographs. Although the locations are not identified, many of the houses shown are recognizable as Lutyens's work, including Hestercombe in Somerset (1906), Folly Farm in Berkshire (1912) and Gledstone Hall in Yorkshire (1922–23). The gardens are laid out with formal terraces and spacious lawns; there are sunken, paved gardens with lily ponds and rills, pergolas and rustic summerhouses. They are in a style we think of today as quintessentially Edwardian, rather than of the '20s. In his introduction to the book Taylor mentioned the exciting opportunities presented by new architecture using concrete, steel and glass, but it is only in the introduction that he illustrates Modern Movement architecture. The houses shown were designed in a style which today we might call 'minimalist'. They consisted of sculptural, stepped blocks and drums of white concrete, the walls broken by horizontal, rectangular windows.

One of the houses illustrated was 'Joldwyns' in Surrey, designed in 1930 by Oliver Hill. Sadly the house has since been demolished. It sat into a slope, with its crisp, clean angles and curves like a monumental sculpture against a background of dark, massed pine trees. Modern architecture was often spoilt by having an inappropriate traditional garden tacked on, but at 'Joldwyns' the house and garden were fully integrated into the landscape with sweeping retaining walls of *in situ* concrete construction, balconies, paved sitting areas, circular steps of white concrete, and an austere rectangular pool. As garden historian and author Jane Brown explains in *The Art and Architecture of English Gardens*, both house and garden were designed for sun-worship and for enjoying varied views of the surrounding landscape. Jane Brown draws a convincing parallel between the spare, simple, outward-looking Modern Movement garden and the eighteenth-century landscape park. In *The Modern Garden* G.C. Taylor pays lip service to modernity:

> Now, with the coming of steel and reinforced concrete that has enabled us so completely to revise our traditional idea of a house, it would appear possible that structural work in formal garden design and treatment, such as terraces, walls and pools, will undergo changes that will remove it far from conventional English style.

The idea didn't catch on, partly because industrial and residential development left less and less landscape on which to gaze, and partly because planning authorities did not look kindly on applications to build private houses in steel and concrete. But the overriding reason was that most house owners wanted a garden they could work in. They wanted to put on their gardening gloves and snip and weed and plant and stake.

Most of Taylor's book caters for this majority, with references to Robinson and Jekyll, and chapters on the herbaceous border, the rock and water garden and the rose garden. He offered no advice on how to fit a tennis lawn or swimming pool into the garden, although the age of Betjemanesque golden sports girls had begun. The most innovative section was the chapter on 'The Wild and Woodland Garden'.

> For some years now there has been a growing movement among gardeners towards what is called wild and woodland gardening… a form of gardening where natural rather than artificial laws are followed, where nothing is evolved on geometrical or symmetrical lines, but where the bones of the design are provided by the natural features of the site,

and clothed and enhanced by an appropriate and well-disposed plant-furnishing....

If its conception was due to the imagination and designs of such pioneers as Miss Gertrude Jekyll and Mr. William Robinson, its translation into practice has been made possible, and has come about all the more rapidly, through the many trophies in the form of trees, shrubs and hardy plants that have reached us from the various plant-hunting expeditions of the last fifty years.

The illustrations show extensive stands of foxgloves, astilbes, funkias (hostas), blue meconopsis and *Lilium giganteum*. It is gardening at its grandest and most expansive, not suitable for everyman's semidetached or terraced garden, nor for his pocket.

The flowers that bloom in the spring, tra la

One wild garden made at this time, and made for a modern house, was at Coleton Fishacre in Devon. Mr. Rupert and Lady Dorothy D'Oyly Carte spotted the site for their house from the sea, while sailing in their yacht. It is situated at the head of a narrow valley running southwards to the sea, watered by a stream, very like the ravines of the great Cornish gardens created farther to the west a century earlier. Rupert D'Oyly Carte was the son of Richard D'Oyly Carte, Gilbert and Sullivan's opera impresario and owner of the Savoy Theatre, Savoy Hotel and Claridges. Rupert inherited his father's wealth and business interests.

In the 1920s he and his wife commissioned the architect Oswald Milne, a pupil of Lutyens, to design their new seaside house. It is comfortable and unpretentious, positioned to take full advantage of the south aspect and views to the sea. The outside of the house is traditional and unobtrusive. Being faced with stone quarried from the valley below, it sits comfortably in the landscape. Inside, it was decorated, and has now been restored, in a style that was the height of fashion, the Art Deco style also used by Milne in the new ballroom wing at Claridges. Textiles used for curtains and covers included Raoul Dufy's black and cream printed linen 'les Arums'.

Coleton Fishacre was more than a weekend and holiday house. Lady Dorothy lived there during the week and her husband would arrive by train from London every Friday, often accompanied by guests. They led an active and informal social life, spending the days out of doors fishing, shooting, sailing, taking their dalmatian and cairn terriers for walks on the cliffs and, in summer, bathing in the tidal swimming pool they had built in Pudcombe Cove below the house. In

the summer they lunched and dined outdoors in the loggia with its view of the sea (now hidden by trees) and in the evenings played bridge or dressed up in costumes from the opera company to perform amateur theatricals.

The garden played an important part in their lives, and Lady Dorothy became an enthusiastic and knowledgeable plantswoman. Their sailing trips sometimes took them to notable Cornish gardens in search of ideas, and weekend guests were expected to do a bit of weeding. Their first priority in the garden was to plant shelter belts against the damaging salt-laden winds, starting with holm oak, Monterey pines and sycamore even before the house was built. The garden immediately around the house was planned by Milne with predictable features in Lutyens's style: a paved terrace, a rill, a concave, recessed semicircular pool, and stout retaining walls containing changes of level.

Away from the house, parallel informal paths offer alternative routes down to the sea, taking in a rustic gazebo with fine seaward views, still close enough to

A plantswoman's garden: the benign coastal climate at Coleton Fishacre in Devon enabled the owner, Lady Dorothy D'Oyly Carte, to develop a distinguished collection of rare plants. These were carefully placed to provide year-round interest and colour.

the house for drinks or tea to be carried out. Lady Dorothy kept a garden diary. It shows that she gradually came to realize that the mild climate and high humidity offered opportunities to grow rare and tender plants. As time went by and her confidence increased, her choice of trees and shrubs became more adventurous. She placed her plants carefully, and now the views from one side of the valley to the other show fine groups of mature plants, offering flowers and scent from early spring to autumn and spectacular leaf colour from autumn into winter. Lush, leafy vegetation follows the course of the stream below.

We made a garden

At East Lambrook Manor in Somerset, at about this time, Margery Fish was making a very different kind of garden. She and her husband Walter bought the charming, golden stone manor house in 1938 when Margery was 46. She spent the 30 years until her death in 1969 developing the garden, initially in partnership with Walter, and after he died, without him. As so often happens in a gardening marriage, he was responsible for imposing order on the garden and setting out a firm structure of paths, lawns and hedges while Margery looked after the plants. This reflected the gardening relationship of Harold Nicolson and Vita Sackville-West and, a little later, the work of David and Rosemary Verey in their garden at Barnsley House in Gloucestershire. Married gardening was not always sweetness and light. Sometimes the irritation factor was strong, as Harold Nicolson noted in his diary of 1946:

> In the afternoon I moon about with Vita trying to convince her than planning is an element in gardening. I want to show her that the top of the moat-walk bank must be planted with forethought and design. She wishes just to jab in the things which she has left over. The tragedy of the romantic temperament is that it dislikes form so much that it ignores the effect of masses. She wants to put in stuff which 'will give a lovely red colour in the autumn'. I wish to put in stuff which will furnish shape to the perspective. In the end we part, not as friends.

Such disagreements will strike a chord with most gardening couples. Walter Fish was so impatient with his wife's magpie plant-collecting instinct that she would try, usually unsuccessfully, to smuggle new plants past him:

> Every gardener knows the fascination of the unknown, and when the ordinary plants are doing nicely there is a great temptation to be a little

more venturesome. That is one of the excitements of gardening, but one which my husband did not share. He pretended not to see me with my nose in catalogues night after night, and though I always tried to intercept the postman when I was expecting plants, he always knew.

Walter also made a fuss about Margery putting eggshells on the compost heap. He thought it was silly when lime could be bought for a few pence. It was presumably Walter who provided the sword which Margery kept sharpened and ready for decapitating daffodils: 'One can slash off a lot of heads in a very short time,' she wrote:

> It isn't only from the point of tidiness that one should remove spent flowers. A plant will go on flowering over much longer periods if every dead bloom is removed at once. Kept in a state of frustrated motherhood it will go on producing flowers in the hope of being allowed to set seed and thus reproduce itself.

She was as much interested in the way plants behaved and the ways in which you could encourage them to give of their best, as she was in designing with plants. Over the years she discovered, by careful and acute observation, what conditions suited them best, and which plants best enhanced each other in colour, texture and form. As a result, Valerie Finnis, herself a distinguished gardener and plantswoman, said, 'Margery had a gift of making plants look comfortable, always choosing just the right plant for the right place.'

The garden at East Lambrook Manor is genuinely and unselfconsciously in the cottage style, therefore immune to the fluctuations of fashion. But it is a style requiring the constant attention of a devoted gardener with a good eye for plants, a role performed after Margery Fish's death by her sister and brother-in-law, Mr and Mrs Boyd-Carpenter. Since their day, it has had its ups and downs, but now, under new and enthusiastic ownership, it is beginning to thrive again.

Margery Fish had a gift for communication. She gave lectures and wrote books recording her gardening experiences. The titles of her books explain her ideas. The first, *We made a Garden* (1956) is an account of how she and her husband initially set about things. It was followed by *Cottage Garden Flowers* (1961), *A Flower for Every Day*, *Ground Cover Plants* (1964) and *Gardening in the Shade* (1964). Christopher Lloyd wrote of her, 'she was a great sharer and proselytizer, one of the warmest and most generous people I have ever known yet with a strong, shrewd personality and a marvellous sense of humour.' She was able to communicate her warmth: her books were immensely popular and visitors flocked to her garden. According to John Sales, the former Chief Gardens Advisor at The National Trust, '…in the second half of the twentieth century no garden has yet had had a greater effect and no garden writer has had a more profound influence.'

She discovered all about gardening by first-hand experience and by trial and error, and in her books she passed on her hard-won knowledge, writing about her failures as well as her successes. Her writing is full of common sense, lively and approachable. She inspires confidence in the reader, and her kind of gardening is accessible to those with the smallest of gardens.

Her garden today is much as Margery Fish designed it. Her vision was of a garden 'as modest and unpretentious as the house, a cottage garden in fact, with crooked paths and unexpected corners.' Elsewhere she wrote,

> Then there is the mystery. The gardens that are remembered are those that lure you on. No one wants to linger in a garden that has no surprises and if the whole garden can be seen at once, there is a tendency to pay less attention to its treasures than if they were discovered in unexpected places under trees, behind walls and round corners.

Into one and a half acres she managed to fit numerous areas of different character, including a white garden, silver garden, terrace garden, ditch garden, rockery, green garden, hellebore garden and orchard, yet the whole never seems fragmented or fussy. It is entirely inward looking, the vistas all being relatively short and contained within the garden. The planting is just on the orderly side of chaos, with plants bursting exuberantly out of their allotted space like Tom Kitten out of his little blue jacket. On the paved paths there is almost nowhere to put your feet without crushing a plant. Margery had a *laisser-faire* attitude to self-seeding plants and would only weed out seedlings if they were a threat to a

Margery Fish in her garden at East Lambrook Manor, Somerset. Through her books and by opening her garden to visitors, she encouraged people to adopt the cottage-garden style, and to grow many of the plants she had saved from extinction.

more delicate neighbouring plant. Plants nearly always grow stronger and look right in their self-chosen position, and this gave the garden a look of well-being and uncontrived informality. As a result of this policy, *Euphorbia wulfenii*, angelica, valerian and fleabane (*Erigeron karvinskianus*) thread themselves through the gardens like musical themes.

Solid structure, in contrast with flowery luxuriance, is supplied by a miniature avenue of clipped lawson cypress (*Chamaecyparis lawsoniana* 'Fletcheri'), recently replaced after outgrowing their positions, and a row of pollarded willows along the ditch. Elsewhere a well-placed tree, a seat or a large stone trough provide punctuation marks. The whole garden is greatly helped by the very fine seventeenth-century malthouse and cowhouse at its centre, the manor house being tucked away in one corner.

Margery Fish's introduction to *Cottage Garden Flowers* gives a vivid picture of the unpretentious village gardens she loved and strove to emulate. The picturesque thatched cottages were already disappearing 'to make way for council houses and modern bungalows' but the flowers still remained.

> The gardens themselves were usually small, sometimes only a slip between the cottage and the road, with a tiny patch behind. They were tidy without being prim and were always packed with flowers. No definite design went to their planting and the treasured flowers were put wherever there was room. There might be a myrtle, grown from a sprig from grandmother's wedding bouquet, pinks from coveted slips, rosemary and Lad's Love, the great red peonies that last so well, and Crown Imperials grown in a row. Wallflowers and Snapdragons grew in the walls, and cheerful red and pink daisies played hide and seek between the shells that edged the path.
>
> Plants are friendly creatures and enjoy each other's company. The close-packed plants in a cottage garden grow well and look happy. They have the shelter of the wall or hedge that screens them from the road, and the comfortable backing of cabbages and leeks. Pansies and Forget-me-nots flower under the currant bushes, nasturtiums frolic among the carrots, and old apple trees give welcome shade.

Margery Fish's books were written after her garden had matured and become famous. But the 1930s, when the garden was in the making, were an anxious time for everybody. Frank Kingdon-Ward, writing in 1935, reminds us what a solace gardening can be to hearts troubled by the world outside:

There is always hope for the man who loves flowers, and I for one will never believe that the bottom has fallen right out of England so long as there are gardens, and men to tend them faithfully…

Any one who seeks the 'peace which passeth all understanding' or, as the Buddhist calls it, Nirvana, might well turn to his garden to distract his mind from the daily anxieties of life. We all love flowers for their graciousness of form, no less than for their delicious colours, and sweet fragrance; and there is nothing which gives so great a return for the labour and money expended on it as a small garden… When the city man comes home, tired after his day's work, it is to his garden that he turns, not only for recreation but for comfort.

Frank Kingdon-Ward, son of Professor Marshall Ward, who was a distinguished Cambridge botanist, went to China in 1907 at the age of 22, to a teaching post in Shanghai. He travelled extensively in China and Tibet, his plant collecting being sponsored from 1911 by Bees Seeds, and yielding, among other plants, seed of *Primula florindae* (named after his wife) and *Meconopsis betonicifolia*, the much loved and coveted (and hard to please) blue Himalayan poppy, originally discovered by Père Delavay. He wrote about most of his 25 exploring expeditions in books like *The Land of the Blue Poppy* (1912) and *Return to the Irrawaddy* (1956). He was a man whose spirit found fulfilment in wild, remote, mountains and valleys, but he also understood the primeval need of all gardeners, to grow plants. He ended his description of the tired city man's garden, quoted above, with these words:

So, even in these hard times, let us not neglect our gardens, but rather sacrifice much else, that we may enjoy the purest and most exquisite pleasure in life: the yield of mother earth in all its strange forms. Truly the cultivation of flowers is something more than a luxury; it is a religion.

Insecticide from your own garden – Mary Tulloch's garden notebook
Gardening was hard work at the time when the Fishes were starting their garden. There were no garden centres where containerized plants could be bought and planted all the year round, and no ready-made products for feeding, weeding and pest control.

A friend gave me her mother-in-law's garden notebook, covering the years from 1934 to 1939. It is foolscap-sized with a hard, black, worn cloth-bound cover. The pages are lined and are arranged alphabetically. Mary Tulloch, whose book it was, has cut out, and pasted into the book, pages or shorter extracts from the weekly paper *Home Gardening*, and added her own hand-written notes. The book is bursting at the seams, and gives a good idea of the practical concerns of gardeners at that time.

'The "Home Gardening" Guide to Garden Pest Control', pasted into the front of the book lists 14 different pests of roses. In order to deal with all of them you would have to have in your poison cupboard, tobacco powder, derris powder, soot water, paraffin, soil fumigant, soft soap wash, nicotine insecticide and some quassia solution. These remedies did not come in handy spray canisters, but had to be measured out, diluted to the required strength and squirted on to the plants with a syringe.

Weedkillers did not exist, neither did proprietary granular or liquid fertilizers. Nevertheless, close attention was paid to the nutritional requirements of each plant. Mary Tulloch noted under 'G':

> Grape Hyacinths feed weekly with soot water to end of flowering to bring out colour. March 23
> Godetias hot sunshine, 1 week liq. man; next 2 parts super-phosphate to 1 of Sul. of Potash, 1oz to sq. yd. No mulch.
> To sow – pail old manure & 2 oz bone meal to sq yd – firm soil dusting of soot.
> Geraniums love sun & soil not too rich – if very rich leave Gs in their pot. Soil manured in autumn dig only 1 ft deep & mix 2 oz Superphosphate to each yd. Gs love superphosphate – if preparing fresh ground – pail of old manure & 2ozs Superphs. Plant Gers: slanting to encourage sideshoots.
> Gooseberries April 16 – 3 Sul of Potash 1 Sul of Ammonia 4oz to sq yd

Gladioli get a whole page of hand-written notes in Mary's book, and there are also notes on Greenhouse shading, Gypsophila, Galtonias, Geums, Genistas, Germination, Gloxinias, Gentians and 'Green sulphur for Carrot fly as soon as they are up.'

All planting had to be planned ahead, and plants ordered for delivery at planting time, either from nurserymen exhibiting at shows, or by post. Mary Tulloch's book is interleaved with order acknowledgements from nurseries, mostly for just two or three plants, one of each kind. When they were delivered they had to be planted or heeled in no matter what the weather.

Mary Tulloch was a regular attender at Southport Flower Show and placed orders for plants with exhibiting nurserymen. When she got home she transferred notes taken at the show to her Garden Book for future reference:

Southport Show August 25. Things I liked but did not order
Bakers Lythrum Brightness – did I order 2 Physostegia Virginia – I want
Helenium Baronin Linden.
Lovely lupins
Keelings Bradford – yellow orchid oncidium – …
Hillier & Son Winchester –
Beautiful Climber Vitis megalophylla – likes lime & soot –
    shrub. Lovely leaves [sketch] Disanthus cercidifolius – no lime –
    lovely Ceratostigma Willmotiana sun dry spot plant 3 –
Abelia grandiflora pink flowers from July to frost

In those days, when men went to work and women stayed at home to look after the house and the children, it was usual for wives rather than husbands to do most of the gardening. Mary Tulloch had a husband and two young children to take care of and was a fairly typical owner-gardener of her time, but compared to most others, she was a perfectionist, and took a great deal of trouble with her garden. As a result, she acquired a vast fund of knowledge and became a very successful gardener. There is nothing in her notes and cuttings about design, or what to plant with what. Her main concern, like that of the majority of gardeners, was to succeed with a wide variety of plants. Her pleasure in gardening lay in

During World War II, under the 'Digging For Victory' scheme, every available plot of land was employed in growing food for the nation. Since all able-bodied young men were in the services, the gardening work was done by women and the elderly.

persuading them to grow well for her. The appearance of the garden was almost a by-product of her success. But she must have had an instinct for placing plants well, because her later garden, which I knew, always looked wonderful.

It is interesting that Mary Tulloch felt the need to keep a Garden Book when there was plenty of published advice available. There is very little in her notes on plant care that she could not have found in, for example, *The Complete Book of Gardening* written by the curators of the Royal Botanic Gardens, Kew, and published by Ward Lock in 1930, with revised editions in 1931 and 1934. But the writing of her own notes was an expression of her strong commitment to her garden, and her determination to achieve the best possible results. Although the book is not full, there are no entries later than 26 August 1939. War was declared on Sunday, 3 September.

Digging for victory

The war changed everything. Men left home to fight or to serve the war effort in other ways. Young women went to work in munitions factories or, as land girls, to replace farm labourers who had been conscripted. The character of gardening changed completely. It was the patriotic duty of those who were left at home, mothers of young children, the elderly and men not deemed physically fit for military service, to 'dig for victory', to produce as much food as their patch of ground was capable of. 'Potatoes and onions were munitions of war as surely as shells and bullets.' In small gardens lawns and flowerbeds were dug over in order to grow them, as well as other vegetable crops.

Plenty of horticultural advice was available. Everyone listened anxiously to the wireless for news of the war, and stayed tuned for broadcasts offering Government advice and a new programme, *Gardener's Question Time*. Newspapers published their weekly gardening articles, Ministry leaflets were distributed and information spread through the invaluable network of Women's Institutes.

In large gardens, open lawns were ploughed and sown with corn, vegetables or fodder crops, or allowed to grow into hay for winter feed for cattle. In some cases, where there was simply no labour available, nature began to reclaim her own. Saplings of sycamore and ash sprang up and brambles and ivy covered the ground and lodged their roots in the crevices of stonework, reducing balustraded terraces and steps, temples and follies to ruins, and prising apart the framework of glasshouses. Except for a few tenacious survivors, rare and precious ornamental plants were unable to compete with aggressively successful weeds, and disappeared. Now that so many historic gardens have been so beautifully restored, it is hard to imagine the devastation caused by wartime neglect.

11 MID-TWENTIETH CENTURY

Postwar Gardening 291

ONE OF THE MOST urgent postwar priorities was to provide housing for returning servicemen and their families, and to replace housing stock lost to wartime bombing. An immediate start was made by the construction of 160,000 prefabs: small, single-storey houses made from prefabricated concrete, asbestos or aluminium units that were quickly erected on site. Although intended to be a partial and temporary solution to the problem, supposed to last for ten years, they were very popular with families who, before the war, had lived in mean back-to-back terraces or slum tenements. Some families were still living in their prefabs after 40 years.

In Bristol, the manufacture of prefabs provided postwar work for the Bristol Aeroplane Company. One group of prefabs was erected at the Sturminster Estate in 1947 on land provided by the Imperial Sports Club. 'They had large gardens and not being directly on the road, were extremely safe places for bringing up children,' one resident remembered some 50 years later. Some families had previously lived in one room and looked back on that time as a golden age. 'We all had young families and they'd play together in the fields. It was just like being in the country.' It would be nice to think Lord Emsworth's 12-year-old

A shared passion for gardening can bring people together in good times as well as at times of crisis.
'The Neighbours', by Stanley Spencer, 1936.

girlfriend, Gladys and her brother Ern, whose visit to the gardens of Blandings Castle was described in the previous chapter (see page 268), were rehoused in such a place. Each prefab had a sitting room and dining room, a kitchen with a fridge, built-in cooker and a wash boiler, two bedrooms, a bathroom and a separate toilet. 'It was pure luxury', specially for families accustomed to using a 'kazi' across the yard in all weathers.

Prefab gardens were mostly laid out on traditional cottage garden lines, with flowers each side of a concrete path leading to the front door and, at the back, a vegetable plot and perhaps a few fruit bushes. Food rationing continued for some years after the war, and home-grown produce helped ease the financial burden of couples with young children to feed. A prefab has been erected and an authentic garden created around it at the Avoncroft Museum of Buildings in Worcestershire.

The provision of gardens for prefabs and for dwellings in the new council housing estates constructed after the war was a policy destined to have wide-reaching repercussions on future land use. Population growth and an increasing assumption that newly married couples were entitled to start life together in a home of their own rather than move in with the in-laws led to a need for new housing that has still not been satisfied 50 years on. Standards of what was acceptable were far higher than before the war, and the idea that every household could have a garden was the starting point for many housing authorities when planning new provision or replacing old, sub-standard housing stock. But in many areas such an ideal could not even be entertained, and high-rise blocks of flats (becoming higher as building technology developed), with ownerless communal spaces below, became the norm.

'…an outrage on Britain's face'

The countryside was shrinking. Land was being taken out of agricultural use for industrial development as well as housing, and new roads were needed to serve the growing population in new housing estates. Expanding industry meant an increase in freight traffic and prosperity meant increased car ownership. Development went snaking out from the cities along new dual carriageways, followed by land-greedy six-lane motorways, ring roads and bypasses. Airports and runways, pylons and wire-scapes further degraded both the rural and the urban landscape of England. Just as the coming of the railways to ruin the Lake District provoked Wordsworth and Ruskin's articulate wrath in the nineteenth century, so the building of new roads and airports generated angry opposition and demonstrations in the twentieth, and still do.

Edward Hyams described the effect of postwar housing estates on the landscape in his book *The Changing Face of Britain*, 1974:

> First they lined the new roads, then they filled in the rectangles
> and triangles between such new roads, until they composed those
> vast 'subtopias' which are and probably always will be an outrage
> on Britain's face.

In other places 'shallow roadside conurbations scores of miles long' left tracts of open farmland between them. Any route out of any major city reveals this kind of development. The lilacs and laburnums seen in front gardens as you go by are hardly compensation for the ugliness of shopping parades and petrol stations. It is difficult to argue with the premise that everyone who wants a garden should

*The rebuilding of bombed Britain after World War II went some way to fulfilling the ideal of
a garden for every family, but many square miles of rural landscape were lost in the attempt.
'The Builders', Harry Bush, 1933.*

have one, but if that ideal is to be fulfilled on Britain's small island without sacrificing more of the already much-diminished countryside, each garden will have to be smaller even than that of the average postwar council house.

The great landscape architect Geoffrey Jellicoe, in his appendix to Miles Hadfield's *A History of British Gardening*, covering the years 1939 to 1978, wrote of the small town garden:

> The Chinese laid down that the garden must have privacy and be such that its owner could commune with nature and converse with his friends. Here for a short time man can escape and return to the rhythms of nature for which his perceptive faculties were originally fashioned. Such a garden is fundamental to a modern democratic society; it occupies so little space that it has been calculated that the entire population of the British Isles could be housed in this way within a circle with a radius of thirty-five miles from Charing Cross.

A perfunctory tour of any council-owned housing estate will reveal that a fairly high proportion of tenants is not interested in using their gardens to grow plants. As Polly Garter, a character in Dylan Thomas's play *Under Milk Wood* (1953), says 'Nothing grows in our garden, only washing. And babies. And where's their fathers live, my love? Over the hills and far away.'

The same applies today in some gardens, front gardens being used not only to park prams and bicycles, but also to repair and service cars and motorcycles, while back gardens are allowed to become overgrown, scrubby wildernesses. This can be accounted for in two ways. First, there was no gardening tradition among families rehoused from slums in the centre of industrial towns. For several generations their only gardening experience may have been growing a few geraniums in pots on a sooty windowsill. The second reason for the neglect of council-house gardens is the fact of council ownership. Unless you own your plot or at least have long-term security of tenure, there is not much incentive to cultivate and improve it. This is borne out by the fact that, since the law was changed to enable tenants to buy their homes at very favourable prices, there has been a surge of interest in gardening among former council tenants. Their interest has been fed by gardening television programmes showing instant 'makeovers' of small gardens, and these programmes have inspired viewers to become interested in making over their own gardens, thereby providing material for more television programmes to give them the advice they need. It is hard to decide which is the chicken, which the egg.

'Hoof and horn, superphosphate of lime and sulphate of potash'

In the immediate postwar decades, few households owned a television set, and keen gardeners looked to books and magazines for advice. In the years leading up to World War II there had been a rapid increase in literacy, and therefore in readership of books, newspapers and magazines. In 1939, 27 million books were bought; three times more than ten years earlier. 247 million books were borrowed from public libraries in 1939, compared to 85 million in 1924.

By 1939 nearly 70 per cent of the population over 16 years old read a national daily newspaper, and for Sunday papers this went up to 80 per cent. Newspapers from *The Daily Telegraph* to the *News of the World* and weekly and monthly magazines like *Woman's Own*, *Woman's Journal*, *The Lady*, *Country Life* and *The Field*, all had regular columns offering gardening advice, so expertise was available to virtually all literate gardeners, from the readers of the *Sunday People* to those of *The Observer*. There were also specialist gardening magazines: *Amateur Gardening* has flourished from its inception in 1884 up to the present day.

Crazy paving is bad enough…

Until the end of the nineteenth century, most gardening advice had been directed at the owners of country gardens: these might be attached to a wide variety of houses, mansions, manors, rectories, farmhouses or cottages, but they all had in common their rural situation. But, as we have seen, this had changed and would continue to change. Suburban and urban gardeners now outnumbered country gardeners and this trend would increase. Suburban houses were designed for small families, with a breadwinner who travelled by train to the office each day and a housewife who stayed at home. Their houses were designed with gardens just the right size for two amateurs to maintain and improve in their spare time, without feeling oppressed by the amount of work involved. It was, in the main, this couple, Mr and Mrs Commuter of 'The Laburnums', Chestnut Close, who subscribed to magazines such as *Amateur Gardening* and bought gardening books.

Gardens looked inwards again, as they had in medieval times, attempting to exclude a hostile world and to give privacy from prying neighbours. Behind the walls and fences, the privet hedges and the dripping laurels, most gardens had no exciting secrets to hide. In fact a look at the layouts recommended in gardening books, and visits to one or two typical small gardens today, suggest that one town or suburban garden was very like another, and has changed very little in the past 40 years. For most householders, the pleasure their gardens offered lay in the plants they grew and tended rather than in changing and updating the structure and furnishings. For some, the goal might be a velvety weed-free lawn, for others a prize-winning half dozen pansies, onions or runner beans at the local flower show.

The advice offered in books and magazines was mostly practical. They catered for readers who wanted to get out there and get on with it. Armchair gardening became a popular leisure activity (inactivity might be a better description) only later, when better and cheaper reproduction of colour photographs made possible the inclusion of alluring, glossy pictures of unattainable gardens.

For more than half a century the standard reference book was *Sanders' Encyclopaedia of Gardening*. The first edition came out in 1895, having been serialized between 1890 and 1895 in *Amateur Gardening*, which Thomas Sanders edited from 1887 until his death in 1926. Apart from having attended the village school at Martley in Worcestershire, he was entirely self-taught. He became a distinguished horticulturalist and writer with some 40 books to his credit. The 22nd edition, revised by A.G.L. Hellyer, came out in 1960. It consists of an alphabetical list of plant descriptions with instructions for the culture and propagation of each. The text is in small print, densely set out and there are no pictures.

A few years later, in 1966, came *Ward Lock's Complete Gardening* edited by C.E. Pearson. Although not many pages longer than 'Sanders' it is twice the size and, with numerous coloured and black-and-white photographs, twice as alluring. Like 'Sanders', 'Ward Lock's' consists mainly of an alphabetical plant list. But there are also chapters on Garden Tools; Basic Operations; Construction of Garden Features; and Greenhouses and Frames. In the chapter on Planning and Designing, five layout plans are shown, all for quite small gardens. Three of the five have vegetable gardens, two have rose gardens, one has a rockery. The one element they all have in common is extensive areas of crazy paving: 'There is no doubt that the most attractive kind of stone path is that formed with crazy paving, but its siting needs choosing with discretion. It is not at home alongside an ultra-modern house…'

Sir William Lawrence, President of the RHS Conference on Landscape Design, held a different opinion on the subject: 'Crazy pavement is bad enough, but intolerable when stuck over with little plants and looking like galantine.' He expressed this opinion in his introduction to *Landscape Gardening* by Richard Sudell, a founder member of the Institute of Landscape Architects in 1927. This book, published in 1933 and revised in 1939, is addressed as much to professional designers as to amateur gardeners, and is much concerned with design, both of the layout and the planting of gardens. Much of his advice follows Gertrude Jekyll's principles, particularly on the subject of colour. Sudell himself declares:

The modern tendency in garden design may, briefly, be stated to be a drift towards simplification and specialization… Popular taste in colour and form has definitely improved. The habits of the modern generation – the desire for games, and appreciation of outdoor life in general – make it imperative that the outdoor area of each homestead shall be really usable in the same manner as the indoor rooms, and the pleasure lawn, with privacy obtained by a surround of trees and shrubs is now given prior consideration.

Landscape Gardening, Richard Sudell, 1933

The simplification he refers to is not evident in the complex layouts illustrated in his book. In one example he has managed to fit into one acre a rose garden, lavender garden, herbaceous borders, annual borders and a lily pond, not to mention a kitchen garden, fruit garden, heather garden, rock garden, glade and woodland walk. Additional space was somehow found for a greenhouse, service yard and car wash.

Richard Sudell was also the author of *Herbaceous Borders and the Waterside, Town & Suburban Garden*, and *Garden Planning*, and he edited Odhams' *New Illustrated Gardening Encyclopaedia*. As a curious sideline, in 1939 W.D. and H. O. Wills commissioned him to select the pictures and write the descriptions for a set of 50 cigarette cards of 'Garden Flowers'.

The great smog of 1952

Several books addressed the many problems of gardening in towns including Richard Sudell's *The New Garden*, written for the novice gardener with a new plot attached to a new house. His approach is realistic and practical. The first chapter, 'Consider your site', is illustrated with two 'before' photographs taken on newly built housing estates. The captions read 'Builders leave the ground littered with brick bats, tins and bits of wood' and '…unsightly backs of houses, fences and sheds which need to be screened.' The author is optimistic that, by helping the new householder solve these problems, he will make a convert. 'I have no fears for the future,' he writes, 'for "once a gardener, always a gardener" is a sound maxim, and the garden fever is very infectious on a new housing estate.' *The New Garden* was one of the first books to encourage people to draw up a plan on paper and design their own gardens. It included instructions on making a simple but accurate survey of the plot.

In older industrial areas, and on those new housing estates that were built to provide factory workers with homes close to the source of employment, the

greatest difficulty for gardeners was air pollution. The problem, originally caused by the burning of coal on domestic as well as industrial premises, was not a new one. In 1661 John Evelyn in *Fumifugium* drew attention to the 'Hellish and dismall cloud of sea-coale' blanketing London. His call for 'noisome trades' to be banned within the city was ignored.

The Industrial Revolution of the nineteenth century added to the pollution problem, with factory chimneys all over the British Isles belching gases and corrosive acids into the atmosphere. The corrosion visible on stone buildings and ironwork also worked invisibly on the lungs of people who breathed the polluted air. The worst effects occurred in winter, when the poisonous smoke and soot hung suspended in damp fog for days at a time and sometimes for a whole week, and coughs, colds and other winter ailments made the population weak and vulnerable to more serious fevers, bronchitis and pneumonia.

'Pea-souper' fog, or smog as it came to be known, occurred regularly every winter, but in some years it was more serious than others. In the last week of December 1813 the London fog was so dense that people could not see from one side of the street to the other, and the London to Birmingham mail coach took seven hours to reach Uxbridge. During a fog which lasted from 7 to 13 December 1873, the death rate in London was 40 per cent higher than normal. There were more serious fogs than usual in London, and increased death rates in the winters of 1880, 1882, 1891 and 1892. The sinister atmosphere created by London fog, metaphorically as well as literally, was described by Charles Dickens in *Bleak House*, by Sir Arthur Conan Doyle in some of Sherlock Holmes's adventures, and by Robert Louis Stevenson in *The Strange Case of Dr Jekyll and Mr Hyde*.

Nothing was done to improve matters in London or elsewhere until 1952 when The Great Smog hit London. The smoke-laden fog brought road, rail and

Before the Clean Air Acts of 1956 and 1968 were introduced, it would not have been possible to grow healthy, edible vegetables in a city garden. 'A Woman Watering the Garden', needlework by Tirzah Ravilious (1908–51).

air transport in the capital almost to a standstill. It infiltrated the auditorium at Sadler's Wells Theatre, making conditions so unpleasant for the audience and performers that the performance was suspended. Cattle at Smithfield Market died of asphyxiation. A far more serious result of the smog was the death, as a direct result, of at least 4000 Londoners, and quite probably many more.

The 1952 smog was the catalyst that finally prompted action. The first Clean Air Act was passed by Parliament in 1956, introducing smokeless zones. It was followed by a further act in 1968, and today winter sunshine levels in London, formerly 30 per cent lower in some urban districts than in rural areas, are now almost the same as those in the country.

During the years of pollution, lack of light and layers of acid and soot on their leaves caused much stress to garden plants in industrial towns and often killed them. By the 1930s a hundred years of sooty deposits carrying chemical impurities had fallen on to the soil and been washed in, making the soil acid and sour. The choice of flowering plants and evergreens that would thrive in such hostile conditions was strictly limited. This problem was tackled head-on by H.H. Thomas, the editor of *Popular Gardening* and *Good Gardening*, in his book *Gardening in Towns* (1936). He wrote:

> One has only to watch the sky at about six o'clock on a fine morning, to see how quickly the smoke pall gathers over a crowded city as the domestic fires are lit…
>
> As an acid soil is unwelcome to most plants, one of the first things a town gardener must do… is to correct soil acidity. The few plants that will tolerate an acid soil are mostly plants that also demand a clean pure atmosphere, so that they cannot be grown in towns.

Thomas also noted the importance of trees to purify the atmosphere, if they can themselves survive. 'The March flowering almond is one of the best. Mountain Ash, Purple-leaved Plum, False Acacia, double pink Cherry, double pink Hawthorn, white Beam [sic], and pink Horse Chestnut are trees that thrive in many of the inner London districts.' All these can be seen in city gardens today, planted, perhaps, in the 1930s and 1940s by gardeners following Thomas's recommendations. Conifers, he said, would only grow in pure air but he recommended, among the few evergreen shrubs able to cope with impure air, *Euonymus japonicus*, *Acuba japonica*, *Mahonia* and holly.

His list of suitable deciduous shrubs is short and not much different from that made by John Claudius Loudon a hundred years earlier: four kinds of berberis,

Cotoneaster horizontalis, buddleja, forsythia, lilac, flowering currant, deutzia, philadelphus, *Fuchsia* 'Riccartoniii', hydrangea and yucca; if you stroll down almost any street today you will still see these shrubs. Recommended climbers are also predictable: ivy, pyracantha, Virginia creeper, winter-flowering jasmine, and, for a south wall, wisteria, ceanothus and two climbing roses, 'Scarlet Climber' and 'Dr Van Fleet'. Thomas has a whole chapter on dahlias, since, apparently, they grow well in smoky districts, and dahlias grown in a tiny London garden have competed successfully against entries from all parts of the country at the National Dahlia Society's shows. Roses, too, get a chapter to themselves. Today it is known that a certain amount of air pollution actually helps to ward off blackspot and mildew, and deters aphids. Rust on hollyhocks is also seen off by soot in the atmosphere, according to Thomas.

The problem of pollution is also recognized by Lady Seton in *My Town Garden* (1927), although she herself gardened first in the relatively salubrious air of Kensington and then in the bracingly pure atmosphere of Hampstead. She identified the drawbacks of town gardening as wall, air, cats and soil, in that order. Her advice on what to wear when gardening gives an idea of the breezy tone of her book:

> …for a great part of the year an ideal gardening dress for women is a short tweed skirt, made very wide, so that one can step across plants without injuring them, a loose jumper made of khaki or brown flannel (for half an hour in wet weather will take the shine off a romantically becoming jumper in pale colours), a gardening apron all pockets, a pair of thick shoes or boots, and a light scarf tied over one's hair. Hats are dreadfully in the way, and if quite uncovered and unshingled, our hair catches in every twig, like Absolom's, and the result is very painful and untidy.

Many of the plants she lists overlap with H.H. Thomas's choice. Both suggest *Clematis jackmanii* (Lady Seton recommends feeding it with crushed oyster shells), and she adds white jasmine to her list of climbers. She says bulbs grow well in difficult conditions, since they bring their own nourishment with them, but they may need to be replaced every year. Flag irises can always be relied on and auriculas do well in smoky air, 'even in the great industrial towns of the North.' Lady Seton considers nasturtiums to be a great stand-by when other things fail, '…and until you have tried it you cannot believe what a lovely dinner-table decoration can be carried out with nasturtium blooms and maidenhair or asparagus fern.'

Bringing flowers into the house

The art of flower arranging has always been inextricably interlinked with the art of gardening, and has influenced the planting of gardens in many ways besides requiring the almost ubiquitous cutting bed in the Victorian and Edwardian walled kitchen garden. In the houses of the gentry of the eighteenth and nineteenth centuries, one of the duties of the head gardener was to decorate the house, not only with pots of orchids, gardenias or ferns from the stove house, but also with cut flowers arranged in vases. This is still the case in some grand houses. *Cassells Popular Gardening*, published in the 1870s, and written as much for professional gardeners as for garden owners, had plenty of advice on the subject. In Volume II, James Hudson, gardener to the Rothschilds at Gunnersbury Park wrote chapters on 'Decorative Use of Flowers', 'Dinner and other Table Decorations', 'Drawing Room and Boudoir, Entrance Halls and Corridors', and 'Personal Decorations – Bouquets'. Each chapter was illustrated with engravings showing arrangements of great complexity.

William Robinson's *The English Flower Garden* first published in 1883 also deals with flower arranging, but his chapter, 'The Flower Garden in the House' takes a different line. It is illustrated by a small bowl of pansies, not arranged at all, just stuck in anyhow, a branch of wild rose alone in a Japanese bronze basin, and groups of peonies, hellebores, choisya and the leaves of epimedium, each species separate and alone in its simple container. Robinson wrote:

> It is not merely the first impression of flowers, good as it may be, that we have to think of, but the charms which intimacy gives to many of the nobler flowers – some opening and closing before our eyes, and showing beauties of form in doing so that we never suspected when passing them in the open air. In the changing and varied lights of a house we have many opportunities of showing flowers in a more interesting way, particularly to those who do not see them much out of doors.

He goes on to be fiercely critical of ugly, modern, over-decorated vases. He recommends keeping a great variety of pots, basins and jars, including Munstead glasses (plain vases shaped like broad, shallow goblets):

> It is well to use a variety of other things in any simple ware that comes in our way, very often things on the way to the rubbish heap, such as Devonshire cream jars in brown ware. Nassau seltzer bottles… old ginger pots… and other articles made for use in trade, come in very well.

He points out that if branches of sloe, plum, or apple trees are cut when in bud they will open indoors.

Gertrude Jekyll, inventor of the Munstead vase, was equally in favour of simplicity. In *Roses for English Gardens* (1902) she had a chapter on 'Roses as Cut Flowers', illustrated with 13 photographs of roses arranged in simple pots, jugs or vases. On the whole, she liked to use roses by themselves, but would sometimes put Cabbage, Moss and Damask roses with honeysuckle and white pinks. She thought the scents as well as the form and colour of these flowers mingled beautifully. She also used the young red shoots of oak as a background to roses. Miss Jekyll was always practical and pointed out that

> Large Roses are top-heavy and every one who is used to arranging flowers, must at some time or other have been vexed by a bunch of Roses carefully placed in a bowl conspiring together to fling themselves out of it all round at the same moment.

Her remedy is to have wire frames made for your vases or to place three garden pots of graduated sizes inside each other in a china bowl, thus making three concentric rings to hold the stalks.

With the advent of owner-gardeners and the development of suburbia, interest in flower arranging grew and grew. By the early 1950s it seemed appropriate to Richard Sudell to introduce *The New Illustrated Gardening Encyclopaedia* with a preliminary section on 'The Art of Flower Arrangement'. He offers it as an answer to the gardener's question, 'what are we to do with our flowers when we have got them? How can we make the most of their beauty and get most pleasure from them?' His ideas are based on the creation of pictures. Just as gardeners use their skills to create large-scale outdoor pictures, so they can create small scale indoor pictures using flowers, fruit and foliage. He explains:

> Modern Flower Arrangement is something quite apart from the casual business of 'doing the vases,' which in the past has been handed over all too frequently to someone who has had neither the inspiration nor the training necessary for successful picture making. A flower arrangement today means the creation of something that has good composition, line, form and colour, just as much as any picture that another artist might put on canvas... Even a brief study of the art of flower arrangement must inspire a desire to grow and use a much wider range of flower, leaf, and fruit than shops and markets normally produce.

A how-to lesson follows, with step-by-step diagrams, and finally there are a few pages of black-and-white photographs showing the kind of rather stiff flower arrangements that might win prizes at local horticultural shows.

The flower-arranging section is still immensely popular at local, regional and national flower shows. Competitions are run under the aegis of NAFAS – the National Association of Flower Arrangers' Societies. This is an umbrella organization for some 1500 clubs, founded in 1959 'to encourage the love of flowers and demonstrate their decorative value.' Of all the societies concerned with flowers and gardens it has, apart from the Royal Horticultural Society, by far the biggest and most active membership. At Chelsea Flower Show you may have to queue for half an hour or more to get into the NAFAS exhibition tent. Competitors are given a theme to interpret in their arrangement. In a recent competition there were classes entitled 'Ocean Deep', 'Teapot Trail', 'Receding Contours of this Land' and 'Emerging Chrysalis' to name but a few. Men as well as a women are members. In a random survey of competition winners, four out of twelve were men.

Constance Spry

The undisputed pioneer and queen of flower arrangers was Constance Spry. This formidable but charming woman's first career was in the Ministry of Munitions, where she was head of women staff in the department of aircraft production during World War II. In 1929 she opened a flower shop in Mayfair, London, followed in the 1930s by a school of flower arranging, where her own elegant and distinctive style was taught. It was a style William Robinson and Gertrude Jekyll would have recognized, mixing garden flowers in airy confections with cow parsley, grasses, twigs or branches of hazelnuts, blackberries or ivy berries. Her ideas no longer seem innovative, but in the beginning they were quite unlike anything that had gone before, and executed with such confidence and panache that those who wished to be fashionable rushed to imitate her style in their own flower arrangements.

Constance Spry's books on flower arranging, *How to do the Flowers* and *Party Flowers* became best sellers. If, in a book or a magazine article, she showed a new way of using alchemilla or astrantia or purple cotinus leaves, people would rush to buy those plants for their gardens, just as, today, Delia Smith only has to use cranberries or prunes in a recipe on television for supermarket shelves to empty of those items. So Constance Spry was the obvious choice to mastermind the flower arrangements for Princess Elizabeth's wedding to Philip Mountbatten and then, in 1952, the flowers for her coronation as Queen Elizabeth II.

When she wanted roses for her flower arrangements, Constance Spry liked to use, not florists' Hybrid teas with their scentless, pointed buds, but the big, cabbagey, fragrant blooms that came to be known as 'old-fashioned roses' or simply 'old roses': the roses of Empress Josephine and Malmaison, and of Edwardian hostesses, whose big hairstyles poised on slender necks resembled the full-blown flowers of damask, gallica and hybrid perpetual roses. They had fallen out of favour until Constance Spry rescued them and made them her signature. Her passion was shared by Vita Sackville-West and Graham Stuart Thomas. These three very different personalities united, with a select few fellow enthusiasts, in what Graham Thomas referred to as the Quest.

Old-fashioned roses had become rare, and enthusiasts sought them in tangled corners of neglected gardens, in libraries where they were to be found delicately and accurately represented in the drawings of Redouté, and in the gardens of fellow-connoisseurs such as Mrs Messel at Nymans, and A.T. Johnson in North Wales. Nancy Lindsay had collected old roses in Persia and France, and at Highdown in Sussex Sir Frederick Stern was growing them successfully on chalk. In *The Old Shrub Roses* (1955) Graham Thomas tells how

> Towards the end of the war my interest was greatly quickened by a visit
> from Mrs Constance Spry. The long French names flowed from her,
> enthusiasm was at bursting point; a few glances at the little lot we had
> collected drew forth some remarks that, while they were not disparaging,
> made me realise I had little to shew. There were no half measures with
> Mrs Spry – a long and growing friendship proved this over and over again
> – and she had assiduously collected her roses from French and American
> nurseries, and from gardens here and there, in days before the war.

'bloomy as a bunch of grapes': old roses

The Quest for old roses took Graham Thomas on a tour of botanic gardens, nurseries in Europe and America and private gardens. The latter included Chetwode Manor in Buckinghamshire where Mrs Louis Fleischmann had in her collection the rare Autumn Damask and a fine, floriferous 'Tour de Malakoff'; High Trees, Chalfont St Peter, where he found 'Cramoisi Picotée'; and the Honourable Robert James's garden at Richmond, Yorkshire, after whom the

The rose 'Constance Spry', bred by David Austin and introduced in 1961 by Sunningdale Nurseries, is named after the doyenne of flower arrangers, who also helped rescue old-fashioned roses from obscurity and made them fashionable.

deliciously scented, rampant rambler, 'Bobbie James' is called. Each garden yielded up one or two rarities. At Weston Hall near Towcester, Sacheverell Sitwell had in his collection the sumptuous crimson-purple 'Maréchal Davoust'. Naturally, Major Lawrence Johnston's Hidcote and Mrs Muir's garden next door at Kiftsgate were on the route, and were much admired by Thomas.

Sissinghurst was an inevitable treat on the southern tour. Vita Sackville-West wrote the Foreword to Thomas's *The Old Shrub Roses*. She compared the colours of old roses to those of the carpets of Isfahan, Bokhara and Samarkand, 'rich as a fig broken open, soft as a ripened peach, freckled as an apricot, coral as a pomegranate, bloomy as a bunch of grapes.' The sensuality of her description is persuasive, but she also makes it clear that these are the aristocrats of roses. A taste for them is, like a taste for oysters, acquired. Such a rose

> …bears little resemblance to the highly coloured Hybrid Teas and polyanthas and floribundas of the modern garden. It is a far quieter and more subtle thing, but oh let me say how rewarding a taste it is when once acquired, and how right is Mr Thomas when he implies that they have all the attraction that sentiment, history, botany, or association can lend them.

In other words, these roses were not for any old gardener. They were for the cultured, well-read, discerning few: only the sort of people who could tell a Helford Native from a Colchester would be admitted to the charmed circle where the merits of 'Président de Sèzes' and 'Tricolore de Flandres' were compared, rose names dropped and cuttings swapped.

The point of old-fashioned roses was that they were plants for connoisseurs. Graham Thomas himself admitted that they 'did not immediately appeal to me, their mauve-pinks and purples being so unexpected that, like many others newly approaching this class of rose, I was almost repelled.' But in due course their strange colouring became one of the things that attracted him most, and he wrote of losing his heart to the extraordinary mixture of cerise, violet and lilac-grey in the perfectly shaped Gallica 'Belle de Crécy'.

Graham Thomas followed up with *Shrub Roses of Today* (1962) and *Climbing Roses Old and New* (1965); the reputation of Constance Spry as the doyenne of domestic elegance continued to increase, and Vita Sackville-West's Sissinghurst grew in beauty as its plants matured. The triumvirate of good taste brought the unwanted Cinderellas of the rose garden out into the limelight and waved a magic wand. Old roses became all the rage for the remaining decades of the twentieth century. Soon, nobody who aspired to good taste would allow a hybrid tea or floribunda rose into their garden.

Colour schemes

The fashion for old roses had far-reaching effects. Gardeners who did not have a single Gallica, Damask or Bourbon rose in their garden were unconsciously influenced by the old rose cult in their choice of plants. Only a limited range of other colours flattered the dusky purples, magentas and mauves that Graham Thomas initially found so difficult to enjoy, and this limited colour range, with the roses they enhanced, became indicators of good taste. The only admissible orange-related shades were the pinky apricot and peach range exemplified in some of the hybrid musk roses such as 'Buff Beauty' or the China rose 'Mutabilis', neither of which are, strictly speaking, old roses, but they were acceptably refined in appearance. Harsher shades of orange and any yellow with the faintest hit of brassiness were greeted with an involuntary shudder, although the pale yellows of verbascum and *Digitalis grandiflora* were recognized as the perfect complement to dark crimson and purple roses.

For nearly 50 years the gardens people envied and emulated were pink, blue, mauve and white with lots of grey and silver-leaved plants. Touches of purple, crimson and pale yellow provided daring highlights. It was a winning formula, and many of the most admired gardens today still adhere to it. Old roses, lightly pruned so as to produce billowing masses of colour in June, were an ideal component in formal beds with luxuriant informal planting in the Sissinghurst style. And, to emphasize the formal structure, the Tudor habit of edging beds with clipped box or lavender was revived. The style and colour scheme seems so completely suited to the English climate and light, and to the English temperament, that it has become a classical kind of gardening, from which gardeners may from time to time make adventurous sorties, but to which they will always return, as English women return, in the cycle of fashion, to flowery summer frocks and pastel-coloured cardigans.

It would be wrong to give the impression that a majority of gardeners embraced the fashionable style of the time, or took a fancy to old-fashioned roses. Roses were certainly the best-loved flower and could be found in one of their many forms in almost every garden. But most rose enthusiasts still grew hybrid tea and floribunda roses, in bush form, as standards and as climbers. Many gardeners were members of the Royal National Rose Society, formed in 1876. One of the services the Society provided was the trial of the numerous new roses introduced each year by hopeful breeders, amateurs as well as professionals.

The popularity of many new varieties was short-lived, their faults becoming apparent after a few years.

Of the many roses introduced in the 1950s and 1960s, those that have stood the test of time include the coral-scarlet 'Fragrant Cloud', yellow 'Grandpa Dickson', and 'Pascali', one of the loveliest ever white roses. The showy and perennially popular multicoloured red and yellow climber, 'Masquerade' was introduced in 1958, and the even gaudier 'Superstar', with its neon vermilion flowers, came in 1960. 'Who', the more fastidious gardeners asked, 'would want a rose with the vulgar colouring of a geranium?' The answer seemed to be, 'Almost everyone.' Among the best of the floribundas, bright, floriferous and healthy but mostly lacking in scent, were the brilliant red 'Evelyn Fison', 'Pink Parfait', the tall, pink 'Queen Elizabeth' and two good yellow roses, 'Arthur Bell' and 'Chinatown'.

The legendary 'Peace', the most popular rose of all time on account of its symbolic significance as well as its huge, pink-flushed yellow blooms, was bred by the French grower Francis Meilland at his nursery near Lyons in France, in 1939.

The tradition of specialized plant collecting, begun in the late nineteenth century by Florists' Societies in the industrial cities of the North and Midlands, still thrives. 'Cacti in the Greenhouse at Cookham Dean', Stanley Spencer.

Before the outbreak of World War II he was able to ensure a future for his promising, as yet unnamed, new rose, no. 3-35-40, by sending propagation material to colleagues in Germany and Italy. Also, by great good fortune, the American consul in Lyons was a rose-fancier, and when he had to leave in November 1939 he volunteered, in spite of a strict baggage allowance, to take a package from Meilland to the Pennsylvanian rose grower Robert Pyle. At the end of the war Meilland discovered that his rose had swept the board in trials in Italy and Germany and earned the highest rating ever in the All American Rose Selection trials. With a surge of postwar optimism, it was decided to launch the wonder-rose under the name 'Peace' in 1945. Since then, well over 100 million plants of 'Peace' have been sold worldwide, assuring its place in garden history.

'Iceberg' was another rose that changed the look of gardens. Wilhelm Kordes bred the immensely successful white floribunda in Germany and introduced it in 1958. It is taller than most floribunda roses, with a loose, informal, shrubby habit making it ideal for mixed planting, for planting in a mass, or for linking old and modern roses in the same scheme. Another great triumph of Kordes's work was the introduction of the 'Frühling' (meaning 'spring') series of early-flowering shrub roses. They have greatly encouraged the use of shrub and species roses in wild and informal gardens.

Special interests

Some gardeners like to specialize in a particular plant species, whether or not they seek recognition of their success on the show bench. Their interests are served by specialist societies, where they can get advice and enjoy the camaraderie of a shared passion. The Alpine Garden Society, founded in 1929 became one of the most popular and successful. Some societies have been around for a long time: the National Chrysanthemum Society since 1846, the National Auricula and Primrose Society since 1876, The National Dahlia Society since 1881 and the National Sweet Pea Society since 1900. Postwar improvements in transport made it easier to attend meetings, and meant that members could travel farther afield to meet local groups and exchange news, views and plants. The National Begonia Society began in 1948, the British Pelargonium and Geranium Society in 1951, and the Heather Society in 1963.

The art of imitation

In the decades after World War II, the advance of techniques in colour photography and the lower cost of colour reproduction in books and magazines meant that advice on the cultivation of individual species, or on garden plants in general, was presented more attractively than ever before. Earlier books had shown images of ideal gardens in the form of charming and picturesque watercolours by such artists as Beatrice Parsons, George Elgood and Ella du Cane. Eventually coloured photographic flower portraits took their place. *The Border in Colour* (1944 revised in 1947 and 1948) by T.C. Mansfield consists mainly of an alphabetical list of herbaceous plants with brief descriptions of each, illustrated by colour photographs of the flowers. It is one of a series by same author, his other books dealing with *Alpines, Roses, Shrubs, Annuals* and *Carnations*. Each volume has 80 full-page colour plates.

Site-specific advice for gardeners also became available in books such as *A Chalk Garden* (1960) by Sir Frederick Stern and *Gardening on Chalk and Limestone* (1965) by E. Bertram Anderson.

Garden visiting

Improved rail and road communications, relatively cheap fares and increased car ownership led to an increase in the popularity of garden visiting as a leisure activity. The result was an unprecedented interchange of garden design ideas, suggestions for plant combinations and sometimes the exchange of actual plants. The National Gardens Scheme began in 1927, with the opening of 600 private gardens up and down the country, in aid of charity. Since then the N.G.S. has gone from strength to strength, and now lists, in its famous Yellow Book, more than 3600 gardens, mostly designed and looked after by their owners. Many of these gardens, not necessarily big or grand in style, set standards of excellence that are either inspiring or depressing, according to the temperament of the visitor.

In 1948 The National Trust made its first acquisition of a garden without a house: Hidcote. As soon as it was recognized that some gardens merited preservation for the nation regardless of the quality of the house they belonged to, others quickly followed. Among the earliest were Nymans and Sheffield Park in Sussex and Trengwainton in Cornwall, with its wonderful collection of camellias, magnolias, rhododendrons and other trees and shrubs, many of them tender. Owners of historic houses also began to open their gardens to paying visitors, as a way of helping to finance their upkeep.

Group tours bringing visitors in charabancs were organized by local horticultural societies and other interested groups. Garden visitors usually came equipped with cameras, and from the 1950s onwards, loaded them with colour film. From this time, many enthusiasts saw gardens almost exclusively through a lens, and judged gardens mainly according to their pictorial quality.

Flower shows

Chelsea Flower Show became an annual mecca for keen gardeners. Many went to Chelsea equipped with their cameras and were able to show friends who could not make it to the event photographs of what they had seen there. Chelsea and other shows fed the acquisitiveness that is part of human nature. Impulse buying was irresistible; everyone's garden has room for just one more plant, and the newest and rarest could be ordered on the spot. Many nurseries still take up to one-third of their annual orders at Chelsea. It is their opportunity to meet their customers and it is the customers' opportunity to chat to the experts and enjoy a knowledgeable glow.

The themes of gardens exhibited at Chelsea Flower Show have always reflected current gardening fashions. Designed by Marney Hall for Chelsea 1998, this Butterfly Conservation garden is planned with flowering plants that will attract many different species of butterfly.

Garden furniture, ornaments, tools and equipment were all exhibited and could be ordered at Chelsea. In the postwar decades the demonstration gardens became a more and more popular feature, to be photographed and copied at home. Many visitors to the Show had gardens about the same size as the demonstration plots, so if they wished to, and could afford to, they could imitate the designs in every detail.

Gardening was now a serious leisure pursuit, and the horticultural industry was becoming a serious earner. Surveys in Allan Patmore's *Land and Leisure* (1970) showed that for married men interest in gardening started between the ages of 23 and 30, and at that age gardening occupied 7 per cent of their leisure time. Thereafter, the percentage rose steadily to a peak of 20 per cent of the leisure time of men over 61. For all age groups, gardening was second only to watching television as a leisure pursuit. Perhaps surprisingly, women spent less of their leisure time gardening: 3.5 per cent for married women between 23 and 30 rising to 10 percent at over 61.

Out of a total of 18.3 million homes, 14 million had gardens; that is, four out of five. These gardens occupied about 620,000 acres – an area about the size of Dorset – of which almost 500,000 acres were lawn.

For a predominantly urban population, gardens now became sanctuaries; more traffic moving at faster speeds made the world outside unsafe and unpleasant. Noise and atmospheric pollution could not be kept out, but they could be ignored, and, what was more important, children could be kept safely inside the garden. Children became important, perhaps the most important, users of gardens, and the planning of the garden and its elements began to centre on them. Many gardens became playgrounds equipped with sand pits, paddling pools, swings, climbing frames, and paved areas for riding tricycles and scooters. In his book *Down to Earth Gardening* (1967) Lawrence D. Hills recognized other practical requirements for gardens, including the need for access across flowerbeds for the window cleaner, space for a clothes line, and hard standing for a car. He was concerned with helping ordinary people make gardens properly suited to modern family life.

Large gardens:
One of the results of two world wars was that men and women were no longer available, willing, or trained for domestic service in the house or the garden. 'You can't get the staff' was a recurrent moan among owners of large houses with large gardens, and even if you could, fewer employers could afford to pay them than in the past. Wages had risen, although, compared to other work,

domestic service and gardening were still poorly paid; and the new generation of owners of large family houses were impoverished by taxation in the form of punitive death duties.

Hazelbury Manor in Wiltshire was a fairly typical example. Its eight acres of garden were laid out in the early twentieth century by George Kidston. Having private means (his family had made their fortune from shipbuilding on the Clyde in Glasgow), Kidston was able to retire early from the diplomatic service and buy Hazelbury, then a tumbledown farmhouse with no garden at all to speak of. A connoisseur of art and an amateur antiquarian, he planned to spend his long retirement restoring the house in authentic early Tudor style. He employed the architect Harold Brakspeare, an expert in medieval architecture who had worked on restoration projects at Battle Abbey in Sussex, St Nicholas Priory at Exeter and Haddon Hall in Derbyshire. Nearer to Hazelbury, Brakspeare had restored Great Chalfield Manor near Bath (now owned by The National Trust), a project very similar to that at Hazelbury.

Every year gardeners flock to Chelsea Flower Show and the Hampton Court Show to see what is new. Millions more watch television programmes about Chelsea and the increasing number of other garden shows held all over Britain.

There is no evidence that Brakspeare advised on the garden layout, but he and George Kidston together may have been responsible for the masterly division of the ground around the manor into walled rectangular spaces of different sizes and at different levels. At the heart of the house there was a courtyard enclosed on all four sides. This was kept as an unornamented grass space, like a monastic cloister. On the entrance front, to the south, steps led down from a broad, deep, balustraded terrace to a large, walled forecourt, and, on the west side, there was a croquet lawn on a higher level, shaded at one end by a group of mature beech trees. During and immediately after World War II there was invariably a pram under the beech trees with one of the Kidstons' grandchildren mesmerized by the shifting pattern of sunlight through the luminous beech leaves.

At a still higher level, a flight of broad, shallow stone steps led to a small orchard dominated by an ancient mulberry tree with branches touching the ground. A group of older grandchildren could often be found perched in its leafy canopy, their mouths, hands and clothes stained purple-black with mulberry juice. Above the mulberry garden a bowling green was backed by a narrow bed of irises against a high, south-facing boundary wall with plum and pear trees trained against it. At one end of the wall a stone lookout tower gave a view across cornfields to beech woods in the distance.

At the opposite end of the bowling green you could enter, through a faded green wooden door, a garden on the north side of the house surrounded by high stone walls. In one wall there was a massive wooden double door which was never opened. It was surmounted by an elaborate stone arabesque known to the grandchildren as 'The Big Eye'. In the Big Eye garden, lavender and clipped box hedges surrounded beds of cabbages and sprouts. Big Roman snails inhabited the box hedge, and the children's rabbits and bantams kept the grass short in the centre of the garden. Steep steps led down to a back yard outside the kitchen scullery, where trugs of muddy potatoes and carrots were deposited by the head gardener for the cook's attention.

The most striking part of the garden was to the east of the house and divided from the house by the driveway and a large stone-built garage block. Known as the Long Garden, it consisted of a very large lawn, about a quarter of which was marked out as a tennis court during the summer. At the farthest end of the lawn a swing hung from the branches of one of a pair of ancient walnut trees. The lawn was sunk between broad grass walks lined with yew topiary pieces, which might pass for chess men although none bore any resemblance to an actual knight, bishop, castle or pawn. Some of the yews seemed to be wearing cardinals' hats. These walks along the upper level were punctuated by various incidents, including a rose garden, herbaceous borders, an apple orchard, some vegetable patches and netted strawberry beds hidden behind espaliered fruit trees, stone summer houses with beds of regale lilies along their walls and a nuttery. The Long Garden was surrounded by dry-stone walls with beech hedges on stilts rising above them. There was a row of unkempt plots at the furthest boundary. These were the children's 'gardens'. Each grandchild was given his or her own plot, and they were all always left neglected and weed-infested. 'We're growing groundsel and dandelions to feed our rabbits,' the children would say if a grown-up complained.

In 1939, the grandchildren's presence became permanent for the duration of the war, when George and Lilian Kidston's three eldest daughters brought their families to Hazelbury while their husbands were away with the army. Two gardeners, where there had once been half a dozen, managed to produce enough vegetables to feed the large, extended family, but the Long Garden became a hay field, the glasshouses remained empty and many beds and borders became overrun by weeds.

Peace restored

When peace came, petrol was in due course available for mowing machines, and the lawns were restored. The greenhouses were never used again and it became a struggle to keep beds and borders tidy. The two gardeners could never quite cope with the workload. Adults in the family weeded and deadheaded and grandchildren were pressed into service and bribed to weed (sixpence for a sack of weeds, and not too much earth on the roots) and to collect windfall fruit (tuppence a pound). The gardens were still beautiful and romantic, but they never recovered their prewar glory.

When George Kidston died, his son sold the estate to pay death duties. A local landowner bought it for the sake of the 180-acre home farm, and let the house to a girls' finishing school. Later, in the 1980s, it became a family house again when it was bought by the architect Ian Pollard. He had his own vision of a renaissance for Hazelbury's gardens. Keeping George Kidston's layout more or less intact, he superimposed water features and a massive rockery and planted the beds and borders in dramatic and flamboyant style. His personal, idiosyncratic vision was expressed beyond the boundaries of the original gardens in a modern interpretation of a prehistoric stone circle and two bosom-like mounds on one side of the front drive. Now Ian Pollard has moved on, to make a highly individual garden at Abbey House at Malmesbury in Wiltshire, another medieval house where Harold Brakspeare worked.

The only unusual thing about the story of Hazelbury's garden is its restoration. Hazelbury was lucky to find such an owner as Ian Pollard. But after World War II hundreds of other large country houses became schools, nursing homes or other institutions when their owners could no longer afford their upkeep. Often the greater part of their gardens was sold for housing development. Even when the garden remained intact, and in spite of the labour-saving advantages of new technology such as motor mowers, lawn edgers, hedge trimmers and chainsaws, the need for a new, low-maintenance form of gardening was apparent. Owners started by grassing over the elaborate beds that had been cut into the lawns of prewar gardens, but that only added to the amount of mowing that had to be done. Larger lawns also reduced the amount of flowering plants that could be grown, thereby, in the eyes of some people, making the garden less interesting.

'…an undergrowth… at all seasons pleasing to look upon'

There was an alternative. Arthur Tysilio Johnson, who, with his wife Nora made an informal woodland garden in North Wales, aiming at naturalistic plant groupings, wrote in 1950:

> We had begun to focus most of our energies on shrubs long before the war came to step up that need for economy, which falling dividends, rising taxation and increasing labour difficulties, had made imperative… It was [also] the problem as to how to maintain the garden by our own labours that was the snag to be overcome….
>
> Thus, some of our older shrub plantations, which now rarely get more than a few hours' attention in the course of the year… once interplanted with innocuous ground covering plants, bulbs and other plants, now have an undergrowth that may be anything but disciplined, but which is at all seasons pleasing to look upon…
>
> In no other department of gardening is that all-season provision of colour and form so pronounced as that in which shrubs and trees prevail. None other does so much in so brief a period to endow the garden with that grace of ripeness which is, or should be, the primary objective of each one of us.

The plantsman and garden designer, Michael Haworth-Booth's *Effective Flowering Shrubs* was published in 1951, with revised editions in 1958 and 1962. He also makes a strong case for shrubs, carefully selected:

Throughout this book I am out for flowers – large, bold, beautiful flowers, equal to, or surpassing, those borne by herbs, bulbs, annuals, orchids or anything else. I have no use for dowdy shrubs… I hold that the finest, most effective, gardenable flowers are borne by flowering shrubs and, in the following pages, I shall do my best to prove it.

Haworth-Booth's book recommends an informal layout:

Rectangular beds and straight lines do not take advantage of the natural, year-round symmetry and beauty of the plantings possible with shrubs. Island-like curving shapes are much more pleasing… a lawned glade stretching away as far as possible in a curving line with informal beds of shrubs at the sides.

He took the reader through the seasons from camellias, chaenomeles and magnolias in early spring to hydrangeas, eucryphias and fuchsias in late summer. He recommended planting the main shrubs at their ultimate distances and filling in with expendable or short-lived shrubs such as common broom, heathers, tree lupins, cistus and ceanothus. He recommended pegging down shrubs to ensure symmetrical growth, well clad right down to the ground, and mulching with fresh fallen leaves or bracken fronds to feed the shrubs and prevent weed germination. To describe his system he coined the phrase 'close boskage'. As well as writing on gardening subjects (notably hydrangeas and tree peonies) he was the author of a manual on the French game of *boules*.

Haworth-Booth's shrubs were carpeted with mulch until they became knitted into close boskage, with no underplanting. But other garden writers turned their attention to A.T. Johnson's 'innocuous ground covering plants.' Margery Fish published *Ground Cover Plants* in 1964. Ground cover, she wrote, 'helps the plants as well as the gardener' by conserving moisture. 'After all this is nature's way. There is no bare soil in the wild; it is only man who keeps scratching away to keep clean the naked soil he has produced artificially.' Her book is organized by types of ground cover (foliage plants, herbaceous, carpeters, annuals, evergreens, trailers, etc.) and by garden situations (woodland, acid soil, sun, banks, damp places, poor soils).

The phrase 'ground cover' was new but the idea was not. Canon Ellacombe had already touched on the desirability of emulating 'nature's way' as early as 1895 in his book *In a Gloucestershire Garden*, where he suggested growing herbaceous plants and alpines among shrubs.

It is too much the fashion to keep every plant in a border as separate as possible from its neighbour; but we have only to go to the nearest hedgerow to see how plants flourish by nestling into each other; and on the barest Alpine hillsides the plants love to get near the shelter of the low shrubs, and even to grow so much among the roots as to appear almost parasitical. To dwell under the shadow of something better and stronger than one's self is as good for flowers as it is for man…

Vita Sackville-West also wrote on the subject of ground cover:

The more I prowl round my garden at this time of year [May], especially during that stolen hour of half-dusk between tea and supper, the more do I become convinced that a great secret of good gardening lies in covering every patch of the ground with some suitable carpeter… with little low things that will crawl about, keeping weeds away and tucking themselves into chinks that would otherwise be devoid of interest or prettiness.

She suggests violets, *Arenaria balearica* and *Cotula squalida*. Elsewhere she describes an underplanting of sweet woodruff, star of Bethlehem (*Ornithogalum nutans*), wood anemones, lily of the valley and Solomon's seal in a small grove of birch or whitebeam 'It must all be green and white; cool, symmetrical, and severe.'

Plants for Ground-Cover by Graham Stuart Thomas was published in association with the Royal Horticultural Society in 1970. In his introduction he sets out precepts worth taking with us into the next chapter:

If you are like me you wish for a large garden where you can rest and gain refreshment for the mind, with a constant succession of beauty in one form or another throughout the twelve months; in spite of all this the garden should cause the least work. To achieve this I ask you to think on these precepts:

1. That leaves are more important than flowers.
2. That green in its many variations is a colour that deserves the closest attention and appraisal in a garden.
3. That a plant or shrub should be assessed on all its points – its stance and character (usually known in horticulture as its 'habit'), its foliage (colour, shape, size, texture), as well as the colour of its flowers, its flowering period and its fruiting propensities.
4. That a mulch of dead leaves or other decomposing vegetable matter is

an asset of incalculable value in regard to fertility and is not to be eschewed on account of untidiness.

5. That it is unnecessary to dig and hoe to ensure the good health of your plants.

Russell Page, perhaps the finest British garden designer in the second half of the twentieth century, would have endorsed these precepts. Much of his work was done abroad and can still be seen in France and Switzerland. But gardens, as we know only too well, are ephemeral and it is his writing that reverberates down the years. He wrote only one book, *The Education of a Gardener* (1962), describing his work up till that date (he continued working until his death in 1985) and setting out his design philosophy. The most thoughtful book about garden design of his generation, it is also perhaps the most inspirational, and it is written in a straightforward, easy style. Almost all the outstanding gardeners of his time, when asked what has influenced them most, mention Russell Page's book.

People as well as plants benefit from summer sun and shelter in the garden. A lazy afternoon spent in the company of beautiful plants and flowers is a rare indulgence for gardeners. 'Figure in the Garden', by David Inshaw, 1989.

12   Y ESTERDAY AND
      T OMORROW

Full Circle    321

B Y THE 1960S, INCREASED general prosperity and
shorter working hours meant that people had more
money and more time to spend on their gardens. Their
horticultural shopping requirements were served by a
revolution in retailing that had started in the 1950s in
America. The rise of garden centres was made possible by
an insatiable demand for plants and other garden needs,
and the means to satisfy the demand all the year round. Traditionally, plants
were marketed by the nurseries that grew them. Customers placed their orders
at shows or chose their plants from catalogues. The plants were dug and sent out
in the planting season, between October and April. The new technique that
brought about the revolution was the raising of plants in pots, making it possible
to sell them throughout the year.

One of the nurserymen who spotted the way things were going was Walter
Pennell. His family business was a nursery on the outskirts of Lincoln, founded
by Richard Pennell in 1780, and latterly specializing in clematis. Among their
introductions were 'Vyvyan Pennell', 'Walter Pennell' and 'Veronica's Choice'.
Walter Pennell's first 'garden centre', opened in 1966, was a small shop with
ad-jacent beds of plants growing in old crisp tins from the nearby Smith's Crisp

*The Beth Chatto gardens at Elmstead Market in Essex. Beth Chatto has had a great influence on
gardeners, helping them to choose plants suited to local conditions and place them to best advantage.*

Factory. He went on to develop purpose-built centres at Doncaster, Grimsby and Lincoln. Competition from the new garden centres caused a number of all-purpose, old-fashioned nurseries to go out of business. But Pennells, being specialists, responded to the challenge by stepping up their production of clematis and other climbing plants and supplying them in containers to the growing number of garden centres.

Another family firm who now own and run six garden centres, started with just three greenhouses in Gloucester, growing cut flowers which they sold from a stall in Gloucester market. Alfred Hurran had left school at 14, and, after working at a rose nursery in Essex, came to Gloucester to start his own business in 1909 when he was 25. The family business prospered and in due course they had six florists' shops in the area. In the 1960s, Stewart Hurran, the youngest of Alfred's four sons, opened their first garden centre, launched by the BBC's gardening star, Percy Thrower.

The biggest success story was that of Harry Williamson of King's Acre near Hereford. He started with a 5-acre rose field and, in 1961, having visited garden centres in the USA, opened his own. For the Pennells, it was crisp tins. At Williamson's first Wyevale Garden Centre the plants were grown in jam tins from a local factory. The Wyevale group's success was phenomenal. By 1987 they had 14 garden centres and the company was floated on the stock exchange. Since then, they have been gobbling up other companies including Cramphorns PLC, Kennedy's and, in the year 2000, Country Gardens PLC. They now operate 120 garden centres and command the lion's share of what is still an increasingly lucrative market.

The value of sales of horticultural products in the United Kingdom in 1999 has been estimated at £2.83 billion, of which 31.4 per cent was sales of plants. The overall market is forecast to go on growing by 4–5 per cent per annum up to 2003. The UK gardening industry is an important one, employing over 80,000 people. There are already an estimated 20 million regular gardeners, all existing or potential customers, and if the socio-economic trend towards increasing home ownership, higher disposable incomes and an ageing (leisured) population continues, the industry will go on expanding.

Already, as happens in other industries, the big fish are swallowing the minnows. But, just as the takeover of small breweries by the big operators led to the formation of the Campaign for Real Ale, followed by the rise of new small breweries making traditional beer for discerning drinkers, so there are also many small nurseries setting up in business to grow the unusual plants so many gardeners want, which cannot be mass-produced for the large garden centres.

All tastes can be catered for it seems. Some families enjoy a weekend outing to a large garden centre where there is play equipment for the children and a restaurant for lunch, and where you can buy not only enough plants to make an instant garden, but also a greenhouse or a shed, tools and a mowing machine, furniture, fountains and fish, barbecues and ornaments. You can buy outdoor clothes, books not only about gardening but also about cooking, biscuits, jams and fudge; in season, you can visit Santa's Grotto.

Other gardeners prefer to visit a small nursery specializing in their own obsession – auriculas, perhaps, or gentians. The nursery will probably have a pretty garden where you can see the plants growing, and pick up a few ideas. It may also have a knowledgeable owner on hand to chat about the plants and their requirements. There may be time to look in at a nearby garden listed in the 'Yellow Book' as open that day under the National Gardens Scheme.

'…to search out and cultivate old flowers which have become scarce'

There have always been gardeners with special interests in particular plants, and there are specialist nurseries to serve their enthusiasms. But from the 1980s to the end of the twentieth century, the expansion in the market for unusual plants, particularly herbaceous perennials, has been remarkable. Herbaceous plants, the stalwarts of colourful borders for half a century, were relegated to the wilderness or, worse, the compost heap, during the period when the fashion for labour-saving shrubs and ground cover ruled. But like all fashions, it has changed, helped perhaps by an increased number of retired people who actually enjoy working in their gardens and have the time for it. Now that labour-saving is no longer an issue, some people have grown tired of what has become a banal and boring formula and are looking in a new direction.

The new direction, for many gardeners, has been backwards. Some of Gertrude Jekyll's and Margery Fish's books were reissued in paperback in the early 1980s. Miss Jekyll's use of herbaceous plants had great appeal for gardeners whose nostalgia for the gardens of the past was combined with a love of, and an interest in, colour. The two writers shared an appreciation of the artless simplicity of cottage gardens, and were eloquent in their pleas to save cottage plants before they disappeared for ever. Gertrude Jekyll could be described as an early advocate of conservation.

But she was not the first. Mrs Horatia Ewing was there a short time before her with *Mary's Meadow*, serialized in *Aunt Judy's Magazine* between 1883 and 1884. It is a story for children about the rescue of an old hose-in-hose cowslip from a cottage garden. She also wrote *Letters from a Little Garden* (1885), in which she regretted that in earlier decades gardeners had got rid of herbaceous plants on to rubbish heaps to make way for bedding plants. The old plants, she wrote, could only be found in cottage gardens:

> It is such little gardens which have kept for us the Blue Primroses, the highly fragrant summer roses (including Rose de Meaux and the red and copper Brier), countless beautiful varieties of Daffy-down-dillies, and all the best of sweet, various and hardy flowers which are now returning… from the village to the hall.
>   It is still in the cottage gardens chiefly that the Crown Imperial hangs its royal head. One may buy sheaves of it in the Taunton market-place on early summer Saturdays. What a stately flower it is! And in the paler variety, of what an exquisite yellow!

Mrs Ewing founded the Parkinson Society (it no longer exists) 'to search out and cultivate old flowers which have become scarce.' In 1978 the NCCPG was founded, under the patronage of HRH the Prince of Wales, for the same purpose, expressed at greater length. Its full name is the National Council for the Conservation of Plants and Gardens, its remit to 'conserve, document, promote and make available Britain and Ireland's great biodiversity of garden plants for the benefit of horticulture, education and science.' The Hardy Plant Society has been going longer, for 40 years. Its aim is similar, to 'help conserve older, rarer and unusual plants to make them more available to gardeners.' The Hardy Plant Society has a flourishing membership of 12,000, perhaps because it organizes, on a local basis, extremely popular plant sales where the keen gardener might pick up something not commercially available, grown by a fellow member.

Thanks to these and a few other conservation organizations, the future of an enormous number of garden plants is assured. At the same time, every year a large number of new plant varieties are launched on the market. Whatever the commodity, the word 'new' means increased sales, and the plant breeders and garden centres are well aware of this. The market for plants never seems to get saturated. But there must come a time when a new plant becomes an old one, and a decision has to be taken about whether it deserves to be conserved.

Gardening with a conscience

Another branch of the conservation movement was concerned with wild British plants, particularly herbaceous flowers growing in meadows and hedgerows. Dr Miriam Rothschild was one of the most influential conservationists. A scientist of great distinction, largely self-taught, she had wide-ranging interests. Before World War II she studied marine biology, specializing in snails and their parasites. Her war work began with a government project to produce chicken food from seaweed, and continued with code-breaking at the now celebrated secret centre at Bletchley Park. But she became best known as the 'Flea Lady', for her continuation of the research of her father, Charles Rothschild, who had discovered, in Egypt, the species responsible for spreading bubonic plague. She became the leading international authority on fleas and parasites, somehow managing to combine her work with bringing up six children.

As far as gardening was concerned, Dr Rothschild took a very different direction from her forebears at Exbury, Gunnersbury and Waddesden. Initially, she retained the conventional, formal garden at her home, Ashton Wold in Northamptonshire. But in the 1970s she had her house altered to make it smaller and more manageable and remade the garden, replacing flowerbeds with fruit trees and flowering shrubs. The garden became wilder as her concern for the wild flowers she had loved but taken for granted as a child, developed. In a television interview she described the moment when she first realized they were at risk:

> I woke up suddenly one morning and looked at the fields. Not a flower in sight. Modern agriculture had bulldozed, weed-killed and drained all the flowers out of the fields that I'd known as a child. We were living on a snooker table. So we let the grass grow and sowed flower seeds taken from disused local airfields: ninety-six species grew up, some of them self-sown and quite rare, including orchids. Anyone with non-acid soil can do it.

Within the garden she began her wildflower experiments on the poor, free-draining, limy soil of the old tennis courts. After 15 years of experimentation and research, she was able to go into commercial production, selling wild-flower plants in containers and wild-flower seed mixes for meadows, woodland and other habitats. In due course, she covered about 150 acres at Ashton Wold with wild-flower meadow to make a nature reserve. Butterflies and dragonflies, more glamorous than fleas to most of us, were another passionate interest of Dr Rothschild, and the National Dragonfly Reserve has been set up there.

The other great ambassador for native flowers was John Chambers, a seedsman who had the vision, and the sound commercial instinct, to put all his resources into the production of wild-flower seed in 1980. He had been working for Mommersteeg International, a large company based in Northamptonshire, supplying grass-seed mixes to local authorities, farmers and landscapers. The first indication of the way things were changing came from customers who wanted to put back into the land the plants that modern farming practices and landscape maintenance methods had taken out.

In due course, John Chambers left to start his own business, packaging wild-flower seeds for sale to gardeners. The packets had attractive pictures of the contents, and gave cultural instructions, and John was adept at promoting them. His first Chelsea Flower Show exhibit attracted a great deal of attention. His stand was simply covered with species-rich turf, the grass hardly visible among the flowers. Nothing like it had been seen before. Gardeners visiting the Chelsea Show received a further shock to the system in 1993 when Julie Toll's design for a wild garden won the sword of honour for Best Garden in the Show. It was the most imaginative award the Royal Horticultural Society had ever made. Her exhibit consisted simply of a sand dune and its vegetation removed from the seaside to the show site. It called into question the generally accepted idea of what a garden is, and liberated gardeners to follow their own inclinations.

There are now a great many nurseries specializing in wild-flower seeds and plants, and many gardeners interested not only in creating flowery meadows but also in using native plants in beds and borders. Some gardeners grow them to ensure their survival now that there are so few wild places left for them. Since World War I, 95 per cent of British lowland and 80 per cent of upland unimproved species-rich grassland has gone, 80 per cent of chalk downland, 50 per cent of broadleaved and coppiced woodland and unmeasurable miles of hedgerow. Other gardeners simply enjoy the pretty, garden-worthy flowers of many native species, finding their quiet charm better suited to the English light and climate, and to the surrounding landscape, than the strong, bright colouring of exotic species. But the overriding motive for growing native wild plants is probably nostalgia. David Bellamy, the naturalist and conservationist, expressed this in his foreword to John Chambers' book *Wild Flower Garden*, 1987:

> One of the most pleasant memories of my childhood was being able to go into the old brickfields opposite my home on the outskirts of London to pick a bunch of wild flowers to give to my mother.
> It was in this way that I soon learned that the petals fall off Buttercups, how Dog daisies got their first name and why my granny would never allow May Blossom in the house… In the post-war years it was possible to cycle from London to Brighton and it was flowers all the way, roadside verges, small fields with cows grazing contentedly on floriferous salads and

in autumn the hedgerows groaning with Hips, Haws, Filberts, Sloes, Geans and Crabs, a surfeit of fruits to feed the birds and small mammals alike... The countryside of my youth was indeed a place of great variety, dazzling beauty and, we then thought, everlasting interest. Now sadly much of that has gone, swept away by a thing called progress.

Most gardeners' ideal wild garden would consist of nature without the stinging nettles, brambles and briers. But for others, the purpose is to support wild life in the garden, providing food and breeding places for birds, butterflies and other insects, hedgehogs and other small mammals, amphibians such as frogs and newts. A successful wildlife garden is less orderly than most, and nettles and brambles are essential components.

The organic movement
Wildlife is important to the increasing number of gardeners who wish to avoid using chemical preparations in the garden, whether pesticides, fungicides or fertilizers. They need ladybirds to feed on aphids, hedgehogs to eat slugs, thrushes to deal with snails, and other birds to get rid of a variety of undesirable insects and creepy-crawlies. They also need to make as much compost and leaf mould as they can, to provide nutritious mulches for their plants. If provision for these requirements is made in a small garden, it will look a little different from a garden where the plants, plant food and pesticides are bought seasonally from the local garden centre. The character of the organic garden is distinctive.

Today's organic gardeners owe a great debt to Lawrence Hills, the founder of the Henry Doubleday Research Association. This visionary man started out as a horticulturalist and freelance journalist writing for *The Observer* for seven years, for *Punch*, and *The Countryman*. In the 1950s he became interested, to the point of obsession, in the plant Russian comfrey and its properties. It is indeed something of a wonder-plant. Hills' research led him to promote it as a plant food rich in potash. Its great advantage was (and is) that it could be cut, left to wilt for 48 hours, then used to feed garden crops, without going through a composting process. Soaked in water for four weeks, the leaves make an excellent food for potatoes, tomatoes and roses. Medicinally, comfrey ointment is used to sooth eczema and other skin inflammations, bruises, sprains and swellings. Hills

Overleaf: *In the last few decades, awareness of the threat to Britain's native plants and native creatures has caused gardeners to bring wild plants into their gardens, as well as to campaign for their conservation in the wild. A bluebell wood at Coton Manor, Northamptonshire.*

carried out his experiments with comfrey on an acre of land he bought for £300 at Bocking in Essex. In 1958 he decided to set up a charity to continue studying the uses of comfrey and to improve organic methods of growing plants.

He called the charity the Henry Doubleday Research Association after a Quaker smallholder who, in the nineteenth century, had as strong a belief in comfrey as Hills himself, and had devoted his life to promoting its use. With equal devotion, Lawrence Hills and his wife Cherry worked unpaid for the Association. By 1970 it had attracted some 17,000 subscribing members and was able to employ a young couple, Alan and Jackie Gear, both scientists. Now the membership has swelled to 28,000 and the Association is run from its own 22-acre research establishment at Ryton-on-Dunsmore near Coventry and has two other display gardens at Yalding in Kent and in the 250-year-old walled kitchen garden at English Heritage's Audley End in Essex. Among HDRA's assets is its Heritage Seed Library, where old and rare vegetable varieties are saved for posterity and distributed to the members to grow in their gardens.

Lawrence Hills's books include *Comfrey Past, Present and Future*, *Grow your own Fruit and Vegetables* and *Down to Earth Gardening*.

'Garden with nature, not struggle against her'

Beth Chatto has been one of the most influential gardeners of the 1980s and 1990s. She and her husband Andrew began making their garden at Elmstead Market in Essex in 1960, attached to a nursery from which they sold the plants they grew. Conditions on their site were far from ideal: there were damp, boggy areas and areas of dry, poor soil, in baking sun or deep shade. Beth Chatto wrote, describing her scree garden, 'as with all new gardens, we expect the planting to evolve as we learn what will do and look well or otherwise.' By their sensitive method of trial and error they discovered which plants were happy in which conditions. Their experiments made them pioneers of what has come to be known as 'ecological gardening'.

Their expertise was disseminated on three fronts. The first was the Chelsea Flower Show. Beth Chatto won a gold medal for her first exhibit of plants from the nursery, and went on to win more gold medals year after year. Her discerning eye for good plants and her sure, creative touch in arranging them, made her exhibit quite unlike any other. At a time when brilliant, sometimes harsh colours were the norm, her stand was a gentle harmony of silvery foliage, soft creamy variegation and flowers in shades of pink, mauve and pale yellow. Visitors to the show would make a beeline for it, notebooks in hand.

The second front was the garden itself. Beth Chatto's knowledge of plant habitats and her respect for their requirements and preferences meant that everything she planted thrived. She made a garden where gardeners could always learn something new, worth visiting even at the most unpromising times of year.

Third, her books passed on her knowledge. *The Damp Garden*, *The Dry Garden* and *Beth Chatto's Gravel Garden* encouraged her readers to 'Garden with nature, not struggle against her,' the same advice, in a different time and context, as Pope's 'In all consult the Genius of the place.'

Marrying the past with the present

As far as the design of gardens is concerned, gardeners can choose from the cumulative style bank of the past, or they can have a stab at predicting the future. There have been several inspiring examples showing how to interpret past styles in a modern garden, and none has been more persuasive than Rosemary Verey in her books and in her own garden at Barnsley House in Gloucestershire. Her garden and some of her designs for the gardens of her clients are rooted in a scholarly knowledge of historic styles; she had a fine collection of antique gardening books in her library, and frequently referred to them. The most photographed and imitated features at Barnsley House are interpretations of the past: her Tudor knot, laburnum walk and potager, inspired by the reconstructed medieval garden at Villandry in France, have spawned countless others, not always in an appropriate context.

Rosemary Verey had a gift for communication, and she and Alvilde Lees-Milne, who herself made two gardens of great beauty and charm, hit upon a winning formula with *The Englishwoman's Garden*. In this best-selling book and its followers *The New Englishwoman's Garden* and *The Englishman's Garden*, they asked 25 or so garden owners to write descriptions of their gardens, explaining what they were trying to achieve and how they set about it. Almost without exception, they were 'gentry' gardens laid out and planted in variations on a traditional country-house style based on Sissinghurst and Hidcote, with a dash of Margery Fish's Lambrook Manor added: timeless, classic English gardens which continue to be admired and imitated.

Wollerton Old Hall Garden in Shropshire is an outstanding example of this kind of garden, made since 1984 for a house dating from about 1530. The owners' aim, to make a garden that will 'excite and stimulate, comfort and soothe, appealing to the senses as well as one's emotion', is realized in a series of linked, formal compartments in tune with the intense romantic spirit inherent in a site that has been occupied for 500 years.

A new approach to garden design

The English are a conservative nation and gardening is a conservative occupation. It is, therefore, quite an achievement for a radical modern designer to break through the reserve of English gardeners and gain their confidence. The landscape architect and designer John Brookes succeeded with his book *Room Outside – a new approach to garden design* (1969). He recognized that the majority of gardens were small and urban, and that their owners did not necessarily want to spend their time weeding, pruning and mulching. His approach had more in common with modern Scandinavian and Californian design than with the English gardening tradition practised by elderly and middle-aged householders. John Brookes designed town gardens with spare, clean lines for young families. They were rooms to live in as an extension of the house.

He continues to put many of his ideas into practice in his own garden at Denmans in Sussex. In his guide to the garden, Brookes asks visitors to note at the entrance a grouping of English native plants contrasted with a planting of some introduced species:

> These are planted in the newer, wilder way as increasingly, it is this inter-action between garden and wild, between plants native and introduced, and how things grow in the wild that we are exploring at Denmans.

Although there are subdivisions within the garden, there are no formal paths and beds at Denmans. A river of gravel flows through the garden and disappears under the plants, sometimes narrowed by creeping, encroaching plants, sometimes opening out into a glade with a well-placed, bright blue seat facing a view towards a half-concealed sculpture. Foliage colours and shapes are as important as flowers. Plants are allowed to seed themselves, and the seedlings are thinned and edited in spring to achieve the desired effects. The garden has a modern feeling, but also, after 20 years, a mature and settled atmosphere.

John Brookes's *The Small Garden* followed in 1977, showing photographs and plans of the gardens, and giving instructions how to carry out much of the construction work. It came at a time when DIY superstores were beginning to prosper and to double up as garden centres. The DIY element and John Brookes' design style were in due course echoed in television gardening programmes. At first there was just one weekly programme, the BBC's *Gardener's World*. Its style was initially cautious and traditional. The presenter from the programme's inception in 1969 was Percy Thrower followed, after he blotted his copybook in 1976 by appearing in a television commercial, by Peter Seabrook.

The best-loved of all the *Gardener's World* presenters, from 1990 until his untimely death in 1996 at the age of 60, was Geoff Hamilton. He was a cockney boy from Stepney who loved plants from an early age. After studying horticulture at Writtle College in Essex, he became a self-employed landscape gardener, then started his own garden centre at Kettering in Northamptonshire. The occasional article written for *Garden News* led in due course to Geoff editing *Practical Gardening* magazine. From 1979 he was a member of the BBC *Gardener's World* team, eventually becoming presenter of the programme. His friendly, straightforward style and obvious expertise won him loyal viewers. Being a man of his time, he preached the organic gospel and gained plenty of converts. Although his programmes showed a certain amount of DIY making of trellis arches and laying of paving, they were mainly about plants and how best to grow them.

The late 1990s saw a proliferation of television gardening programmes of a very different kind. Throughout the twentieth century the pace of life had accelerated, fashions in various aspects of social and cultural life succeeding each other at an alarming rate. Those who liked to follow fashion (and, indeed, those who liked to lead it) found that no sooner were they up to date than it was time to change again. Now, as the twenty-first century begins, the fashionable discover that their clothes, hair, car, children, holidays, house, are ready for another make-over as soon as they have grown accustomed to the last one.

It seems that television viewers just cannot get enough of 'make-over' programmes. 'Ordinary' people with ordinary homes are chosen for the experts to work their magic on. Gardens as well as houses are redesigned and rebuilt. The producers of, and performers in, television gardening programmes and the publishers of gardening magazines and books are peddlers of dreams. And for the chosen few, their dreams really can come true

For viewers inspired to make-over their own plot there has never before been so much advice on garden design so widely available, nor such a diversity of plants, garden furniture, ornaments and aids to creating garden décor in any style that takes their fancy, all to be had instantly.

Into the twenty-first century

We don't know to what extent television gardens are copied in real life, because most gardens are hidden away behind terraced or semidetached houses. Research has shown that television cooking programmes, although they are immensely popular, do not inspire viewers to go into the kitchen and cook the recipes shown on the screen. The programmes are viewed as entertainment rather than inspiration, to be watched while munching some takeaway food, or oven-baked chips. The same may be true of garden making: television gardens may be more wondered at than imitated. On the other hand, the increasing turnover at garden centres and DIY stores is evidence that at least some householders are responding to the innovative garden design ideas presented on television.

Today's gardeners have grown up in a culture where fashion is for everyone, not just for the rich and well educated. The culture of the second half of the twentieth century is illustrated by popular styles of music and dress. They came and went in rapid succession, from rock and roll to mods and rockers to flower power to punk to grunge. People listened to the music, dressed the part and danced the dances of Bill Haley and his Comets, The Who, Bob Dylan, the Sex Pistols. Pop culture was not reflected in garden design because it was a youth culture, and the nearest its aficionados might have got to gardening would have been a few cannabis plants in a window box. But it was a culture with no interest in tradition or traditional social values: a culture advocating change for the sake of change, and encouraging the expectation of instant gratification. When mods and rockers, hippies and punks grew up, and had houses of their own, would they make a new kind of garden?

The Sunday sound of the mower or strimmer and the scent of the barbecue, are evidence that families today spend their leisure time in the garden much as their parents did. For some, a garden as seen on television, designed for minimum upkeep, with paving or decking, a water feature and a few carefully selected plants with sculptural foliage, may make the perfect labour-saving and practical outdoor space. One of the advantages of such a garden is that it can be changed and up-dated to stay in fashion: a coat of paint on fences and trelliswork, an aluminium plant container to replace a terracotta pot, a tree fern instead of a phormium, can bring the garden to the forefront of fashion.

But the same people may, in due course, come to ask more from their garden. They may find that they need, from time to time, an active relationship with nature and they may find fulfilment by experimenting with the three elements that compose the natural landscape: stone, water and plants, combining them in different ways. Most people live in cities and for them the landscape beyond the garden fence is not beautiful. It brings no spiritual refreshment, no stimulation to the senses. These essentials must therefore be sought within the garden, however small it may be. There is a need for the garden to exclude the world outside, as there was in the Middle Ages. Medieval gardens were safe havens from a dangerous and savage wilderness. Modern gardens are safe havens from the noise and pollution of industry and transport, and sometimes also

from a dangerous and savage street life. The possibility of creating, in the most unpromising places, a personal paradise, makes gardening a joy in any century.

Sir Geoffrey Jellicoe explained, in his appendix to Miles Hadfield's *A History of British Gardening*, that small modern town gardens fall into the timeless categories of classical and romantic. The classical garden is designed as an outwards extension of the interior of the house, geometrical in form, where nature can be restrained by training and clipping the plants, or allowed to grow free. It can be subdivided for different uses:

> The formal or classical garden is concerned with the finite: that is to say that the limiting boundaries are apparent, as they are in the house. The informal or romantic garden is concerned with the infinite, where the boundaries are subdued or eliminated and the imagination is encouraged to roam at will beyond the confines of the site. This is an especially English concept and not only inspired Bridgeman and Kent to 'leap the fence and see that all nature was a garden,' but led such later writers as Uvedale Price to establish Picturesque principles for parks and gardens which may equally apply to the small gardens of the present day. Philosophically,

A garden for the twenty-first century: stone seats, walls and paving form elemental sculptural shapes in a naturalistic setting combining native and exotic plants. Tom Stuart-Smith's design for the Laurent-Perrier Harpers & Queen garden at Chelsea Flower Show, 2001.

the romantic garden is not so much an extension of the house as an incursion of nature into the site. This is the ancient Chinese concept of a town garden and is symbolic, not a copy, of nature. Today the design is an art form that symbolizes what the western mind conceives to be the most beautiful in nature, varying in its contents from one individual to another.

Successful realization of the ideal has never had anything to do with the size of the garden. Writing in 1877, Grant Allen postulated in *Physiological Aesthetics*:

> All our sense perceptions are based on those of man the forest dweller… The owner of a small garden in a dense urban area has in fact only to lie on his back on a summer's day, and look upwards through foliage to the sky, to realise that he is able to reach back to his origins.

Sources of inspiration

The technical side of gardening has never been easier. Plants can be bought in any size from rooted cutting to fully-grown, dormant, in bud or in full flower. Each plant comes with its printed label telling you what conditions it prefers, and how to care for it. Plant food is clean, easy to handle and does not smell. Control of pests and diseases is yours at the touch of a spray button. Advice on every conceivable aspect of plant care and garden design is readily accessible in books, magazines and newspapers, on television and on the internet. Gardeners can also look before they buy and consult the experts at numerous Flower Shows held up and down the country every year.

Many gardening books today present much the same information (although not always as comprehensive, albeit updated) as is found in John Parkinson's *Paradisi in Sole Paradisus Terrestris* (1629) or John Claudius Loudon's *An Encyclopaedia of Gardening* (1822). By far the most successful of the current books of practical advice, much to the chagrin of authors and publishers of other gardening manuals, is the series of 'Expert' titles by Dr. Hessayon. His worldwide sales amount to more than 40 million books and he holds the Guinness Record as best-selling living writer of the 1990s. *The Garden Expert*, *The Flowering Shrub Expert*, *The Rock & Water Garden Expert* and numerous other titles are inexpensive, unglamorous and packed with information presented clearly and simply.

Dr Hessayon read Botany at Leeds University and, after a brief spell lecturing on horticulture in Ghana and Manchester, joined Pan Britannica Industries as chief scientist. 1n 1959 he persuaded PBI, manufacturers of Bio garden and houseplant fertilizers and pesticides, to back his first book *Be Your Own Gardening*

Expert. They did so reluctantly, on condition that, if the book failed, he would repay their investment. Hessayon based the philosophy and format of his book on that of cigarette cards, the aim being to get as much information as possible into the space available. It succeeded spectacularly.

As pretty as a picture

From the 1980s on, most books and magazine articles about gardens have been celebrations of the advances in photographic techniques and the skill of specialist photographers, as much as the gardens they illustrate. The photographers are highly talented and completely professional. They often take the trouble to be in the garden at dawn, when the light is best, capturing for readers an image of the garden that even the owner seldom sees. Such ravishing images are a reminder of the eighteenth-century ideas about the picturesque, when ladies and gentlemen of taste would hold up rectangular cardboard frames through which to view the landscape.

Fortunately, people have always made images of gardens. If they had not, if there were no medieval Books of Hours, no Stoke Edith embroidered hangings, and no nineteenth-century watercolours, there would be no garden history and no foundations for English gardening traditions. But looking at endless delightful photographs of impossibly beautiful gardens can be frustrating and inhibiting for someone struggling to make an unpromising plot into a garden. The camera can lie; some of the loveliest photographs are taken by a photographer standing on a chair or even a stepladder; or, for a worm's eye view, he has his chin on the ground. How many people see their garden from these positions?

Most garden visitors go round with a camera, and it is a useful tool for recording ideas and impressions. But the trend towards seeing gardens always through a lens, as a series of pictures, means that many people now think of a garden as entirely a visual experience, and when they work on their own garden that is what they try to make. But some gardens offer a more complete experience, giving pleasure to all the senses, gardens where you can smell and touch the plants, and hear the sound of birdsong and the wind rustling the leaves of bamboos or aspens. They are places to be in as well as pictures to look at, and just a few have an intangible quality, impossible to design for: the ability to stir the emotions. Such gardens are outside fashion and, in a way, outside history.

Overleaf: *Land, wood and water sculpted into a landscape garden, rich in allegory and symbolism, as radical as the great landscapes of Kent, Hamilton and Hoare were in the eighteenth century. The Garden of Cosmic Speculation at Portrack, Dumfriesshire.*

The visionary's garden

A rare few gardens have all these qualities and one more. They not only please the senses and touch the heart, they also engage the mind on a poetic or philosophical level. Two such are in Scotland, so strictly speaking they are outside the scope of this book. But they are inspirational and may indicate a direction which garden making in Britain might take in the future.

At his house at Portrack in Dumfriesshire, Charles Jencks and his wife the late Maggie Keswick made 'The Garden of Cosmic Speculation'. The garden is rich in symbolism designed to be read on two levels, the first open and accessible to most observers, the second understandable only to those who share the designer's knowledge of art, mythology and astrophysics. There is also a third, which might be called the zero level, at which no intellectual effort is required at all, and the garden is simply enjoyed as a beautiful place to be in. But to be unaware of any meaning in the garden is to miss out on a large part of its interest. There are references to Maggie Keswick's interest in China (she wrote the best book available on Chinese gardens) and Charles Jencks's passion for cosmic

Geometry meets nature in a harmonious composition in Charles Jencks's beautiful and symbolic garden at his house in Portrack. This area is called the Black Hole Terrace, The Garden of Cosmic Speculation.

science. The two elements meet in the Giant Dragon Ha-Ha, its wall built in undulating bands of stone in two colours. Landform, sculpture and plants separate and flow together to symbolize the creation of energy, matter, life and consciousness. Sharply sculpted grass terraces divided by elliptical lakes form a landscape of complex twisting and undulating landforms, including a double-spiral Snail Mound and a capricious Snake Mound. There is a geometric Kitchen Garden of the Six Senses, the sixth being the sense of anticipation. Throughout the garden there are sculptures, including one of DNA. Charles Jencks's garden practises what he preached when he wrote '…it is time artists and designers reclaimed the territory that was customarily theirs and the obligations to portray a more interesting, beautiful, dynamic and tragic universe.'

The poet Ian Hamilton Finlay's garden at Little Sparta in Lanarkshire is in the tradition of Alexander Pope and the eighteenth-century gardens he inspired, William Shenstone's *ferme ornée* at The Leasowes, or Kent's Rousham. Finlay has divided his 9 acres in the Pentland Hills into groves, glades and pools as settings for his poetic and sculptural inscriptions. Some make reference to the classical Arcadia, some to other literary themes, to the garden of Rousseau's lovers, Julie and Saint-Preux, for example; others are Ian Finlay's own sometimes cryptic, sometimes punning, sometimes disturbing compositions.

A serious intention behind symbolism and allusions to the other arts (literature, music, sculpture, even painting) can underpin the design of a garden, giving it a depth and mystery that are felt even when the allusions are not understood. Geoffrey Jellicoe, the one English landscape and garden designer to achieve international status in the twentieth century believed this. He wrote, 'Allegory and analogy will have their own invisible part to play, …for in essence they subconsciously relate a design to something that has already been accepted in the abstract as a work of art; and if not an art, landscape design is nothing.'

His two great American projects of the 1980s (when Jellicoe himself was in his 80s) were both conceived as allegories: the Moody Gardens at Galveston, Texas, were intended to describe the history of human civilization through the evolution of landscape and garden history. The gardens were to be a realization of Jellicoe's book *The Landscape of Man*. The continuous landscape Jellicoe designed for the Historic Center at Atlanta, Georgia, was called 'The Academic Journey'.

Of his work in England, two outstanding gardens have survived. At Shute House in Wiltshire, he described the garden he made for Michael and Anne Tree, who were ideal clients, as 'The Metamorphosis of Classicism into Romanticism'. He retained existing Classical features including an 'ivy-consumed temple' and a laurel tunnel and hedge, and introduced the romantic elements of 'giants' in yew, a steeple in ivy, a large, reflective crystalline rock, and a box of clipped box, captioned on his drawing for the garden 'mythical chest. What does it contain?' It is Pandora's box, perhaps. Water moves through the garden in a classical canal and rill and a romantic pool with rocky cascades, the classical and romantic streams finally uniting in the bog garden.

The garden at Shute House also represented a journey through time which, Jellicoe noted,

> …ends with one of the oldest ideas in the relation of man to environment – the Chinese philosophy of a analogy between man and the rock from which he emerged, and the human significance of the stone itself. Three stones were chosen, for their personality, from a near-by disused quarry, and after discussion, were disposed on the site in a relationship that was unaccountably agreeable.

As a young man, Jellicoe had studied Italian Renaissance gardens, measuring them and drawing them until he knew them inside out. He also knew and loved classical Latin literature and the art of the Renaissance. With such a background, it is surprising that his gardens were not more traditional, but a strong and deep knowledge of tradition is often an aid to artists in striking out beyond their traditions. Jellicoe's other interests, in twentieth-century philosophy and ancient Chinese philosophy, and in the art of Paul Klee, Kandinsky and Picasso, of Henry Moore and Anthony Caro, are evidence of the breadth of his horizons. The layout of his rose garden for Lord Astor at Cliveden in Berkshire, hidden in the woods, is based on Paul Klee's painting *The Fruit*. The shapes of the beds are abstract and sinuous, and Jellicoe's specially designed arches are a friendly, abstracted human shape.

The garden at Sutton Place in Surrey, made for Stanley Seeger, is also rooted in allegory, the themes being *creation*, *life* and *aspiration*. Many of the references are enigmatic. Jellicoe explained:

> Behind each part with its seductive delights lurks an idea that reflects, or is intended to reflect, either a lighter or a darker mood of the subconscious… Thus Pluto's grotto is recognisably a return to Greek myth, yet the subconscious appeal is not the myth itself, but the direct analogy with man's place in the cosmos. Similarly, all can see that the lake is in the shape of a fish, but few that the hills around are composed as the man, woman, child complex immemorial in art; and that the whole

concept – water into hills into sculpture – is an analogy of the emergence
of civilisation.

The east walled garden is a concentration of ideas emanating from
Stanley Seeger and processed by myself. You must fathom how it is that
hazardous stepping stones across the moat are more satisfying than a
sensible bridge; why the pleasure garden with its conversation arbours,
flowers and the sound of water is now called the Paradise garden; why the
secret garden beyond contains two hidden circles, one of grass and the
other of moss; outside the east wall garden, why on earth surrealism

*In his garden at Little Sparta, Lanarkshire, the poet Ian Hamilton Finlay expresses his ideas
literally by means of words inscribed on stone or wood, and metaphorically by means of his
arrangement of stone, water and plants in the landscape.*

should be a fitting end to the sensible long south walk; and, on beyond this, not on earth, cogitate upon the Nicholson wall and its two circles.

Jellicoe designed The Kennedy Memorial at Runnymede in Surrey. It is based on John Bunyan's *The Pilgrim's Progress* and symbolizes man's journey through adversity to 'a happy issue out of all our afflictions'. A path of 60,000 granite setts laid randomly, each one representing a traveller on life's path, winds upwards through close, sometimes forbidding woodland, to emerge into an open, sunlit meadow where the memorial stone is set. To walk the path is a moving and uplifting experience.

Intuition, without which no art exists.

It is always interesting to see what kind of garden professional designers make for themselves. Sir Frederick Gibberd, a friend and contemporary of Sir Geoffrey Jellicoe, was an architect, town planner and landscape architect. His biggest project, and the one for which he is best known, was as master-planner of Harlow New Town. He looked for a property near his work, where he could make a garden from scratch, and found a 1907 bungalow just outside Harlow with 16 acres of woodland and scrub. His first work after moving there in 1956 was to clear scrub and fell trees to create paths and glades. In his own words, 'I consulted the genius of the place and then exercised some intuition, without which no art exists.' His wife later recalled that 'He used to say it's one of the delights of being your own client that you don't have to prepare drawings and you don't have to make up your mind; you can change it umpteen times and it doesn't cost anybody anything.'

Part of the garden's *raison d'être* is the collection of modern sculptures made by Sir Frederick and Lady Gibberd. There are 85 pieces in the garden and yet, so skilful is the design, that it always feels like a garden and not an art collection. Each work is carefully placed to surprise or please, and each appears to be in its inevitable right position. Apart from a strong axis from the house and its main terrace, based on a mature lime avenue already established when the Gibberds bought the house, the garden is informal with meandering paths crossing meandering streams, tributaries of the Pincy brook. The brook is also diverted to form a moat for the castle built by Sir Frederick for his grandchildren.

Sir Geoffrey Jellicoe's design for the gardens at Shute House in Dorset makes use of the natural springs and ponds on the site to construct a water garden of canals, fountains and waterfalls, including a musical cascade.

A garden like the Gibberd Garden, which has evolved rather than being transferred from the drawing board to the ground, has a special, timeless quality. The designer's touch is light, to the point of being almost invisible, but the garden is nevertheless based on strong theoretical foundations: Gibberd said,

> Garden design is an art of space, like architecture and town design.
> The space, to be a recognisable design, must be contained and the plants and walls enclosing it then become part of the adjacent spaces. The garden has thus become a series of rooms, each with its own character from small intimate spaces to large enclosed prospects.

The 'Yellow Book'

There is a delightful element of 'lucky dip' about the English recreation of garden visiting. You never know when you may stumble into someone's personal paradise and find yourself completely at home there. I have already mentioned the garden visitor's *vade mecum*, the 'Yellow Book'. In the year 2001, £1.5 million raised from garden openings organized through The National Gardens Scheme was donated to charities.

It is interesting to see that recent fashions in garden design and planting, as described in books and magazines, have passed most of the Yellow Book gardens by, though it does seem that ornamental grasses are here to stay. Gardeners who take pleasure in sharing their gardens seem to be firmly rooted in a recognizable English gardening tradition, in which the plants are the most important element, and among plants, preference is given to flowers over foliage. If you visit some of the gardens and talk to their owners you will be left in no doubt that their love affair is with plants. Their satisfaction comes first from growing and nurturing their chosen plants, and second from devising the best settings in which to display them and their best relationship with each other.

These simple objectives have been interpreted in an astonishing diversity of garden types and styles, a culmination of the riches of nearly 1000 years. A browse through the Yellow Book will show that the historic past is an inspiration to many gardeners. There are knot gardens, arbours, herb gardens, walks shaded by pleached limes or hornbeam, potagers, parterres, topiary, rills, fountains and cascades. The descriptions of the gardens are written by their owners, and have to be brief. This concentrates the mind and, reading the brief notes on each garden, you learn what each gardener thinks is most important and interesting about his garden, and gain an insight into the aspirations of the present generation of garden makers, even if these are not always successfully realized.

Open the Yellow Book at random and you will probably find the following descriptions occurring at least once on each page: 'A plantsman's garden' (sometimes 'plantswoman's' or 'plantsperson's'), 'plantaholic', 'plant lover'. During the past decade 'potager' (a tribute to Rosemary Verey), 'cottage garden' and 'wildlife garden' have cropped up with increasing regularity. Many of the gardens are 'planted for year-round interest'. Some owners are proud of particular plants; not surprisingly, roses and clematis feature again and again, and, in the West Country and other areas with suitably acid soil, camellias, magnolias, azaleas and rhododendrons.

In other gardens there are more unusual plant collections. One owner lists, in a half-acre suburban garden, 'hostas and other shade-loving plants; euphorbias, dicentras, rhododendrons, phlox, hebes and grasses.' On the same page the following garden is described

> Plantsman's garden 70ft x 35ft. Sloping site with steps and walls. Large
> mixed border at front. Planted for year-round interest. Galanthus,
> crocus, helleborus, old dianthus, geranium, penstemon, alpine scree,
> hyssop, satureja, camomile lawn. National Collection of Thymus.

This is by no means the smallest garden in the Yellow Book. It is almost inconceivable how many thriving, healthy plants some gardeners can cram into a small space. Adjectives that recur in the descriptions include 'romantic', 'scented', 'secret', 'tranquil', indicating the atmosphere people like to create in their gardens.

Scanning the 3500-odd descriptions in the Yellow Book you receive an overwhelming impression of respect for England's garden history. Owners of period houses are making and remaking gardens that interpret the history of their houses with accuracy and sensitivity. Others, with less remarkable houses, show their love of English gardening traditions by creating, in some cases, gardens suffused with poignant nostalgia. And a few, taking those traditions as their starting point, are developing new and exciting ideas.

If you were short of time, with the Yellow Book as your guide you could devise a comprehensive time-tour covering 1000 years of English garden making; it could be completed in less than a week and cover a remarkably compact area. You would come to the conclusion that most gardeners today are confident and happy making gardens firmly rooted in tradition; but it is a tradition so rich, so complex and so diverse that you could spend a lifetime visiting gardens and never empty the cornucopia.

WHERE TO SEE HISTORIC GARDENS OR GARDENS WITH HISTORIC FEATURES

NB *For up to date opening times and other information, see the latest edition of* Gardens of England and Wales Open for Charity (*the* Yellow Book) *or 'The Good Gardens Guide'. 'Grade I' refers to English Heritage's assessment.*

MEDIEVAL GARDENS
Recreated gardens
BAYLEAF AND HANGLETON at The Weald and Downland Open Air Museum, West Sussex.

BEDE'S WORLD HERB GARDEN, Jarrow, South Tyneside. Herb garden attached to museum and laid out according to the St. Gall Monastery plan.

CHENIES MANOR Buckinghamshire. Physic garden, penitential maze.

HALF MOON HOUSE, Manaton, Devon. Enclosed Mary garden.

MICHELHAM PRIORY, Hailsham, East Sussex. Stew ponds, physic garden, Mary garden.

THE PREBENDAL MANOR HOUSE, Nassington, Northamptonshire. A series of garden enclosures around a C13 house.

QUEEN ELEANOR'S GARDEN, The Castle, Winchester, Hampshire. *Hortus conclusus.*

THE SHREWSBURY QUEST, Shrewsbury, Shropshire. Monastic herb garden.

TRETOWER COURT, Crickhowell, Powys. Pleasure garden.

Gardens with medieval features
BEAULIEU ABBEY, Hampshire. Founded 1204, cloister garth, physic garden.

BENINGTON LORDSHIP, Stevenage, Hertfordshire. Norman fish ponds, moat

BERKELEY CASTLE, Gloucestershire. C12 terrace and bowling green.

BROUGHTON CASTLE, Banbury, Oxfordshire. Moated and fortified C14 manor house.

DEAN'S COURT, Wimborne Minster, Dorset. Stew pond.

ECCLESHALL CASTLE, Staffordshire. Moat with 650-year-old walls.

EDMONDSHAM HOUSE, Cranborne, Dorset. Grass cockpit, possibly medieval.

FORDE ABBEY, Chard, Somerset. Ponds.

MANNINGTON HALL, Saxthorpe, Norfolk. Moat.

MAPPERCOMBE MANOR, Powerstock, Dorset. Monks' rest house, stew pond, dovecote.

STANTON HARCOURT, Oxfordshire. Stew ponds, moat.

TUDOR GARDENS
ABERGLASNEY, Llangathen, Carmarthenshire, Wales. Cloister garden possibly dating from 1600s.

ATHELHAMPTON, Dorchester, Dorset. Garden designed by Francis Inigo Thomas in 1891 in Tudor style. Grade I.

DALEMAIN, Penrith, Cumbria. Tudor walled knot garden and gazebo.

DODDINGTON HALL, Lincolnshire. Early C20 gardens in the Elizabethan style, House designed by Smythson.

ELSING HALL, East Dereham, Norfolk. Romantic planting round moat and stew pond.

GREYS COURT, Henley-on-Thames, Oxfordshire. 'Archbishop's Maze', enclosed knot garden.

HARDWICK HALL, Chesterfield, Derbyshire. Formal walled and hedged gardens. Grade I.

HATFIELD HOUSE, Hertfordshire. Knot garden, Lime *allée* and other Tudor and Jacobean elements (see under 17th century below). Grade I.

HELMINGHAM HALL, Stowmarket, Suffolk. Moat, knot garden, and more recent outstanding garden design, retaining Elizabethan atmosphere.

HOLDENBY HOUSE, Northampton-shire. Elizabethan layout, period planting by Rosemary Verey.

IGHTHAM MOTE, Sevenoaks, Kent. A C19 interpretation of a Tudor garden for a medieval house.

LITTLE MORETON HALL, Congleton Cheshire. Moat, mound, knot garden, orchard, herbs, vegetables.

LYVEDEN NEWBIELD, Oundle, Northamptonshire. The ghost of a garden.

MONTACUTE HOUSE, Somerset. Formal terraces, topiary, raised

walk with original pavilions. Grade I.

PACKWOOD HOUSE, Solihull, Warwickshire. C16—C17 layout intact, sympathetically developed in 1850s and 1930s, including famous 'Sermon on the Mount' yew topiary. Grade I.

PENSHURST PLACE, Tonbridge, Kent. Tudor gardens restored and developed in C20. Grade I.

THE TUDOR HOUSE MUSEUM, Bugle Street, Southampton. Meticulous reconstruction of small town garden.

Gardens with Tudor features
CRANBORNE MANOR, Wimborne Dorset. Mount, knot garden.

HADDON HALL, Bakewell, Derbyshire. Terraced layout. Grade I.

LYME PARK Disley, Stockport, Cheshire. Some original Tudor and Jacobean features.

ROCKINGHAM CASTLE, Market Harborough, Northamptonshire. Moat, mount, terraces, yew hedges (restored in 1660s after civil war).

NORTON CONYERS, Ripon, North Yorkshire. Bowling green.

17TH-CENTURY GARDENS
ALBURY PARK, Guildford, Surrey. John Evelyn's design.

BODYSGALLEN HALL, Llandudno, Gwynedd, Wales. Beautifully restored, steeply terraced formal gardens.

BRAMHAM PARK, Wetherby, Yorkshire. A rare survival of a formal landscape in the French style.

BRICKWALL, Northiam, East Sussex. Stuart garden made 1680 to 1720 reconstructed with authentic planting.

CHELSEA PHYSIC GARDEN, London. Medicinal herb collection started in 1673.

HADDON HALL, Bakewell, Derbyshire. C17 garden teraces reconstructed.

HAM HOUSE, Surrey. 1670s layout, planting and ornaments restored.

HAMPTON COURT PALACE, London. Extensive royal gardens include William III's Privy Garden faithfully restored, the Yew maze (part of Wren's 'wilderness') and Jean Tijou's wrought iron screen. Grade I.

HATFIELD HOUSE, Hertfordshire. The Marchioness of Salisbury's faultless interpretation of the garden laid out for Robert Cecil by John Tradescant in the early C17.

LEVENS HALL, Kendal, Cumbria. 1694 design still intact including topiary and first known ha-ha. Grade I.

MAPPERTON, Beaminster, Dorset. 1920s interpretation of a C17 garden.

MELBOURNE HALL, Derbyshire. Late C17, early C18 garden laid out with London & Wise's advice; Birdcage arbour erected in 1706. Grade I.

POWIS CASTLE, Welshpool, Powys, Wales. Spectacular terraced gardens, late C17/early C18.

THE RED LODGE, Bristol. Reconstruction of a prosperous merchant's town garden.

TREDEGAR HOUSE, Newport, Gwent, Wales. Authentic mineral parterre restored in the Orangery garden.

WESTBURY COURT, Gloucester. Beautifully restored water garden in the Dutch style.

WHITBY ABBEY, Yorkshire. Recently excavated 1670s formal paved garden with raised walkway.

Gardens with 17th-century features

ADLINGTON HALL, Macclesfield, Cheshire. Lime walk planted in 1688

BODRHYDDAN, Clwyd, Wales. 1612 Inigo Jones pavilion, housing St Mary's Well.

CHATSWORTH, Bakewell, Derbyshire. London and Wise's cascade, willow tree fountain, 1692. Grade I.

EUSTON HALL, Thetford, Norfolk. Pleasure grounds laid out with John Evelyn's advice 1670

GRIMSTHORPE CASTLE, Bourne, Lincolnshire. Formal 1660s layout, as shown in Kip engraving.

HAUGHLEY PARK, Stowmarket, Suffolk. Much of 1620 layout

survives.

HUTTON-IN-THE-FOREST, Penrith, Cumbria. Terraces, dovecote.

KENTWELL HALL, Suffolk. Layout, moat, dovecote.

SMEDMORE HOUSE, Kimmeridge, Dorset. 1620 layout survives.

WILTON HOUSE, Wiltshire. Cedars of Lebanon planted 1636

18TH-CENTURY GARDENS

BLAISE CASTLE, Bristol. Repton's 1766 landscape (recorded in his Red Book) including the Sham Castle, and, Nash's early C19 dairy, orangery and estate hamlet.

Bowood House, Calne, Wiltshire. 'Capability' Brown's park, orangery by Robert Adam, hermit's cave and cascade by Charles Hamilton of Painshill. Grade I.

BRAMHAM PARK, Wetherby, West Yorkshire. Formal avenues in the Versailles style, water and buildings. Grade I.

CALKE ABBEY, Ticknall, Derbyshire. walled garden (1773) and orangery.

CANON'S ASHBY, Daventry Northamtonshire. Formal layout untouched by the landscape movement.

CASTLE BROMWICH HALL, Birmingham. Continuing restoration of late C17/early C18 formal gardens and informal landscape.

CASTLE HOWARD, Yorkshire House and grounds designed by Sir John Vanbrugh 1700-50. Grade I.

CHISWICK HOUSE, London. Lord Burlington's and William Kent's 'Roman villa' garden. Grade I.

CLAREMONT LANDSCAPE GARDEN, Esher, Surrey. Vanbrugh, Bridgeman and Kent worked here for the Duke of Newcastle, and later, 'Capability' Brown for Clive of India. Beautifully restored. Grade I.

CORBY CASTLE, Carlisle, Cumbria. Early (1720s) romantic landscape. River walks, cascade.

CROWE HALL, Bath, Somerset. Landscape garden with restored grotto and more recent features looking towards Prior Park.

DUNCOMBE PARK, Helmsley, North Yorkshire. Terraces and temples.

ERDDIG, Wrexham, Clywd, Wales. Rare early C18 formal garden

design, fully restored.

FARNBOROUGH HALL, Banbury, Oxfordshire. 1740s curved terrace walk with temples and obelisk. Grade I.

FOUNTAINS ABBEY, Studley Royal, Ripon, North Yorkshire. Landscaped by John Aislabie, 1722–42. Grade I.

THE GEORGIAN GARDEN, Bath, Somerset. 1760s garden restored to archaeological evidence.

GILBERT WHITE'S GARDEN, Selborne Hampshire. Restored as he designed it.

GOLDNEY HALL, Bristol. Restored gardens including outstanding grotto.

INKPEN HOUSE, Newbury, Berkshire. Early C18 4-acre formal avenues and shrubberies.

ISLAND HALL, Godmanchester, Cambridgeshire. Restored to mid-C18 formal design.

MOUNT EDGCUMBE, Torpoint, Cornwall. Formal gardens and Grade I landscaped park, grotto.

PAINSHILL LANDSCAPE GARDEN, Cobham, Surrey. Charles Hamilton's vision realized (see pp146–47). Grade I.

PAINSWICK ROCOCO GARDEN, Stroud, Gloucestershire. Restored to design shown in Thomas Robins's 1748 paintings.

PRIOR PARK, Bath, Somerset. Landscape with Palladian bridge, restored by National Trust.

PETWORTH HOUSE W Sussex. 1751–1763. Capability Brown created outstanding landscape.

RABY CASTLE, Darlington, Durham. Medieval castle with walled garden by Thomas Wright (1740s) Joseph Spence advised on landscaping (ha-ha, lake, pond, hedges). Ischia fig planted. 1786.

RIELVAUX TERRACE, Helmsley, North Yorkshire. c.1754 grass terrace from which to view the landscape and ruined abbey, with a classical temple at each end. Grade I.

ROUSHAM HOUSE, Steeple Aston, Oxfordshire. 'Kentissimo'. William Kent's 1738 landscape still intact, and earlier walled gardens and dovecote. Grade I.

SCOTTS GROTTO, Ware, Hertfordshire. Well-restored grotto is all that survives.

349

ST PAUL'S WALDEN BURY, Hitchin, Hertfordshire. The 1730s layout of formal *allées* in the French style, over 40 acres, remains intact. Grade I.

SQUERRYES COURT, Westerham, Kent. Restored to formal Anglo-Dutch plan shown in 1719 drawing.

STANWAY HOUSE, Winchcombe, Gloucestershire. *c.*1720 sensational baroque water garden under restoration. Grade I.

STOURHEAD, Warminster, Wiltshire. Henry Hoare's famous landscape garden around a lake. Grade I.

WEST WYCOMBE PARK, Buckinghamshire. Landscape influenced by Sir Francis Dashwood's Grand Tour with lake, bridges, temples and follies. Grade I.

WREST PARK, Silsoe, Bedfordshire. Early C18 formal gardens on grand scale, parts by Bridgeman, later work by 'Capability' Brown

18TH-CENTURY FEATURES

ARBURY HALL, Nuneaton, Warwickshire. Water garden & cascade by Sanderson Miller.

BURTON CONSTABLE HALL, Hull, Yorkshire. Orangery by Thomas Atkinson of York. 1770s 'Capability' Brown park.

CLANDON PARK, Guildford, Surrey. Landscaped park, grotto.

CORBY CASTLE, Cumbria. 1720s romantic landscape developed in Inglewood Forest.

GRIMSTHORPE CASTLE, Bourne, Lincolnshire. Layout of pleasure gardens modified by Stephen Switzer and later by Lancelot Brown.

HOLKER HALL, Cumbria. Part of the formal gardens replaced by naturalistic landscape.

LYME PARK, Stockport, Cheshire. *Parterre de broderie* in 1720s Sunken Dutch garden.

MINTERNE, Dorchester, Dorset. 1768: Admiral Digby planted shelter belts and made lake and cascades.

MUNCASTER CASTLE, Ravenglass, Cumbria. 1783: long terrace, new woodlands.

STONOR PARK, Henley-on-Thames, Oxfordshire. Italianate terraces. Grade I.

WARWICK CASTLE, Warwickshire. 1750s: 'Capability' Brown landscape. 1786: gothic conservatory.

WILTON HOUSE, Wiltshire. The Earl of Pembroke designed Palladian bridge (1737) and classical landscape. Grade I.

EARLY TO MID-19TH CENTURY

ASHRIDGE MANAGEMENT COLLEGE, Berkhamsted, Hertfordshire. Much of Repton's design shown in his Red Book of 1813 can still be seen.

CHILLINGHAM CASTLE, Northumberland. Grounds landscaped by Jeffry Wyatville in 1828.

CHOLMONDLEY CASTLE, Malpas, Cheshire. 1801: house built, park landscaped.

EASTNOR CASTLE, Ledbury, Herefordshire. Arboretum of conifers and deciduous trees planted 1812-1818

ENDSLEIGH HOUSE, Tavistock, Devon. Repton's garden for Wyatville's Cottage Orne. Grade I.

HAREWOOD HOUSE, Leeds, W Yorkshire. In the 1840s Sir Charles Barry and altered the house and designed formal terraces. Grade I.

LYME PARK CHESHIRE. Wyatt's 1815 orangery, planted with figs and camellias.

MOUNT EDGCUMBE, Plymouth, Cornwall. English, French, Italian formal gardens, shell grotto, landscaped park. Grade I.

PENCARROW, BODMIN, Cornwall.1830s: Sir William Molesworth's formal Italian garden, granite rockery and plant collection in woodland garden.

RIPLEY CASTLE, Harrogate, Yorkshire. Elaborate formal gardens restored, palm house etc.

SCOTNEY CASTLE, Tunbridge Wells, Kent. William Sawrey Gilpin advised Hussey on the romantic, picturesque landscape garden. Grade I.

SEZINCOTE, Moreton-in-Marsh, Gloucestershire. Repton and Daniell's design in the Mogul style. Grade I.

STANCOMBE PARK, Dursley, Gloucestershire. 1840s Gothick tunnels and grottoes. Grade I.

SOMERLEYTON HALL, Lowestoft,

Suffolk. Nesfield's 1846 layout includes a maze, pagoda, and 90m pergola. Paxton's glass houses, winter garden.

TATTON PARK, Knutsford, Cheshire. Lewis Wyatt's flower garden1814, orangery 1818, vista to classical folly 1820, Paxton's fernery 1850.

WOBURN ABBEY, Bedfordshire. Repton's plans implemented 1804-1810. Grade I.

Gardens with early to mid 19th-century features

BENINGTON LORDSHIP, Stevenage, Hertfordshire. 1830 Pulhamite neo-Norman folly.

BOWOOD HOUSE, Wiltshire. Pinetum started in 1820s.

CHATSWORTH, Derbyshire. Paxton's 'Conservative Wall' completed 1848.

HOLKER HALL, Cumbria. William Lobb brought Monkey Puzzle seed from Chile in 1844.

ROCKINGHAM CASTLE, North-amptonshire. 1820: rose garden laid out on site of castle keep.

SYON PARK, Middlesex. 1827-30: Dr Charles Fowler built the 'Great Conservatory'

MID TO LATE 19TH CENTURY

ARLEY HALL, Northwich, Cheshire. 12 acres include herbaceous borders first planted in 1846.

ASCOTT, Wing, Buckinghamshire. Stylish Rothschild opulence.

ATHELHAMPTON, Dorset. See under 'Tudor gardens' above.

BIDDULPH GRANGE, Stoke-on-Trent, Staffordshire. Complex, imaginative, typically Victorian series of linked theme gardens.

BODRHYDDAN, Denbighshire, Wales. Nesfield's 1875 parterre, restored 'Pleasance'.

BORDE HILL, Haywards Heath, W Sussex. Col. Stephenson Clarke's world-wide collection of rare trees and shrubs, started in 1893.

BRANTWOOD, Coniston, Cumbria. John Ruskin's Lakeland garden, being restored.

CHILLINGHAM CASTLE, North-umberland. 1880s rockery and wellingtonias.

CHIRK CASTLE, Wrexham, Clwyd, Wales. 1870s yew-enclosed formal garden, topiary, rock garden, pleasure-ground wood, C18 park. Grade I.

CLIVEDEN, Maidenhead, Berkshire. Large, elaborate terrace and parterre. Park. Grade I.

CRAGSIDE, Rothbury, Northumberland. Flamboyant Victorian garden.

ELTON HALL, Peterborough, Cambridgeshire. Formal gardens laid out in the 1850s.

HOLME PIERREPONT HALL, Radcliffe-on-Trent, Nottinghamshire. Restored 1875 box parterre, possibly by Nesfield.

HUGHENDEN MANOR, High Wycombe, Buckinghamshire. Mrs Dsraeli's 1860s garden includes bright Victorian bedding.

KNEBWORTH, Hertfordshire. 1887 wilderness planted including 27 hawthorn varieties.

LAMPORT HALL, Northampton. Huge ironstone rockery, home of the first garden gnome.

LEONARDSLEE, Horsham, W Sussex. 240-acre woodland garden with seven lakes, started by Sir Edmund Loder in 1889.

NYMANS, Haywards Heath, W Sussex. The Messel family's varied and romantic garden, started in 1890.

RAGLEY HALL, Alcester, Warwickshire. Formal and informal gardens laid out in 1874.

RIVERHILL HOUSE, Sevenoaks, Kent. John Rogers planted trees and shrubs collected by Robert Fortune, 1840-60.

RYDAL MOUNT, Ambleside, Cumbria. William Wordsworth's Lakeland garden.

WARWICK CASTLE, Warwickshire. Parterre and rose garden designed by Robert Marnock in 1869.

WEST DEAN, W Sussex. In 1891 Ernest George & Harold Peto enlarged the house and extended the gardens. 90M pergola. Walled fruit garden maintained to Victorian standards.

WADDESDON MANOR, Aylesbury, Buckinghamshire. Grand, elaborate Rothschild gardens.

EARLY TO MID-20TH CENTURY

BLENHEIM PALACE, Oxfordshire. Achille Duchene laid out the formal gardens, 1910-30. Grade I.

BODNANT, Colwyn Bay, Conwy, Wales. Beautiful and varied gardens and plant collection developed by

four generations of the Aberconway family from 1874 onwards.

BUSCOT PARK, Faringdon, Oxfordshire. Harold Peto's water garden laid out in 1912.

CHARLESTON, Firle, East Sussex. Bloomsbury Group garden.

COLETON FISHACRE, Kingswear, Devon. The D'Oyly Cartes' ravine garden, begun 1926.

DYFFRYN GARDENS, St Nicholas, Glamorgan, Wales. Important Edwardian garden designed by Thomas Mawson for the knowledgable plantsman Reginald Cory in 1904.

EXBURY, Southampton, Hampshire. Lionel de Rothschild's 200-acre woodland garden, made 1919-1935.

FOLLY FARM, Sulhamstead, Berkshire. Lutyens/Jekyll partnership.

GODINGTON HOUSE, Ashford, Kent. Blomfield's 1902 formal gardens for Jacobean house.

GRAVETYE MANOR, East Grinstead, W Sussex. William Robinson's own garden restored.

HESTERCOMBE, Taunton, Somerset. Best example of Lutyens-Jekyll partnership; also newly restored C18 park. Grade I.

HIGH BEECHES, Handcross, W Sussex. 20 acres of water, woodland and rare plants begun by Colonel Loder in 1906.

HEVER CASTLE, Edenbridge, Kent. Elaborate gardens laid out in the Italian style 1904-08 by William Waldorf Astor. Grade I.

HIDCOTE MANOR, Gloucestershire. Influential garden with rooms.

IFORD MANOR, Bradford-on-Avon, Wiltshire. Architect and garden designer Harold Peto's own garden. Grade I.

KIFTSGATE COURT, Chipping Camden, Gloucestershire. Created by three generations of the same family. Fine features include late C20 water garden.

LUTON HOO, Bedfordshire. Romaine Walker designed Italianate terrace gardens for Julius Wernher in 1903.

THE MANOR HOUSE, Upton Grey, Hampshire. Meticulously restored Jekyll design.

1920s MAPPERTON HOUSE, Dorset Italianate sunken gardens.

MOUNDSMERE MANOR, Preston Candover, Hampshire. Reginald

Blomfield's 1908 formal design.

1912 MOUNT EPHRAIM, Kent. Garden laid out, inc. Japanese garden.

POLESDEN LACEY, Dorking, Surrey. Edwardian garden made for Mrs Ronald Greville from 1906.

PUTTERIDGE BURY, Luton, Hertfordshire. Lutyens/Jekyll restored by Herts Gardens Trust.

RENISHAW HALL, Sheffield, Derbyshire. Sir George Sitwell's Italianate terraces.

RODMARTON MANOR, Cirencester, Gloucestershire. Designed by Ernest Barnsley (Arts & Crafts Movement).

SISSINGHURST CASTLE, Cranbrook, Kent. Vita Sackville-West and Harold Nicolson's garden.

SIZERGH CASTLE, Kendal, Cumbria. Superb 1920s rock garden.

TATTON PARK, Knutsford, Cheshire. 50 acres restored by National Trust including 1890s Italian formal garden, Edwardian rose garden, 1910 Japanese garden.

TREBAH, Mawnan Smith, Cornwall. Archetyal Cornish ravine garden.

TREWITHEN, Truro, Cornwall. 30 acres of wonderful plants, many collected by Ward and Forrest, developed 1912 to 1960.

WAYFORD MANOR, Crewkerne, Somerset. Harold Peto's 1902 design for 3-acre garden of Elizabethan house, enhanced by today's owners.

MID- TO LATE 20TH CENTURY

ABBEY HOUSE GARDENS, Malmesbury, Wiltshire. Exuberant, uninhibited colour in formal structure.

ANGLESEY ABBEY, Cambridge. Superb 100-acre National Trust garden.

THE BETH CHATTO GARDENS, Elmstead Market, Essex. Influential garden based on an understanding of plants' requirements.

BIDE-A-WEE COTTAGE, Stanton, Northumberland. Rich planting in an old quarry.

BROADLEAS, Devizes, Wiltshire. Distinguished collection of trees and shrubs in a steep dell.

BUSCOT PARK, Faringdon, Oxfordshire. Lord Faringdon's formal gardens with informal planting.

CLINTON LODGE, Fletching, East Sussex. Garden of nostalgia with medieval, Elizabethan, Victorian and Pre-Raphaelite gardens and Reptonian landscape.

COTHAY MANOR, Greenham, Somerset. Exuberant and stylish modern planting in a series of enclosures laid out in the 1920s in tune with the unspoiled medieval manor house.

COTTESBROOKE HALL, Northamptonshire. A series of formal gardens around a Queen Anne House set in a fine park.

THE COURTS, Holt, Wiltshire. Fine C20 planting in an Edwardian garden.

CROSSING HOUSE, Shepreth, Hertfordshire. Small, individualistic garden packed with plants.

DENMANS, Fontwell, West Sussex. John Brookes's 1980s layout and planting, in truly modern style.

EAST LAMBROOK MANOR, South Petherton, Somerset. Margery Fish's garden being restored. Grade I.

EAST RUSTON OLD VICARAGE, Norwich, Norfolk. A series of vistas and enclosures, exotically planted.

THE GARDEN HOUSE, Buckland Monachorum, Devon. Imaginative and innovative design and planting.

THE GIBBERD GARDEN, Harlow, Essex. Sir Frederick Gibberd's own design and collection of C20 sculpture.

GREAT COMP, Sevenoaks, Kent. 7 acres beautifully planned and planted since 1957.

GREAT DIXTER, East Sussex. Christopher Lloyd's garden; house restored and garden layout planned by Lutyens.

GRESGARTH HALL, Caton, Lancashire. Designer Arabella Lennox-Boyd's own garden.

HODNET HALL, Market Drayton, Shropshire. Lakes with exceptional marginal and bog planting.

KNIGHTSHAYES, Tiverton, Devon. Formal and woodland gardens made from 1950s onwards.

THE MANOR HOUSE, Bledloe, Buckinghamshire. Formal and informal, traditional yet modern.

MARWOOD HILL, Barnstaple, Devon. Distinguished plant collections and outstanding bog garden.

MOTTISFONT ABBEY, Romsey, Hampshire. National Trust's collection of old roses in walled

garden.

NEWBY HALL, Ripon, North Yorkshire. 25 acres of outstanding restored and more modern gardens around C18 family house.

THE OLD RECTORY, Burghfield, Berkshire. Plant-lover's garden started in 1950.

SALING HALL, Braintree, Essex. Hugh Johnson's 12-acre garden of wonderful trees.

SHUTE HOUSE, Donhead St Mary, Dorset. Geoffrey Jellicoe's design.

THE SKIPPET, Chipping Norton, Oxfordshire. 2 acres crammed with unusual plants.

STICKY WICKET, Buckland Newton, Dorset. Designed for wildlife conservation.

STONE HOUSE COTTAGE GARDENS, Kidderminster, Worcestershire. Small-scale towers and follies add charm and originality to a garden started in the 1970s.

SUTTON PARK, Sutton-in-the-Forest, Yorkshire. Terraced gardens developed from Percy Cane's 1962 design.

SUTTON PLACE, Guildford, Surrey. Geoffrey Jellicoe's 1980s design for Stanley Seeger, now restored.

TINTINHULL HOUSE, Yeovil, Somerset. Phyllis Reiss's 2-acre 1930s garden further developed by Penelope Hobhouse.

WEST GREEN HOUSE, Hartley Wintney, Hampshire. Modern planting in a traditional formal layout.

WESTWELL MANOR, Burford, Oxfordshire. 6 acres of separate rooms with imaginative different themes.

WOLLERTON OLD HALL, Hodnet, Shropshire. 3 acres of beautifully planted rooms pierced by vistas, in tune with the medieval house.

WYKEN HALL, Bury St Edmunds, Suffolk. A series of garden rooms full of colour and scent.

YORK GATE, Adel, Yorkshire. Masterly design and planting in just over one acre, made since 1951.

21ST CENTURY

ALNWICK GARDENS, Alnwick Castle, Northumberland. New 12-acre project includes spectacular water garden with programmed fountains run by up-to-the-minute computerized technology.

INDEX

352

357

BIBLIOGRAPHY

AMHERST, HON. ALICIA, A *History of Gardening in England*, 1896

ANDERSON, E. BERTRAM, *Gardening on Chalk & Limestone*, 1965

BACON, FRANCIS, *Of Gardens*, 1625

BAGOT, SUSAN, *Levens Hall and Gardens*,1999

BARON, JOHN, *Life of Dr Jenner*, 1827

BATEY, MAVIS, *Alexander Pope – the Poet and the Landscape*, 2001. *Regency Gardens*, 1995

BEAN, W.J., *Trees & Shrubs Hardy in the British Isles*, 1976

BONIFACE, PRISCILLA (ed), *In Search of English Gardens – the Travels of John Claudius Loudon and his Wife Jane*,1987

BROOKES, JOHN, *Room Outside*, 1969 *The Small Garden*, 1977

BROWN, JANE, *The Art and Architecture of English Gardens, 1989 Gardens of a Golden Afternoon, 1982 The Pursuit of Paradise*, 1999

BURNETT, FRANCES HODGSON, *The Secret Garden*, 1911 Cassell's *Popular Gardening*

CHAMBERS, JOHN, *Wild Flower Garden*, 1987

CHAMBERS, SIR WILLIAM, *Designs of Chinese Buildings*, 1757

CHAMBERS, SIR WILLIAM, *A Dissertation on Oriental Gardening*, 1772

CLARE, JOHN, *Selected Poems* ed. Ian Hamilton, 1996

COBBETT, WILLIAM, *Rural Rides*, 1830

COLBORN, NIGEL, Dr Miriam Rothschild [article in *Hortus* 9], 1989

DEFOE, DANIEL, *Tour through the Whole of England & Wales*, 1724

DRURY, ELIZABETH & LEWIS, PHILIPPA, *The Victorian Garden Album*, 1993

EARLE, MRS C.W, *Pot-Pourri from a Surrey Garden*, 1897

EATES, MARGOT, *Gardening in Cities*, 1955

ELLACOMBE, CANON, *In a Gloucestershire Garden*, 1895

EVELYN, JOHN, SYLVA, *A Discourse of Forest Trees*, 1664

FEARNLEY-WHITTINGSTALL, JANE, *Historic Gardens*, 1990

FISH, MARGERY, *Cottage Garden Flowers*, 1961 *Gardening in the Shade*, 1964 *Ground Cover Plants*, 1964

FISK, DOROTHY, *Dr Jenner of Berkeley*

FITZHERBERT, MASTER, *The Booke of Husbandrie*, 1534

FLEMING, LAURENCE & GORE, ALAN, *The English Garden*, 1979

FOSBROKE, THOMAS DUDLEY, *Berkeley Manuscripts*, 1821

GERARD, JOHN, *The Herball or General Historie of Plantes*, 1579

GILBERT, REV SAMUEL, *The Florists's Vade Mecum*, 1683

GOODY, JACK, *The Culture of Flowers*, 1993

GROSSMITH, GEORGE AND WEEDON, *The Diary of a Nobody*, 1892

HADFIELD, MILES, HARLING, ROBERT, HIGHTON LEONIE, *British Gardeners – A Biographical Dictionary*, 1980

HADFIELD, MILES, *A History of British Gardening*, 1979

HANMER, SIR THOMAS, *Garden Book* [first published 1933] written 1659

HARVEY, JOHN, HARDY *Plants of the Late Eighteenth Century*, 1988 *Medieval Gardens*, 1981 *Restoring Period Gardens*, 1993

HAWORTH-BOOTH, MICHAEL, *Effective Flowering Shrubs*, 1951

HAYDEN, RUTH, *Mrs Delany – her life and her flowers*, 1980

HESSAYON, DR D.G., *The Garden Expert*, 1986

HIBBERT, CHRISTOPHER, *The English – A Social History 1066-1945, 1987*

HIBBERD, SHIRLEY, *The Town Garden*, 1859

HILLS, LAWRENCE D., *Down to Earth Gardening*, 1967

HOBHOUSE, PENELOPE, *The National Trust - A Book of Gardening, 1986 Plants in Garden History*, 1992

HOLE, DEAN S. REYNOLDS, *A Book about Roses*, 1901

HOSKINS, W.G., *The Making of the English Landscape*, 1955

HYAMS, EDWARD, *The Changing Face of Britain*, 1977

JACKSON-STOPS, GERVASE, *An English Arcadia 1600-1990*, 1992

JAMES, JOHN (tr from French), *The Theory & Practice of Gardening*, 1712

JEKYLL, GERTRUDE, *Colour Schemes for the Flower Garden*,1908

JEKYLL, GERTRUDE & MAWLEY, EDWARD, *Roses for English Gardens*, 1901

JEKYLL, GERTRUDE & WEAVER, LAWRENCE, *Gardens for Small Country Houses*, 1912

JELLICOE, GEOFFREY & SUSAN (ED), *The Oxford Companion to Gardens*, 1986

JOHNSON, GEORGE W., *The Cottage Gardener,* 1857

JON THE GARDENER, *The Feate of Gardening,* c1440

KING, PETER (ED), *The Good Gardens Guide 2001*

KEEN, MARY, *The Glory of the English Garden*, 1989

KEMP, EDWARD, *How to Lay out a Garden*, 1850

KNIGHT, RICHARD PAYNE, *An Analytical Enquiry into the Principles of Taste*, 1794

LANDSBERG, SYLVIA, *The Medieval Garden*

LANDSBERG, SYLVIA, *The Recreation of Small Period Gardens for Museums and Public Spaces in Britain*, 1995

LANDSBERG, SYLVIA, BAYLEAF – 'A medieval yeoman's garden' *The Garden* Vol 121 no. 6 1996

LANGLEY, BATTY, *The New Principles of Gardening*, 1728

LAWSON, WILLIAM, *A New Orchard and Garden*, 1618

LEAPMAN, MICHAEL, *The Ingenious Mr Fairchild*, 2000

LEES-MILNE, ALVILDE, VEREY, ROSEMARY, *The Englishwoman's Garden*, 1980

LLOYD, CHRISTOPHER, *The Well-Tempered Garden*, 1970

LONGSTAFFE-GOWAN, TODD, *The London Town Garden 1700-1840*, 2001

LOUDON, JANE, *The Ladies' Flower Garden of Ornamental bulbs, 1841 The Ladies' Flower Garden of Ornamental Perennials*, 1849

LOUDON, JOHN CLAUDIUS, *The Manual of Cottage Gardening and Husbandry*, 1830 *An Encyclopaedia of Gardening*, 1834 *The Suburban Gardener and Villa Companion*, 1836

MABEY, RICHARD, *Flora Britannica*, 1996

MACCARTHY, FIONA, *William Morris – a Life for our Time*, 1994

MCDOUGALL, ELISABETH B. (ED), *Medieval Gardens: Dumbarton Oaks,* Colloquium, 1986

MADDOCK, JAMES, *The Florists' Directory*, 1792

MARKHAM, GERVASE, *The English Husbandman*,1613

MARKHAM, GERVASE, *Cheap and Good Husbandry*, 1614

MEAGER, LEONARD, *The English Gardener*, 1670

M'INTOSH, CHARLES, *The New and Improved Practical Gardener*, 1855

MOUNTAINE, DIDYMUS (THOMAS HILL), *The Gardeners Labyrinth*, 1577

NATIONAL TRUST, *The National Trust Handbook*, 2001

OSBORN, A, *The Complete Book of Gardening*, 1930

PAGE, RUSSELL, *The Education of a Gardener*, 1962

PAINSHILL PARK TRUST, *A Guide to Painshill*, 2000

PARKINSON, JOHN, *Paradisi in Sole. Paradisus Terrestris*, 1629

PATMORE, J. ALLAN, *Land and Leisure*, 1970

POPE, ALEXANDER, *An essay on Criticism*, 1715

PRICE, SIR UVEDALE, *An Essay on the Picturesque*, 1794

QUEST-RITSON, CHARLES, *The English Garden – a Social History*, 2001

REA, JOHN, FLORA, *Ceres and Pomona*, 1665

ROBINSON, WILLIAM, *The English Flower Garden*, 1883
The Wild Garden, 1894

SACKVILLE-WEST, V., ED. LANE FOX, Robin, *The Illustrated Garden Book - a New Anthology*, 1986

SAVAGE, ROBERT J.G., 'Natural History of the Goldney Garden Grotto' *Journal of the Garden History Society* vol 17 no.1 1989

SCHAMA, SIMON, *Landscape and Memory*, 1995

SCOTT-JAMES, ANNE, *The Cottage Garden*, 1981

SETON, LADY, *My Town Garden*, 1927

SITWELL, OSBERT, *Laughter in the Next Room*, 1949

SLATER, JOHN, *The Amateur Florists' Guide*, 1840

SPENS, MICHAEL, *The Complete Landscape Designs and Gardens of Geoffrey Jellicoe*, 1994

STEMBRIDGE, P.K., *Thomas Goldney's Garden*, 1996

STRONG, ROY, *The Artist and the Garden*, 2000

SUDELL, RICHARD, *Landscape Gardening*, 1933
The New Garden, 1935
The New Illustrated Gardening Encyclopaedia

SUFFOLK GARDENS TRUST, 'Pastime of Pleasure': *a Celebration of Suffolk Gardens from the Seventeenth Century to the Present Day*, 2000

SWITZER, STEPHEN, *The Nobleman, Gentleman & Gardener's Recreation*, 1718

SYMES, MICHAEL, *The English Rococo Garden*, 1991

TAYLOR, G.C., *The Modern Garden*, 1936

TAYLOR, GLADYS, *Old London Gardens*, 1953

THACKER, CHRISTOPHER, *The Genius of Gardening – the History of Gardens In Britain and Ireland*, 1994
The History of Gardens, 1979

THOMAS, GRAHAM STUART, *Gardens of the National Trust*, 1979
The Old Shrub Roses, 1957
Perennial Garden Plants or The Modern Florilegium, 1976

THOMAS, H.H., *Gardening in Towns*, 1936

THOMPSON, FLORA, *Lark Rise to Candleford*, 1945

TULLOCH, MARY, *Garden notebook* (unpublished), 1935-1939

TUSSER, THOMAS, *A Hundreth Good Points of Husbandry*, 1557

TUSSER, THOMAS, *Five Hundred Points of Good Husbandry*, 1573

VEREY, ROSEMARY, *Classic Garden Design*, 1984

WALMSLEY, R. CHARLES, *Albury Park, Guildford, Surrey*, 1986

WALPOLE, HORACE, *Essay on Modern Gardening*, 1785

WAUGH, EVELYN, *Put out More Flags*, 1942

WEIR, ALISON, *Eleanor of Aquitaine*, 1999

THE WELSH HISTORIC GARDENS TRUST, *Guide to the Historic Parks and Gardens of Wales*, 2001

WHATELY, THOMAS, *Observations on Modern Gardening*, c1765

WHEELER, DAVID (ED), *The Penguin Book of Garden Writing*, 1996

WHITE, GILBERT, *The Garden Kalendar* ed. John Clegg, 1976
The Natural History of Selborne, 1788-9

WHITTLE, ELIZABETH, *The Historic Gardens of Wales*, 1992

WILLIAMSON, TOM, *Polite Landscapes – Gardens & Society in Eighteenth-Century England*, 1995

WODEHOUSE, P.G., *Blandings Castle*, 1935

YORKSHIRE GARDENS TRUST, *Temple Grounds, Richmond*

QUOTATIONS

The author is most grateful for permission to quote from the following works. Every effort has been made to contact the copyright holders and the publishers would welcome any errors or omissions being brought to their attention.

Acton, Harold, *Memoirs of an Aesthete*, 1948; Chambers, John, *Wild Flower Garden*, 1987; Fish, Margery, *We Made a Garden*, 1956; *Cottage Garden Flowers*, 1961; Hadfield, Miles, *A History of British Gardening*, 1979; Haworth-Booth, Michael, *Effective Flowering Shrubs*, 1951; Hibbert, Christopher, *The English – A Social History 1066-1945*, 1987; Hyams, Edward, *The Changing Face of Britain*, 1977; Jellicoe, Geoffrey & Susan *Appendix to a History of British Gardening*, 1979; Kipling, Rudyard, *The Glory of the Garden*, 1911; Lloyd, Christopher, *Guide to the Garden at Great Dixter*, MacCarthy, Fiona, *William Morris – a Life for our Time*, 1994; Nicolson, Nigel (ed.) *Harold Nicolson's Diaries. 1966-8*; Sackville-West, V., *The Garden*, 1946; Scott-James, Anne, *The Cottage Garden*, 1981; Seton, Lady, *My Town Garden*, 1927; Sitwell, Osbert, *Laughter in the Next Room*, 1949; Spens, Michael, *The Complete Landscape Designs and Gardens of Geoffrey Jellicoe*, 1994; Sudell, Richard, *Landscape Gardening*, 1933; *The New Illustrated Gardening Encyclopaedia*; Taylor, G.C., *The Modern Garden*, 1936; Thomas, Dylan, *Under Milk Wood*, 1953; Thomas, Graham Stuart, *The Old Shrub Roses*, 1957; *Plants for Ground Cover*, 1970; Thomas, H.H., *Gardening in Towns*, 1936; Thompson, Flora, *Lark Rise to Candleford*, 1945; Waugh, Evelyn, *Put out More Flags*, 1942; Williamson, Tom, *Polite Landscapes – Gardens & Society in Eighteenth-Century England*, 1995; Wodehouse, P.G., *Blandings Castle*.

First published in the United
Kingdom in 2002

Text copyright © Jane Fearnley-
Whittingstall, 2002
Design and layout copyright ©
Weidenfeld & Nicolson, 2002

360

This edition produced for
The Book People Ltd
Hall Wood Avenue,
Haydock,
St Helens WA11 9UL

A CIP catalogue record for this book
is available from the British Library
ISBN 0 297 843079

Design director David Rowley
Editorial director Susan Haynes
Designed by Clive Hayball
Edited by Jinny Johnson
Picture research by Tom Graves
Proofread by Gwen Rigby
Index by Elizabeth Wiggans

PICTURE CREDITS

Every effort has been made to
contact the copyright holders for
images reproduced in this book.
The publishers would welcome any
errors or omissions being brought to
their attention.-

AKG London 25 (Biblioteca Estense,
Modena Ms. Cat. 209); John Bethell
146; Mark Bolton 192; Bridgeman Art
Library:- Fig. 21, 28 (Osterreichische
Nationalbibliothek, Vienna) 31
(British Library) 33 (British Library)
36-37 (Louvre/Giraudon) 39, 40 (Yale
Centre for British Art: Paul Mellon
Collection) 44 (Photo Mark Fiennes),
50, 69, 74-75, 83 (Kunsthistorisches
Museum, Vienna) 101, 107, 112 (John
Bethell) 115, 122, 126 (Wallace
Collection, London) 128 (National
Gallery, Victoria, Austraila) 132, 136-
137, 143 (De Morgan Foundation,
London) 149, 154. 155 (British
Library) 180 (Bristol City Museum
and Art Gallery) 190-191 (Harris
Museum and Art Gallery, Preston)
198 (Royal Botanical Gardens, Kew)
199 (Linnean Society, London) 210,
213 (Worthing Museum and Art
Gallery) 216, 229, 230 (The Art
Workers' Guild Trustees Ltd.,
London) 239 (Abbot Hall Gallery,
Kendal) 233, 273 John Bethell) 290
(Stanley Spencer Gallery, Cookham)
293 (Fine Art Society London) 298,
310, 319; Jonathan Buckley 277; The
Beth Chatto Gardens, Essex (Photo
Steve Wooster) 320; Christie's Photo
Library 43, 88; Country Life Picture
Library 221; English Heritage Photo
Library (James Austin) 156; Mary
Evans Picture Library 10, 163, 164-165,
266; The Garden Picture Library 99,
104 (Clay Perry) 110-111 (Clay Perry)
250 (Rex Butcher); Grosvenor
Museum, Chester (Photo Simon
Warburton); Harpur Garden Library,
Jerry Harpur: end papers, 47, 152, 195,
249, 264, 303, 305, 313, 335 Marcus
Harpur: 8, 9, 161; Charles Jencks 338-
339, 340; Edward Jenner Museum,
Berkeley, Glos. (Photos David
Mullin) 174, 175; Andrew Lawson
Picture Library 236, 243, 328-329, 343,
345; © National Gallery, London 70;

National Trust Photographic Library
60-61 (Nick Meers) 76, 102 (John
Hammond) 134-135 (David Noton)
182 (Stephen Robson) 202-203
(George Wright) 207 (Ian Shaw) 208
(Nick Meers) 254-255 (Stephen
Robson) 261 (Clive Boursnell) 281
(Stephen Robson) 81 (Upton House
Bearsted Coll./Angelo Hornak);
Popperfoto 288; Royal Horticultural
Society (Lindley Library/Photo
Valerie Finnis) 284; Victoria and
Albert Museum 65, 96; Weidenfeld
Archive 177.

290 © Estate of Stanley Spencer 2002.
All Rights Reserved DACS
308 © Estate of Stanley Spencer 2002.
All Rights Reserved DACS

298© 2002. All Rights Reserved
DACS

AUTHOR'S ACKNOWLEDGEMENTS

I would like to thank John Borron of
Cumbria Gardens Trust, Polly Burns
of Suffolk Gardens Trust, Godfrey
Carter for drawing my attention to
'The Girl Friend' in P.G.
Wodehouses's Blandings Castle, Tessa
Hayward, Ian and Val Hepworth of
the Yorkshire Gardens Trust, Charles
Jencks for supplying the
photographs of Portrack, Anne and
Peter Lascelles for their hospitality,
Fanny Oglander for giving me access
to Sir John Oglander's Diaries, Ginny
Scott of Hereford and Worcester
Gardens Trust, and Ferrers Vyvyan
for information about the Cornish
connection. I am also very grateful
to Jinny Johnson for editing the
book with great skill and tact, to
Clive Hayball for his brilliant design,
to Tomas Graves for finding such
apposite illustrations and to Susan
Haynes for looking after the project
from start to finish.